TAJIKISTAN

EXPORT-IMPORT AND BUSINESS DIRECTORY

International Business Publications, USA
Washington, DC, USA - Tajikistan

TAJIKISTAN

EXPORT-IMPORT AND BUSINESS DIRECTORY

Editorial content: International Business Publications, USA
Editor-in-Chief: Dr. Igor S. Oleynik
Editor: Natasha Alexander
Managing Editor: Karl Cherepanya

Published by
International Business Publications, USA
P.O.Box 15343, Washington, DC 20003
Phone: (202) 546-2103, Fax: (202) 546-3275, E-mail: rusric@erols.com

UPDATED ANNUALLY

Databases & Information: **Global Investment Center, USA**
Cover Design: **International Business Publications, USA**

We express our sincere gratitude to all government agencies and international organizations which provided information and other materials for this *directory*

2004 International Business Publications, USA
ISBN 0-7397-6013-0

This guide provides basic information for starting or/and conducting business in the country. The extraordinary volume of materials covering the topic, prevents us from placing all these materials in this guide. For more detailed information on issues related to any specific investment and business activity in the country, please contact Global Investment Center, USA
Please acquire the list of our business intelligence and marketing reports and other business publications. We constantly update and expand our business intelligence and marketing materials. Please contact the center for the updated list of reports on over 200 countries.

in the USA: **Global Investment Center, USA.**
P.O.Box 15343, Washington, DC 20003
Phone: (202) 546-2103, Fax: (202) 546-3275, E-mail: rusric@erols.com

For additional analytical, marketing and other information please contact Global Investment Center, USA

Printed in the USA

TAJIKISTAN

EXPORT-IMPORT AND BUSINESS DIRECTORY

TABLE OF CONTENTS

STRATEGIC & BUSINESS PROFILES

COUNTRY OVERVIEW

President: Emomili Rakhmonov
Prime Minister: Abdujalil Samadov
Independence: September 9, 1991 (from Soviet Union)
Population (1994E): 6.0 million
Location/Size: Central Asia/143,100 sq. miles, slightly smaller than Wisconsin
Major Cities: Dushanbe (capital)
Languages: Tajik (official), Russian
Ethnic Groups: Tajiks (64.9%), Uzbek (25%), Russian (3.5%), other (6.6%)
Religions: Sunni Muslim (80%), Shi'a Muslim (5%), other (15%)
Defense (1993): Army (2,500), CIS Forces (mostly Russian) (25,000), National Guard (NA), Security Forces (NA)

ECONOMIC OVERVIEW

Currency: Ruble
Commercial Exchange Rate: N/A
Gross Domestic Product (Purchasing Power Equivalent) (1993E): $6.9 billion
Real GDP Growth Rate (1993E): -21%
Inflation Rate (Consumer Prices) (1993 Average): 38% per month
Merchandise Exports (1993): $263 million to non-FSU
Merchandise Imports (1993): $371 million from non-FSU
Major Export Products: Cotton, aluminum, fruits
Major Import Products: Fuel, chemicals, machinery

Current issues: Tajikistan has experienced three changes of government since it gained independence in September 1991. The current president, Emomali RAHMONOV, was elected in November 1994, yet has been in power since 1992. The country is suffering through its fourth year of a civil conflict, with no clear end in sight. Underlying the conflict are deeply rooted regional and clan-based animosities that pit a government consisting of people primarily from the Kulob (Kulyab), Khujand (Leninabad), and Hisor (Hissar) regions against a secular and Islamic-led opposition from the Gharm, Gorno-Badakhshan, and Qurghonteppa (Kurgan-Tyube) regions. Government and opposition representatives have held periodic rounds of UN-mediated peace talks and agreed in September 1994 to a cease-fire which has been periodically extended. Russian-led peacekeeping troops are deployed throughout the country, and Russian-commanded border guards are stationed along the Tajikistani-Afghan border.

GEOGRAPHY

Location: Central Asia, west of China

Geographic coordinates: 39 00 N, 71 00 E

Map references: Commonwealth of Independent States

Area:
total : 143,100 sq km
land: 142,700 sq km
water: 400 sq km

Area - comparative: slightly smaller than Wisconsin

Land boundaries:
total: 3,651 km
border countries: Afghanistan 1,206 km, China 414 km, Kyrgyzstan 870 km, Uzbekistan 1,161 km

Coastline: 0 km (landlocked)

Maritime claims: none (landlocked)

Climate: midlatitude continental, hot summers, mild winters; semiarid to polar in Pamir Mountains

Terrain: Pamirs and Alay Mountains dominate landscape; western Fergana Valley in north, Kofarnihon and Vakhsh Valleys in southwest

Elevation extremes:
lowest point: Syrdariya 300 m
highest point: Qullai Kommunizm 7,495 m

Natural resources: significant hydropower potential, some petroleum, uranium, mercury, brown coal, lead, zinc, antimony, tungsten

Land use:
arable land : 6%
permanent crops: 0%
permanent pastures: 25%
forests and woodland: 4%
other: 65% (1993 est.)

Irrigated land: 6,390 sq km (1993 est.)

Natural hazards: NA

Base 802370 (R00627) 8-95

Environment - current issues: inadequate sanitation facilities; increasing levels of soil salinity; industrial pollution; excessive pesticides; part of the basin of the shrinking Aral Sea suffers from severe overutilization of available water for irrigation and associated pollution

Environment - international agreements:
party to: none of the selected agreements
signed, but not ratified: none of the selected agreements

Geography - note: landlocked

PEOPLE

Population: 5,945,903 (July 1997 est.)

Age structure:
0-14 years: 42% (male 1,263,725; female 1,234,730)
15-64 years : 53% (male 1,578,940; female 1,599,458)
65 years and over: 5% (male 114,118; female 154,932) (July 1997 est.)

Population growth rate: 1.18% (1997 est.)

Birth rate: 27.93 births/1,000 population (1997 est.)

Death rate: 7.74 deaths/1,000 population (1997 est.)

Net migration rate: -8.42 migrant(s)/1,000 population (1997 est.)

Sex ratio:
at birth : 1.05 male(s)/female
under 15 years: 1.02 male(s)/female
15-64 years: 0.99 male(s)/female
65 years and over: 0.74 male(s)/female
total population: 0.99 male(s)/female (1997 est.)

Infant mortality rate: 109.5 deaths/1,000 live births (1997 est.)

Life expectancy at birth:
total population: 64.68 years
male : 61.55 years
female: 67.97 years (1997 est.)

Total fertility rate: 3.58 children born/woman (1997 est.)

Nationality:
noun: Tajikistani(s)
adjective: Tajikistani

Ethnic groups: Tajik 64.9%, Uzbek 25%, Russian 3.5% (declining because of emigration), other 6.6%

Religions: Sunni Muslim 80%, Shi'a Muslim 5%

Languages: Tajik (official), Russian widely used in government and business

Literacy:
definition: age 15 and over can read and write
total population: 98%
male: 99%
female: 97% (1989 est.)

GOVERNMENT

Country name:
conventional long form : Republic of Tajikistan
conventional short form: Tajikistan
local long form: Jumhurii Tojikistan
local short form: none
former : Tajik Soviet Socialist Republic

Data code: TI

Government type: republic

National capital: Dushanbe

Administrative divisions: 2 oblasts (viloyatho, singular - viloyat) and one autonomous oblast* (viloyati avtonomii); Viloyati Avtonomii Badakhshoni Kuni* (Khorugh - formerly Khorog), Viloyati Khatlon (Qurghonteppa - formerly Kurgan-Tyube), Viloyati Leninobod (Khujand - formerly Leninabad)
note: the administrative center name follows in parentheses

Independence: 9 September 1991 (from Soviet Union)

National holiday: National Day, 9 September (1991)

Constitution: new constitution adopted 6 November 1994

Legal system: based on civil law system; no judicial review of legislative acts

Suffrage: 18 years of age; universal

Executive branch:
chief of state : President Emomali RAHMONOV (since 6 November 1994; head of state and Assembly chairman since NA November 1992)
head of government: Prime Minister Yahyo AZIMOV (since 8 February 1996)

cabinet: Council of Ministers appointed by the president who proposes them to the Supreme Assembly for approval
elections : president elected by popular vote for a five-year term; election last held 6 November 1994 (next to be held NA 1999); prime minister appointed by the president
election results: Emomali RAHMONOV elected president; percent of vote - Emomali RAHMONOV 58%, Abdumalik ABDULLAJANOV 40%

Legislative branch: unicameral Supreme Assembly or Majlisi Oli (181 seats; members are popularly elected to serve five-year terms)
elections : last held 26 February and 12 March 1995 (next to be held NA 2000)
election results: percent of vote by party - NA; estimated seats by party - Communist Party and affiliates 100, People's Party 10, Party of People's Unity 6, Party of Economic and Political Renewal 1, other 64

Judicial branch: Supreme Court, judges are appointed by the president

Political parties and leaders: People's Party of Tajikistan [Abdumajid DOSTIYEV]; National Revival Bloc [Abdumalik ABDULLOJONOV]; Tajik Communist Party [Shodi SHABDOLOV]; Democratic Party [Jumaboy NIYAZOV, chairman]; Islamic Renaissance Party or IRP [Mohammed Sharif HIMMATZODA, chairman]; Rebirth (Rastokhez) [Takhir ABDUZHABOROV]; Lali Badakhshan Society [Atobek AMIRBEK]; Tajikistan Party of Economic and Political Renewal or TPEPR; Citizenship, Patriotism, Unity Party [Bobokhon MAHMADOV]; Adolatho "Justice" Party [Abdurahmon KARIMOV, chairman]

Political pressure groups and leaders: Tajikistan Opposition Movement based in northern Afghanistan [Seyed Abdullah NURI, chairman]

International organization participation: CIS, EBRD, ECE, ECO, ESCAP, FAO, IBRD, ICAO, IDA, IDB, IFAD, IFC, ILO, IMF, Intelsat, IOC, IOM, ITU, NACC, OIC, OSCE, UN, UNCTAD, UNESCO, UNIDO, UPU, WFTU, WHO, WIPO, WMO, WTrO (observer)

Diplomatic representation in the US: Tajikistan does not have an embassy in the US, but has a mission at the UN: address - 136 East 67th Street, New York, NY 10021, telephone - [1] (212) 472-7645, FAX - [1] (212) 628-0252; permanent representative to the UN is Rashid ALIMOV

Diplomatic representation from the US:
chief of mission: Ambassador R. Grant SMITH
embassy : interim chancery, Oktyabrskaya Hotel, 105A Prospect Rudaki, Dushanbe 734001
mailing address: use embassy street address
telephone : [7] (3772) 21-03-56
FAX: Telex (787) 20116

Flag description: three horizontal stripes of red (top), a wider stripe of white, and green; a gold crown surmounted by seven five-pointed gold stars is located in the center of the white stripe

ECONOMY

Economy - overview: Tajikistan had the next-to-lowest per capita GDP in the former USSR, the highest rate of population growth, an extremely low standard of living, and rampant inflation. Agriculture dominates the economy, with cotton being the most important crop. Mineral resources, varied but limited in amount, include silver, gold, uranium, and tungsten. Industry is limited to a large aluminum plant, hydropower facilities, and small obsolete factories mostly in light industry and food processing. The Tajik economy has been gravely weakened by four years of civil conflict and by the loss of subsidies from Moscow and of markets for its products, which has left Tajikistan dependent on Russia and Uzbekistan and on international humanitarian assistance for much of its basic subsistence needs. Moreover, constant political turmoil and the continued dominance by former communist officials have impeded the introduction of meaningful economic reforms. The regime made initial efforts to stabilize the economy and promote reform in 1996.

GDP: purchasing power parity - $5.4 billion (1996 estimate as extrapolated from World Bank estimate for 1994)

GDP - real growth rate: -17% (1996 est.)

GDP - per capita: purchasing power parity - $920 (1996 est.)

GDP - composition by sector:
agriculture: NA%
industry: NA%
services: NA%

Inflation rate - consumer price index: 65% (1996 est.)

Labor force:
total: 1.9 million (1996)
by occupation: agriculture and forestry 52%, manufacturing, mining, and construction 17%, services 31% (1995)

Unemployment rate: 2.4% includes only officially registered unemployed; also large numbers of underemployed workers and unregistered unemployed people (December 1996)

Budget:
revenues: $NA
expenditures : $NA, including capital expenditures of $NA

Industries: aluminum, zinc, lead, chemicals and fertilizers, cement, vegetable oil, metal-cutting machine tools, refrigerators and freezers

Industrial production growth rate: -20% (1996 est.)

Electricity - capacity: 4.44 million kW (1994)

Electricity - production: 16.8 billion kWh (1994)

Electricity - consumption per capita: 2,135 kWh (1995 est.)

Agriculture - products: cotton, grain, fruits, grapes, vegetables; cattle, sheep, goats

Exports:
total value: $768 million (1996 est.)
commodities : cotton, aluminum, fruits, vegetable oil, textiles
partners: FSU 78%, Netherlands (1994)

Imports:
total value: $657 million (1996 est.)
commodities: fuel, chemicals, machinery and transport equipment, textiles, foodstuffs
partners : FSU 55%, Switzerland, UK (1994)

Debt - external: $635 million (of which $250 million to Russia) (1995 est.)

Economic aid:
recipient : ODA, $22 million (1993)
note: commitments, $885 million (disbursements $115 million) (1992-95)

Currency: the Tajikistani ruble (TSR) = 100 tanga; Tajikistan introduced its own currency in May 1995

Exchange rates: Tajikistani rubles (TJR) per US$1 - 350 (January 1997), 284 (January 1996)

Fiscal year: calendar year

COMMUNICATIONS

Telephones: 303,000 (1991 est.)

Telephone system: poorly developed and not well maintained; many towns are not reached by the national network
domestic: cable and microwave radio relay
international: linked by cable and microwave radio relay to other CIS republics, and by leased connections to the Moscow international gateway switch; Dushanbe linked by Intelsat to international gateway switch in Ankara (Turkey); satellite earth stations - 1 Orbita and 2 Intelsat

Radio broadcast stations: 1 state-owned radio broadcast station

Radios: NA

Television broadcast stations: 1
note : 1 Intelsat earth station provides TV receive-only service from Turkey

Televisions: NA

TRANSPORTATION

total: 480 km in common carrier service; does not include industrial lines (1990)

Highways:
total: 32,752 km
paved: 21,119 km (note - these roads are said to be hard-surfaced, meaning that some are paved and some are all-weather gravel surfaced)
unpaved: 11,633 km (1992 est.)

Pipelines: natural gas 400 km (1992)

Ports and harbors: none

Airports: 59 (1994 est.)

Airports - with paved runways:
total : 14
over 3,047 m: 1
2,438 to 3,047 m: 5
1,524 to 2,437 m: 7
914 to 1,523 m: 1 (1994 est.)

Airports - with unpaved runways:
total: 45
914 to 1,523 m: 9
under 914 m : 36 (1994 est.)

MILITARY

Military branches: Army, Air Force, Presidential National Guard, Security Forces (internal and border troops)

Military manpower - military age: 18 years of age

Military manpower - availability:
males age 15-49: 1,393,416 (1997 est.)

Military manpower - fit for military service:
males : 1,143,159 (1997 est.)

Military manpower - reaching military age annually:
males: 60,832 (1997 est.)

Military expenditures - dollar figure: 180 billion rubles (1995); note - conversion of defense expenditures into US dollars using the current exchange rate could produce misleading results

Military expenditures - percent of GDP: 3.4% (1995)

TRANSNATIONAL ISSUES

Disputes - international: boundary with China in dispute; territorial dispute with Kyrgyzstan on northern boundary in Isfara Valley area; foreign support to Islamic fighters based in northern Afghanistan in Tajikistan's civil war

Illicit drugs: limited illicit cultivation of cannabis and opium poppy, mostly for domestic consumption; increasingly used as transshipment point for illicit drugs from Southwest Asia to Russia and Western Europe

IMPORTANT INFORMATION FOR UNDERSTANDING TAJIKISTAN

PROFILE

OFFICIAL NAME: Republic of Tajikistan

GEOGRAPHY

Area: 143,100 sq. km.
Capital: Dushanbe.
Terrain: Pamir and Alay mountains dominate landscape; western Ferghana valley in north, Kofarnihon and Vakhsh Valleys in southwest.
Climate: Mid-latitude continental, hot summers, mild winters; semiarid to polar in Pamir mountains.

At 36'40' northern latitude and 41'14' eastern longitude, Tajikistan is nestled between Kyrgyztsan and Uzbekistan to the north and west, China to the east, and Afghanistan to the south. Tajikistan is home to some of the highest mountains in the world including the Pamir and Alay ranges. Ninety-three percent of Tajikistan is mountainous with altitudes ranging from 1,000 feet to 27,000 feet, with nearly 50% of Tajikistan's territory above 10,000 feet. Earthquakes are of varying degrees and are frequent. The massive mountain ranges are cut by hundreds of canyons and gorges at the bottom of which run streams which flow into larger river valleys where the majority of the country's population lives and works. The principal rivers of Central Asia, the Amu Darya and the Syr Darya, both flow through Tajiksitan, fed by melting snow from mountains of Tajikistan and Kyrgyztsan. Flooding sometimes occurs during the annual Spring thaw.

PEOPLE

Nationality: Tajikistani.
Population (2000 est.): 6.1 million .

Population growth rate (2000 est.): 1.5%.
Ethnic groups: Tajik 67%, Uzbek 23%, Russian 3.5%, other 6.5%.
Religion: Sunni Muslim 80%, Shi'a Muslim 5%, other 15%.
Language: Tajik (sole official language as of 1994), Russian widely used in government and business, 77% of the country, however, is rural and they speak mostly Tajik.
Education: *Literacy* (according to Tajikistan official statistics, 2000)--99%. The Tajik education system has suffered greatly since independence.
Health: *Life expectancy*--60.95 years men; 67.38 years women. *Infant mortality rate*--117.42 deaths/1,000 live births (2000 est.).
Work force: No recent data available.

Contemporary Tajiks are the descendants of ancient Eastern Iranian inhabitants of Central Asia, in particular the Soghdians and the Bactrians, and possibly other groups, with an admixture of western Iranian Persians and non-Iranian peoples, Mongols, and Turkic peoples, and reports of Alexander the Great's army. Until the 20th century, people in the region used two types of distinction to identify themselves: way of life--either nomadic or sedentary--and place of residence. By the late 19th century, the Tajik and Uzbek peoples, who lived in proximity for centuries and often used--and continue to use--each other's languages, did not perceive themselves as two distinct nationalities. The division of Central Asia into five Soviet Republics in the 1920s imposed artificial labels on a region in which many different peoples lived intermixed.

HISTORY

The current Tajik Republic hearkens back to the Samanid Empire (A.D. 875-999), that ruled what is now Tajikistan as well as territory to the south and west, as their role model and name for their currency. During their reign, the Samanids supported the revival of the written Persian language in the wake of the Arab Islamic conquest in the early 8th century and played an important role in preserving the culture of the pre-Islamic persian-speaking world. They were the last Persian-speaking empire to rule Central Asia.

After a series of attacks beginning in the 1860s during the Great Game, the Tajik people came under Russian rule. This rule waned briefly after the Russian Revolution of 1917 as the Bolsheviks consolidated their power and were embroiled in a civil war in other regions of the former Russian Empire. As the Bolsheviks attempted to regain Central Asia in the 1920s, an indigenous Central Asian resistance movement based in the Ferghana Valley, the "Basmachi movement," attempted to resist but was eventually defeated in 1925. Tajikistan became fully established under Soviet control with the creation of Tajikistan as an autonomous Soviet socialist republic within Uzbekistan in 1924, and as one of the independent Soviet socialist republics in 1929.

GOVERNMENT AND POLITICAL CONDITIONS

Type: Republic.
Independence: September 9, 1991 (from Soviet Union).

Constitution: November 6, 1994.
Branches: *Executive*--Chief of state: President Emomali RAHMONOV since November 6, 1994; head of state and Supreme Assembly chairman since November 19, 1992; head of government: Prime Minister Oqil OQILOV since January 20, 1999. Cabinet: Council of Ministers appointed by the president, approved by the Supreme Assembly. Elections: president elected by popular vote for a 7-year term; election last held November 6, 1999 (next to be held NA 2006); prime minister appointed by the president. Election results: Emomali RAHMONOV elected president; percent of vote: Emomali RAHMONOV 96%, Davlat USMONOV 4%. *Legislative*--Bicameral Supreme Assembly or Majlisi Oli (181 seats; next election 96 seats; members are elected by popular vote to serve 5-year terms).

Elections held February 26 and March 12, 1995 (next were held February 27 and March 23, 2000). Election results: percent of vote by party, NA. Estimated seats by party: Communist Party and affiliates 100; People's Party 10; Party of People's Unity 6; Party of Economic and Political Renewal 1; Islamic Rebirth Party 2; other 62. *Judicial*--Supreme Court, judges are appointed by the president. Political parties and leaders: Democratic Party or TDP [Mahmadruzi SKANDDAROV, chairman]; Islamic Rebirth Party [Said Abdullo NURI]; National Unity Party--evolved from the People's Party and Party of People's Unity; Party of Justice and Development Rahmatullo ZOIROV]; People's Democratic Party of Tajikistan or PDPT [Abdulmajid DOSTIEV]; Rastokhez (Rebirth) Movement [Tohiri ABDUJABBOR]; Tajik Communist Party or CPT [Shodi SHABDOLOV]; Tajikistan Party of Economic and Political Renewal or TPEPR [leader NA].
Suffrage: 18 years of age, universal.

Defense: military manpower (availability): 1,253,427 (2000 est.).
Flag: three horizontal stripes of red (top), a wider stripe of white, and green; a gold crown surmounted by seven gold, five-pointed stars is located in the center of the white stripe.

The Republic of Tajikistan gained its independence during the breakup of the U.S.S.R. on September 9, 1991 and promptly fell into a civil war from 1992-97 between old-guard regionally based ruling elites and disenfranchised regions, democratic liberal reformists, and Islamists loosely organized in a United Tajik Opposition (UTO). Other combatants and armed bands that flourished in this civil chaos simply reflected the breakdown of central authority rather than loyalty to a political faction and continue to remain unreconciled with the Tajik Government. The height of hostilities occurred between 1992-93. By 1997, The predominantly Kulyabi-led Tajik Government and the UTO successfully negotiated a powersharing peace accord and implemented it by 2000.

Tajikistan is slowly rebuilding itself with an integrated government and continues to permit a Russian military presence to guard their border with Afghanistan and the basing of the Russian 201st Motorized Rifle Division--that never left Tajikistan when it became independent. Most of these Russian-led forces, however, are local Tajik noncommissioned officers and soldiers.

Both Tajikistan's presidential and parliamentary elections, in 1999 and 2000, respectively, were widely considered to be flawed and unfair but peaceful. The inclusion of an overtly declared Islamic party committed to secular government (Islamic Rebirth Party) and several other parties in the Parliamentary elections represented an improvement in the Tajik people's right to choose their government. Tajikistan is the only Central Asian country in which a religiously affiliated political party is represented in Parliament. President Rahmonov, while no longer specifically obliged--as he was under the peace accords--to allocate one-third of government positions to the UTO, has kept some former UTO officials in senior cabinet-level positions. While the government and the now incorporated former opposition continue to distrust each other, they have often found a way to work with each other and are committed to peacefully resolving their differences.

Tajikistan's fragmented neighbor to the south, Afghanistan, continues to be a base of international terrorism, a scene of civil conflict between the Taliban and their opponents, and the world's largest producer of opium. This combination of negative factors produces crossborder effects that regularly threatens to destabilize Tajikistan's fragile and hard-won peace. In the summers of 1999 and 2000, the Islamic Movement of Uzbekistan, an officially declared terrorist organization by the U.S. Government, used Tajikistan as a staging ground for an insurgency campaign against the Government of Uzbekistan. At the same time, Taliban advances in northern Afghanistan threatened to inundate Tajikistan with thousands of refugees. All the while, a constant flow of illegal narcotics continue to transit Tajikistan from Afghanistan on its way to Russian and European markets, leaving widespread violent crime, corruption, increased HIV incidence, and economic distortions in its wake.

Principal Government Officials
President--Emomali Rahmonov
Prime Minister--Oqil Oqilov
Foreign Minister--Talbak Nazarov
Ambassador to the United Nations--Rashid Alimov

MAJLISI OLI OF THE REPUBLIC OF TAJIKISTAN (PARLIAMENT)

Majlisi Oli - the parliament of the Republic of Tajikistan is a higher government and legislative body of the Republic of Tajikistan. Majlisi Oli consists of two Majlises - Majlisi Milli and Majlisi Namoyandagon.

Term of powers of Majlisi Oli is 5 years. The powers of Majlisi Milli and Majlisi Namoyandagon ends at the day, when Majlisi Oli of new convocation starts its activity. Organization and activity of Majlisi Oli is determined by Constitutional law. Majlisi Namoyandagon is elected on the basis of general, equal and direct elective right under a secret voting. Majlisi Namoyandagon acts on a constant and professional basis. The deputy of Majlisi Namoyandagon can be elected a citizen not younger 25.

Three fourth parts of Majlisi Milli is elected by an indirect way, by secret voting on a joint meeting of people deputes of Gorno-Badakhshan autonomous region and its cities and regions, areas and their towns and regions, Dushanbe city and its regions, the cities and regions of Republic subordination. In Majlisi Milli, the Gorno-Badakhshan autonomous region, the areas, Dushanbe city, cities and regions of republican subordination have an equal number of representatives. One fourth part of the members of Majlisi Oli is to be appointed by the president of the Republic of Tajikistan.

Majlisi Milli acts on convocation basis. The member of Majlisi Oli can be elected and appointed a citizen who is 35 and who has a higher education. Each former president of the Republic of Tajikistan is the member of Majlisi Oli forever in case if he doesn't refuse having this right. The number of members of Majlisi Milli and Majlisi Namoyandagon, order of their election, non-election and incompatibility with a mandate of members of Majlisi Oli is determined by constitutional law. (full text about Majlisi Oli).

THE PRESIDENT OF THE REPUBLIC OF TAJIKISTAN

Rahmonov Imam Ali Sharipovich.

Imam Ali Rahmonov is tajik, was born in October 5th, 1952 in Dangara settlement of Kulob region. In 1992 - graduated from the Tajik State University, is an economist by specialty. A Deputy of the Supreme Soviet of the Republic of Tajikistan of XII convocation.

His professional activity Imam Ali Rahmonov began in 1971 as an electrician of the creamery of Kurgan-Tube city. Since 1972-1974 - served in the Soviet Army. After demobilization he continued working at the creamery. In 1976-1988 - held a post of the secretary of the governing and the Chairman of the trade union committee of collective farm of Dangara region, after that he used to work in the Party boards.
Since June, 1988 - a director of Lenin state farm of Dangara region. In November, 1992 he was elected a chairman of the executive committee of Kulob regional Council of people deputies. In November, 19th in the XVI session of the Supreme Soviet of the Republic of Tajikistan of XII convocation Imam Ali Rahmonov was elected a chairman of the Supreme Soviet of the Republic of Tajikistan. In November,6th 1994 - was elected a President of the Republic of Tajikistan. In November 16th , 1994 - was put on oath. In Novembert 16th, 1994 - was reelected a President of the Republic of Tajikistan for a period of seven years in accordance with the changes introducted in the Constitution of the Republic of Tajikistan in 26th of September,1999.

He is married and have nine children.

ECONOMY

GDP nominal: $955 million.
GDP per capita (2000): $154/per capita.
GDP (2000. est.): Real growth rate: 8.3%.
Inflation rate: 33%.
Natural resources: Hydropower, some petroleum, uranium, gold, mercury, brown coal, lead, zinc, antimony, tungsten.
Unemployment rate: 54.1% (1998), under-employment also is high; 80% live under the poverty line (2001).
Agriculture: *Products*--cotton, grain, fruits, grapes, vegetables; cattle, sheep, goats.
Industry: *Types*--aluminum, zinc, lead, chemicals and fertilizers, cement, vegetable oil, textiles, metal-cutting machine tools, refrigerators and freezers.
Trade: *Exports*--$792 million (2000): aluminum (49%), electricity (23%), cotton (12%), gold, fruits, vegetable oil, textiles. *Partners*--Europe 43%, Russia 30%, Uzbekistan 13%, Asia 12%, other CIS 2% (1997). *Imports*--$839 million (2000.): electricity, petroleum products, aluminum oxide, machinery and equipment, foodstuffs. *Partners*--Other CIS 41%, Uzbekistan 27%, Russia 16%, Europe 12%, Asia 4% (2000).
External debt total (2000): $1.2 billion. Bilateral external debt: total --$509 million: Uzbekistan $130 million, Russia $288 million, U.S. $22 million, Turkey $26 million, Kazakhstan $19 million, Pakistan $16 million; multilateral debt: total--$365 million: World Bank $153 million, IMF $113 million, ADB $19 million (2000).
Debt/GDP ratio (2000): 129.

Tajikistan is the poorest NIS country and one of the poorest countries in the world. With foreign revenue precariously dependent upon exports of cotton and aluminum, the economy is highly vulnerable to external shocks. In FY 2000, international assistance remained and essential source of support for rehabilitation programs that reintegrated former civil war combatants into the civilian economy, thus helping keep the peace. International assistance also was necessary to address the second year of severe drought that resulted in a continued shortfall of food production.

Despite resistance from vested interests, the Government of Tajikistan continued to pursue macroeconomic stabilization and structural reform in FY 2000. In December 1999, the government announced that small-enterprise privatization had been successfully completed, and the privatization of medium-sized and large-owned enterprises (SOEs) continued incrementally. The continued privatization of medium-sized and large SOEs, land reform, and banking reform and restructuring remain top priorities. Shortly after the end of FY 2000, the Board of the International Monetary Fund gave its vote of confidence to the government's recent performance by approving the third annual Poverty Reduction and Growth Facility Loan for Tajikistan.

U.S.-TAJIK RELATIONS

The United States remains committed to helping Tajikistan in any way it can develop their economy, recover from their war and 2 years of severe drought, and rebuild its infrastructure so that the Tajik people may prosper in a stable, productive, democratic, and tolerant society.

In FY 2000, the U.S. Government provided an estimated $49.30 million in assistance to Tajikistan, including $33.90 million in U.S. Department of Agriculture (USDA) food aid through Food for Progress and Section 416(b) Programs, $9.93 million in FREEDOM Support Act (FSA) assistance, $140,000 in other U.S. Government assistance, and $5.33 million in U.S. Defense Department excess and privately donated humanitarian commodities. USAID programs, which accounted for about $7.5 million of FSA-funded assistance to Tajikistan, were focused on the broad areas of democracy and governance, economic restructuring, health sector support, humanitarian assistance, and energy and environment assistance. In addition to providing FSA-funded assistance, USAID also provided $25,000 in assistance through Child Survival and Matching Grant Programs of its Office of Foreign Disaster Assistance. The U.S. State Department's Public Diplomacy exchange programs accounted for approximately $1.0 million.

Over the past several years, U.S. Government assistance to Tajikistan has focused heavily on supporting political reconciliation and the establishment of a stable, pluralistic government. This has included direct support for the now-completed peace process, for demobilizing combatants, and for political party development and election administration. The U.S. Government also has promoted the development of a more active civil society in Tajikistan in order to build demand for democratic practices. To facilitate Tajikistan's transition to a market economy, the U.S. Government has helped the Government of Tajikistan rewrite laws and recast the public institutions needed to foster economic growth in a free market. To spur economic growth, the U.S. Government has promoted privatization, commercial law reform, microcredit programs, agricultural-sector development, and the strengthening of local nongovernmental organizations (NGOs).

The U.S. Government's regional environmental and energy programs have supported Tajikistan's participation in regional water and energy management programs along with its Central Asian neighbors. U.S. Government-funded assistance in the health-care sector has demonstrated the openness of the Tajik medical community to quality improvements and the willingness of the Ministry of Health to support needed health-sector reforms. In FY 2000, U.S. Government-funded humanitarian assistance programs continued to target vulnerable groups throughout the country. Through extensive U.S. Government-funded training programs, thousands of Tajik citizens from a wide range of sectors have gained the skills needed to move forward with reforms in the public sector and to build a prosperous private-sector economy.

The United States recognized Tajikistan on December 25, 1991, the day the U.S.S.R. dissolved, and opened a temporary embassy in a hotel the capital, Dushanbe, in March 1992. After the bombings of U.S. embassies in Africa in 1998, Embassy Dushanbe American personnel were temporarily relocated to Almaty, Kazakhstan, due to heightened embassy security standards. American Embassy Dushanbe personnel continue to work in Tajikistan on an unscheduled and intermittent basis. The embassy can be reached 24 hours a day, by calling either the Dushanbe or Almaty offices.

Principal U.S. Embassy Officials
Ambassador--Franklin "Pancho" Huddle, Jr.
Deputy Chief of Mission--James Boughner
DAO--Maj. David Brigham
USAID--Micheal Harvey

Almaty Office: 531 Seyfullin Prospect, Almaty, Kazakhstan 480091, tel. 7-3772-21-03-56, fax 7-3772-21-03-62. Dushanbe Office: 10 Pavlova Street, Dushanbe, Tajikistan 734003, tel. 992-372-21-03-48/50/52, fax 992-372-24-15-62.

TRAVEL AND BUSINESS INFORMATION

The U.S. Department of State's Consular Information Program provides Consular Information Sheets, Travel Warnings, and Public Announcements.

Consular Information Sheets exist for all countries and include information on entry requirements, currency regulations, health conditions, areas of instability, crime and security, political disturbances, and the addresses of the U.S. posts in the country.

Travel Warnings are issued when the State Department recommends that Americans avoid travel to a certain country.

Public Announcements are issued as a means to disseminate information quickly about terrorist threats and other relatively short-term conditions overseas which pose significant risks to the security of American travelers. Free copies of this information are available by calling the Bureau of Consular Affairs at 202-647-5225 or via the fax-on-demand system: 202-647-3000. Consular Information Sheets and Travel Warnings also are available on the Consular Affairs Internet home page: http://travel.state.gov. Consular Affairs Tips for Travelers publication series, which contain information on obtaining passports and planning a safe trip abroad are on the internet and hard copies can be purchased from the Superintendent of Documents, U.S. Government Printing Office, telephone: 202-512-1800; fax 202-512-2250.

Emergency information concerning Americans traveling abroad may be obtained from the Office of Overseas Citizens Services at (202) 647-5225. For after-hours emergencies, Sundays and holidays, call 202-647-4000.

Passport information can be obtained by calling the National Passport Information Center's automated system ($.35 per minute) or live operators 8 a.m. to 8 p.m. (EST) Monday-Friday ($1.05 per minute). The number is 1-900-225-5674 (TDD: 1-900-225-7778). Major credit card users (for a flat rate of $4.95) may call 1-888-362-8668 (TDD: 1-888-498-3648). It also is available on the internet.

Travelers can check the latest health information with the U.S. Centers for Disease Control and Prevention in Atlanta, Georgia. A hotline at 877-FYI-TRIP (877-394-8747) and a web site at http://www.cdc.gov/travel/index.htm give the most recent health advisories, immunization recommendations or requirements, and advice on food and drinking water safety for regions and countries. A booklet entitled Health Information for International Travel (HHS publication number CDC-95-8280) is available from the U.S. Government Printing Office, Washington, DC 20402, tel. (202) 512-1800.

Information on travel conditions, visa requirements, currency and customs regulations, legal holidays, and other items of interest to travelers also may be obtained before your departure from a country's embassy and/or consulates in the U.S. (for this country, see "Principal Government Officials" listing in this publication).

U.S. citizens who are long-term visitors or traveling in dangerous areas are encouraged to register at the U.S. embassy upon arrival in a country (see "Principal U.S. Embassy Officials" listing in this publication). This may help family members contact you in case of an emergency.

STRATEGIC INFORMATION FOR CONDUCTING BUSINESS

U.S. AND MULTILATERAL INSTITUTIONS ACTIVE IN TAJIKISTAN

STATUS OF U.S.-TAJIK COMMERCIAL AGREEMENTS

On November 24, 1993 a trade agreement and a bilateral assistance treaty went into effect. Within the bilateral assistance treaty, Tajikistan has been granted MFN (Most Favored Nation) trading status which allows for lower tariffs on exports from Tajikistan to the United States. However, Tajikistan is not a member of the Generalized System of Preferences (GSP), which provides preferential duty-free entry to over 4,000 products from designated beneficiary countries. For further information on GSP, please (202) 395-6971.

Overseas Private Investment Corporation (OPIC). OPIC has signed a bilateral agreement with Tajikistan authorizing it to provide loan guarantees and insurance to U.S. companies establishing business ventures in the country. OPIC's Project Development Program provides U.S. businesses with up to 50% financing for evaluations to determine commercial viability of projects in Tajikistan. For more information on OPIC's activities in Tajikistan, contact James Gale, regional Director (Tel.: 202- 336-8629; Fax 202-408-5145; E-mail jgale@opic.gov).

Export-Import Bank (EXIM). Although closed for certain routine trade finance transactions, Ex-Im Bank will consider structured financing arrangements such as Ex-Im Bank's project finance program, asset-based aircraft leases, and other financing arrangements that offer a reasonable assurance of repayment, including reliable access to adequate foreign exchange.

U.S. Trade and Development Agency Program (TDA). TDA is authorized to operate in Tajikistan. TDA provides funding for U.S. firms to carry out feasibility studies, consultations, and other planning services related to major projects in developing countries. For more information on TDA funding for Tajikistan, contact Daniel Stein, Regional Director or KelleyAnn Szalkowski, Country Manager (Tel: 703-875-4357; Fax: 703-875-4009).

International Monetary Fund(IMF)/World Bank: Tajikistan joined the IMF and the World Bank in 1993. The World Bank provides financing to Tajikistan for capital infrastructure projects, such as roads and railways, telecommunications, and power facilities. The Multilateral Investment Guarantee Agency (MIGA), an agency of the World Bank that provides investment insurance for noncommercial risks to firms of member countries, including the United States, is also active in Tajikistan.

In June 1998 the IMF announced a three-year $128 million arrangement under an Enhanced Structural Adjustment Facility (ESAF). $48 million were disbursed in 1998. In

December 1997 the Fund had already agreed to provide $20 million in financial assistance. The Fund supported the Consultation Group helping with the stabilization efforts. In May 1996, the IMF also approved a $22 million Stand- by Arrangement. Consequently, total IMF commitment to date amounts to $170 million.

European Bank for Reconstruction and Development (EBRD): U.S. companies investing in Tajikistan are eligible to receive EBRD loans. The EBRD provides counseling, loans, equity investments, and debt guarantees. By the end of 1998, The EBRD had approved investments totaling ECU 13.3 million in Tajikistan. Its first investment project was a SME credit line involving two local private banks. The EBRD has implemented several other projects in Tajikistan such as a project to resurface the runway at Dushanbe airport, one for a packaging plant in Khujand and one for the Obi-Zulol Water Bottling Plant.

Firms seeking involvement in EBRD-funded projects can call the U.S. Government points of contact: Gene Harris, Senior Commercial Officer, in the U.S. Executive Director's Office, in London at 44-71- 558-4027 or fax at 44-71-588-4026 or email at harrisg@ebrd.com.

Central Asian-American Enterprise Fund (CAAEF): The Central Asian-American Enterprise Fund was incorporated in July 1994 to promote the development of emerging private sectors in the five Central Asian countries of Kazakhstan, Uzbekistan, Turkmenistan, Kyrgyzstan, and Tajikistan. The Fund has been capitalized by the U.S. Government at $150 million. The Fund is managed by a private board of directors, and has the authority to make debt and equity investments and offer technical assistance to promote new private enterprises in the Central Asian states. The Fund concentrates mainly on promoting small- and medium-size companies and gives preference to projects in infrastructure sectors such as food processing, textile manufacturing, distribution and transportation, and consumer goods production.

In Tajikistan, the Fund has made three investments: a Pepsi bottler, a carbide plant, and a food company. For more information, contact Brian K. Mercer, Chief Financial Officer (Tel: 202-737-7000; Fax: 202- 737-7077; E-mail: us@caaef.com).

Asian Development Bank (ADB): Tajikistan became the 57th member of the ADB in April 1998. ADB is a development finance institution consisting of over 50 member countries and is engaged in promoting economic and social progress in the Asian and Pacific region. The ADB's principal functions are to make debt and equity investments for the economic and social advancement of developing member countries, to provide technical assistance for the preparation and execution of development projects, to conduct advisory services, and to promote investment of public and private capital for development purposes. As a member of the ADB, Tajikistan is eligible for the full range ADB financing programs. In December 1998, the ADB approved its first project, the Post-Conflict Infrastructure Program Loan amounting to $20 million, and two technical assistance grants totaling $1.65 million.

Primary sectors of ADB lending include energy and power, telecommunications, transportation, and the environment. Firms seeking involvement in ADB-funded projects can call Denny Barnes, Senior Commercial Officer in the U.S. Executive Director's Office, in Manila at +63-2-890-9364 or by fax at 63-2-890-9713; E-mail:dbarnes@doc.gov.

THE WORLD BANK IN TADJIKISTAN

Tajikistan declared independence from the former Soviet Union (FSU) in September 1991, and shares borders with Uzbekistan, the Kyrgyz Republic, China and Afghanistan. Seventy percent of the country's 5.8 million population resides in rural areas. Ethnically, the population is divided among several groups including: Tajiks (62 percent); Uzbeks (23 percent); Russians (8 percent); Tatars (1.4 percent) and Kyrgyz (1.3 percent). The population is large relative to the available arable land. Tajikistan's 143,000 square kilometers are mostly mountainous; 7 percent of its land is arable with 85 percent irrigated. A system of glacier fed rivers provides 3,900 megawatts of hydroelectric power. With a GNP per capita of US$330 in 1996, Tajikistan is the poorest of the FSU republics.

Tajikistan's economy is based on its primary commodities of cotton and aluminum. The country's highly mechanized and irrigated agricultural sector takes advantage of the country's vast and inexpensive water supply. The sector also accounts for 25 percent of output and 50 percent of employment, a higher share than in most FSU republics. The country's main agricultural products are cotton, silk, fruits and vegetables. Industry accounts for 35 percent of output, 12 percent of employment. The country has considerable development potential in gold and silver. The other major component of the industrial sector is textile production which accounts for about one-third of industrial output. While the Tursunzade aluminum smelter is a dominant feature of the country's landscape, its contribution to employment is relatively small. It also requires considerable subsidies and is a source of serious environmental problems in the region. However, the political and social costs of closing the plant would be substantial.

Although aluminum and cotton are unquestionably at the heart of the economy, the structure is such that links between the production of these commodities and other sectors of the economy are comparatively small, reflecting the severity of past policy distortions. For example, although cotton accounts for about 50 percent of total crop production, only 10-15 percent of cotton fiber produced is used by the local textile industry.

Despite Tajikistan's present economic crisis, it has considerable potential for development. Its land, is very fertile and has demonstrated a capacity to produce competitively for international markets. Tajikistan also has an established but idle industrial base with assets that can be deployed more efficiently and productively.

Tajikistan has been wracked by political instability and civil war since its independence. The collapse of the trade and payments system among the FSU countries triggered a precipitous decline in output. Civil war, floods and mud slides took more than 50,000 lives, displaced 850,000 persons and inflicted extensive damage to the country's infrastructure. These external shocks further contributed to inflation, an unprecedented drop in output, loss of control over public finances, rapid deterioration of the financial sector, widening trade deficit and an explosive buildup of external debt.

Recent economic and social indicators reflect the adverse impact of events on the country since its independence. Between 1991 and 1996, output fell by 40 percent, with agriculture and industry the most severely affected. In 1995, output plummeted by 8 percent. Most industrial firms have been operating at less than one-third of their capacity because fuel and other essential imports have been in short supply. Agricultural production is only at about 30 percent of its 1991 level.

The financial sector also deteriorated rapidly due to the poor performance of state-owned enterprises, which are unable to repay most of their loans. Inflation has been rampant, reaching 635 percent in 1995 and 42 percent in 1996. Inflation prior to May 1995 was linked to inflation in Russia. Also, faster than targeted credit and excessive monetary expansion in Tajikistan after the launch of the Tajik ruble also had adverse effects on inflation. In addition, both the state budget and current account deficits have been unsustainably large due to the legacy of dependence on transfers from Moscow during the Soviet era. Budget deficits on an accrual basis averaged over 27 percent of GDP between 1992-1994. For 1995 and 1996, the deficit declined to about 11 percent of GDP. At present, external debt amounts to about $850 million, over 80 percent of which is owed to the CIS countries-mainly Russia, Uzbekistan, and Kazakstan.

In an effort to embark on economic reforms, the government approved an economic program in 1995 that emphasizes stabilization of the economy and the initiation of structural changes that would halt the economic decline and increase foreign exchange earnings as well as budget revenues. The program's near-term strategic priorities are to: reform the agricultural sector and complete small and initiate large-scale privatization; restore production and business activity; create conditions for attracting foreign investments; and maintain a minimum level of social protection.

The Government's reform program has been supported by an IMF stand-by arrangement (May 1996), and IDA Credit in the form of a policy-based Agricultural Recovery and Social Protection (ARSP). Implementation of these programs were satisfactory until late 1996 when renewed violence caused the government to increase its defense expenditures significantly. They were financed by a combination of budget arrears and monetary expansion. Since the Peace Accord was signed in June 1997, there has been tangible progress on several economic issues. Since July 1997, the government has made substantial progress on getting the macroeconomic framework back on track. Inflation is slowing down as a result of stopping credit expansion and controlling the budget deficit.

THE WORLD BANK PROJECTS

Since Tajikistan joined the Bank and the International Development Association (IDA) in June 1993, the Bank's assistance has focused mainly on policy dialogue and support for the government's external assistance policy. Privatization of state-owned enterprises, farm restructuring and financial sector reform have been on the government's agenda for structural change.

Given the widespread poverty, in the country, the government and the Bank Group have agreed that the primary objective of the economic program should be poverty reduction and that this objective will be best achieved in the near-term by focusing on structural reforms, macroeconomic stability, strengthening the social safety net and fostering employment intensive growth. The rationale for this emphasis rests on the massive increase in unemployment and underemployment, accompanied by a decline in household incomes and an increase in poverty since 1991.

In May 1996, the World Bank provided its first credit, a US$5 million International Building Technical Assistance to help Tajikistan initiate privatization and undertake reforms in the financial sector. In September 1996, the World Bank approved a US$50 million Agricultural Recovery and Social Protection Credit to facilitate key agricultural reforms while helping to cushion the social costs of reform. In addition, a third credit, in the amount of US$12 million for a Pilot Poverty Alleviation Project, approved by the Bank in April 1997, will help to revive local economic activity and strengthen community-based social infrastructure and services.

The recent peace agreement between the Government and the opposition on the Terms of a Peace Accord signal a new era in Tajikistan. The Bank Group is responding to the new environment by increasing the number of operation to be implemented in 1998 and 1999.

THE WORLD BANK GROUP ACTIVITIES IN TAJIKISTAN[1]

The World Bank Group, which consists of the International Bank for Reconstruction and Development (IBRD), the International Development Association (IDA), International Finance Corporation (IFC) and the Multilateral Investment Guarantee Agency (MIGA) has one overarching goal: helping its borrowers reduce poverty. The IBRD and IDA make loans to borrower governments for projects and programs that promote economic and social progress by helping raise productivity so that people may live better lives. Along with these loans, the World Bank provides policy advice and technical assistance.

The IBRD was established in 1945 and is now owned by the governments of 180 countries. The IDA was established in 1960 to provide assistance to poorer developing countries that can not meet the IBRD terms. IDA provides credits to poorest countries - mainly those with an annual per capita gross national product of $785 (in 1996 US dollars) or less. By this criterion, about seventy countries are eligible. These are concessional credits: 40 years repayment period, 10 years grace period and interest rate zero.

The Republic of Tajikistan became a member of the World Bank on June 4, 1993. On October 15, 1996 the World Bank Field Office in Dushanbe was established. Since 1994 seven projects have been approved by the World Bank for a total commitment of USD 142 million. In addition, some nearly USD 1.0 million have been made available to Tajikistan for institutional building and post-conflict assistance on a grant basis. Furthermore, IFC contributed USD 15.5 million for the development of a gold mining project. At present, there are two additional projects under active preparation.

[1] Source: The World Bank Group

A summary of the World Bank activities in Tajikistan as well as brief project description are presented below.

I. THE FRAMEWORK FOR BANK ASSISTANCE-- THE COUNTRY ASSISTANCE STRATEGY

The Bank Group's initial assistance strategy for Tajikistan (September 1996) was intended to provide support for meeting Tajikistan's immediate needs. The Bank program began with 3 operations that were intended to a) strengthen institutional capacity to plan and implement a medium-term program of structural reform, b) support the government's efforts to stabilize the economy; and c) moderate the impact of the economy collapse on vulnerable groups.

The second Country Assistance Strategy (July 1998), which covers the period FY99-FY01, focuses on poverty reduction, post-conflict rehabilitation, economic reform and institutional building. The development of the program is linked to the security situation and paced to government's progress with the reform process. Specifically, the CAS addresses the following issues: a) reducing inefficiency by transferring publicly owned enterprises to the private sector; b) restructuring farms under private ownership and investing in rural infrastructure as a means of creating rural growth and livelihoods; c) improving coverage, access and quality of social services; d) targeting assistance to the poorest groups; and e) enhancing institutional capacity. Because most of the poor are in rural areas, a primary theme of the Country Assistance Strategy (CAS) is transferring agricultural assets from public to private hands, enhancing incentives, and investing in rural infrastructure. This would be complemented by investments in health, education, and social funds.

NON-LENDING ACTIVITIES

Emphasis on Institutional Building, Aid Coordination and Policy Dialogue

A. Country Economic and Sector Work and Policy Dialogue

Two economic reports (1994 and 1996) were produced by the Bank since Tajikistan joined the Bank. Two additional reports (Country Economic Memorandum and Public Expenditures Review) are planned for FY99.
Two sector notes (poverty note, health note) were completed and a third note (education) is being prepared.

Policy dialogue with the Government is a continuous process. It is carried out during Bank missions, Government visits to Washington and by the Field Office on a regular basis.

B. Institutional Building

Institutional Development Fund Grants (FY94-FY98). The Bank approved three IDF grants (totaling US$ 827,000) for:
establishment of an external assistance management unit (approved in August 1993 and completed in 1996, US$ 442,000) in collaboration with UNDP;
public procurement reform (approved in June 1996, US$ 178,000). The government is in the process of identifying consultants to carry out the work; and

public debt management (approved in April 1997, US$ 207,000.). Government has already identified a consultant who is expected to begin his work in August 1997.

Post-Conflict Program Grant (FY98). The Bank also approved (in March 1998) a Post-Conflict Program Grant to the CNR in the amount of USD 165,000. The grant is provided from a new facility established by the World Bank specifically for post-conflict countries. Its objective is to support the CNR sub-commission on military issues in the design and preparation of a program for the reintegration of demobilized soldiers. The CNR is expected to set-up a Reintegration Center with an overall coordinating role and to contract to external partners some of the activities to be implemented.

Training activities. Over the past 18 months, about 140 Tajiks have or will have attended 40 World Bank Group (essentially EDI) training courses. The topics include social policy reform, health, agriculture and procurement. Other donors and agencies tend to provide similar training. There is room for coordination between the donor community so as to reduce the degree of overlap, particularly with respect to the selection of candidates.

C. Aid Coordination--Consultative Group Meeting

The World Bank organized the first CGM for Tajikistan in Tokyo on October 31, 1996. Indications of pledges amounting to US$185 million in 1997 were received to help support the balance-of-payments, the investment program and technical assistance needs of Tajikistan. The second CG Meeting was held on May 20, 1998 in Paris. A total of US$280 million of potential commitments for 1998 and 1999 were indicated by the participants. All commitments of assistance are subject to negotiation and signing of agreements between the Government and the concerned parties. The government, through the ACU, is currently in the process of following up on the CGM.

LENDING ACTIVITIES

Emphasis on Poverty Alleviation and Policy Reform

A. Two Completed Operations

1. Agricultural Recovery and Social Protection Credit (FY97). This credit of US$ 50 million was approved by the Bank in September 1996 and was fully disbursed. The main objectives of the credit were:
To support Government's efforts to: (a) stabilize the economy; (b) ease the foreign exchange shortage so that critical imported inputs can be acquired; (c) reform agriculture policy in areas including the pricing and marketing of agricultural commodities, land reform, trade, and privatizing state enterprises; and (d) enhance the social safety net and improve its targeting. Restoring macroeconomic stability and implementing structural reforms in agriculture would be help arrest the collapse in production and employment.

Status: The credit had been fully disbursed by April 1997 (USD 30 million disbursed in 1996 and USD 20 million in 1997). The government used the proceeds of the credit to finance the overall budget, with particular emphasis on the social safety net in 1996. About US$15 million was used to fund the SSN during the fourth quarter of 1996.

2. Post-Conflict Rehabilitation Credit (FY98). The PCRC was designed as a budget support project to help the Government support the peace process in Tajikistan. Total amount of credit is $10 million, of which $7 million are intended to be used by the Government to reduce its compensation arrears, and the rest $3 million will go for implementing the peace accord (expenses on refugees, CNR, etc.). This operation was approved by the World Bank Board of Directors on December 16 1997 and became effective on December 19, 1997. The whole amount of the credit was disbursed to the Government in one tranche.

B. Five Ongoing Operations

1. **Institutional Building Technical Assistance (FY96).** This US$ 5 million credit was approved by the Bank in May 1996. The project consists of three components:

Technical assistance to the SPC: The project provides financing for consultants, training and office equipment to help prepare and implement a comprehensive privatization program. The technical assistance to the SPC will help with design and implementation in the following four sub-components: (i) privatization of small enterprises; (ii) privatization of medium and large enterprises; (iii) mass privatization; and (iv) public information in support of privatization. Training SPC staff in all aspects of privatization will be an on-going activity of each sub-component.

Technical Assistance to the Ministry of Agriculture (MOA): The proposed project supports the Government's farm restructuring program and demonopolization of the cotton processing and marketing channels. It provides consultancy services, training and office equipment to help the MOA to: (i) identify and propose changes in existing laws that are needed to ensure secure land access rights and full transferability to access rights, specify implementation mechanisms for the farm restructuring program and develop voluntary farmer associations; (ii) identify options for revising the legal framework in cotton processing and marketing, work toward design and implementation of a strategy for demonopolizing the state cotton marketing entity and ginneries and provide options for reforming the cotton sector; (iii) train MOA staff in all aspects of farm restructuring and demonopolization of the state cotton marketing entity.

Assistance to the Financial Sector: The major objective of technical assistance for the financial sector s to help upgrade a number of key operations crucial for the success of banking reform. The project supports banking reform by providing technical assistance and training for the NBT and other banks to facilitate transition to a market-based financial system. Technical assistance under this component will be closely coordinated with assistance provided by the IMF and USAID and will consist of the following sun-components: (i) revising the current legal framework for banks; (ii) preparing and implementing new accounting and auditing procedures for banks, based on internationally accepted accounting principles; (iii) developing audit reports for the four sectoral banks; (iv) developing effective supervision of the banking system; and (v) introducing efficient payment mechanisms.

Status: All 3 components--privatization, banking and farm restructuring--are under implementation. All the legal aspects of the privatization component (law on privatization, regulations on valuation, segmentation, and investment funds) are now in place. The database on PEs is being established. The banking component (Arthur Andersen) is on schedule, with the legal component completed. Work on land reform and cotton marketing restructuring (under SOFRECO) begun in May, after some delays related to the security situation.

2. Pilot Poverty Alleviation Project (FY97). The project (US$ 12 million) was approved by the Bank in April 1997 and became effective in July 1997. The project consists of two components:

Expanding Existing Poverty Alleviation Programs of International Non-Governmental Organizations (NGOs) (US$7.5 million) will help to improve the living standards of the most vulnerable through:

The Shelter and Housing Rehabilitation Program, (US$3.2 million), carried out by Save the Children Federation of the United States, which will assist 2,000 poor and previously displaced families in the self-help reconstruction of their homes in the five districts most devastated by the recent civil war, Bokhtar, Vakhsh, kabodien and Shaartuz of the Khatlon region.

The Micro-Credit program (US$ 1.0 million), carried out by the Save the Children of the United States, which will provide access to credit and mobilize savings for 3,750 poor women in the Bokhtar, Vakhsh, Vose, Kurgan-Tube and Kolkhozabad districts of the Khatlon region.

The Program of Support to female-Headed Households (US$1.0 million), carried out by the Save the Children of the United Kingdom, which will provide a total of 3,700 female-headed households (2,100 of them in Vakhsh, and 1,600 in Aini, Penjikent, Dushanbe, and Shaartuz) will access to and ownership of agricultural assets such as livestock, seed and tools, as well as technical advise, and start-up grants for day-care centers and schools.

Agricultural Reform Program (US$0.7 million), carried out by the Aga Khan Foundation, which will help to increase food crop production and productivity, and establish and support private farm management in the Gorno-Badakhshan region.

Future sponsored activities (US$1.6 million) which will provide funding for the above or other NGO programs, and/or additional micro-projects. Tajikistan Social Investment Fund (US$4.2 million) will help to channel new funds to many poor communities through:

Development of the Tajikistan Social Investment Fund (TASIF) (US$1.6 million) which will provide funds for operational support, training, and technical assistance to TASIF staff on participatory community development, contracting, bidding procedures, project management, supervision, and evaluation.
70 Microprojects (US$ 2.6 million) which will primarily improve water supply and sanitation, irrigation canals, local roads, and reconstruct kindergartens, schools, and health facilities.

3. Post-Conflict Emergency Reconstruction Project Credit (FY98). The main objective of the PCERP is to support Tajikistan's recovery from the civil conflict. The amount of this credit is $10 million. The project was approved by the World Bank Board of Directors on January 29, 1998; its implementation started in March 1998 and is expected to be completed in two years, in Spring 2000. It will help the Government in reconstruction of the physical infrastructure and economic assets in war-affected areas (namely Karategin Valley) and has the following components:

Agricultural Support: the emergency purchase and distribution of seed and fertilizer to private farmers for the Spring 1998 planting season (US$0.6 million equivalent, or 6 percent of base cost);

Bridges and Roads: the repair or reconstruction of an estimated 15 destroyed or damaged bridges, and completion of a 4 kilometer by-pass road for the town of Darband to replace the current non-functional road (US$5.1 million equivalent, or 51 percent of base cost);

Small Community Works: the reconstruction, repair and/or rehabilitation of destroyed, damaged or dilapidated schools, health care facilities, and other community facilities, and the implementation of other programs of small works benefiting local communities in the Karategin-Tavildara Valley area (US$2.3 million equivalent, or 23 percent of base cost); and

Other Infrastructure Works: the repair and rehabilitation of war-damaged infrastructure in the power and agriculture sectors (US$1.9 million equivalent, or 20 percent of base cost).

4. Structural Adjustment Credit (FY98)

This policy-based operation of US$50 million (SDR 37.1 million) is designed to focus on privatization, banking sector reform and protecting the social safety net. The operation is underpinned by the analytical work being undertaken under IBTA. Being an adjustment operation, this credit is conditional on having a satisfactory macroeconomic framework.

The project was approved by the Board on July 30, 1998. Specifically the credit will assist in the following:

Privatization of Enterprises. (i) Prepare the necessary legal framework for accelerated privatization and development of the private sector; (ii) develop a comprehensive Privatization Action Plan for 1998; (iii) accelerate privatization of small-scale and large-scale enterprises; (iv) accelerate conversion of large-scale enterprises to open joint-stock companies; (v) protect shareholder rights by establishing a centralized share registry; (vi) sell state-owned unfinished construction; (vii) accelerate privatization of the state-owned trucking fleet; and (viii) restructure the cotton marketing agency, Glavkhlopkoprom, and the Tajik Aluminum Plant.

Financial Sector Reform. (i) Strengthen the banking sector's legal framework; (ii) provide banks with additional mechanisms to protect themselves against borrower

defaults by improving the current Law on Collateral; (iii) ensure that banks manage risk well by improving regulations and supervision; (iv) improve information on banks for shareholders, management, creditors, regulators, and the public; (v) improve the payments system to reduce risk and transaction costs; and (vi) restructure the banking sector and promote savings.
Enhancing Budgetary Provisions for the Social Safety Net, Health and Education. Protect social expenditures by ensuring that education, health and the social safety net receive a reasonable share of the budget.

Status: First tranche (US$ 20 million) was disbursed on August --, 1998. The reforms supported by the second tranche are being implemented.

5. Emergency Flood Assistance Project (FY99). This project was designed to help the Government overcome the consequences of the natural disasters which took place in the country between January and May 1998 (heavy snows and rains, which caused floods, landslides, etc.). The project focuses on rehabilitation of the infrastructure (mainly roads and bridges) in the flood-affected areas. The project, which amounts to US$5 million, was approved by the World Bank on August --, 1998.

IFC

1. Zeravshan Gold Company (IFC, FY97-98). This is the largest foreign joint venture and the first mining project in the country. IFC financial involvement (loan/equity/quasi-equity) amounts to US$ 15.55 million. After a difficult start, the company is operating satisfactorily, with gold exports actually taking place.

B. Two Planned Operations (FY99)

1. Farm Privatization Support Project. Main objective is to support the Government program for land reform and restructuring of the state and collective farms in a systematic and transparent manner and to provide models for wider geographical replicability. The proposed project will have the following components:

provision for essential pre-privatization support services necessary to sustain privatized agriculture, which are: (a) land registration services, (b) farm information and advisory services, and (c) rehabilitation of critical irrigation and drainage infrastructure; and

provision of post privatization support services which are credit and community based social services.

2. Institutional Building Technical Assistance II. (to be defined)

US ASSISTANCE TO TAJIKISTAN

	FY 1998 Actual	FY 1999 Estimate	FY 2000 Request
FREEDOM Support Act	$12,150,000	$11,870,000	$12,000,000
P.L. 480 Title II	4,049	--	--

Tajikistan is a small, but unstable, new state in the center of Asia that is emerging from five years of civil war between regional and ideological factions. The United States is the largest bilateral donor, and a key supporter of the 1997 Peace Accord and an independent and stable Tajikistan. The fragile peace and potential disintegration of Tajikistan threatens regional stability and deflects attention within the region from critical economic and political reforms. The humanitarian situation is dire.

THE DEVELOPMENT CHALLENGE.

Tajikistan is the poorest of the new Central Asian states and the only one in which underlying ethnic, regional, economic and ideological strains led to open warfare and major population displacements. The June 27, 1997 Peace Accord opened a new phase in Tajikistan's short history, formally ending a civil war begun in 1992 which left at least 50,000 dead and 700,000 displaced and a legacy of hatred and suspicion which makes reconstruction tenuous and difficult.

The most important task for Tajikistan is to carry out the Peace Accord. USAID's role is to provide support for the reconciliation process and to rebuild institutional capacity. However, in the fall of 1998, relocation of the U.S. Ambassador and all U.S. employees from Dushanbe to Almaty, Kazakhstan limited USAID's capacity to support the Peace Accord and development change. The security situation had deteriorated to the point where it was unsafe to continue a U.S. physical presence. Official travel was severely curtailed. Neither USAID officers nor contractors have easy access to development partners or clients. USAID must now find ways to provide effective assistance from its regional office in Almaty, Kazakhstan.

By the end of FY 1998, progress had slowed and little if any prospects were on the horizon for improvement. While most of the Tajik refugees who fled to Afghanistan had returned by early 1998, the government and opposition groups continued to face internal obstacles to a sustained peace settlement. On the more positive side, however, proposals for amendments to the constitution are under review and parliamentary elections tentatively planned for mid-1999. These may well be the most important elections within the region.

Likewise, progress on economic reform faltered in 1998. Macroeconomic stability suffered, and the Tajik ruble continued its decline, albeit at a slower pace. By October 1998, the Government of Tajikistan (GOT) was implementing International Monetary Fund (IMF) fiscal austerity policies, and the macroeconomic situation had made up some lost ground. Whereas progress in privatization remained slow, there have been some hopeful signs, such as changes proposed to the antiquated Russian tax laws.

The focus for U.S. assistance remains humanitarian in nature. Private voluntary organizations (PVOs), such as the World Food Program, Mercy Corps, CARE, Save the Children, and the Aga Khan Foundation (AKF), have been innovative in using U.S. assistance and the transition from strictly humanitarian relief to humanitarian-focused economic development which lays a foundation for sustainable development. USAID assistance to other international organizations (e.g., United Nations Mission of Observers in Tajikistan (UNMOT), UNDP, and IBRD is anticipated in order to secure a favorable environment for USAID intervention and to maximize impact. Assistance to the Tajikistan Social Investment Fund's poverty alleviation program provides an opportunity for USAID to support community mobilization around water use issues, institute measures to prevent water-borne diseases, and address policy issues related to water charges and consumer use.

USAID increased its support for the peace process through reconstruction, assistance to civil society development, and constitutional and electoral reform. USAID also continued to provide advice and training on privatization and bank supervision with plans to expand this modest effort, the security situation permitting. Some short-term technical assistance and training is underway in economic restructuring, democratization, and health and family planning. USAID participant training programs both expose Tajik citizens to alternative approaches and systems for managing their country and develop the human resources needed for development once there is greater political stability.

OTHER DONORS.

While the U.S. had taken the lead in responding to the humanitarian crises following the civil war, the IMF and the World Bank (IBRD) provided substantial resources to support macroeconomic stability and reform. Thus far, $22 million has been received from the IMF and $60 million from the IBRD. Their assistance has dropped in recent years, with IBRD currently financing only a $12 million Poverty Alleviation Project. However, at the end of FY 1998, each organization came forward with $10 million to support the peace process. United Nations High Commission of Refugees (UNHCR) has provided significant assistance during the refugee repatriation period, with the United Nations Development Program (UNDP) moving into the field with increasingly significant resources beginning in FY 1995. The European Union (EU), individual EU countries, Turkey, Russia and Iran have also assisted Tajikistan, as has the International Red Cross, supported in part by U.S. Government contributions. Large numbers of Private Voluntary Organizations, including several from the United States, are active and effectively managing their programs in Tajikistan.

FY 2000 PROGRAM.

USAID's involvement in Tajikistan assumes continued progress in the inter-Tajik peace process, which is essential for achieving national reconciliation and holding elections that meet international standards. Under economic restructuring, USAID will focus on two objectives: growth and development of private enterprise and evolution of a commercial legal and regulatory structure. There may also be some assistance to build the private banking sector. Tajikistan is one of the lowest rated countries in the region in terms of macroeconomic policy, and economic growth will be limited until they move forward on reforms.

The size and nature of USAID's programs will be determined by the political and security situation of Tajikistan. USAID will continue to support the development of non-governmental organizations (NGOs), with a focus on those that contribute to the peace process through reconciliation and local community development. USAID is combining humanitarian and economic development efforts by moving forward with a competitive grant process to identify and support the most cost-effective local government activities in communities where there are also opportunities to build reconciliation in the post war period. These grants will be implemented by private voluntary and international organizations.

USAID will continue to support independent electronic media, focussing on how media stations can contribute to public understanding of the peace initiatives, upcoming elections, and proposed constitutional changes. After the election of the new parliament, USAID expects to direct assistance toward building the institutional capacity of the parliament. These elections, scheduled for mid-1999, are considered to be among the most significant and competitive in the region. USAID intends to increase support for this important undertaking. In the social sector, USAID will continue to work closely with other donors, PVOs and NGOs. Special initiatives in reproductive health, infectious disease, and health partnerships will be programmed in a manner which promotes citizen and community involvement as well as achieves needed improvements in health.

TAJIKISTAN FY 1999 PROGRAM SUMMARY*
(in Thousand of Dollars)

Strategic Objectives	Economic Restructuring	Democratic Transition	Social Stabilization	Cross-cutting / Special Initiatives	Total
Privatization	--	--	--	--	--
Fiscal Reform	--	--	--	--	--
Private Enterprise	1,650	--	--	--	1,650
Financial Reform	1,150	--	--	--	1,150
Energy	--	--	--	--	--
Environmental Management	--	--	--	--	--
Citizens' Participation	--	1,800	--	--	1,800
Legal Systems	--	--	--	--	--
Local Government	--	--	--	--	--
Crises	--	--	1,400	--	1,400
Social Benefits	--	--	--	--	--
Environmental Health	--	--	--	--	--
Cross-cutting / Special Initiatives	--	--	--	6,000	6,000
TOTAL	2,800	1,800	1,400	6,000	12,000
*Freedom Support Act (FSA) funds					
USAID Mission Director: Glenn Anders					

SELECTED PROJECTS

ACCELERATED DEVELOPMENT AND GROWTH OF PRIVATE ENTERPRISES, 110-S001.3

STATUS: Continuing
PROPOSED OBLIGATION AND FUNDING SOURCE: FY 2000: $1,650,000 Freedom Support Act
INITIAL OBLIGATION: FY 1995; **ESTIMATED COMPLETION DATE:** FY 2002

Summary: Prior to 1996, the policy environment was not conducive to concentrated technical assistance in the area of economic restructuring. In the wake of the ongoing civil war, training and exchange were the best mechanisms for Tajiks to observe developments elsewhere and to gain international experience. To encourage reform, USAID engaged Tajik counterparts in necessary private sector reforms through training courses and modest, targeted technical assistance.

The objective of this activity is to achieve accelerated development and growth of private enterprises. USAID has sent hundreds of Tajiks to U.S. and other Central Asian countries for short-term training in a variety of economic reform areas. Specialized in-country training has also been effective. Tajiks trained under these programs now form a professional cadre of reform-minded officials who are taking the lead in crafting long-term economic stabilization and structural adjustment programs.

An area of USAID training support that has been well received in Tajikistan is commercial law reform. As in the other countries of Central Asia, the Government of Tajikistan (GOT) has indicated its support for the development of a core set of commercial legislation that will serve as the legal backbone for the nation's emerging private sector. USAID has already demonstrated its capacity to provide expertise in this area through its comprehensive commercial law assistance activities in Kazakhstan and Kyrgyzstan.

Although continued political instability led to the suspension of USAID activity at the end of the year, the security situation permitting, new technical assistance is planned that will constitute a critical element of the peace process. Success in this area will be achieved with an increase in the share of GDP being generated by private enterprises to 75% in 2001.

Entrepreneurs and those involved in private sector development stand to benefit from this initiative. More broadly, the citizens of Tajikistan would benefit from economic reform that leads to sustainable economic growth.

Key Results: Accelerated development and growth of private enterprise hinge on progress toward the following: 1) continued GOT adherence to conditionality of international financial institutions; 2) the dollar volume of joint venture funds invested increasing to $11 million in FY 2001; 3) the share of GDP generated by private enterprise growing to 50% by FY 2001; and 4) the percentage of total capital investment in the private sector also growing to 75% by FY 2001.

Performance & Prospects: During FY 1998, the Central Asian-American Enterprise Fund (CAAEF) made eight loans totaling $730,468 to private businesses in Tajikistan. Winrock Farmer-to-Farmer and USAID-funded International Executive Service Corps advisors have assisted Tajik enterprises in preparing business plans and loan/equity proposals for CAAEF and have acted as consultants on post-investment management.

Subject to continued commitment by the Government of Tajikistan to economic reforms, as well as increased security and political stability in the country, USAID plans to undertake a modest commercial law assistance initiative in FY 1999 and FY 2000 to help the GOT develop a market-oriented commercial infrastructure, including key reforms in the law.

The program will initially focus on drafting the following laws: bankruptcy; collateral law; banking; and foreign investment; areas designed to promote the transfer of productive assets to the private sector and strengthen the rights of private investors. Practical constraints to business formation and operation (*e.g.*, licensing and registration procedures) will also be addressed. In addition to commercial law reform, the activity will provide in-country training to key officials involved with the implementation of a market-friendly regulatory regime, *i.e.*, judges, lawyers, and prosecutors. Work under this strategic objective will promote the rule of law and thereby the solidification of the peace process.

Possible Adjustments to Plans: The most immediate concern is the direction that the country takes with regard to the civil war and violence. USAID closely monitors this issue and will adjust the program accordingly. USAID is interested in restarting efforts in commercial law.

One of the key foci in the coming years will be the Fergana Valley, for it is one of the most dynamic regions for private enterprise growth in Central Asia. Plus, parts of the Valley have been untouched by the civil war. If the opportunity presents itself, USAID will strengthen the IESC activities in this region.

Other Donors Programs: USAID will continue to work closely with the various governmental entities involved in private sector development and economic restructuring issues. The World Bank and IMF are also directly engaged in this effort. USAID coordinates closely with these two institutions on their activities and in some instances, such as in the recent placement of a privatization advisor in Dushanbe, directly supports their programs. Activities are also coordinated with those of other donors such as the European Union and UNDP, as they are interested in economic reform issues.

Principal Contractors/Grantees/Implementing Agencies: USAID assistance activities are implemented through private U.S. firms, such as ARD/Checchi, and U.S. PVOs, IESC and CAAEF.

Selected Performance Measures:

	Baseline	Target
GOT adherence to conditions of international financial institutions	Yes (1997)	Yes (1997)
Dollar value of joint venture funds invested (millions)	$3 (1997)	$11 (2001)
Share of GDP generated by private enterprise	20% (1996)	50% (2001)
Percentage of total capital investment in the private sector	20% (1997)	75% (2001)

A MORE COMPETITIVE AND MARKET RESPONSIVE PRIVATE FINANCIAL SECTOR, 110-S001.4

STATUS: Continuing
PROPOSED OBLIGATION AND FUNDING SOURCE: FY 2000: $1,150,000 Freedom Support Act
INITIAL OBLIGATION: FY 1998; **ESTIMATED COMPLETION DATE:** FY 2000

Summary: Before 1996, the policy environment was not conducive to concentrated technical assistance in the area of economic restructuring. In the wake of the civil war, training and exchanges were the best mechanisms for Tajiks to observe developments elsewhere and to gain international experience. To encourage reform, USAID engaged Tajik counterparts in necessary private sector reforms through training courses and modest, targeted technical assistance.

The objective of this activity is to create a more competitive and market responsive private financial sector. USAID has sent hundreds of Tajiks to the U.S. and other Central Asian countries for short-term training in a variety of economic reform areas. Specialized in-country training has also been effective. Tajiks trained under these programs now form a cadre of reform-minded officials who are taking the lead in crafting long-term economic stabilization and structural adjustment programs.

USAID's targeted training and technical support has sought to maximize its impact on key economic reforms. For example, in early FY 1997, a USAID privatization advisor played a crucial role in initiating privatization reforms that are now being undertaken as part of a comprehensive World Bank program. In early 1998, a USAID bank supervision consultant began an assignment with the Tajik Central Bank. The activity was designed to help the Central Bank establish the capability to effectively supervise the commercial banking sector in Tajikistan through design and training of a modern bank supervision unit. The project appeared to get off to a very rapid start, with the resident advisor quickly establishing credibility with his counterparts.

After only a few weeks, the advisor had already undertaken an on-site commercial bank examination. In addition, the Chairman of the Central Bank requested weekly meetings with the USAID advisor to review progress in implementing the advisor's ambitious work plan. Although continued political instability led to the suspension of USAID activity at the end of FY 1998, further technical assistance is planned for 1999 and beyond and will constitute a critical element of the peace process.

Despite problems related to ongoing political instability in Tajikistan, during the 1996-1998 period, the Government of Tajikistan showed increased commitment to economic reforms. Success in this activity will be achieved if there are increases in the ratio of private sector deposits in Tajikistan's banking system to GDP. To date, however, baseline data have not been gathered.

The direct beneficiary of this activity would be the Central Bank of Tajikistan. More importantly, the citizens of Tajikistan would benefit from economic reform that leads to sustainable economic growth, a critical element of the peace process.

Key Results: This was a new activity in FY 1998. Baseline data and targets will have to be completed. Achievement of financial sector reform will depend upon progress as measured by the following indicators: 1) increases in private sector deposits in Tajikistan's banking system as a percentage of GDP; 2) a positive USAID assessment of regulatory readiness of the Central Bank of Tajikistan; 3) increases in the number of banks converted to international accounting standards by FY 2001; and 4) consideration/adoption of appropriate official laws and regulations.

Performance and Prospects: The political and security situation permitting, USAID's efforts in FY 2000 will continue to be targeted at achieving key results in the legal/regulatory structure of the commercial banking sector, increasing the number and quality of financial services available, and improving Central Bank access to information about the banking system and its capability to enforce prudent norms in the banking sector. These core efforts will likely be complemented by a progressive emphasis on use and strengthening of international accounting standards in the banking sector. USAID will coordinate its Central Bank assistance closely with the IMF and with the advisory assistance from the World Bank. USAID's successful work in banking system development in Kazakhstan and Kyrgyzstan provides a significant advantage in continuation of the program in Tajikistan.

Possible Adjustments to Plans: The most immediate concern is the direction that the country takes with regard to the civil war and violence. USAID closely monitors this issue and will adjust the program accordingly. Based upon an expressed need, USAID may begin to work in the area of accounting conversion for private enterprise, with limited training and technical assistance. This would complement an existing privatization program of the World Bank.

Other Donor Programs: USAID will continue to work closely with the various governmental entities involved in private sector development and economic restructuring issues. The World Bank and IMF are also directly engaged in this effort. USAID has coordinated closely with these two institutions on their activities. Activities are also coordinated with those of other donors such as EU and UNDP, which are interested in economic reform issues.

Principal Contractors, Grantees, or Implementing Agencies: The private U.S. firm of Arthur Andersen has been the primary implementing agency.

Selected Performance Measures: This was a new activity in FY 1998. Baseline data and targets will have to be completed. The indicators to be tracked are listed below:

	Baseline	Target
Private sector deposits in banking system as a percentage of GDP	NA (1997)	NA
USAID assessment of regulatory readiness of Central Bank	NA (1997)	NA
Number of banks converted to international accounting standards	NA (1997)	NA
Consideration/adoption of appropriate official laws and regulations	NA (1997)	NA

INCREASED CITIZEN'S PARTICIPATION IN POLITICAL AND ECONOMIC DECISION-MAKING, 110-SOO2.1

STATUS: Continuing
PROPOSED OBLIGATIONS AND FUNDING SOURCES: FY 2000: $1,800,000 Freedom Support Act
INITIAL OBLIGATION: FY 1995; **ESTIMATED COMPLETION DATE**: FY 2002

Summary: Efforts to bring about political consensus in Tajikistan have proven to be long, arduous and fragile. Nonetheless, provided that the security situation permits international organizations to operate in Tajikistan, opportunities do exist to promote reconciliation through assistance to the election process, enhancement of information flows about the peace process and the upcoming elections, and assistance in increasing the participation of Tajik citizens in the rehabilitation process. The aftermath of civil war and the economic decline have, in a number of instances, left vacuums that can be filled in part by local community groups working together to help in rehabilitating the country. In FY 1999, USAID initiated substantial assistance for the upcoming parliamentary elections. In addition, modest NGO, judicial and media support activities will continue, but with more emphasis on the peace process.

Key Results: Three key intermediate results were concluded to be necessary to achieve the Strategic Objective. NGO participation in civil society must be strengthened, information on domestic economic policies and politics must become more widely available and the Government must become more responsive and accountable to citizens and citizens' organizations.

Performance and Prospects: To date, over 1072 NGOs and local community group representatives have participated in USAID training courses, and USAID has made some 90 small NGO seed grants totaling approximately $239,370 (through Counterpart Consortium and ISAR). USAID assistance through the International Center for Not-for-profit Law (ICNL) helped to facilitate the drafting of revisions to the Public Association Law which was passed by the parliament over this past year. The judicial association of Tajikistan, with the assistance of ABA/CEELI, has played an active role in promoting an independent judiciary as the Council for National Reconciliation considers constitutional amendments. The association adopted an ethics code to which all judges must adhere -- an important step toward transparency and accountability. ABA/CEELI recently convened a successful workshop with Tajik officials on corruption law and intends to follow-up in the near future. Assistance to independent media continues to be required given the government's use of the media law against media outlets and given future demands of the peace process. USAID is supporting the Internews production of Pairachi Zindagi ("The Path of Life"), a first step in supporting more independent media outlets, critical to fostering greater citizen participation.

USAID is looking to continue these successes with the eventual return of American staff to our partner offices (i.e., Internews and ABA). In addition, the upcoming elections in the summer of 1999 in Tajikistan challenge the GOT and our partners to support electoral reforms necessary to convene fraud-free elections. USAID and its partners are working closely with GOT (through legislation reform, election administration training, and voter registration system development) to develop conditions conducive for elections that meet international standards.

Possible Adjustments to Plans: In addition to an increase in election-related assistance this year, USAID anticipates a more intensive strategic focus on conflict/crisis management and the peace process in the upcoming years. In particular, USAID intends to work more closely with other donor partners on cross-sectoral integration and synergies in our programming.

Other Donor Programs: USAID is working closely with UNMOT and the OSCE on coordinating election-related assistance, as well as on specific joint projects. The international community, including USAID, is paying particular attention the country's all-important first post-conflict elections. Joint activities include co-sponsoring a constitutional reform workshop and an upcoming election law seminar. The OSCE and UNMOT have indicated an interest in providing additional commodities to support USAID's voter registration system development activity. Other donors, including the EU and various UN agencies, are also involved in a variety of activities that promote democracy and the peace efforts. Donors meet regularly to discuss areas of common concern, and this coordination will continue.

Principal Contractors, Grantees or Agencies: Several USAID-funded American NGOs, such as the American Bar Association/CEELI, Internews, and the International Foundation for Electoral Systems (IFES), are playing a role in promoting democracy and the peace effort in Tajikistan. The Counterpart International, Aid to Artisans, and the International Center for Not-for-profit Law, which together form the Counterpart Consortium, also participate in local NGO development. Initiative for Social Action and

Renewal in Eurasia (ISAR) will also participate in the development of local environmental NGOs.

Selected Performance Measures:

	Baseline	Target
Number of NGOs involved in advocacy	9/9 (1997)	60/40 (2001)
Average daily minutes of local news programming	5 (1996)	14 (2001)
Number of Parliamentary hearings and committee meetings addressing legislative/policy issues	0 (1994)	5 (2001)

IMPROVED RESPONSE TO AND MANAGEMENT OF HUMANITARIAN CRISES, 110-S003.1

STATUS: Continuing
PROPOSED OBLIGATION AND FUNDING SOURCES: FY 2000 $1,400,000 Freedom Support Act
INITIAL OBLIGATION: FY 1993; **ESTIMATED COMPLETION DATE:** FY 2000

Summary: The U.S. has been a lead donor in providing humanitarian assistance following the 1992 civil war. In FY 1996 and FY 1997, there was a marked shift away from strictly humanitarian assistance toward a program emphasizing economic growth. However, events in 1998, including the worsening of the already fragile political situation, a number of serious security incidents, and set-backs in implementation of the 1997 peace accords, have now required that programming needs to take into account the relative instability of the domestic situation. The closing of the U.S. Embassy in Dushanbe and the withdrawal of USG employees has reinforced this view.

Therefore, support for the peace process has assumed a greater priority for USAID in Tajikistan. Seventy-five percent of the available development resources in 1998 were directed towards this end. USAID expects that the program emphasis on reinforcing the peace process will continue through FY 2000. USAID has therefore chosen to target social development activities that involve members of the local community, contribute to the development of indigenous organizations, encourage sustainability, and provide a strong link to longer-term development within an environment of peace and social harmony.

Key Results: In 1998, USAID's Tajikistan Social Investment Fund (TASIF) started to implement micro projects. The major participants involved in implementing micro projects are: a) the community or group that benefits directly from the micro project in terms of increased job opportunities and income and improved access to services; b) the sponsoring agency, that is, the local government, NGO or community group; and c) the implementing agency.

The implementing agency is an NGO, local government or other community group. More than 40 micro-projects have been implemented already. USAID is also supporting activities that have proven successful in increasing employment and income in the agricultural and agro-processing sector through community participation. USAID supports activities to increase community access to primary health care. USAID actively supported citizen-sponsored government action to meet the challenges facing Tajikistan and coordinated with the Ministries of Health, Education, Agriculture, Finance and the State Committee for Emergencies; helped pass a decree to prohibit the reconstruction of houses in flood plains working closely with flood-affected populations and local and international NGOs; and integrated a peace component into a rehabilitation project for war-affected schools.

Performance & Prospects: Development-oriented humanitarian programs introduced since 1996 have achieved increasingly noteworthy results. A USAID-supported small loan program for farmers permits loan repayment in kind directly to local institutions such as hospitals and orphanages, thereby benefitting not only farmers but vulnerable groups. Other programs have improved access to basic health services for 260,000 people, and established 62 village health committees covering approximately 85,000 beneficiaries. A revolving pharmaceutical fund established with USAID support has enabled 17,000 patients to purchase or receive needed medications.

USAID has provided critically needed funding to the United Nations Mission of Observers in Tajikistan (UNMOT) as a key contribution to maintaining personnel and peacekeeping activities at a critical time in the implementation of the peace process. USAID also provided support for UNDP/UNOPS activities, particularly a UNDP rural reconstruction project for war affected areas. In 1998, USAID initiated assistance to a project of the Aga Khan Foundation (AKF) to support establishment of private farmers in a war-affected area, to promote community-based peace and confidence-building measures in the Gharm region, and supported World Bank assistance to their Poverty Alleviation Project to improve access to social and economic services.

Possible Adjustments: It is expected that assistance through the year 2000 will continue to focus on economic and social development activities which support the peace process.

Other Donor Programs: Donor coordination in Tajikistan is excellent and is regarded as among the most effective in the former Soviet Union. Various donor groups meet weekly to discuss programs and exchange information on important developmental and security issues affecting Tajikistan. Lead organizations include the United Nations (UNDP/UNOPS, UNICEF, WHO, etc.), bilateral donors including various European organizations, and a variety of American and international PVOs. Both the World Bank and the UNDP support initiatives that rely largely on local and foreign non-governmental organizations to deliver badly needed goods and services to many areas of Tajikistan.

Principal Contractors, Grantees, or Implementing Agencies: Groups that have received USAID funds include Save the Children, Relief International, CARE, World Food Program, Mercy Corps International, and AKF.

Selected Performance Measures:

	Baseline	Target
Humanitarian/crises activities	50% (1997)	10% (2000)
Reconciliation/development programs	50% (1997)	90% (2000)

STRATEGIC INFORMATION AND US-TADJIK RELATIONS

POLITICAL DEVELOPMENTS

Tajikistan is a nation undergoing profound political and economic change. It is a newly independent nation still in the process of stabilizing its internal political situation as well as its relations with neighboring states. Although the 1992 civil war, which was caused by regional economic and political differences, largely subsided by March 1993, there continues to be sporadic fighting along the Tajik border with Afghanistan between remnants of the Tajik opposition and Russian border guard forces.

In June 1997 a peace agreement was signed between the government and the United Tajik Opposition (UTO) under which the government promised to lift the ban on all parties of the United Tajik Opposition in order that fair and democratic elections can take place. The signing of the peace agreement opened a new window of opportunity for economic reforms. In spite of this major step for the peace process, Tajikistan is still plagued by occasional outbreaks of violence led by regional warlords and disgruntled UTO guerilla leaders.

In August 1998, four United Nations military observers were killed in the eastern part of the country, and in November 1998, an armed rebellion in Khujand, in the northern part of the country, led by Colonel Mahmud Khudoiberdiyev and former premier Abdumalik Abdullojonov was defeated by government troops after intense fighting. The Tajik peace process suffered an additional blow when, in May 1999, UTO leaders pulled out of the National Reconciliation Commission following the government's refusal of the opposition's demand for greater influence in the power sharing coalition.

Tajikistan is located at a crossroads of major world civilizations--Russia, Turkey, Iran, India-Pakistan, and China--and has been influenced by each. Russia, China and India share an interest in restraining Islamic fundamentalism, while Iran and Pakistan vie to reinforce Tajikistan's Islamic identity. Russia and Tajikistan's fellow Central Asian neighbors--Kazakhstan, Kyrgyzstan, and Uzbekistan--have been concerned about drug and gun running across the borders as well as Islamic fundamentalism, and have mostly supported Tajikistan's secular regime. Russia has been concerned to safeguard the 90,000 ethnic Russians still residing in Tajikistan, and Uzbekistan, to safeguard the 1.5 million ethnic Uzbeks residing there.

Discrimination against ethnic Russians in Tajikistan has increased and fuels a continuing exodus. The only political violence in Dushanbe has been a number of killings of ethnic Russians, usually soldiers, which has been of little comfort to Russian civilians.

Tajikistan's neighbors in the region, in particular Uzbekistan and the Russian Federation, maintain great influence over the course of internal Tajik politics. Russia, which already has 25,000 armed troops in Tajikistan (largely Russian CIS peacekeeping forces), tentatively agreed in April 1999 to the establishment of a military base which would help increase the stability in Tajikistan. Due to the geography of the region and the whims of Soviet planners, Tajikistan is largely at the mercy of Uzbekistan for all overland and rail transport. Tajikistan has moved to reduce its energy dependency on Uzbekistan by signing a tripartite agreement on trade, economic, and cultural relations with Turkmenistan and Iran. Turkmenistan provides Tajikistan with reduced cost fuel and natural gas as part of the agreement.

The government of President Emomali Rakhmonov is dominated by Tajiks from the southern Kulyab region who were victorious in the 1992-93 civil war. The November 1994 Presidential election, while peacefully conducted, was marred by fraud and intimidation, as were the February 1995 parliamentary elections. Tajikistan also adopted a new constitution in November 1994, which, while not a perfect document, is still judged to be a significant improvement over the Soviet-era version.

Political relations with the United States are on a cordial footing in spite of the temporary suspension of Embassy operations in Dushanbe in the fall of 1998. This decision was made due to concerns about threats to U.S. facilities worldwide, turmoil in Tajikistan, and a limited ability to secure the safety of personnel in their facility. This suspension is temporary and the State Department intends to resume operations as soon as a suitable new site is identified and a more secure facility for the Embassy can be built.

ECONOMIC SITUATION

Tajikistan is in a very slow transition from a command economy to a more market-oriented economy. Difficulties abound with the disruption of established trade routes, civil unrest, natural disasters, and an absence of the traditional Soviet-era inputs that came from Moscow for over seventy years.

The collapse of the trade and payment system, the deterioration of the terms of trade, and the absence of union transfers from Moscow, which had been the main method of funding Soviet Republics during the Soviet period, have inflicted significant damage to Tajikistan's economy. The move from a command economy under the Soviet system to a more open and market-oriented economy has been an onerous task, replete with legislative, institutional, and cultural obstacles.

These obstacles have been compounded by civil war and natural disasters. As a result of political instability, Tajikistan has been late in receiving the international monetary assistance and foreign investment that other former Soviet Republics have already received. On the economic front, the government of Tajikistan now appears to be ready to do the work necessary to receive international donor support and to return Tajikistan to the standard of living experienced prior to the outbreak of the civil war.

With the assistance of the IMF, Tajikistan has established a three-stage economic reform process designed to carry the country into the next century. The first stage (mid-

1995/1997) focused on improvement in the legal infrastructure, reforms in the agricultural sector, privatization of small-scale enterprises, and creation of favorable conditions to attract foreign investors. The second stage (1998- 2000) presently focuses on the privatizing of large-scale enterprises, and establishing efficiently- functioning banking, credit and taxation systems. The third stage (2001+) will focus on the further modernization of the economy, the formation of an efficient infrastructure and the implementation of large scale socio-economic programs.

There appears to be a good degree of political will behind the reforms and their implementation. Progress has been slow, but steady. Partially to reward the government's implementation of some economic reforms and to encourage more, international financial organizations such as the IMF and the World Bank have begun an infusion of credit to Tajikistan which should straighten the path of economic reform. On June 15, 1999, the World bank approved three credits worth a total of $31.7 million with $20 million being used to support the privatization of farms.

BASIC STRATEGY OF ECONOMIC REFORM

The basic strategy of the economic reform plan is to move the economy from a command economy to a socially-oriented, market-oriented one which provides for economic growth and the welfare of the population. The current program envisages a set of measures for deepening economic changes and for finding a way out of the crisis to promote stabilization and economic growth.

THE FIRST STAGE OF ECONOMIC REFORM

The first stage of economic reform entails legislative reform. The following laws were adopted in 1995 and 1996 to provide a legal basis for reform:
- On Credit Insurance;
- On Money Circulation;
- On the National Budget for 1996;
- On Copyrights;
- A decree "On Support of Small Business" was also adopted instead of the Law of the Republic of Tajikistan for the Protection of Private Entrepreneurs.

PRIVATIZATION

The Government of Tajikistan has outlined plans to accelerate the pace of privatization and to form a securities market in 1997. While most of the small retail enterprises have already been privatized, only 11 percent of medium and large enterprises have been privatized. In most cases the government has maintained a share of more than 40 percent of privatized enterprises. While leveraged buyout has been the preferred method of privatization, the program has reportedly been plagued by corruption.

The current share of the private sector in GDP is approximately 20-30%. Obstacles to the growth of the private sector include difficult entry and exit rules, lack of finance, limited access to business information, strict labor regulations and an incomplete legal framework.

Enterprise restructuring began in 1991 but stalled as a result of the war and political instability and has yet to gain momentum. A Law on Bankruptcy was passed in June 1992 but few companies have been forced into bankruptcy. The 1995 decree on "The Identification of Bankrupt Enterprises" represents an effort to speed up rehabilitation and restructuring of inefficient enterprises.

Agricultural reform - The goal of the government's plans for agricultural reform is to release a sufficient amount of land to individual farmers so as to reinvigorate agricultural production and generate more commercial activity. At present the agrarian sector is still controlled by large collective farms (kolkhozes) and state farms (sovkhozes). All kolkhozes will be transformed into farms which will be governed by individuals or a group of private farmers having the right of inheritance leasing, which permits the lessor to designate an heir to control the property being leased. One of the difficulties of this type of reform is choosing deserving candidates for land use and giving equitable compensation to those farmers who will be deprived of land.

The government reorganized "Glavkhlopkoprom" (a state organization called "The Main Cotton Industry" which controls all the ginning and part of the selling of cotton fiber) at the end of 1997. The organization was replaced by half a dozen firms which are intermediaries for receiving crop loans from international banks and assisting individual kolkhozes to buy inputs and sell their cotton. The intermediary firms see this as a temporary stage, with some of the kolkhozes already dealing directly with suppliers and buyers. Smaller producers and traders are already dealing directly, but such activity is impeded by the lack of effective international banking facilities.

Concerning other agricultural products, the government has started to liberalize of the marketing system by reducing the share of production being purchased by the state order and giving producers the right to sell the remainder of their products not sold to the state. This creates a more commercial atmosphere.

THE FOREIGN ECONOMIC ACTIVITY.

With the export and import operation in the Republic of Tajikistan are engaged 749 entities of the foreign economic activity officially registered in the Ministry of economy and the foreign economic relations including 515 collective farms and state farms. According to the information of the state statistical agency at the Government of the Republic of Tajikistan, the trade economic partners of Tajikistan are 71 countries of the world , from them 10 countries of CIS. In January-August of 2000, the foreign trade turnover of the Republic of Tajikistan including electrical energy and natural gas made 265,9 million dollars of USA, and has exceeded the level of the last year to 11% or to 92,0 million dollars. There are exported goods for January - August of 2000 on the amount of 522,9million dollars that in 19% is more than in January - August of 1999. There are imported goods to the Republic on the amount 443,0 million dollars that in 2% is more than the last year. For the countries of the CIS in the foreign trade turnover is 66% or 636,8 million dollars and for remote countries is 34%. The deficit of the balance of trade with the countries of the CIS turned out negative and made 94,4 million dollars. In export a little advantage belongs to the countries of the CIS and makes 52% or 271,2 million dollars. In import a considerable share are occupied by the countries of CIS-83% or 365,6 million dollars.

The share of the electrical energy in the foreign trade turnover made 16%. For January-August of 2000 its export made 2855,3 million kilowatt / hours on 85,0 million dollars. The import of the natural gas made 474,9 million cubic metre on the amount of 23,0 million dollars. In the export of the republic 54,5% takes aluminum. For January - August of 2000 it has been sent outside the country 179,7 thousand tones on the amount 285,2 million dollars , from them a considerable part on the amount of 160,0 million dollars are sent to the remote countries. An average cost for one tone in comparison with the last year has increased up to 22% and made 1587 dollars. The export of cotton-fibre has made 36,9 thousand tones on the amount 41,4 million dollars and has decreased with the comparison of the last year on 17,5% or 8,7 mill. dollars. The deliveries to the remote countries has decreased on 27% and to the countries of the CIS has increased up to 86%.

ECONOMIC INDICATORS

I. MACROECONOMIC INDICATORS			
	1999, in actual prices	1999 in % to 1998 (in comparable prices	To the right 1998 to 1997
ECONOMIC INDICATORS			
Operative gross domestic product, milliard roubles	1345	103.7	105
Volume of industrial output, million roubles	852126	105.0	108
Production of national consumer goods, million roubles	218230	90.0	118
Transportation of goods (including private enteprisers), thousand tones	7151,2	88.1	X
Transfered by road of general use, thousand tones	3720,6	83,9	130
Goods turnover by road of general use	1404,1	87,7	X
Including by road of general use, mill. tone. kms	1330,8	87,1	83,1
Million passengers have been carriaged (including private enteprisers)	145,8	105,9	
Million people are transfered by road of	120,9	105,5	108

general use			
Turnover of passengers	1436.8	96,1	X
Turnover of passengers by road of general use	1138,0	82,2	98,4
Gross production of agriculture	412942	103,8	106
Including:			
* public sector	139852	87,6	96,5
* population (farm economy)	273090	114,6	116
Volume of animal production in agricultural undertaking , tone			
- meat	9742	86,9	73
- milk	42315	100,3	107
- hundred eggs	3691	98,1	84
Million roubles at the expense of all financial resources	102900,3	X	X
Million roubles are put into the operation of:			
- main funds,	56168,0	X	X
- dwelling houses	135469	138	74
- comprehensive schools, educational sites	3295	126	66
- hospitals, bunks	240	65	7
-policlinics, visits per shift	308	60	73
- clubs,	150	-	-
SOCIAL INDICATORS			
Retail turnover through all the channels of realisation, million roubles	566479,6	104,0	108
Including:			
-through registered companies	28804,6	82,4	105
Fee paying services through all the channels of realisation: through considered rate	142296,0 30674,2	117,8 83,1	116 113
Foreign trade turnover , hundred $	1353496,4	103	87

- through countries CIS and	830410,0	128	86
- remote countries	522077,4	79	89
Export total - hundred dollars	688669,1	115	80
- through countries CIS	314984,5	155	74
- through remote countries	373684,6	95	83
Import total – hundred dollars	663827,3	93	95
- through countries CIS	515434,5	116	93
- through remote countries	148392,8	56	99
A number of registered unemployed makes hundred people (for December , 1)	53,3	84,4	
An average monthly wages of one employee for January - November			
- Nominal wages	11503	138,8	179
- Real wages	X	110,3	121

MAJOR ECONOMIC AND INDUSTRIAL SECTORS

AGRICULTURE

The agricultural sector is the major employer (45% of the work force) and the most important economic activity in Tajikistan. Agricultural production makes a significant contribution to the balance of payments. Agriculture and agribusiness have helped lead the way towards economic recovery for the country since independence. Agriculture is more mechanized in Tajikistan than in neighboring countries although the country now faces shortages of spare parts and adequate maintenance.

Although the agricultural sector is one of the most modernized in the NIS, total output has been declining sharply during the last five years. Cotton yields, for example, are suffering from a lack of fertilizers, pesticides and herbicides.

The main crop production areas lie in the irrigated valleys of the tributaries of the Amu and Syr Darya rivers. About 9.6 million hectares of land are under cultivation, mainly in the hands of state and collective farms. Cotton, which is the major cash crop accounting for about two thirds of the gross production value of the agriculture sector, takes up 35 percent of the cultivated area. There are unconfirmed reports that the government intends to permit forward sales of cotton for the first time. The state cotton procurement agency, Glavkhlopoprom, has indicated that some of the cotton should be sold from foreign shipment points like Riga, Latvia, and that letters of credit should be used rather than pre- payment terms. The introduction of forward trading would serve to boost foreign confidence in Tajik cotton.

Agriculture in Tajikistan offers virtually unlimited opportunities for investment in terms of capital, joint ventures and the transfer of know-how. This includes improved management techniques, better irrigation practices, the use of basic agricultural chemicals, and more efficient harvesting and distribution. In addition, there are many opportunities to increase the added value of products through more quality control, processing and packaging. The first loan signed by the Dushanbe office of the Central Asian-American Enterprise Fund was for a cannery on the outskirts of Dushanbe. A visit by BISNIS in May 1996 revealed an intense interest in both northern and southern Tajikistan for food processing ventures and food packaging ventures to take advantage of the country's rich agricultural output and export the products to Russia, the NIS, and surrounding countries.

Cotton Production - The 1998 cotton harvest of approximately 350,000 tons fell below 1997's 358,000 tons, due to inadequate inputs, reduced acreage and poor weather. Productivity also dropped in terms of kilograms per hectare. In 1996, a total of 95,000 tons of cotton, with an estimated value of $146 million, was exported to more than 18 countries. The state cotton procurement agency Glavkhlopkoprom was recently liquidated and some of its functions were taken over by the Ministry of Agriculture.

Tursunzade consumes nearly 40 percent of the total power output in the country, employs 12,000 workers and indirectly supports a community of 100,000. The only downstream industries at present are a cable and foil plant. Aluminum is one of the two main exports. The government is seeking foreign investment in the aluminum plant itself as well as opportunities for downstream projects. There have been instances of fighting near the plant as different factions have tried to assert control over the plant's production and lucrative exports.

The Government of Tajikistan has decided to include the plant in its privatization program. The government would retain a controlling block of shares, while the remaining assets could be purchased by foreign investors. The plant has, however, accumulated an estimated $120 million in debt to foreign creditors which is likely to make it less attractive to foreign investors.

The Republic of Tajikistan is an agrarian country. Early in nineties, the total floorspace of an agricultural arable of Tajikistan exceeded 4,3 million hectares. 82% of an arable lands (over 660 thousand hectares) had been irrigating. Crop-growing had been giving over 65% of gross production. The basic article of Tajik export is cotton. There had been producing up to 1 million tone of seed-cotton in Tajikistan before. In 1997, more than 360 thousand tones of cotton were collected in the Republic. The Tajik cotton is highly valued in the world. Both fine-fibre and average-fibre grades of cotton, which go to various needs, are grown in the Republic of Tajikistan. The Tajik cotton fibre is divided into seven categories from which the first, second and the third kinds refer to fine-fibre, deduced from the cotton of Gossypium barbadense L's kind. The other four kinds of the fibre are from the Gossypium brisytum L's type, which was deduced by Soviet scientists.

According to impurity, the fibre is divided into five classes: the supreme, good, average, usual and weed, depending on which there changes also the price from +5 up to -55 percents in Liverpool cotton exchange. After demobilisation of the cotton market, the cotton-growing economies have received the right to dispose independently the collected crop i.e. to sell a production inside the Republic or export it outside the Republic. There acts a cotton exchange in the Republic of Tajikistan, on which there are carried out bargains on purchase and sale of cotton fibre and other cotton production. During the last years, there are widely spread so-called future bargains in the Republic of Tajikistan. According to the contracts, the foreign firms provide crop-growing economies means for future crop as the petroleum Products, tractors, chemical weed-killers, fertilisers and money to cotton-growers for their labour.

The greatest investors and buyers, working actively with Tajik producers of cotton are: the Switzerland firm "Paul Reinkhard", Trade Department of Switzerland bank "A credit Swiss Fest Boston". The Tajik cotton is also exported to Hungary, Austria, Italy, Poland, Cyprus and USA. There is also grown grain and other crops: potatoes, fruit, grape, vegetable and water-melons. There were developed meat and milk cattle breeding, meat and wool sheep farming and silkworm breeding.

MINING AND MINERALS

Underneath Tajikistan's ever-present mountains lie a wide array of natural resources, many of which have not yet been exploited because of their geographical location or geological depth. For its size, Tajikistan is relatively blessed with silver and gold deposits. Total silver ore deposits are estimated at 60,000 tons and the largest, in Bolshoi Kanemansur, is around 38,000 tons. There are more than 30 known gold deposits, of which only a few have been prospected. Several potentially important coal deposits have been identified but have not yet been exploited. May of the mineral deposits are suitable for relatively inexpensive open-pit mining, but they are found in mountainous regions where extreme weather conditions prevail and transportation routes are difficult or non-existent. There is some coal extraction at the Yagnob mine in the Leninabad Region, while a number of other coal deposits have not yet been exploited.

A large antimony deposit has been discovered in the Khovland district southeast of Dushanbe. Japan has tentatively agreed to provide financing for the mine with an initial sum of $2 million earmarked for planning and feasibility study.

ALUMINUM

During the Soviet era, Tajikistan was famous for its aluminum smelter. The largest enterprise in Tajikistan, the Tursunzade Aluminum Smelter (Tadaz) is in the south-west of the country. It has an overall capacity of over 520,000 tons a year and accounting for 53 percent of total exports making it one of the largest in the world. Tajikistan produced 131,900 tons of aluminum and earned $210 million in export revenues. However, This is small compared with 450,000 tons in 1990. The aluminum is exported to countries including the Netherlands, Finland, England, Hungary, South Korea, Turkey and Belgium. Among NIS countries, Russia and Turkmenistan are the largest importers of Tajik aluminum. An estimated 5,000 tons of aluminum was consumed domestically to produce kitchenware and other household necessities.

Tursunzade consumes nearly 40 percent of the total power output in the country, employs 12,000 workers and indirectly supports a community of 100,000. It has a capacity of 520,000 tons and accounts for more than 30 percent of total exports. By 2005 Tursunzade plans to increase its production levels to 346,000 tons. The only downstream industries at present are a cable and foil plant. Aluminum is one of the two main exports. The government is seeking foreign investment in the aluminum plant itself as well as opportunities for downstream projects. There have been instances of fighting near the plant as different factions have tried to assert control over the plant's production and lucrative exports.

The Government of Tajikistan has decided to include the plant in its privatization program. The government would retain a controlling block of shares, while the remaining assets could be purchased by foreign investors. The plant has, however, accumulated an estimated $120 million in debt to foreign creditors, which is likely to make it less attractive to foreign investors.

SILVER AND GOLD

Tajikistan produced 1.5 tons of gold during the first eight months of 2000, a 15 percent increases over the same period in 1999 and worth about $35.8 million. Tajikistan has big plans for its silver sector. The country has plans to establish a joint venture with Indian companies to develop the Bolshoi Kinimansur silver deposit. The Indian companies plan to inject US $ 100 million into the deposit, which is home to 53,000 tons of silver.

ENERGY

Tajikistan is the world's third largest producer of hydroelectric power after the U.S. and Russia. Hydroelectric generation accounts for 76 percent of total energy output in the country. Energy consumption per capita is among the lowest in the NIS. An estimated 3.8 billion kWh of electricity was exported to other Central Asian countries in 1996, generating approximately $177 million in export earnings. The primary consumer was Uzbekistan, which consumed 3.4 billion kWh at a cost of nearly $170 million. Tajikistan is also an importer of electricity and in 1996 imported electricity worth $135 million, which amounted to almost 3 billion kWh, the bulk of which came from Uzbekistan.

The hydroelectric power station at Norwalk is one of the largest in Central Asia. Another major power station, a legacy of Soviet ‘gigantism', is the Rogun dam which is under construction. Rogun is designed to have a capacity of 3,6000 megawatts, which would produce an average annual output of 13.3 billion kilowatt hours. The Government of Tajikistan is anxious to identify foreign financing to finish the construction of the Rogun complex to address the country's critical energy shortages that result in only a few hours a day of electricity in the winter and has shut down much of the country's industry. Upon completion, the Rogun Dam would have an estimated annual output of 13.3 billion kWh.

Tajikistan also consumes significant quantities of oil, natural gas and coal but is self-sufficient for less than 50 percent of its total energy needs. Tajikistan imported more than $64 million of oil products in 1996, of which 35 percent was supplied by Turkmenistan, with 22 percent supplied by Uzbekistan and 21 percent by Kazakhstan. Indigenous oil and gas production provides six percent of demand, the remainder coming from imports.

In the past, Tajikistan relied on Uzbekistan for its supply of natural gas but payment arrears and political difficulties have resulted in frequent shut-offs and drastically reduced supplies. The government has identified several gas fields for development and is seeking foreign investors.

INDUSTRY AND POWER ENGINEERING.

During the decades, past after 1924, as a result of social-economic transformations, Tajikistan has turned into advanced agro-industrial state. Active population makes 34,4% of all inhabitants of the Republic (67,8% of which are men). 97,7% of the population are literates. 55% of them have secondary education and 7,5% Higher Education.

INDUSTRY.

On a boundary of nineties, about 400 industrial enterprisers acted in Tajikistan, in which there were occupied about 215 thousand workers, engineers and employees. The branch of heavy industry had about 40% of industrial production; light and food industry - 60%. The main branches of heavy industry are: electric power engineering, mining industry, non-ferrous metallurgy (enterprisers in Tursunzade and Isfara), engineering (enterprisers in Dushanbe and Khujand), metal processing, manufacture of building materials (Nurek), chemical industry (enterprisers in Dushanbe, Kurgan-Tube, Yavan). The basis of non-ferrous metallurgy are the factories in Tursunzade (in Gissar valley) and in Isfara (Leninabad region). There are extracted and concentrated ores of non-ferrous and rare metals, such as: lead-ore, zinc, bismuth, stibium, mercury, tungsten, molybdenum and gold. The brown coal is extracted in Shurab (Leninabad region).

There are also extracted oil (in the north and south regions of Tajikistan) and natural gas (in Gissar and Vaksh valley). The main branches of light industry are: food, cotton - cleaning, boot and shoe industry, silk and carpet industry. During last years, there is observed a volume of production's manufacture in industry. The growth in industry manufacture is mainly reached due to Tajik aluminium factory. The production's volume of this factory makes 108,9%.

POWER ENGINEERING.

Tajikistan, according to indexes of hydropower resources, takes the first place in the world and by absolute indexes (300 milliard kilowatt/hour per year) the eighth. The Republic could be the largest exporter of hydropower energy in the region, in case of using it outside the country. The basis of electric power engineering of Tajikistan make hydroelectric power stations: the Nurek hydroelectric power station (2700) enters into 30 the most powerful hydro stations of the world.

According to the level of dam's height, Nurek is the world leader - 300metres above sea level. Except for Nurek's hydroelectric power station, there also exists Golovnaya and Baipazin (in Vaksh river) and Kairakum hydroelectric power station in Sirdarya river. There also acted a hydroelectric power station near Khorog in GBAO. In 1989, a construction of the large hydroelectric power station in Vaksh-Rogumskaya river started. The Sangtuda hydroelectric power station is also under construction. There act the large thermal power stations in Dushanbe and Yavan.

TRANSPORT AND TELECOMMUNICATIONS

MOTOR TRANSPORT.

In Tajikistan despite the absence of good roads , motor transport is the most popular kind of movement. About 90% from the total volume of passengers carriages (537386,9 thousand persons within 8months of 2000) and more than 80% of internal cargo carriage (1350,5 thousand ton cargo within 8 months of 2000)are the duty of motor car. The network of highways of general use makes in Tajikistan about 13 thousand kilometers. And moreover the road network is distributed unevenly at the territory of the republic and its structure depends on population density, geographical factors. There is a developed rail network with a good surface in the valley of Sirdarya river (the north of the republic) of Kulob region, Gissar and Vaksh valleys. In the mountainous Badakhshan and in Garm group of regions and Zerafshan valley because of the complex mountain relief, the road network is less developed and has a bad surface.. Because of the climatic conditions and technical characteristics two more important arterial roads " Dushanbe-Aini" and "Kalaikhumb- Khorog" are opened for transport only six months in a year.

AIR TRANSPORT.

111,2 thousand passengers and 1,1 thousand ton of cargoes are carried by air transport within 8 months of 2000. The air transport has a great value for the republic which has not yet a direct way to sea and developed network of motor roads. At the present time the air transport considers as a "bridge" connecting it with the external world. The air company " Tojikiston" that acts independently since October 1992 and have a state status was created on the base of the air technique inherited from the soviet "Air company". There work more than 3 thousand persons in the company. At the beginning of 1998 the park of the air company of "Tajikistan" consisted of 14 planes TY-154M, 11units - TY-154A, 12-liners YAK-40, 3-AN-28. The other air vessels At the present time the air company is in the scheduled service to Moscow(four times in a week), Alma-Ata (three times), Novosibirsk (one time), Bishkek(one time), Samara(one time), Ashkhabad (once in a week) to Khujand and Khorog daily. There also carries out a charter flights to Karachi, Mashhad, Dubai and Shardgu.

Railway transport.

Because of the complex relief conditions the railways didn't develop in the republic. The total extent of the railways makes altogether 474 kms. The basic part of these roads is located in the south part of the country connecting the capital of the state with the industrial zones of Gissar, Vaksh valley and the external world. In Tajikistan within 8 months of the current year, 322,6 thousand persons and 409,1 ton of cargo have been carried by railway transport.

TELECOMMUNICATION.

At the present time the total capacity of the local telephone stations of the Republic of Tajikistan make 247thousand numbers, serviced by 80 urban stations (202thousand numbers) and by majority of small stations located in the rural areas (45 thousand numbers). The national density of telecommunication services is equal to 4,1 telephone for 100 persons. According to this information Tajikistan occupies the last place among the countries of the CIS and the Central Europe. Until very recently Tajikistan

hadn't hot automatic line with remote countries. Beginning from 1994 the Ministry of Finance provides to those who wish the service by means of connecting the subscriber to the state station of satellite communication. It became possible after opening in Dushanbe the 60-channel ground station of communication satellite and the modern digital automatic telephone station on 2,5 thousand numbers. All this equipment was delivered to Tajikistan by Turkish government. Because of the high cost of the direct communication satellite, nowadays a limited circus of subscribers use this service-they are missions of international organizations, diplomatic structures and a large commercial organizations.

The overwhelming majority of users of international communication have to book a coupon beforehand in the post department and call the subscriber through the (switchboard) operator. The new kinds of communication services have appeared in Dushanbe recently, they are mobile communication, mobile radio-link and radio paging. The operator of the mobile radio-link in Dushanbe since 1996 is joint enterprise " Tajik Tel", radio paging is provided by joint enterprise "Jakhon Page". Since June 1995 there acts an Electronic mail(E-mail) in the republic. In December 1998 Internet-link has appeared.

The national company "Telecomm Technology" became its parent. Nowadays almost all international organizations, large banks, commercial structures, the President apparatus of the Republic of Tajikistan, a number of ministries, departments, the largest highest educational establishments and private persons use the services of the company "Telecomm Technology". At the present time the company introduces Internet-link in a larger industrial- developed region of the republic - Sogd (the former Leninabad) region and this year is also going to open Internet - unit in Khatlon region that allows to cover all large regions of the country with Internet- link. Besides the company "Telecomm Technology" the Internet providers in Dushanbe are the companies "Tajiktelecomm", "Babilon-T" and " Intercom".

INVESTMENT AND BUSINESS CLIMATE

BASIC STRATEGY OF ECONOMIC REFORM

Economic Strengths: Tajikistan is blessed with abundant natural resources that could make the country an important producer of gold and other precious metals. It is currently a major-hydro-electric power producer, with a potential to increase capacity considerably. A relatively strong agricultural sector allows export opportunities for high quality cotton and processed food products. Tajikistan maintains a skilled industrial labor force at competitive wage rates, and has the potential to be a major exporter of aluminum. With mountains, valleys, lakes, and numerous rivers, the eco-tourism industry in Tajikistan is just waiting to be developed.

The basic strategy of the economic reform plan is to move the economy from a command economy to a socially-oriented, market-oriented one which provides for economic growth and the welfare of the population. The current program envisages a set of measures for deepening economic changes and for finding a way out of the crisis to promote stabilization and economic growth.

THE FIRST STAGE OF ECONOMIC REFORM

The first stage of economic reform entails legislative reform. The following laws were adopted in 1995 and 1996 to provide a legal basis for reform:

- On Credit Insurance;
- On Money Circulation;
- On the National Budget for 1996;
- On Copyrights;
- A decree "On Support of Small Business" was also adopted instead of the Law of the Republic of Tajikistan for the Protection of Private Entrepreneurs.

AGRICULTURAL REFORM

The goal of the government's plans for agricultural reform is to release a sufficient amount of land to individual farmers so as to reinvigorate agricultural production and generate more commercial activity. In the past agrarian sector has been controlled by large collective farms (kolkhozes) and state farms (sovkhozes). All kolkhozes will be transformed into farms, which will be governed by individuals or a group of private farmers having the right of inheritance leasing, which permits the lesser to designate an heir to control the property being leased. The issue of land use certificates is planned, by the Land Reform Committee, to affect 120 large state-owned farms and more than 9,000 farmers by September 2001. However, the farms can choose whether to reorganize as collective farms or to be broken up into privately held farms. One of the difficulties of this type of reform is choosing deserving candidates for land use and giving equitable compensation to those farmers who will be deprived of land.

Around 55 percent of all agricultural land was estimated to be in private hands by the end if 2000, up from 25 percent in 1997. However, this process of transitioning state-owned farms into privatized farms has not always run smoothly. Farmers have remained very dependent on the old Kolkhoz and Sovkhoz management for key and use of former collective assets, such as tractors. Also, old collectivized farm debts place an extra weight upon privatized farms in the cotton industry.

The government reorganized "Glavkhlopkoprom" (a state organization called "The Main Cotton Industry" which controlled all the ginning and part of the selling of cotton fiber) at the end of 1997, was replaced by half a dozen firms which are intermediaries for receiving crop loans from international banks and assisting individual kolkhozes to buy inputs and sell their cotton. The intermediary firms see this as a temporary stage, with some of the kolkhozes already dealing directly with suppliers and buyers. Smaller producers and traders are already dealing directly, but such activity is impeded by the lack of effective international banking facilities.

Concerning other agricultural products, the government has started to liberalize of the marketing system by reducing the share of production being purchased by the state order and giving producers the right to sell the remainder of their products not sold to the state. This creates a more commercial atmosphere.

FOREIGN INVESTMENT AND TRADE ENVIRONMENT

The Tajik Government welcomes foreign investment, and Tajikistan offers genuine opportunities for those willing to consider innovative forms of financing for trade and investment which usually involve significant risk. Numerous barriers to U.S. exports and trade are more a result of geography and the general economic crisis than any deliberate targeting of U.S. goods and services which are highly regarded and desired in the country. Tajikistan's geographical isolation, devastated economy and, most importantly, lack of currency, largely crimp its ability to trade effectively, even with neighboring NIS states.

Great interest in U.S. products is hindered by the lack of banking transfers or cash payments with which to purchase them. Another hindrance is a business culture which emphasizes personal contacts over competitive bidding, a concept American companies are frequently slow to acknowledge. In general, legislation encourages foreign investment but contradictory decrees and an expanded tax burden make doing business in Tajikistan a labyrinthine process.

There were almost 200 registered joint ventures in Tajikistan in 1996, a minority of which are currently operational. Seventy percent of existing joint ventures are involved in production, and the remainder are mostly in trading and services. The two largest joint ventures are with British mining companies, Zarafshan and Darvoz. There is one Italian joint venture, Giavoni, with Carrera jeans which started in 1995, and one South Korean cotton processing joint venture, Koobal.

There were six registered Tajik- American joint ventures and four American representative offices, Interfur and Karakum Oil Ltd. being the most active. Due to financial and bureaucratic problems, 229 joint ventures and foreign companies closed in 1996. Among these, 19 involved some level of American capital: 13 Tajik-American joint ventures, 2 American companies, and 4 Tajik-American joint ventures with British, Russian, and Ukrainian capital. At present there are only seven companies with American capital officially present in Tajikistan. Most joint ventures are located where the raw materials are found, and therefore, many are in the northern part of the country.

INVESTMENT BARRIERS

There are difficulties with repatriation of profits and capital, due to a lack of legislation protecting foreign profits; currency convertibility problems; and prohibition on land ownership (only leases are allowed). Foreign investors have equal access to government contracts, although the Bilateral Investment Treaty between Tajikistan and the U.S. is still in the process of negotiation.

ATTRACTING FOREIGN INVESTMENT

As prescribed in the law "On Foreign Investments in the Republic of Tajikistan," foreign investors and enterprises with foreign investments are allowed to conduct business in the free economic zones, despite the fact that the law "On Free Economic Zones" has not been adopted yet.

Major efforts have been done to inform potential foreign investors of business opportunities in Tajikistan through the intermediary of the internet:

- The State Property Committee of the Republic of Tajikistan has put together a list a major investment projects as well as comprehensive information on the privatization process in Tajikistan.
http://privatization.tajikistan.com/

- The External Resources Management Division (ERMD) within the Office of the Prime Minister of the Republic of Tajikistan provides information related to economic life and business opportunities in Tajikistan.
http://www.glasnet.ru/~ermdtaj/index.htm

BEST PROSPECTS FOR U.S. EXPORTS AND INVESTMENT

U.S.-Tajikistan trade has been small since Tajikistan's independence. U.S. exports to Tajikistan amounted to $12 million in 1998 down from $18.5 million in 1997. U.S. imports went up from $9 million in 1997 to $33 million in 1998, $30 million being import of aluminum.

Non-Agribusiness Sectors - Mining and related equipment, medical and pharmaceutical supplies, textile machinery, telecommunications, oil/gas extraction equipment and eco-tourism.

Agribusiness and Related Sectors - Canning/food processing equipment, grain/flour, fertilizers, and farm equipment (ginning and harvesting equipment and tractors).

In the agribusiness sector excellent opportunities exist in the food processing and packaging industry, particularly for packaging of tomato paste and dried fruit, as well as bottling of juices and wine. Currently, 40-50 percent of fruits and vegetables harvested goes to waste due to the lack of preservatives and portion technology for producing smaller packaging.

In the mining sector, there are significant reserves of rare and non-ferrous metals, as well as silver and gold quarries. Western technology is needed to develop these deposits. Tajikistan has made public its desire to seek foreign partners to rapidly develop its gold deposits and is actively courting foreign mining firms. In addition, the Government of Tajikistan has made strenuous efforts to attract foreign investment to the hydroelectric energy industry, with some projects already under construction.

As part of its effort to attract foreign investment to the mining sector, a September 1995 Presidential decree created the Committee on Precious Metals and Semi-Precious Stones ("Tajikdrag- metsamotzvety"). The goal of this committee is to develop and coordinate state policy on the extraction, processing, and use of precious metals and stones. The committee is based upon a combination of the previous government structures regulating gold extraction and production and "Pamirquartzsamotzvety".

There are no quantitative restriction on imports, but there is a list of commodities which can only be imported after the Ministry of Economy and Foreign Economic Relations has examined the contract. This list includes trucks, oil and oil products, fertilizers, wheat, flour, rice, tea, sugar, and vegetable oil. There is also a list of commodities which need government permission to import, including natural gas, uranium and other radioactive substances, narcotic and psychotropic substances, weapons and other military equipment, ammunition, cipher equipment, and electric power.

Standards - Standards, testing, labeling, and certification for export goods are in accordance with the standards of the Russian Federation. Quality certificates for import goods are checked by three government agencies: the Trade Industrial Agency, the State Committee on Standards, and the State Veterinary Control. Phyto-sanitary control was recently introduced. Ecological requirements for import goods are in the process of development.

VAT and fees - All companies, regardless of ownership or forms of property are subject to the value added tax (VAT) of 20 percent. In cases where other CIS republics have higher VAT rates Tajikistan imposes a reciprocal VAT.

Intellectual Property Rights - Tajikistan joined the World Intellectual Property Organization's permanent committee in the field of industrial property protection in 1994, thereby recognizing all international conventions in this area. The departments of copyright at the Ministry of Culture and Information and the National Center for Patents and Information have been charged with the administration of intellectual property rights in the country.

BANKING IN TAJIKISTAN

While banks in Tajikistan have not been rated by the major rating agencies and it is not as easy to transfer money in and out of the country as it may be in other NIS countries, there are signs that the banking sector is improving. In the past year, the National Bank of Tajikistan (NBT) has instituted measures to reform and improve the sector. These measures include raising capital requirements and signing reorganization agreements with larger banks. In addition, international technical assistance is aimed at improving the regulation of the sector and increasing working capital available from banks to businesses.

CAPITAL REQUIREMENTS

As in most NIS countries, many Tajikistani "banks" started operating with little capital. The NBT has taken an active role in closing down such banks by gradually raising the minimum capital requirements in order to establish a more sound and reliable banking system. The board of the NBT set the present minimum capital requirement for existing banks on April 17, 1998 (in its instruction No. 79). The minimum capital requirement will be raised gradually to: US$500,000 as of January 1, 1999; US$750,000 as of July 1, 1999; and US$1 million as of January 1, 2000. Banks created in 1998 have been required to meet the US$1 million statutory minimum from the time of their establishment.

The NBT declared bankrupt and closed certain banks that have failed to meet the 1998 requirements. These banks included Bahtovar, Toribank, and Ziroat. Two others, Ilhom and Rishta, were transformed into branches of Agroinvestbank. In addition, as a result of the more stringent requirements, the NBT has not been receiving any applications for banking activity licenses or the establishment of new banks.

REORGANIZATION AGREEMENTS

The NBT signed reorganization agreements with four large commercial banks: Agroinvestbank, Tajikbankbusiness, Sberbank, and Vnesheconombank. According to the guidelines set out in the agreements, these four banks had until November 30, 1998, to increase their statutory capital, reduce expenditures, try harder to collect earlier-issued loans, pay back overdue debts and loans, and liquidate unprofitable branches.

Another important requirement of the agreements (with these banks) is the transition to International Accounting Standards (IAS). All other banks in Tajikistan have until December 31, 1998, to convert to IAS. The transition has been facilitated by the requirement, as of November 1, 1996, that all banks prepare parallel financial statements in accordance with IAS.

CORRESPONDENT RELATIONSHIPS AND MONEY TRANSFER

Almost all Tajikistani banks have correspondent relationships with Western banks, with the three largest banks having the most relationships of this type. For instance, Orienbank has relationships with around 50 foreign banks, including one with a U.S. bank (Citibank in New York). Vnesheconombank has correspondent relationships with 35 Western banks, but no direct relationships with U.S. banks. Sberbank's corresponding relationships are limited to Russian banks.

An ordinary money transfer usually takes two to three days, while an urgent transfer can take up to one and a half days. Usually, a bank charges a commission of 0.1 percent. Vnesheconombank charges US$50 for a transfer plus a 0.1 percent commission; Orienbank's commissions range from US$40 to US$150.

Regional branches of banks usually do not perform money transfers themselves; instead they send transfer instructions to their headquarters in Dushanbe. This procedure can add one to three days to the transfer process. However, some banks have authorized their branches to make transfers themselves. Tajikbankbusiness granted such a right to its branch in Khojand.

There are no monetary amount restrictions for currency transfers by individuals or legal entities. However, the transfer must be justified: for individuals, the client must have written confirmation from the local tax authorities that the individual is a law-abiding taxpayer; for legal entities, proof of existence of a contract or another legal document is required.

OUTSIDE ASSISTANCE

Financial assistance by multilateral institutions, such as the World Bank, the International Monetary Fund, and the European Bank for Reconstruction and Development (EBRD), kicked off the reform of the banking system in Tajikistan in 1994. The EBRD has granted lines of credit totaling US$4 million to Orienbank, enabling it to lend to private sector small and medium-sized enterprises or to privatizing state-owned companies. Loans range in size from US$10,000 to US$250,000.

CHOOSING A BANK

Investors and depositors should exercise caution when choosing a bank in Tajikistan, especially considering that the major rating agencies have not rated any banks in Tajikistan. Currently, all banks in Tajikistan that have been issued a license by NBT to carry out banking operations and that have met and can meet the minimum capital requirements could be considered reliable. However, the existence of a correspondent account with a foreign bank should not be considered a sure sign of a bank's reliability. As a guideline, one should first consider those banks already using IAS and meeting the future US$1 million minimum capital requirement. A potential client can utilize financial statements prepared in accordance with IAS to assess the future viability of the bank considered.

PROCEDURES FOR ESTABLISHING A JOINT VENTURE

Registering a joint venture conservatively takes about three weeks of hard work by a local representative savvy to the machinations of the Tajikistan bureaucracy. There is no restriction on the percentage of foreign ownership in a joint venture and there are no prohibitions against a foreign enterprise establishing wholly owned subsidiary in Tajikistan. However, several bureaucratic hoops must be negotiated.

I. First, a joint venture must register with the Ministry of Finance. In order to register with the Ministry, the following steps and documents are required:

A) Application by the Tajik partner;
B) Copies of the charter and agreement of the future joint venture, certified by a local notary;
C) Bank certificates confirming the foreign and Tajik partners' solvency;
D) Registration fee to be paid at the Foreign Economic Bank into the Republican Hard Currency Fund.

Following review by a special commission of the Ministry of Finance which is to take place within a two week period, a certificate is issued which permits the joint venture to open a bank account.

II. Second, a joint venture must register with the State Statistical Committee. The following documents and steps are required before issuance of the Statistical Committee certificate:

A) Certificate from the Ministry of Finance;
B) Copy of the charter and agreement;
C) Registration fee.

III. Third, the joint venture should inform the local regional, district, or city executive committee by official letter of its existence.

IV. Fourth, the joint venture should register with local tax authorities.

V. Fifth, any joint venture for a foreign firm planning to engage in foreign economic activity must register with the Ministry of Foreign Economic Relations as a "participant in foreign economic activity." The following steps and documents are necessary to complete the process:

A) An application;
B) Copy of charter and agreement certified by notary;
C) Certificate of the State Statistical Committee;
D) Certificate of the Ministry of Finance;
E) Three copies of a registration form;
F) Registration fee paid to the Foreign Economic Bank Republic Hard Currency Fund.

A special commission of the Ministry of Foreign Economic Relations will study all the submitted documentation and, subject to approval, will register the joint venture and issue a license of "participant of foreign economic activity."

ESTABLISHING AN OFFICE

To register a branch office or representative of a foreign firm, the following documents must be presented to the Ministry of Foreign Economic Relations:

A) Application describing the objectives of opening the branch or establishing representation and a description of the firm;
B) Copy of the charter, which should be certified by an original stamp from a consulate of the Republic of Tajikistan (or Russian Consulate) in the firm's country of registration;
C) Extract on the firm from the trade register of the firm's home country;
D) Letter-guarantee from the firm's bank;
E) Registration paid to the Foreign Economic Bank Republic Hard Currency Fund.

A special commission of the ministry of Foreign Economic Relations will examine the submitted documents and, subject to approval, register and issue the license for a branch or representative office.

EXPORT AND CURRENCY LIBERALIZATION

President Rahmonov of Tajikistan signed a decree in February 1996 liberalizing currency and export operations. All export customs duties were canceled effective March 1, 1996. This move was designed to stimulate exports in order to reduce the trade deficit and attract foreign exchange that has been fleeing the country. Local exporters may freely use their currency profits but payments on export-import operations of Tajik enterprises with foreign partners cannot be held in offshore banks. All export articles shall be sold at world market prices or at those determined by the Republican Commodity Exchange.

As a result of this decree, all hard currency profits of Tajik exporters are free of any taxes except those of cotton and aluminum, with sales taxes of 5 and 25 percent respectively. The government of Tajikistan hopes by this decree to encourage exporters to return their hard currency earnings to Tajikistan instead of hiding them abroad. The government stipulates that exporters may use them for their own purposes. However, the government would prefer they be used for purposes meeting the interests of Tajikistan and developing further production.

Perhaps the most important feature of the decree is the cancellation of the obligation for exporters to sell 30 percent of their hard currency profits to the gold-currency fund to the Tajik National Bank. This onerous requirement had encouraged Tajik enterprises to hide their profits abroad. Now all foreign exchange will be sold and purchased through the Republican Currency Exchange.

The government estimates that it will lose about one billion Tajik rubles in customs duties but hopes to offset the losses through better regulation of taxes and the introduction of taxes on profits on exporting cotton and aluminum.

BUSINESS TRAVEL TO TAJIKISTAN

COUNTRY DESCRIPTION: Tajikistan, a newly independent country in central Asia, has been undergoing profound political and economic changes since the break-up of the Soviet Union. After the civil war in 1992, sporadic fighting continued, largely in remote areas, the comprehensive peace accords were signed in June 1997, some armed clashes involving renegade forces still take place. Tourist facilities are undeveloped, and many goods and services taken for granted in other countries are unavailable.

ENTRY REQUIREMENTS: A passport and visa are required. Entry into Tajikistan at points along the Gorno-Badakhshan border requires special authorization in advance. Without a visa, travelers cannot register at hotels and may be required to leave the country immediately. In the U.S., the Russian Embassy, Consular Division, 1825 Phelps Place NW, Washington, D.C. 20008, telephone (202) 939-8907, or the Russian Consulates in New York, San Francisco or Seattle issue visas for Tajikistan. Tajik visas granted by these offices are valid for a stay of three days in Tajikistan. Visas issued for other CIS countries (except Turkmenistan) are also valid for up to a three-day stay in Tajikistan. If travelers plan a longer stay, they may apply for a longer visa at the Ministry of Foreign Affairs after arriving in the country.

Note: Travelers who intend to visit Tajikistan should obtain double entry Russian, Kazak and Uzbek visas prior to departure, depending on intended transit points. There is no Uzbek embassy in Tajikistan.

INTERNAL TRAVEL: Travel to, from, and within Tajikistan is difficult and unreliable. Flights may be cancelled or substantially delayed. Return commercial charter flights are frequently overloaded with merchandise. International train connections are dangerous because of criminals operating on board.

AVIATION SAFETY OVERSIGHT: As there is no direct commercial air service at present, or economic authority to operate such service, between the U.S. and Tajikistan, the U.S. Federal Aviation Administration (FAA) has not assessed Tajikistan's civil aviation authority for compliance with international aviation safety standards for oversight of Tajikistan's air carrier operations. For further information, travelers may contact the Department of Transportation within the U.S. at 1-800-322-7873, or visit the FAA internet home page at http://www.faa.gov/avr/iasa/index.htm. The U.S. Department of Defense (DOD) separately assesses some foreign air carriers for suitability as official providers of air services. For information regarding the DOD policy on specific carriers, travelers may contact DOD at 618-256-4801.

ROAD CONDITIONS AND TRAFFIC SAFETY: Road travel can be made difficult by checkpoints, where police or soldiers are armed and known to shoot if vehicles do not stop. Some checkpoints, operated by independent armed groups that have targeted foreigners in the past, exist on the road east of Dushanbe. For this reason, road travel to the East is strongly discouraged. Vehicles with Tajik license plates have frequently been refused permission to enter Uzbekistan, so a change of vehicles at the border may be required. Road travel should be done only in daylight hours, and on routes known to the traveler or with a reliable escort.

AREAS OF INSTABILITY: Due in part to the actions of those opposed to the implementation of the June 1997 peace accords,the situation in the capital and its environs remains insecure. In November 1997 two French citizens were taken hostage by a semi-independent armed group operating to the east of Dushanbe. One was released after two weeks, but the other was killed during a rescue attempt. The group that took these hostages has reportedly been eliminated, but the general security situation is not stable. Also in the fall of 1997, there were a number of explosions, some on public transport, in which some local persons were killed or injured. In August 1997 there was an outbreak of fighting between government factions within Dushanbe and to the south

and west. Smaller clashes between paramilitary gangs took place in Dushanbe in September 1997 and May 1998 as well. In July 1998, four United Nations personnel were murdered in the Karotegin Valley. The identity of the murderers is still unknown.

To date, Americans have not been targeted but bystanders have been hurt in some of these attacks. Because of this unpredictability, U.S. travelers should avoid demonstrations, crowds, and places where military personnel congregate. Americans should remain inside during hours of darkness. Security forces are visible in the capital and the southern half of the country. U.S. citizens should check with the U.S. Embassy Almaty in Kazakhstan for current information before traveling outside of Dushanbe, and should observe strict security precautions while moving about, at their work sites, and at their homes. The situation in Leninabad Province, in the northern part of the country, and in Gorno Badakhshan, in the east has been generally quiet.

MEDICAL FACILITIES: The medical infrastructure of Tajikistan is significantly below western standards. Many trained medical personnel have left the country. Medical equipment and medicines are scarce, and significant disease outbreaks are possible due to population shifts and the breakdown in immunization activity. There have been outbreaks of typhoid in the Dushanbe area and in the south, and the risk of cholera and water-borne illnesses is high.

U.S. medical insurance is not always valid outside the United States. Travelers have found that supplemental medical insurance with specific overseas coverage, including air evacuation, has proved useful. The government of Tajikistan requires visitors who remain in country for more than 90 days to present a medical certificate showing that they are AIDS-free, or to submit to an AIDS test in Tajikistan. This testing requirement has not been implemented, but could be at any time. Because of the lack of medical supplies, submitting to an AIDS test in Tajikistan could be risky. Further information on health matters can be obtained from the Centers for Disease Control and Prevention's (CDC) international travelers' hotline, tel: 1-800-232-3228; fax:

1-800cdc-faxx, or via the CDC home page on the Internet:http://www.cdc.gov.

CRIME INFORMATION: Tajikistan is a country with a struggling economy and widespread unemployment, which have resulted in a high rate of street crime. There has been a recent surge in pickpocketings, muggings, and armed robberies in the homes of persons perceived as having money, including foreigners. Travelers should not travel alone or on foot after dark. The loss or theft abroad of a U.S. passport should be reported immediately to the local police and the nearest U.S. Embassy or Consulate.

The Department of State's pamphlet A Safe Trip Abroad provides useful information on guarding valuables and protecting personal security while traveling abroad. Additional information on the region can be found in the brochure Tips for Travelers to Russia and the Newly Independent States. Both publications are available from the Superintendent of Documents, U.S. Government Printing Office, Washington D.C. 20402, and via the internet athttp://www.access.gpo.gov/su_docs.

Currency Regulations: Tajikistan is a cash-only economy. International banking services are not available. Credit cards and traveler's checks are not accepted. Travel with large amounts of cash can be dangerous. Tajikistan has introduced its own currency, the Tajik ruble, which is convertible.

DRUG PENALTIES: U.S. citizens are subject to the laws of the country in which they are traveling. Penalties for possession, use, or trafficking in illegal drugs in Tajikistan are strict, and convicted offenders can expect jail sentences and fines.

REGISTRATION AND EMBASSY LOCATION: U.S. citizens are urged to register with the Consular Section of the U.S. Embassy Almaty, Kazakhstan and obtain updated information on travel and security within Tajikistan.

The U.S. Embassy in Almaty is located at 99/97A Furmanov Street, telephone 7(3272)63-39-05. Limited information is available in Dushanbe at telephone 7(3772)21-03-56.

TADJIKISTAN INDUSTRY: LARGEST COMPANIES ALPHABETICAL LISTING

1 ADRASMAN LEAD and ZINC WORKS

Ownership: ***state***
Industry: ***Ore mining industry***
Number of Employees:
CEO: **Yevgeny N.Bondarevsky**
Address: 735780, Republic Tadjikistan, Leninabad Reg., Kairakkum, pos. Adrasman, Leninabad Gertsen St., 72

Phone: **27-30**
Products: **unwrought lead 3,800 tons**
silver 27.2 tons

2 ADRASMAN LOW-VOLTAGE ELECTRIC EQUIPMENT WORKS

Ownership: ***state***
Industry: ***Electrical engineering***
Number of Employees: ***529.00***
CEO: **Amon E.Eshbaev**
Address: 735780, Republic Tadjikistan, Reg., Kairakkum, pos. Adrasman, Leninabadskaya St., 9

Phone: **3-34-38**
Products: **low-voltage apparatus**

3 AGROINDUSTRIAL GRAIN PROCESSING PRODUCTION COMPANY

Ownership: ***state***
Industry: ***Food & food processing***
Number of Employees:
CEO: **Sobir Rakhimov**
Leninsky
Address: 735140, Repiblic Tadjikistan, Khatlon Reg., Kurgan-Tyube, Sverdlov St., 43

Phone: **(37744) 2-25-24, 2-25-54**
Products: **flour, mixed fodder**

4 AINI GINNERY

Ownership: ***state***
Industry: ***Textile industry***
Number of Employees: ***650.00***
CEO: **Lyambir Z.Shoyev**
Address: 735100, Republic Tadjikistan, Dist., pos. Novabad

Phone: **31-18-83**
Products: **cotton 7,514 tons**
seeds 14,291 tons
lint 1,859 tons

5 ANZOBSKY ORE CONCENTRATING MILL

Ownership: ***state***
Industry: ***Ore mining industry***
Number of Employees: ***985.00***
CEO: **Ivan F.Glazunov**
Address: 735522, Republic Tadjikistan, Leninabad Reg., Aini Dist., pos. Zeravshan-2
Leninabad
Solprom

Phone: **24-43, 1-69**
Products: **antimony concentrate**
mercury concentrate

6 ASHTI SALT WORKS n2

Ownership: ***state***
Industry: ***Mining industry (building mateirlas)***
Number of Employees: ***190.00***
CEO: **Azamdzhon Karimov**
Address: 735790, Republic Tadjikistan, Reg., Ashti Dist., pos. Shaidon, St., 1

Phone: **2-20-51, 2-11-67**
Products: **salt 28,454 tons**

7 BAIRAZA HYDROELECTRIC STATION

Ownership: *state*
Industry: *Power industry*
Number of Employees: *10.00*
CEO: **A. N.Kozlov**
Address: 735300, Republic Tadjikistan, Nurek, post box 43

Phone: **(37738) 2-17-35, ext. 3-60**
Products: **electric power supply 2,289 mln kWh**

8 BAKERY "NONPAZ"

Ownership: *state*
Industry: *Food & food processing*
Number of Employees: *178.00*
CEO: **Muzafarkhon Kamolov**
Address: 735360, Repiblic Tadjikistan, Khatlon Reg., Kulyab, Lenin St., 100

Phone: **(37713) 3-27-43, 3-27-40, 3-22-46**
Products: **bakers' wares 6,415 tons**
confectionery 362 tons
corn sticks

9 BUSTON GINNERY

Ownership: *state*
Industry: *Textile industry*
Number of Employees: *383.00*
CEO: **Abdurasul Khikmatov**
Address: 735800, Republic Tadjikistan, Leninabad Reg., Matchinsky Dist., pos. Buston,

Phone: **2-20-68**
Products: **cotton 7,320 tons**
seeds 13,626 tons
lint

10 CENTRAL ELECTRIC POWER TRANSMISSION NETWORK

Ownership: *state*
Industry: *Power industry*
Number of Employees: *1,237.00*
CEO: **Umar A.Ashrapov**
Address: 734045, Republic Tadjikistan, Dushanbe,
Kalinin St., 1/3

Phone: **(3772) 36-46-43, 36-62-13**
Products: **electric power supply 96 mln kWh**

11 CLOSED JOINT-STOCK COMPANY "BOFANDA"

Ownership: *joint-stock*
Industry: *Textile industry*
Number of Employees: *480.00*
CEO: **Tursunpulot Khodzhimatov**
Address: 735790, Republic Tadjikistan, Leninabad Reg., Ashti Dist., pos. Shaidon, S.Niyazov St., 13

Phone: **2-25-00**
Products: **carpets 54 ths sq m**
floor coverings
vests

12 CLOTHING FACTORY "FIRUZA"

Ownership: *state*
Industry: *Clothing industry*
Number of Employees: *550.00*
CEO: **Amadkhon Amonov**
Address: 735360, Repiblic Tadjikistan, Khatlon Reg., Kulyab, Kalinin St., 40

Phone: **(37713) 3-26-91, 3-37-96, 3-42-43**
Products: **articles of apparel and clothing accessories**
trousers for children
bed-linen

13 CLOTHING FIRM "GULISTAN" WORKS

Ownership: *state*
Industry: *Clothing industry*
Number of Employees: *1,668.00*
CEO: **Valentina R.Krayushkina**
Address: 734025, Republic Tadjikistan, Dushanbe, Dushanbe, Tegron St., 21
Phone: **(3772) 22-31-42, 22-55-96, 22-56-09**
Products: **bathrobes 0.3 ths pcs**
suits 317.7 ths pcs

14 COMPUTING APPARATUS REPAIR

Ownership: *state*
Industry: *High-tech products, PC, research & design services*
Number of Employees: *132.00*
CEO: **Mikhail E.Uryadov**
Address: 734030, Republic Tadjikistan, Dushanbe, Aini St., 259
Phone: **(3772) 25-27-03, 25-26-49**
Products: **repair of automatic data processing machines**

15 CONFECTIONERY FACTORY "MAISHAT"

Ownership: *joint-stock*
Industry: *Food & food processing*
Number of Employees: *80.00*
CEO: **Rustam R.Abdullo-zade**
Address: 735700, Republic Tadjikistan, Leninabad Reg., Khudzhand, Teatralnaya St., 1
Phone: **(37922) 6-01-70**
Products: **confectionery 1,430 tons**
preserved fruit 100 ths tins
milk and dairy products

16 CONFECTIONERY FACTORY "SHIRIN"

Ownership: *joint-stock*
Industry: *Food & food processing*
Number of Employees: *644.00*
CEO: **Saida F.Mirazorova**
Address: 734009, Republic Tadjikistan, Dushanbe, Dzh.Rasulov Ave., 10
Phone: **(3772) 36-17-70, 36-95-57**
Products: **sugar confectionery**

17 DUSHANBE AGRARIAN PRODUCTION COMPANY "NONPAZ"

Ownership: *state*
Industry: *Food & food processing*
Number of Employees: *1,146.00*
CEO: **Davon Ibragimov**
Address: 734013, Republic Tadjikistan, Dushanbe, Dushanbe, P.Lumumba St., 28
Phone: **(3772) 22-87-66**
Products: **bakers' wares**
pasta

18 DUSHANBE AGROINDUSTRIAL PRODUCTION COMPANY

Ownership: *state*
Industry: *Food & food processing*
Number of Employees: *275.00*
CEO: **Umed Dusmatov**
Address: 734032, Republic Tadjikistan, Firdousi St., 8
Phone: **(3772) 31-44-44**
Products: **bakers' wares 7,038 tons**

19 DUSHANBE BRICK YARD PRODUCTION COMPANY

Ownership: ***state***
Industry: ***Building materials industry***
Number of Employees: ***300.00***
CEO: **Gies K.Nazirov**
Address: 734002, Republic Tadjikistan, Dushanbe, Dushanbe,
Surkhob St., 5

Phone: **(3772) 24-77-56**
Products: **building bricks 17,801 ths pcs**

20 DUSHANBE CABLE PLANT "TADZHIKKABEL"

Ownership: ***state***
Industry: ***Electrical engineering***
Number of Employees: ***271.00***
CEO: **Fakhriddin A.Alekberov**
Address: 734033, Republic Tadjikistan,

GSP, Oktyabrya St., 210

Phone: **(3772) 33-49-63, 33-49-43, 33-21-54**
Products: **cables**

21 DUSHANBE CHEESE PLANT

Ownership: ***joint-stock***
Industry: ***Food & food processing***
Number of Employees: ***93.00***
CEO: **Khairali M.Saidov**
Address: 734011, Republic Tadjikistan, Dushanbe,
40 let Tadzhikistana St., 35
Dushanbe,

Phone: **(3772) 22-22-71, 22-52-54**
Products: **butter 124 tons**
cheese 692 tons
milk and dairy products

22 DUSHANBE CLOTHING PRODUCTION COMPANY "CHEVAR"

Ownership: ***state***
Industry: ***Clothing industry***
Number of Employees: ***1,196.00***
CEO: **Igor A.Fraidin**
Address: 734010, Republic Tadjikistan,

Dzh.Rasulov Ave., 71/7

Phone: **(3772) 33-38-26, 33-31-67**
Products: **industrial clothing**
suits 256 ths pcs

23 DUSHANBE COMPANY "GULDAST" "TADZHIKATLAS"

Ownership: ***state***
Industry: ***Clothing industry***
Number of Employees: ***426.00***
CEO: **Karomat Sharipova**
Address: 734067, Republic Tadjikistan, Dushanbe, Dushanbe,
Gagarin St., 19

Phone: **(3772) 24-57-07, 24-57-20, 24-27-46**
Products: **dresses 41.1 ths pcs**
dresses of silk 24.8 ths pcs

24 DUSHANBE COMPANY

Ownership: ***state***
Industry: ***Textile industry***
Number of Employees: ***958.00***
CEO: **Rano O.Umarova**
Address: 734018, Republic Tadjikistan,

N.Karabaev St., 8

Phone: **(3772) 33-39-94**
Products: **fabrics of silk 3,064.8 ths m**
twisted threads of silk 38.2 ths m
folk handicraft articles

25 DUSHANBE CONFECTIONERY FACTORY "LAZZAT" (JOINT-STOCK COMPANY)

Ownership: ***joint-stock***
Industry: ***Food & food processing***
Number of Employees: ***52.00***
CEO: **Alexander Ya.Dorovskikh**
Dushanbe,
Address: 734015, Republic Tadjikistan, Dushanbe,
1-i Pr. Afzali, 17

Phone: **(3772) 27-73-31**
Products: **sugar confectionery 112.7 tons**

26 DUSHANBE DAIRY

Ownership: ***state***
Industry: ***Food & food processing***
Number of Employees: ***439.00***
CEO: **Mirzo M.Kamildzhanov**
Address: 734043, Republic Tadjikistan,

Dzh.Rasulov Ave., 9

Phone: **(3772) 36-96-77, 36-95-87**
Products: **butter 226 tons**
cheese 29 tons

milk and dairy products

27 DUSHANBE EXCAVATOR REPAIR WORKS

Ownership: *state*
Industry: *Metal-working industry*
Number of Employees: *82.00*
CEO: Galina V.Solovyeva
Address: 734033, Republic Tadjikistan, Dushanbe, Dushanbe,
Borbad St., 23-a

Phone: (3772) 33-50-41, 33-67-79
Products: welded metal structures 898 tons
repair of motor vehicles

28 DUSHANBE EXPERIMENTAL PLANT "SISTEMAVTOMATIKA"

Ownership: *state*
Industry: *Medical equipment industry*
Number of Employees: *65.00*
CEO: Vladimir I.Gavrilov
Address: 734024, Republic Tadjikistan,
Druzhby narodov Ave., 62

Phone: (3772) 23-04-83, 27-09-39
Products: instruments and apparatus
maintenance of instruments and automated equipment

29 DUSHANBE FERROCONCRETE STRUCTURES and BUILDING ARTICLES PLANT n1

Ownership: *state*
Industry: *Building materials industry*
Number of Employees: *288.00*
CEO: President
Address: 734029, Republic Tadjikistan, Dushanbe, Dushanbe,
K.Tsetkin St., 2

Phone: (3772) 36-72-05
Products: pre-cast ferroconcrete 25.2 ths cu m
pipes
concrete

30 DUSHANBE FERROCONCRETE STRUCTURES and BUILDING ARTICLES PLANT n2

Ownership: *state*
Industry: *Building materials industry*
Number of Employees: *132.00*
CEO: Takhir K.Mukhitdinov
Address: 734065, Republic Tadjikistan,
9-i km Kofarnikhon Shosse

Phone: (3772) 25-10-77, 25-07-84, 25-05-54
Products: pre-cast ferroconcrete
articles of concrete, not reinforced concrete

31 DUSHANBE FERROCONCRETE STRUCTURES and BUILDING ARTICLES PLANT n3

Ownership: *state*
Industry: *Building materials industry*
Number of Employees: *216.00*
CEO: Rasul K.Kasymov
Address: 734055, Republic Tadjikistan, Dushanbe, Dushanbe,
Borbad St., 36
Ordzhonikidzeabad

Phone: (3772) 31-22-51, 31-26-97
Products: pre-cast ferroconcrete
wall panels
m

32 DUSHANBE FERROCONCRETE STRUCTURES and BUILDING ARTICLES PLANT n6

Ownership: *state*
Industry: *Building materials industry*
Number of Employees: *178.00*
CEO: Victor V.Fundurakin
Address: 734063, Republic Tadjikistan,
p/o Guliston, 9-i km
Shosse

Phone: (3772) 29-85-06
Products: pre-cast ferroconcrete 6.2 ths cu

33 DUSHANBE FERROCONCRETE STRUCTURES and PRE-CAST PARTS PLANT

Ownership: *state*
Industry: *Building materials industry*
Number of Employees: *467.00*
CEO: **Victor M.Nasyrov**
Dushanbe,
Address: 734060, Republic Tadjikistan, Dushanbe, Lomonosov St., 377/1

Phone: **(3772) 33-11-63**
Products: **pre-cast ferroconcrete 16.8 ths cu m**
articles of concrete, not reinforced

concrete

34 DUSHANBE FOLK DECORATIVE HANDICRAFT COMPANY "DILOROM"

Ownership: *state*
Industry: *Textile industry*
Number of Employees: *938.00*
CEO: **Lyutfiya R.Bakoyeva**
Address: 734018, Republic Tadjikistan,

Sherozi Ave., 11

Phone: **(3772) 33-63-78, 33-25-91**
Products: **articles of apparel and clothing accessories** fabrics of cotton

fabrics of silk

35 DUSHANBE FOOD PROCESSING ENTERPRISE

Ownership: *state*
Industry: *Food & food processing*
Number of Employees: *300.00*
CEO: **Akhmad Kh.Radzhabov**
Address: 734002, Republic Tadjikistan, Dushanbe,
Dushanbe,
Shotemur St., 60

Phone: **(3772) 27-27-83, 27-47-32**
Products: **beer 1,082 ths dal**
non-alcoholic beverages 216 ths dal
mineral waters

36 DUSHANBE FURNITURE PLANT

Ownership: *state*
Industry: *Consumer goods, furniture, household & cultural goods*
Number of Employees: *537.00*
CEO: **Yury D.Volchinsky**
Address: 734012, Republic Tadjikistan,

Korgar St., 130

Phone: **(3772) 22-49-43**
Products: **furniture**

37 DUSHANBE GRAIN PROCESSING PLANT

Ownership: *state*
Industry: *Food & food processing*
Number of Employees: *243.00*
CEO: **Rakhmetdin Sh.Davlyatov**
Address: 734029, Republic Tadjikistan, Dushanbe, Vose St., 12
Dushanbe,

Phone: **(3772) 25-19-69, 25-18-91**
Products: **wheat flour 110,390 tons**

38 DUSHANBE JEWELLERY PLANT

Ownership: *state*
Industry: *Consumer goods, furniture, household & cultural goods*
Number of Employees: *401.00*
CEO: **Isak Burkhanov**
Address: 734033, Republic Tadjikistan,

Shestopalov St., 7

Phone: **(3772) 33-25-18, 33-15-78**
Products: **articles of jewellery**
metal haberdashery
fittings

39 DUSHANBE JOINT-STOCK LEATHER FOOTWEAR COMPANY "RAFIK"

Ownership: *joint-stock*
Industry: *Footwer & tanning industry*
Number of Employees: *3,928.00*
CEO: **Arkady P.Rokhman**
Dushanbe,
Address: 734005, Republic Tadjikistan, Dushanbe, Charm-Garon St., 10-a

Phone: **(3772) 22-84-84, 22-32-80**
Products: **footwear 2,005 ths pairs**

40 DUSHANBE KNITTING MILL

Ownership: *state*
Industry: *Textile industry*
Number of Employees: *743.00*
CEO: **Davlyat S.Boboyev**
Address: 734005, Republic Tadjikistan,

40 let Tadzhikistana St., 123

Phone: **(3772) 27-48-96, 27-55-66**
Products: **knitted linen**

41 DUSHANBE LEATHER HABERDASHERY FACTORY "CHARMDUZ"

Ownership: *state*
Industry: *Footwer & tanning industry*
Number of Employees: *143.00*
CEO: **Leonid D.Khovansky**
Dushanbe,
Address: 734060, Republic Tadjikistan, Dushanbe, Dzh.Rasulov Ave., 71/7

Phone: **(3772) 33-49-26, 33-78-11**
Products: **suitcases 7.5 ths pcs**
satchels 18.9 ths pcs
bags 118.6 ths pcs

42 DUSHANBE MEAT PROCESSING PLANT

Ownership: *state*
Industry: *Food & food processing*
Number of Employees: *562.00*
CEO: **Bakhtier Kh.Gadoyev**
Address: 734005, Republic Tadjikistan,

Fuchik St., 4

Phone: **(3772) 22-64-76, 22-36-74**
Products: **meat 2,558 tons**

43 DUSHANBE OILERY and FAT PLANT

Ownership: *state*
Industry: *Food & food processing*
Number of Employees: *917.00*
CEO: **Said Kh.Radzhabov**
Address: 734009, Republic Tadjikistan, Dushanbe, Dzh.Rasulov Ave., 9

Dushanbe,
Phone: **(3772) 36-95-35**
Products: **vegetable oil 11.2 ths tons**
hydrogenated fat 3.5 ths tons
household soap 5 ths tons

44 DUSHANBE PAINTS and VARNISHES PLANT "RANGINKAMON"

Ownership: *state*
Industry: *Chemical, pharmaceutical & micribiology industry*
Number of Employees: *290.00*
CEO: **Khairullo A.Abdulloyev**
Address: 734008, Republic Tadjikistan,

Rudaki Ave., 205

Phone: **(3772) 24-85-51, 24-28-53**
Products: **paints and varnishes 996 tons**
floor oil paints
pottery articles

45 DUSHANBE PILOT-PRODUCTION and EXPERIMENTAL PLANT "REMSTROIDORMASH"

Ownership: *state*
Industry: *Metal-working industry*
Number of Employees: *141.00*
CEO: Odildzhon M.Abdullaev
Address: 734036, Republic Tadjikistan, Dushanbe, 40 let Tadzhikistana St., 45

Phone: (3772) 33-48-09, 33-27-42
Products: structural aluminium 172 tons
welded metal structures 6.7 tons

46 DUSHANBE PILOT-PRODUCTION and EXPERIMENTAL PLANT "SELEKTSIONNAYA TEKHNIKA"

Ownership: *state*
Industry: *Machine building industry*
Number of Employees: *10.00*
CEO: Sadullo S.Giyasov
Address: 735100, Republic Tadjikistan, pos. Leninsky, kolkhoz "Leningradsky"

Phone: 27-54-76
Products: warehousing equipment

47 DUSHANBE PIPE APPLIANCES PLANT NAMED AFTER ORDZHONIKIDZE

Ownership: *state*
Industry: *Metal-working industry*
Number of Employees: *1,328.00*
CEO: Aktam A.Akbarov
Dushanbe,
Address: 734036, Republic Tadjikistan, Dushanbe, Dzhami Pr., 2/1

Phone: (3772) 31-07-67
Products: appliances for pipes, boilers, etc
equipment
gate valves of steel
cast articles of pig iron

48 DUSHANBE PLANT "STROMMASH"

Ownership: *state*
Industry: *Machine building industry*
Number of Employees: *98.00*
CEO: Fazlidin T.Abdusamiev
Address: 734008, Republic Tadjikistan,

Rudaki St., 204

Phone: (3772) 24-27-42, 24-57-92
Products: oxygen 61 ths cu m
non-standard machinery and

343.7 tons

49 DUSHANBE PLANT "TADZHIKTEKSTILMASH"

Ownership: *state*
Industry: *Machine building industry*
Number of Employees: *1,400.00*
CEO: Rufik M.Biktimirov
Dushanbe,
Address: 734042, Republic Tadjikistan, Dushanbe, Shapkin St., 7

Phone: (3772) 23-44-57, 22-31-72
Products: winding machinery and spare parts
200 pcs
electric cabinets

trade equipment

50 DUSHANBE PLANT "TORGMASH"

Ownership: *state*
Industry: *Machine building industry*
Number of Employees: *493.00*
CEO: Vladimir G.Koknaev
Address: 734000, Republic Tadjikistan,

Navruz St., 161

Phone: (3772) 22-33-73
Products: trade equipment and spare parts
electric ovens 23,911 pcs
textile spinning machines 152 pcs

51 DUSHANBE PRINT-SHOP n18

Ownership: *state*
Industry: *Publishing & printing*
Number of Employees:
CEO: **Rasima I.Osipova**
Address: 734017, Republic Tadjikistan, Dushanbe,
Dushanbe,
Nosir-Khisrav St., 6

Phone: **(3772) 24-56-14**
Products: **printed matter**

52 DUSHANBE PRINTING WORKS

Ownership: *state*
Industry: *Publishing & printing*
Number of Employees: ***382.00***
CEO: **Vladimir Sh.Mansurov**
Address: 734063, Republic Tadjikistan,

Aini St., 126

Phone: **(3772) 25-10-46**
Products: **printed matter**

53 DUSHANBE SILK MILL

Ownership: *state*
Industry: *Textile industry*
Number of Employees: ***1,986.00***
CEO: **Abdurakhman T.Khabibov**
Address: 734007, Republic Tadjikistan, Dushanbe,
Akhmadi Donish St., 5

Dushanbe,
Phone: **(3772) 27-02-36, 27-45-57, 29-07-61**
Products: **threads of silk, unbleached 70 tons**
fabrics of silk
twisted threads of silk

54 DUSHANBE SOUVENIR FACTORY "ARMUGON"

Ownership: *joint-stock*
Industry: *Consumer goods, furniture, household & cultural goods*
Number of Employees: ***96.00***
CEO: **Bagrad A.Mardoyants**
Address: 734014, Republic Tadjikistan,

Druzhby narodov Ave., 78

Phone: **(3772) 27-09-91, 27-24-88**
Products: **folk handicraft articles**

55 DUSHANBE SPECIALIZED ENGINEERING DESIGN BUREAU

Ownership: *state*
Industry: *Machine building industry*
Number of Employees: ***174.00***
CEO: **Abdurakhim K.Avganov**
Dushanbe,
Address: 734018, Republic Tadjikistan, Dushanbe,
N.Karabaev St., 54

Phone: **(3772) 34-82-77**
kWh
Products: **designing**
non-standard machinery and equipment

56 DUSHANBE THERMOELECTRIC STATION

Ownership: *state*
Industry: *Power industry*
Number of Employees: ***748.00***
CEO: **Alisher I.Arifov**
Address: 734054, Republic Tadjikistan,

40 let Tadzhikistana St., 39

Phone: **(3772) 27-67-19, 23-38-32**
Products: **electric power supply 680 mln**

heating 3,245 ths Gcal

57 DUSHANBE TOBACCO FACTORY

Ownership: *state*
Industry: *Tobacco industry*
Number of Employees: ***235.00***
CEO: **Kamar D.Mirazorov**
Address: 734002, Republic Tadjikistan, Dushanbe,
Telman St., 31
Dushanbe,

Phone: **(3772) 27-46-64, 24-60-07, 24-60-13**
Products: **cigarettes 2,607 mln pcs**

58 DUSHANBE TOWN ELECTRIC POWER TRANSMISSION NETWORK

Ownership: *state*
Industry: *Power industry*
Number of Employees: ***380.00***
CEO: **Dzhamshed M.Mansurov**
Address: 734060, Republic Tadjikistan,

1-i Ostrovsky pr.

Phone: **(3772) 22-69-21, 22-67-64, 22-67-91**
Products: **electric power supply**

59 DUSHANBE WINE PLANT

Ownership: *state*
Industry: *Food & food processing*
Number of Employees: *260.00*
CEO: **Abduvose A.Bakiev**
Address: 734013, Republic Tadjikistan, Dushanbe, Druzhby narodov Ave., 106
Dushanbe,

Phone: **(3772) 22-89-89, 23-08-82, 22-31-54**
Products: **vodka 258 ths dal**
wine 110 ths dal
brandy

60 DUSHANBE WOOD-WORKING PLANT

Ownership: *state*
Industry: *Forestry & timber processing industry*
Number of Employees: *121.00*
CEO: **Oleg Kh.Sabirov**
Address: 734063, Republic Tadjikistan,

9-i km Ordzhonikidzeabad Shosse

Phone: **(3772) 25-27-10, 25-24-38**
Products: **window assemblies 9.4 ths sq m**
door assemblies 3.5 ths sq m
floor panels

61 DUSHANBE WOOD-WORKING PLANT

Ownership: *state*
Industry: *Forestry & timber processing industry*
Number of Employees: *294.00*
CEO: **Ulyashbai F.Muminov**
Address: 734029, Republic Tadjikistan, Dushanbe,
Dushanbe,
Zebunisso St., 5

Phone: **(3772) 25-18-81, 25-16-16**
Products: **window assemblies 25.5 ths sq m**
door assemblies 14.7 ths sq m
wood sawn lengthwise

62 DUSHANBE WOOD-WORKING PLANT

Ownership: *state*
Industry: *Forestry & timber processing industry*
Number of Employees: *74.00*
CEO: **Akram N.Uzakov**
Address: 734005, Republic Tadjikistan,

Fuchik St., 88

Phone: **(3772) 22-36-17, 22-48-00**
Products: **window assemblies 4.9 ths sq m**
door assemblies 1.9 ths sq m
PVC pipes

63 DUSHANBEPRESSURE PIPES and FERROCONCRETE ARTICLES PLANT

Ownership: *state*
Industry: *Building materials industry*
Number of Employees: *221.00*
CEO: **Alexander V.Kiryushin**
Address: 734050, Republic Tadjikistan, Dushanbe, 9-i km Ordzhonikidzeabad Shosse

Phone: **(3772) 25-18-13, 25-24-23, 25-25-91**
Products: **pre-cast ferroconcrete**
chutes
power transmission line supports

64 DZHILIKUL FISHING FARM

Ownership: *state*
Industry: *Fishing & fish processing*
Number of Employees: *90.00*
CEO: **Vladimir S.Bulychev**
Address: 735218, Repiblic Tadjikistan, Khatlon Reg., pos. Dzhilikul

Phone: **5-52-99**
Products: **live fish 600 tons**
smoked fish 190 tons

65 DZHILIKUL FISHING FARM

Ownership: *state*
Industry: *Fishing & fish processing*
Number of Employees: *89.00*
CEO: Valery D.Golikov
Address: 735207, Repiblic Tadjikistan, Khatlon Reg., Dzhilikul Dist., s. Pakhtakor, uch. Dushanbe, 40

Phone: 5-52-99, 82-48
Products: fish

66 ENTERPRISE "TADZHIKENERGOREMONT"

Ownership: *state*
Industry: *Electrical engineering*
Number of Employees: *268.00*
CEO: Vyacheslav M.Palatov
Address: 734011, Republic Tadjikistan, Sherozi Ave., 26

Phone: (3772) 23-16-58, 27-37-09
Products: repair of power equipment
spare parts for power machinery

67 FACTORY "ZARDUZ"

Ownership: *state*
Industry: *Textile industry*
Number of Employees: *462.00*
CEO: Khalimdzhon Okhundzhanov
Address: 735702, Republic Tadjikistan, Leninabad Reg., Khudzhand, Lenin St., 223

Phone: (37922) 6-78-02, 6-37-85, 6-47-48
Products: textile haberdashery 240 mln pcs
articles of apparel and clothing accessories 100 mln pcs

68 FARKHOR GINNERY

Ownership: *state*
Industry: *Textile industry*
Number of Employees:
CEO: Rakhmonzon Tetaboev
Address: 735390, Repiblic Tadjikistan, Khatlon Reg., pos. Farkhor, Lenin St., 25

Phone: 2-35-91, 2-20-95, 3-35-92
Products: cotton 6,048 tons
seeds 10,361 tons
lint

69 FERMENTED TOBACCO PLANT

Ownership: *state*
Industry: *Tobacco industry*
Number of Employees: *85.00*
CEO: President
Address: 734024, Republic Tadjikistan, Dushanbe, Dushanbe, Shapkin St., 157

Phone: (3772) 23-29-24
Products: fermented tobacco 1,186 tons

70 FIRM "BORCHOMA"

Ownership: *state*
Industry: *Pulp & paper industry*
Number of Employees: *133.00*
CEO: Karim S.Kadyrov
Address: 734060, Republic Tadjikistan, pos. Rokhi-Nav, 208

Phone: (3772) 33-48-94, 33-50-64, 33-50-38
Products: articles of plastics
packing containers of paperboard
articles of polyethylene and cellophane

71 FIRM "DOVUD"

Ownership: *joint-stock*
Industry: *Scrap & waste processing industry*
Number of Employees: *96.00*
CEO: **President**
Dushanbe,
Address: 734000, Republic Tadjikistan, Dushanbe, Dzh.Rasulov Ave., 60

Phone: **no data**
Products: **processing of metal scrap 40,234 tons**

72 FIRM "NAFISA"

Ownership: *joint-stock*
Industry: *Textile industry*
Number of Employees: *1,702.00*
CEO: **Ismon O.Obidov**
Address: 734024, Republic Tadjikistan,

Popov St., 11

Phone: **(3772) 27-30-77**
Products: **stockings 4,260 ths pairs**
panty hoses
socks

73 FISHING FARM "CHUBEK"

Ownership: *state*
Industry: *Fishing & fish processing*
Number of Employees: *80.00*
CEO: **Rustam Salimov**
Address: 735370, Repiblic Tadjikistan, Khatlon Reg., Moskovsky Dist., kishlak Tudaboen
Leninabad

Phone: **2-24-92**
Products: **live fish 90 tons**
chilled fish 8 tons
m

74 GAFUROV FERROCONCRETE STRUCTURES PLANT n7

Ownership: *state*
Industry: *Building materials industry*
Number of Employees: *164.00*
CEO: **Nematzhon Domulloyev**
Address: 735690, Republic Tadjikistan,

Reg., Khodzhent Dist., Gafurov

Phone: **3-29-28, 3-26-56, 3-21-08**
Products: **pre-cast ferroconcrete 26,763 cu**

concrete 1,331 cu m

75 GAFUROV MEAT PROCESSING PLANT

Ownership: *state*
Industry: *Food & food processing*
Number of Employees: *390.00*
CEO: **Abdurazak Latipov**
Address: 735690, Republic Tadjikistan, Leninabad
Leninabad
Reg., Khodzhent Dist., Gafurov, 119-i
Gogolya
kvartal

Phone: **3-15-49**
Products: **hides**
dal
meat 2,657 tons
sausages

76 GAFUROV WINE PLANT

Ownership: *state*
Industry: *Food & food processing*
Number of Employees:
CEO: **Mullodzhon Oglukov**
Address: 735690, Republic Tadjikistan,

Reg., Khodzhent Dist., Gafurov,

St., 63-a

Phone: **3-39-36, 3-12-54**
Products: **wine of fresh grapes 368.1 ths**

vodka

77 GANCHI BRICK YARD

Ownership: *state*
Industry: *Building materials industry*
Number of Employees: *240.00*
CEO: Maruf Khakimov
Address: 735620, Republic Tadjikistan, Leninabad Reg., pos. Ganchi
Leninabad

Phone: 7-76
Products: building bricks 15,844 ths pcs

78 GANCHI CLOTHING and KNITWEAR FACTORY

Ownership: *state*
Industry: *Textile industry*
Number of Employees: *471.00*
CEO: Kurbonali Boboyev
Address: 735620, Republic Tadjikistan,

Reg., pos. Ganchi

Phone: no data
Products: knitted outerwear 687 ths pcs

79 GISSAR COMPANY "GIDROSTROIMATERIALY"

Ownership: *state*
Industry: *Oil refining & gas processing*
Number of Employees: *800.00*
CEO: Abdurakhmon Tabarov
Address: 735020, Republic Tadjikistan, pos. Gissar

Phone: (37739) 2-59-52
Products: linoleum 355.6 ths sq m
roll roofing materials 1,811 ths sq m
building bricks

80 GISSAR GINNERY

Ownership: *state*
Industry: *Textile industry*
Number of Employees: *10.00*
CEO: President
Address: 735020, Republic Tadjikistan, Gissar Dist., pos. Sharora

Phone: no data
Products: cotton 1,035 tons
seeds 1,831 tons
lint

81 GISSAR GRAIN INTAKE PLANT

Ownership: *state*
Industry: *Food & food processing*
Number of Employees: *64.00*
CEO: Razok K.Kadyrov
Address: 735020, Republic Tadjikistan, pos. Gissar, K.Marks St., 4

Phone: (37739) 2-62-10, 2-65-15
Products: wheat flour 44 ths tons
bran 11 ths tons

82 GISSAR TEXTILE MILL

Ownership: *state*
Industry: *Textile industry*
Number of Employees: *20.00*
CEO: President
Address: 735020, Republic Tadjikistan, pos. Gissar, K.Marks St., 54

Phone: (37739) 2-61-67
Products: fabrics, unbleached 3,207 ths m

83 GISSAR TRAINING and PRODUCTION POWER
WORKS

Ownership: *joint-stock*
Industry: *Food & food processing*
Number of Employees:
CEO: President
Address: 735020, Republic Tadjikistan, pos. Gissar
Region,

Phone: no data
Products: lids for preserves 15,801 ths pcs
crown corks 3,724 ths pcs

84 GORNO-BADAKHSHAN ELECTRIC

TRANSMISSION NETWORK

Ownership: *joint-stock*
Industry: *Power industry*
Number of Employees: *570.00*
CEO: Safar M.Dzhumaev
Address: 736100, Republic Tadjikistan, Gorno-Badakhshan Autonomous

Khorog, Gulmamad St., 75

Phone: (377910) 28-10, 29-15
Products: electric power supply 93,500 ths

kwh

folders

85 GRAIN INTAKE PLANT

Ownership: ***state***
Industry: ***Food & food processing***
Number of Employees: ***126.00***
CEO: **Miron K.Sakhibov**
Address: 735320, Repiblic Tadjikistan, Khatlon Reg., pos. Dangara

Phone: **2-28, 2-20, 2-19**
Products: **mixed fodder 31 ths tons**

86 GRAIN INTAKE YARD

Ownership: ***state***
Industry: ***Food & food processing***
Number of Employees: ***20.00***
CEO: **Nemat Rakhmankulov**
Address: 735500, Republic Tadjikistan, Leninabad Reg., Pendzhikent

Phone: **(37775) 2-34-74**
Products: **cereal meal 4,974 tons**
rice meal 947 tons

87 GRAIN PROCESSING PLANT

Ownership: ***state***
Industry: ***Food & food processing***
Number of Employees: ***513.00***
CEO: **K. T.Turaev**
Address: 735400, Republic Tadjikistan, Kofarnikhon, Rabochaya St., 19

Phone: **2-37-31, 2-24-93**
Products: **wheat flour 142 ths tons**
bran 40 ths tons
semolina

88 ILIYCHEVSKY FEED MILL

Ownership: ***state***
Industry: ***Food & food processing***
Number of Employees: ***37.00***
CEO: **Amir Kh.Khudoidodov**
Address: 735131, Repiblic Tadjikistan, Khatlon Reg., Iliychevsky Dist., s. Obi-Kiik

Phone: **2-11-61, 2-12-58**
Products: **mixed fodder**

89 INDUSTRIAL and COMMERCIAL FIRM "ISMAIL"

Ownership: ***state***
Industry: ***Consumer goods, furniture, household & cultural goods***
Number of Employees: ***10.00***
CEO: **Ismail Gulov**
Address: 735400, Republic Tadjikistan, Kofarnikhon, Guliston St., 2

Phone: **2-28-19, 2-44-23**
Products: **kitchen furniture**
stools 86.6 ths rbls 865 pcs
dinner-tables

90 INDUSTRIAL and TRADING FIRM "SIMO"

Ownership: ***state***
Industry: ***Footwer & tanning industry***
Number of Employees: ***262.00***
CEO: **Abdullo Khusainov**
Address: 735500, Republic Tadjikistan, Leninabad Reg., Pendzhikent, K.Marks St., 72

Phone: **(37775) 2-50-07, 2-50-52, 2-51-69**
Products: **footwear 500 ths pairs**

91 ISFARA BAKERY

Ownership: ***state***
Industry: ***Food & food processing***
Number of Employees: ***125.00***
CEO: **Abdurakhim T.Timurkhanov**
Address: 735920, Republic Tadjikistan, Leninabad Reg., Isfara, Lenin St., 62

Phone: **2-15-63, 2-45-43**

92 ISFARA BUILDING MATERIALS PLANT

Ownership: ***state***
Industry: ***Building materials industry***
Number of Employees: ***508.00***
CEO: **Abdullo Gafurov**
Address: 735920, Republic Tadjikistan, Leninabad Reg., Isfara Dist., pos. Khonobad

Products: bakers' wares

Phone: 2-32-04, 2-18-51, 2-31-03
Products: gypsum, building bricks

93 ISFARA CANNERY
Ownership: *state*
Industry: *Food & food processing*
Number of Employees: *941.00*
CEO: Atakhon Abdukadyrov
Address: 735920, Republic Tadjikistan, Leninabad Reg., Isfara, Lenin St., 143
Phone: 2-12-71, 2-13-81, 2-17-64
Products: preserved vegetables 6,657 ths tins

94 ISFARA CHEMICALS PLANT
Ownership: *state*
Industry: *Chemical, pharmaceutical & micribiology industry*
Number of Employees: *1,609.00*
CEO: Ilyes Aslamov
Address: 735920, Republic Tadjikistan, Leninabad Reg., Isfara Dist., pos. Novobad
Phone: no data
Products: household chemicals
paints and varnishes
mineral fertilizers

95 ISFARA CONFECTIONERY FACTORY
Ownership: *state*
Industry: *Food & food processing*
Number of Employees: *106.00*
CEO: Abdugafar Kadyrov
Address: 735920, Republic Tadjikistan, Leninabad Reg., Isfara, Abdullaev St., 2
Phone: 2-36-02, 2-41-89
Products: caramel

96 ISFARA CREAMERY
Ownership: *state*
Industry: *Food & food processing*
Number of Employees: *79.00*
CEO: Abdusamad Sh.Shomirsaadov
Address: 735920, Republic Tadjikistan, Leninabad Reg., Isfara Dist., pos. Istaravshan
Phone: 2-54-00, 2-13-76
Products: butter 465.4 tons
milk 2,138.6 tons
fermented milk products

97 ISFARA FERROCONCRETE STRUCTURES and BUILDING ARTICLES PLANT n5
Ownership: *state*
Industry: *Building materials industry*
Number of Employees: *310.00*
CEO: Ibragim Mukhamadov
Address: 735920, Republic Tadjikistan, Leninabad Reg., Isfara, Zavodskaya St., 20
Phone: 2-47-31, 2-32-69, 2-28-80
Products: pre-cast ferroconcrete
structural components for house construction 3.3 ths sq m

98 ISFARA FURNITURE PLANT
Ownership: *state*
Industry: *Consumer goods, furniture, household & cultural goods*
Number of Employees: *52.00*
CEO: Abdulafiz Abdusattarov
Address: 735920, Republic Tadjikistan, Leninabad Reg., Isfara, Lenin St., 49
Phone: 2-15-43, 2-48-07
Products: furniture
tables
beds
supports for power transmission lines

99 ISFARA HYDROMETALLURGICAL PLANT
Ownership: *state*
Industry: *Metallurgy*

100 ISFARA MEAT PROCESSING PLANT
Ownership: *state*
Industry: *Food & food processing*

Number of Employees: *10.00*
CEO: **Abduzhabar R.Kataev**
Address: 735920, Republic Tadjikistan, Leninabad Leninabad
Reg., Isfara, Lenin St., 132-a

Phone: **2-42-84**
Products: **barium metal 9,812 kg**
chemical products 6,555 tons
precious metals

Number of Employees: *122.00*
CEO: **Farkhad A.Abdullaev**
Address: 735920, Republic Tadjikistan,
Reg., Isfara, Lenin St., 71

Phone: **2-42-98, 2-43-38**
Products: **meat 545.5 tons**

101 ISFARA MEDICAL PREPARATIONS and FEED PROTEIN PLANT

Ownership: *state*
Industry: *Chemical, pharmaceutical & micribiology industry*
Number of Employees: *125.00*
CEO: **Bakhram S.Boboyev**
Address: 735920, Republic Tadjikistan, Leninabad Leninabad
Reg., Isfara, Ashurbibi Azimov St., 86

Phone: **2-88-77, 2-48-39**
Products: **crude alcohol 286.7 ths dal**

102 ISFARA MINERAL PAINTS PLANT "NILUFOR"

Ownership: *state*
Industry: *Chemical, pharmaceutical & micribiology industry*
Number of Employees: *244.00*
CEO: **Domullo Kadyrov**
Address: 735920, Republic Tadjikistan,
Reg., Isfara, Lenin St., 55

Phone: **2-48-46, 2-14-83**
Products: **dry ochre 5,980 tons**
silicate paints
paints and varnishes

103 JOINT-STOCK COMPANY "BOFANDA"

Ownership: *joint-stock*
Industry: *Textile industry*
Number of Employees: *2,281.00*
CEO: **Saidullo M.Makhsumov**
Address: 734011, Republic Tadjikistan, Dushanbe, Leninabad
Sherozi Ave., 6

Phone: **(3772) 27-76-91, 22-36-73, 29-94-36**
Products: **yarn of cotton 6,371 tons**

104 JOINT-STOCK COMPANY "FAIZ"

Ownership: *joint-stock*
Industry: *Textile industry*
Number of Employees: *1,055.00*
CEO: **Khamdam F.Khodzhibaev**
Address: 735610, Republic Tadjikistan,
Reg., Ura-Tyube, Fabrichnaya St., 14

Phone: **2-20-24, 2-10-84**
Products: **socks for men 7 ths pairs**
socks for children
panty hoses for children

105 JOINT-STOCK COMPANY "KOLINKHO"

Ownership: *joint-stock*
Industry: *Textile industry*
Number of Employees: *5,429.00*
CEO: **Yakhye N.Azimov**
Address: 735750, Republic Tadjikistan, Leninabad Leninabad
Reg., Kairakkum, Tekstilshchikov St., 1

Phone: **2-20-01, 2-12-17**
Products: **carpets and other textile floor coverings 8,297.5 ths sq m**
8,000 ths pcs

106 JOINT-STOCK ENTERPRISE "LACHP"

Ownership: *joint-stock*
Industry: *Building materials industry*
Number of Employees: *495.00*
CEO: **Mirzokhalim Mirzokarimov**
Address: 735702, Republic Tadjikistan,
Reg., Khudzhand, Lenin St., 262

Phone: **(37922) 6-45-94**
Products: **cans 100 mln pcs**
twisted yarn 4,014.5 tons bottles
paperboard boxes

yarn in skeins

107 KAIRAKKUM AGROINDUSTRIAL PRODUCTION COMPANY

Ownership: *state*
Industry: *Food & food processing*
Number of Employees: *442.00*
CEO: **Abduzhalil M.Khamidov**
Address: 735750, Republic Tadjikistan, Leninabad
Leninabad
Reg., Kairakkum

Phone: **2-28-41**
Products: **wheat flour 93,206 tons**
pasta 7,701 tons
bran

108 KAIRAKKUM FISHING INDUSTRY ENTERPRISE

Ownership: *state*
Industry: *Fishing & fish processing*
Number of Employees:
CEO: **Tatyana I.Divitskaya**
Address: 735750, Republic Tadjikistan,
Reg., Kairakkum

Phone: **2-15-30, 2-17-34**
Products: **fish 497 tons**
live fish 298 tons
smoked fish

109 KAIRAKKUM MECHANICAL REPAIR WORKSHOP

Ownership: *state*
Industry: *Metal-working industry*
Number of Employees: *60.00*
CEO: **Valery I.Shtorts**
Leninabad
Address: 735750, Republic Tadjikistan, Leninabad
Reg., Kairakkum, Lenin St., 108

Phone: **2-15-64, 2-13-22**
Products: **welded metal structures 447 tons**
repair of building machinery

110 KAIRAKKUM MINE

Ownership: *state*
Industry: *Ore mining industry*
Number of Employees:
CEO: **Rakhim N.Nurmatov**
Address: 735750, Republic Tadjikistan,
Reg., Kairakkum

Phone: **no data**
Products: **precious metals**

111 KAIRAKKUM SUBSIDIARY ENTERPRISE

Ownership: *state*
Industry: *Building materials industry*
Number of Employees: *397.00*
CEO: **Kamil Kh.Kabanov**
Address: 735750, Republic Tadjikistan, Leninabad
Reg., Kairakkum, Kovrovshchikov St., 3

Phone: **2-11-32, 2-12-09, 2-23-46**
Products: **pre-cast ferroconcrete**

112 KALININABAD FERROCONCRETE STRUCTURES PLANT n1

Ownership: *state*
Industry: *Building materials industry*
Number of Employees: *202.00*
CEO: **Yevgeny I.Ababkov**
Address: 735147, Repiblic Tadjikistan, Khatlon
Reg., Kalininabad

Phone: **(37744) 6-13-57**
Products: **pre-cast ferroconcrete**

113 KALININABAD FERROCONCRETE STRUCTURES PLANT n8

Ownership: *state*
Industry: *Building materials industry*
Number of Employees: *150.00*
CEO: **Akhmatkul V.Khalikov**
Address: 735147, Repiblic Tadjikistan, Khatlon Reg., Kalininabad

Phone: **(37744) 6-13-44, 2-55-05, 2-13-57**
Products: **pre-cast ferroconcrete 7.7 ths cu m**
welded metal structures 639 tons
bars and rods for use in construction

114 KALININABAD GRAVEL SIZING MILL

Ownership: *state*
Industry: *Mining industry (building mateirlas)*
Number of Employees: *50.00*
CEO: **Ivan I.Skuneman**
Address: 735147, Repiblic Tadjikistan, Khatlon Reg., Kalininabad

Phone: **(37744) 2-12-83**
Products: **crushed stone 22.2 ths cu m**
natural sands 12.8 ths cu m

115 KANIBADAM BAKERY

Ownership: *state*
Industry: *Food & food processing*
Number of Employees: *159.00*
CEO: **Ikram A.Abdullaev**
Address: 735900, Republic Tadjikistan, Leninabad
Leninabad
Reg., Kanibadam, Lenin St., 533

Phone: **2-27-94, 2-28-57**
Products: **bakers' wares**

116 KANIBADAM BRAKE EQUIPMENT PLANT

Ownership: *state*
Industry: *Metal-working industry*
Number of Employees: *1,682.00*
CEO: **Yusuf Akhmedov**
Address: 735900, Republic Tadjikistan,
Reg., Kanibadam, Lenin St., 257

Phone: **2-22-55, 2-21-75, 2-23-24**
Products: **metal-working tools**
machining attachments
consumer goods

117 KANIBADAM CANNERY

Ownership: *joint-stock*
Industry: *Food & food processing*
Number of Employees: *730.00*
CEO: **Gaffar Aliev**
Address: 735900, Republic Tadjikistan, Leninabad Reg., Kanibadam, Madaniyat St., 19
Leninabad

Phone: **2-45-11**
Products: **preserved vegetables 4,232 ths tins**
preserved fruit 13,501 ths tins

118 KANIBADAM CLOTHING PRODUCTION COMPANY "KHUSNORO"

Ownership: *state*
Industry: *Clothing industry*
Number of Employees: *1,791.00*
CEO: **Nematzhon U.Umatov**
Address: 735907, Republic Tadjikistan,
Reg., Kanibadam, Aini St., 260

Phone: **2-28-25, 2-27-20**
Products: **industrial clothing**
dresses, bathrobes 696.7 ths pcs

119 KANIBADAM FERROCONCRETE STRUCTURES PLANT n2

Ownership: *state*
Industry: *Building materials industry*
Number of Employees: *100.00*
CEO: Ibragim B.Islamov
Address: 735900, Republic Tadjikistan, Leninabad Reg., Kanibadam

Phone: 2-52-91
Products: pre-cast ferroconcrete 4.3 ths cu m
ferroconcrete articles
concrete

120 KANIBADAM GINNERY

Ownership: *state*
Industry: *Textile industry*
Number of Employees: *951.00*
CEO: Israil Z.Obidzhanov
Address: 735903, Republic Tadjikistan, Leninabad Reg., Kanibadam, Aini St., 64

Phone: 2-27-80, 2-58-86
Products: cotton 17,499 tons
seeds 32,492 tons
lint 2,641 tons

121 KANIBADAM OILERY and FAT PLANT MILL

Ownership: *state*
Industry: *Food & food processing*
Number of Employees:
CEO: Karim Kenzhaev
Address: 735900, Republic Tadjikistan, Leninabad Reg., Kanibadam, pos. Dusti

Phone: 2-22-59, 2-38-32
Products: vegetable oil 18,457 tons

122 KANIBADAM SPINNING and WEAVING

Ownership: *state*
Industry: *Textile industry*
Number of Employees: *1,722.00*
CEO: Nemat N.Toshmatov
Address: 735900, Republic Tadjikistan, Leninabad Reg., Kanibadam, Dzerzhinsky St., 45

Phone: 2-23-03, 2-23-98
Products: yarn of cotton 4,473 tons
unbleached fabrics of cotton 3,840 tons
finished fabrics of cotton

123 KANIBADAM TRAINING and PRODUCTION ENTERPRISE

Ownership: *joint-stock*
Industry: *Consumer goods, furniture, household & cultural goods*
Number of Employees:
CEO: President
Address: 735900, Republic Tadjikistan, Leninabad Reg., Kanibadam, Leninabadskaya St., 35

Phone: 2-48-03
Products: floor coverings of cotton 134 ths sq m
carpets1.2 ths sq m
mattresses

124 KANSAI NON-METALLIFEROUS and FACING MATERIALS PLANT

Ownership: *state*
Industry: *Building materials industry*
Number of Employees: *78.00*
CEO: Vladimir I.Kondratov
Address: 735744, Republic Tadjikistan, Leninabad Reg., Kairakkum, pos. Chorukh-Dairon

Phone: 5-42-74
Products: facing tiles 19.5 ths sq m

125 KHODZHENT GINNERY

Ownership: *state*
Industry: *Textile industry*
Number of Employees: *586.00*
CEO: **Mirzoakhmad Ismatov**
Address: 735690, Republic Tadjikistan, Leninabad Reg., Khodzhent Dist., Gafurov Region,

Phone: **3-35-55, 3-24-75**
Products: **cotton 11,439 tons**
seeds 19,391 tons
lint 2,081 tons

126 KHOROG BAKERY

Ownership: *state*
Industry: *Food & food processing*
Number of Employees:
CEO: **President**
Address: 736000, Republic Tadjikistan, Gorno-Badakhshan Autonomous

Khorog

Phone: **(377910) 23-57**
Products: **bakers' wares**

127 KHOROG CLOTHING FACTORY n3 and "KHAIET"

Ownership: *state*
Industry: *Clothing industry*
Number of Employees: *545.00*
CEO: **Davlater Khumorikov**
Address: 736000, Republic Tadjikistan, Gorno-Badakhshan Autonomous Region, Region,
Khorog, Lenin St., 90

Phone: **(377910) 37-27**
Products: **articles of apparel and clothing accessories**

128 KHOROG MEAT PROCESSING PLANT DAIRY

Ownership: *state*
Industry: *Food & food processing*
Number of Employees:
CEO: **Kimatys Ilolov**
Address: 736001, Republic Tadjikistan, Gorno-Badakhshan Autonomous

Khorog, Karalishoyev St., 59

Phone: **(377910) 23-09**
Products: **meat**
butter
milk and dairy products

129 KHUDZHAND AUTOMOBILE REPAIR WORKS n4

Ownership: *state*
Industry: *Automobile industry*
Number of Employees: *86.00*
CEO: **Kholikdzhon I.Ibragimov**
Leninabad
Address: 735712, Republic Tadjikistan, Leninabad Reg., Khudzhand, Gagarin St., 62

Phone: **(37922) 6-25-11, 4-35-11**
Products: **repair of motor vehicles**

130 KHUDZHAND BAKERY

Ownership: *state*
Industry: *Food & food processing*
Number of Employees: *344.00*
CEO: **Mubin A.Kholmatov**
Address: 735700, Republic Tadjikistan,

Reg., Khudzhand, Shark St., 84

Phone: **(37922) 4-48-75**
Products: **bakers' wares**
confectionery
pasta

131 KHUDZHAND CANNERY

Ownership: *state*
Industry: *Food & food processing*
Number of Employees: *824.00*
CEO: **Vasily A.Averin**
Address: 735700, Republic Tadjikistan, Leninabad Reg., Khudzhand, Lenin St., 252

Leninabad

Phone: **(37922) 6-37-55, 6-32-11**
Products: **preserved fruit and vegetables 39,085 ths tins**

132 KHUDZHAND CLOTHING PRODUCTION and TRADE COMPANY NAMED AFTER N.K.KRUPSKAYA

Ownership: *state*
Industry: *Clothing industry*
Number of Employees: *2,650.00*
CEO: **Abdukadyr Kamilov**
Address: 735708, Republic Tadjikistan,

Reg., Khudzhand, K.Tsetkin St., 2

Phone: **(37922) 6-42-81, 6-78-34**
Products: **dresses, bathrobes 638.2 ths pcs**

133 KHUDZHAND CONTAINER REPAIR WORKS

Ownership: *state*
Industry: *Consumer goods, furniture, household & cultural goods*
Number of Employees: *125.00*
Leninabad
CEO: **Dzhumabai Manadzhanov**
Vostochnaya
Address: 735690, Republic Tadjikistan, Leninabad Reg., Khodzhent Dist., Gafurov, Chekhov St., 54

Phone: **3-16-44, 3-20-37**
Products: **repair of containers**

134 KHUDZHAND DAIRY

Ownership: *state*
Industry: *Food & food processing*
Number of Employees: *225.00*
CEO: **Olim Sh.Akhmedov**
Address: 735714, Republic Tadjikistan,

Reg., Khudzhand, Severo-

promzona

Phone: **(37922) 5-41-98, 5-42-47**
Products: **butter 613 tons**
milk and dairy products
cheese of sheep's milk

135 KHUDZHAND ELECTRIC POWER TRANSMISSION NETWORK ENTERPRISE

Ownership: *state*
Industry: *Power industry*
Number of Employees: *900.00*
CEO: **Akobir K.Umarov**
Address: 735750, Republic Tadjikistan, Leninabad
Leninabad
Reg., Kairakkum, Lenin St., 113
4

Phone: **5-15, 3-14, 2-17-01**
Products: **electric power supply 692 mln kWh**

136 KHUDZHAND FURNITURE PLANT

Ownership: *state*
Industry: *Consumer goods, furniture, household & cultural goods*
Number of Employees: *600.00*
CEO: **Takhir A.Radzhabov**
Address: 735700, Republic Tadjikistan,

Reg., Khudzhand, K. Khudzhandi St.,

Phone: **(37922) 6-45-71, 6-46-71**
Products: **furniture**

137 KHUDZHAND GAS EQUIPMENT ENGINEERING WORKS

Ownership: *state*
Industry: *Machine building industry*
Number of Employees: *367.00*
CEO: **Yevgeny I.Yantsen**
Address: 735700, Republic Tadjikistan, Leninabad Leninabad
Reg., Khudzhand

Phone: **(37922) 2-75-07, 2-76-07**
Products: **consumer goods**
gaseous hydrocarbons
ths

138 KHUDZHAND LEASING-BASED ENTERPRISE "EMALIROVSHCHIK"

Ownership: *state*
Industry: *Metal-working industry*
Number of Employees: *484.00*
CEO: **Abdusamad Kh.Samadov**
Address: 735700, Republic Tadjikistan,
Reg., Khudzhand, Pravyi bereg, 3-i Microraion

Phone: **(37922) 2-87-10, 2-89-43, 2-87-12**
Products: **steel enamelled tableware 946.3**
pcs

139 KHUDZHAND PLANT "TORGMASH"

Ownership: *state*
Industry: *Metal-working industry*
Number of Employees: *812.00*
CEO: **Gafarkhon N.Mukhitdinov**
Address: 735700, Republic Tadjikistan, Leninabad Leninabad
Reg., Khudzhand, Suleimani Pr., 4
6

Phone: **(37922) 6-42-92, 6-06-17**
Products: **electric cookers 13,459 pcs**
spoons

140 KHUDZHAND SHOE FACTORY n2

Ownership: *state*
Industry: *Footwer & tanning industry*
Number of Employees: *1,835.00*
CEO: **Abdukhamid Samadov**
Address: 735708, Republic Tadjikistan,
Reg., Khudzhand, K.Khudzhandi St.,

Phone: **(37922) 6-06-61, 6-83-61, 6-70-63**
Products: **footwear**

141 KHUDZHAND SILK MILL PRODUCTION

Ownership: *state*
Industry: *Textile industry*
Number of Employees: *8,960.00*
CEO: **Takhir Babaev**
Address: 735702, Republic Tadjikistan, Leninabad
Reg., Khudzhand, Lenin St., 238

Leninabad

St.,
Phone: **(37922) 4-34-20, 6-31-27,**
Products: **silk yarn 683.1 tons**
twisted articles
fabrics of silk, unbleached
sq

142 KHUDZHAND TRAINING and

ENTERPRISE

Ownership: *joint-stock*
Industry: *Consumer goods, furniture, household & cultural goods*
Number of Employees:
CEO: **Boltukhon Rakhimov**
Address: 735700, Republic Tadjikistan,
Reg., Khudzhand, Chernyakhovsky
19

Phone: **(37922) 6-34-10**
Products: **floor coverings of cotton 35.9 ths**
m lids 13 mln pcs

143 KHUDZHAND TRAINING and PRODUCTION WORKS n2

Ownership: *joint-stock*
Industry: *Consumer goods, furniture, household & cultural goods*
Number of Employees: *234.00*
CEO: Saidvali Abasov
Kofarnikhon
Address: 735700, Republic Tadjikistan, Leninabad Reg., Khudzhand, Engels St., 1

Phone: (37922) 5-67-32, 5-66-51
Products: wadding of cotton 1,916 tons
machines
articles of apparel and clothing accessories

144 KOFARNIKHON MECHANICAL REPAIR WORKS

Ownership: *state*
Industry: *Machine building industry*
Number of Employees: *870.00*
CEO: Boris I.Galich
Address: 735400, Republic Tadjikistan,

Phone: 6-94
Products: auxiliary mechanized devices
electric cranes 344 pcs
spare parts for road building

145 KOFARNIKHON MECHANICAL WORKS "ZARFSOZ"

Ownership: *state*
Industry: *Metal-working industry*
Number of Employees: *390.00*
CEO: Anvar Kh.Rakhmonov
Address: 735400, Republic Tadjikistan, Kofarnikhon

Phone: 2-54-45
Products: table and kitchen articles of aluminium 620 tons
trays of aluminium

articles of alloys

146 KOFARNIKHON RICE PLANT

Ownership: *state*
Industry: *Food & food processing*
Number of Employees: *65.00*
CEO: D.Sh.Erkabaev
Address: 735400, Republic Tadjikistan, Kofarnikhon, Privokzalnaya St.

Phone: 2-27-00, 2-87-00
Products: meal of rice 14 ths tons

147 KOFARNIKHON TRAINING and PRODUCTION ENTERPRISE

Ownership: *joint-stock*
Industry: *Consumer goods, furniture, household & cultural goods*
Number of Employees: *700.00*
CEO: President
Address: 735400, Republic Tadjikistan, Kofarnikhon

Phone: no data
Products: floor coverings of cotton 32 ths sq m
carpets 1,051 ths pcs

ropes of cotton

148 KOLKHOZABAD GRAIN PROCESSING PLANT

Ownership: *state*
Industry: *Food & food processing*
Number of Employees:
CEO: Madzhid Khafizov
Address: 735200, Repiblic Tadjikistan, Khatlon Reg., pos. Kolkhozabad

Phone: (37747) 4-34-90, 4-47-08
Products: flour, mixed fodder

149 KUIBYSHEVSK FISHING FARM

Ownership: ***state***
Industry: ***Fishing & fish processing***
Number of Employees: ***130.00***
CEO: **Saidbek Sharipov**
Address: 735120, Repiblic Tadjikistan, Khatlon Reg., pos. Kuibyshevsk

Phone: **37-65**
Products: **live fish 1,116 tons**
smoked fish 19 tons

150 KULYAB BRICK YARD

Ownership: ***state***
Industry: ***Building materials industry***
Number of Employees: ***320.00***
CEO: **President**
Address: 735360, Repiblic Tadjikistan, Khatlon Reg., Kulyab, pos. Tuto

Phone: **(37713) 3-23-21**
Products: **building bricks 7,886 ths pcs**

151 KULYAB CREAMERY

Ownership: ***state***
Industry: ***Food & food processing***
Number of Employees: ***100.00***
CEO: **Abdulkazi Sharifov**
Address: 735360, Repiblic Tadjikistan, Khatlon Reg., Kulyab, Frunze St., 122
234

Phone: **(37713) 2-20-06**
Products: **cotton seed oil 2,738 tons**
oil-cake 12,735 tons
hulls

152 KULYAB DAIRY

Ownership: ***state***
Industry: ***Food & food processing***
Number of Employees: ***160.00***
CEO: **Abdurakhim Kholov**
Address: 735360, Repiblic Tadjikistan, Khatlon Reg., Kulyab, Charm-Gorm-Poen St.,

Phone: **(37713) 3-35-61**
Products: **butter 494 tons**
milk and dairy products
fermented milk products

153 KULYAB EXPERIMENTAL MACHINING ATTACHMENTS PLANT

Ownership: ***state***
Industry: ***Metal-working industry***
Number of Employees: ***389.00***
CEO: **Abdukarim Abdurakhimov**
Address: 735360, Repiblic Tadjikistan, Kulyab-4, Krasnykh partizan St.

Phone: **(37713) 2-25-02, 3-15-88**
Products: **metal-working tools**
consumer goods
parts of agricultural machines

154 KULYAB GINNERY

Ownership: ***state***
Industry: ***Textile industry***
Number of Employees: ***558.00***
CEO: **Mirzo Rasulov**
Address: 735360, Repiblic Tadjikistan, Khatlon Reg., Kulyab, Kirov St., 101

Phone: **(37713) 2-26-07, 2-26-13**
Products: **cotton 6,055 tons**
seeds 10,537 tons
lint 889 tons

155 KULYAB GRAIN PROCESSING PLANT

Ownership: ***state***
Industry: ***Food & food processing***
Number of Employees: ***118.00***
CEO: **Manaim K.Kasymov**
Address: 735360, Repiblic Tadjikistan, Khatlon Reg., Kulyab, Lenin St., 1

Phone: **(37713) 2-47-37, 2-25-09, 2-22-84**
Products: **flour 60 ths tons**
bran 13 ths tons
mixed fodder

156 KULYAB MEAT PROCESSING PLANT

Ownership: ***joint-stock***
Industry: ***Food & food processing***
Number of Employees: ***170.00***
CEO: **Khakim Karimov**
Address: 735360, Repiblic Tadjikistan, Khatlon Reg., Kulyab, Khati-rokh St., 324

Phone: **(37713) 2-27-25, 2-27-23**
Products: **meat, incl. edible offal 1,304 tons**
sausages 2,110 ths rbls 70.9 tons
fat

157 KULYAB OIL EXTRACTING ENTERPRISE

158 KULYAB TRAINING and PRODUCTION

n2

Ownership: *state*
Industry: *Oil & gas industry*
Number of Employees:
CEO: D.Negmatova
Address: 735360, Repiblic Tadjikistan, Khatlon Reg., Kulyab, Kuibyshev St., 398

Phone: (37713) 2-32-03, 2-20-58
Products: crude petroleum oils 7 ths tons
gas condensate
sq m
gaseous hydrocarbons

ENTERPRISE

Ownership: *joint-stock*
Industry: *Consumer goods, furniture, household & cultural goods*
Number of Employees: *202.00*
CEO: President
Address: 735360, Repiblic Tadjikistan, Khatlon Reg., Kulyab, Lenin St., 111

Phone: (37713) 2-33-07
Products: floor coverings of cotton 54 ths

pile carpets

ropes of cotton

159 KURGAN-TYUBE BAKERY

Ownership: *state*
Industry: *Food & food processing*
Number of Employees:
CEO: A. Kayumov
Address: 735140, Repiblic Tadjikistan, Khatlon Reg., Kurgan-Tyube, Sverdlov St., 10

Phone: (37744) 2-26-24, 2-25-24
Products: bakers' wares
2,566

160 KURGAN-TYUBE CANNERY

Ownership: *state*
Industry: *Food & food processing*
Number of Employees: *290.00*
CEO: M I.Mugadov
Address: 735140, Repiblic Tadjikistan, Khatlon Reg., Kurgan-Tyube, Dzhalilov St., 15

Phone: (37744) 2-27-65
Products: preserved fruit and vegetables

ths tins

161 KURGAN-TYUBE CLOTHING FACTORY

Ownership: *state*
Industry: *Clothing industry*
Number of Employees: *1,100.00*
CEO: Subkhon K.Rakhimov
Address: 735140, Repiblic Tadjikistan, Khatlon Reg., Kurgan-Tyube, Gafurov St., 7/9

Phone: (37744) 2-20-54
Products: trousers
skirts
shorts

162 KURGAN-TYUBE CONFECTIONERY FACTORY "LAZZAT"

Ownership: *state*
Industry: *Food & food processing*
Number of Employees: *40.00*
CEO: Abdurakhmon Talbonov
Address: 735147, Repiblic Tadjikistan, Khatlon Reg., Kurgan-Tyube, Aini St., 22

Phone: (37744) 2-21-43, 2-34-06
Products: confectionery 1,223 tons

163 KURGAN-TYUBE COTTON SPINNING MILL

Ownership: *state*
Industry: *Textile industry*
Number of Employees:
CEO: Akhmad Makhkamov
Address: 735140, Repiblic Tadjikistan, Khatlon Reg., Kurgan-Tyube, Aini St., 2-a

Phone: (37744) 2-73-64
Products: yarn of cotton

164 KURGAN-TYUBE EXPERIMENTAL FURSKIN FACTORY "MUINNA"

Ownership: *state*
Industry: *Clothing industry*
Number of Employees: *102.00*
CEO: President
Address: 735140, Repiblic Tadjikistan, Khatlon Reg., Kurgan-Tyube

Phone: no data
Products: sheepskins 843 ths sq dm
men's anoraks 2,230 pcs
short coats

165 KURGAN-TYUBE FOLK DECORATIVE HANDICRAFT FACTORY

Ownership: *state*
Industry: *Textile industry*
Number of Employees:
CEO: **President**
Address: 735140, Repiblic Tadjikistan, Khatlon Reg., Kurgan-Tyube, Abu-Ali ibn Sin St.

Phone: **no data**
Products: **articles of apparel**
hosiery 2.4 ths pcs
knitwear articles

166 KURGAN-TYUBE GINNERY

Ownership: *state*
Industry: *Textile industry*
Number of Employees:
CEO: **Tavarali Davlyatov**
Address: 735140, Repiblic Tadjikistan, Khatlon Reg., Kurgan-Tyube, Aini St., 39

Phone: **(37744) 2-32-54**
Products: **cotton**

167 KURGAN-TYUBE MEAT PROCESSING PLANT and DAIRY

Ownership: *state*
Industry: *Food & food processing*
Number of Employees: *156.00*
CEO: **Vadim S.Tsoi**
Address: 735140, Repiblic Tadjikistan, Khatlon Reg., Kurgan-Tyube, Kosmonavtov St., 1

Phone: **(37744) 2-30-52**
Products: **meat, incl. edible offal**
building
sausages 90 tons
ferrous metals
semi-prepared products

168 KURGAN-TYUBE MECHANICAL REPAIR WORKS

Ownership: *state*
Industry: *Machine building industry*
Number of Employees: *60.00*
CEO: **Yury D.Alimbetov**
Address: 735140, Repiblic Tadjikistan, Khatlon Reg., Kurgan-Tyube, Lenin St., 152

Phone: **(37744) 2-25-25**
Products: **metal structures**
repair and maintenance of road
machinery and spare parts ucts of

169 KURGAN-TYUBE NON-ALCOHOLIC BEVERAGES and MINERAL WATER PLANT

Ownership: *state*
Industry: *Food & food processing*
Number of Employees: *100.00*
CEO: **Nasreddin Ibragimov**
Address: 735140, Repiblic Tadjikistan, Khatlon Reg., Kurgan-Tyube, Nekrasov St., 3

Phone: **(37744) 2-21-06**
Products: **mineral waters 19 ths bottles**
beer
wine

170 KURGAN-TYUBE OIL EXTRACTING ENTERPRISE n1

Ownership: *state*
Industry: *Oil & gas industry*
Number of Employees:
CEO: **R. T.Sharafutdinov**
Address: 735147, Repiblic Tadjikistan, Khatlon Reg., Kalininabad

Phone: **2-13-90, 2-40-55**
Products: **crude petroleum oils 19 ths tons**
gaseous hydrocarbons 1 mln cu m

171 KURGAN-TYUBE OILERY

Ownership: *state*
Industry: *Food & food processing*
Number of Employees: *220.00*
CEO: **Dzhamildin Tolibov**
Address: 735140, Repiblic Tadjikistan, Khatlon Reg., Kurgan-Tyube, Aini St., 37

Phone: **(37744) 2-29-57, 2-29-54**

172 KURGAN-TYUBE TRANSFORMER PLANT

Ownership: *state*
Industry: *Electrical engineering*
Number of Employees: *583.00*
CEO: **Rakhmatullo Kalandarov**
Address: 735140, Repiblic Tadjikistan, Khatlon Reg., Kurgan-Tyube, Gafurov St., 7

Phone: **(37744) 2-22-16**

Products: cotton oil 10,657 tons

Products: **high-voltage apparatus 1,705 pcs**
electric transformers 45 ths pcs
power transformers 489 ths kWh

173 LEASE-HOLDER COLLECTIVE "VREMYA"

Ownership: *state*
Industry: *Mining industry (building mateirlas)*
Number of Employees: *130.00*
CEO: **Amon Eshboyev**
Address: 735750, Republic Tadjikistan, Leninabad Leninabad
Reg., Kairakkum

Phone: no data
Products: **crushed stone 186 ths cu m**
natural sands 156 ths cu m
blocks of stone

174 LEASING-BASED ENTERPRISE "SHARBAT"

Ownership: *state*
Industry: *Food & food processing*
Number of Employees: *339.00*
CEO: **Mavlon Mirzoyev**
Address: 735500, Republic Tadjikistan,
Reg., Pendzhikent, Lenin St., 6

Phone: (37775) 2-33-50
Products: **jam 6,379 ths rbls 202 ths tins**
fruit juices
grape juice

175 LENINABAD RARE METALS PLANT

Ownership: *state*
Industry: *Metallurgy*
Number of Employees: *720.00*
CEO: **Makhmudzhon Khalikov**
Address: 735744, Republic Tadjikistan, Leninabad Reg., Kairakkum Dist., pos. Chorukh-Dairon, Lenin St., 108

Phone: 5-65-91
Products: **alloys**

176 LENINSKY NON-METALLIFEROUS MATERIALS PLANT

Ownership: *joint-stock*
Industry: *Building materials industry*
Number of Employees: *10.00*
CEO: **President**
Address: 735100, Republic Tadjikistan, pos. Leninsky

Phone: no data
Products: **crushed stone 80 ths cu m**
natural sands 84.6 ths cu m
ferroconcrete articles 868 cu m

177 MATCHINSKY RURAL CONSTRUCTION PLANT

Ownership: *state*
Industry: *Building materials industry*
Number of Employees: *113.00*
CEO: **Khadzhi M.Mukhamadiev**
Address: 735800, Republic Tadjikistan, Leninabad Reg., Matchinsky Dist., pos. Buston

Phone: 5-65-25
Products: **pre-cast ferroconcrete**

equipment

178 MECHANICAL WORKS "KHLOPKOZAPCHAST"

Ownership: *state*
Industry: *Machine building industry*
Number of Employees:
CEO: **President**
Address: 735400, Republic Tadjikistan, Kofarnikhon, Shestopalov St., 1

Phone: 2-30-64
Products: **wire 991 tons**
repair of electric motors
non-standard machinery and

179 MINE "FAN-YAGNOB"

Ownership: *state*
Industry: *Coal mining & peat industry*
Number of Employees:
CEO: **Zakhid M.Fazylov**
Address: 735520, Republic Tadjikistan, Leninabad
Leninabad
Reg., Aini Dist., pos. Zeravshan

Phone: **21-90**
Products: **coal 29 ths tons**

180 MINING ENTERPRISE "TADZHIKSKOYE"

Ownership: *state*
Industry: *Coal mining & peat industry*
Number of Employees: *10.00*
CEO: **Azimboi Azizov**
Address: 735930, Republic Tadjikistan,
Reg., Isfara Dist., pos. Shurab

Phone: **37-49, 41-61**
Products: **coal 177.7 ths tons**

181 MOSKOVSKY FERROCONCRETE STRUCTURES PLANT n1

Ownership: *state*
Industry: *Building materials industry*
Number of Employees:
CEO: **Amrokhon Saidov**
Address: 735370, Repiblic Tadjikistan, Khatlon
15
Reg., Moskovsky Dist., kishlak Rossiya

Phone: **2-21-63, 2-21-60**
Products: **pre-cast ferroconcrete**
structural components for house construction crushed stone

182 MOSKOVSKY GINNERY

Ownership: *state*
Industry: *Textile industry*
Number of Employees: *460.00*
CEO: **Sikandor Sakhibnazarov**
Address: 735370, Repiblic Tadjikistan, Khatlon Reg., pos. Moskovsky, K.Marks St.,

Phone: **2-20-12**
Products: **cotton 4,433 tons**
seeds 8,184 tons
lint 853 tons

183 NAU BUILDING MATERIALS and STRUCTURES PLANT

Ownership: *joint-stock*
Industry: *Building materials industry*
Number of Employees:
CEO: **Anvar Kh.Usmanov**
Leninabad
Address: 735830, Republic Tadjikistan, Leninabad Reg., pos. Nau, Saidov St., 42

Phone: **2-35-50**
Products: **pre-cast ferroconcrete**
crushed stone 34.2 ths cu m
natural sands

184 NAU GINNERY

Ownership: *state*
Industry: *Textile industry*
Number of Employees: *387.00*
CEO: **Abdullo F.Ubaidullaev**
Address: 735830, Republic Tadjikistan,
Reg., pos. Nau, Volkov St., 22

Phone: **2-28-38**
Products: **cotton 10,289 tons**
seeds 18,670 tons
lint 1,747 tons

185 NAU GRAIN PROCESSING PLANT

Ownership: ***state***
Industry: ***Food & food processing***
Number of Employees: ***498.00***
CEO: **Makhsud S.Saliev**
Address: 735830, Republic Tadjikistan, Leninabad Reg., pos. Nau

Phone: **2-24-16**
Products: **wheat flour 132 ths tons**
bran 35 ths tons
mixed fodder

186 NAU MECHANIZED QUARRY

Ownership: ***state***
Industry: ***Mining industry (building mateirlas)***
Number of Employees: ***92.00***
CEO: **Abdukhalil A.Abdusattarov**
Address: 735830, Republic Tadjikistan, Leninabad Reg., pos. Nau, Volkov St., 52

Phone: **2-24-01**
Products: **crushed stone 34 ths cu m**
gravel 32.3 ths cu m
natural sands

187 NEFTEABAD OILFIELD

Ownership: ***state***
Industry: ***Oil & gas industry***
Number of Employees: ***362.00***
CEO: **A. A.Kakharov**
Address: 735920, Republic Tadjikistan, Leninabad Reg., Isfara, pos. Nefteabad

Phone: **2-52-42, 2-52-44**
Products: **crude petroleum oils 38 ths tons**
gas condensate
gaseous hydrocarbons

188 NON-ALCOHOLIC BEVERAGES and MINERAL WATER PLANT

Ownership: ***state***
Industry: ***Food & food processing***
Number of Employees: ***102.00***
CEO: **Uchkun T.Yusupov**
Address: 735690, Republic Tadjikistan, Leninabad Reg., Khodzhent Dist., Gafurov, Vokzalnaya St., 13

Phone: **3-26-48, 3-25-48**
Products: **beer 120 ths dal**
non-alcoholic beverages 46 ths dal
mineral waters

189 NUREK CLOTHING FACTORY

Ownership: ***state***
Industry: ***Clothing industry***
Number of Employees: ***20.00***
CEO: **Rakhmatullo Asoyev**
Address: 735300, Republic Tadjikistan, Nurek, Aini St., 1

Phone: **(37738) 2-28-58, 2-21-81**
Products: **shirts of cotton 633.3 ths pcs**

190 NUREK EXPERIMENTAL MECHANICAL WORKS

Ownership: ***state***
Industry: ***Machine building industry***
Number of Employees: ***10.00***
CEO: **Khamrokul Sh.Erov**
Address: 735300, Republic Tadjikistan, Nurek, Promzona

Phone: **(37738) 2-28-29, 2-28-39, 2-28-27**
Products: **spare parts for road building machines**
metal structures for use in construction 194 tons
non-standard machinery and equipment

191 NUREK HYDROELECTRIC STATION

Ownership: *state*
Industry: *Power industry*
Number of Employees:
CEO: **Abdullo E.Erov**
Address: 735300, Republic Tadjikistan, Nurek, Lenin St., 14

Phone: **(37738) 2-25-36, 2-14-11**
Products: **electric power supply 11,541 mln kWh**

192 OIL ASPHALT PLANT

Ownership: *state*
Industry: *Oil refining & gas processing*
Number of Employees: *150.00*
CEO: **President**
Address: 735202, Repiblic Tadjikistan, Khatlon Reg., Kolkhozabad Dist., pos. Isoeva

Phone: **4-30-00, 4-30-03**
Products: **oil asphalt**

193 OKTYABRSKY COTTON PROCESSING MILL

Ownership: *state*
Industry: *Textile industry*
Number of Employees:
CEO: **I.K.Safarov**
Leninabad
Address: 735162, Repiblic Tadjikistan, Khatlon Reg., pos. Oktyabrsky

Phone: **2-13-74**
Products: **cotton**

194 PENDZHIKENT BRICK YARD

Ownership: *state*
Industry: *Building materials industry*
Number of Employees: *133.00*
CEO: **K. Shodiev**
Address: 735500, Republic Tadjikistan,

Reg., Pendzhikent

Phone: **(37775) 2-24-36, 2-39-02**
Products: **wall materials 7,720 ths pcs**

195 PENDZHIKENT FERMENTED TOBACCO PLANT
PLANT

Ownership: *joint-stock*
Industry: *Tobacco industry*
Number of Employees: *500.00*
CEO: **Akhmat Yarboyev**
Leninabad
Address: 735500, Republic Tadjikistan, Leninabad Reg., Pendzhikent, Khudoiberdyev St., 3

Phone: **(37775) 2-22-90**
Products: **unmanufactured tobacco 6,559 tons**

196 PENDZHIKENT FISH PROCESSING

Ownership: *state*
Industry: *Fishing & fish processing*
Number of Employees: *32.00*
CEO: **Kobir Eshondzhanov**
Address: 735500, Republic Tadjikistan,

Reg., Pendzhikent

Phone: **(37775) 2-39-58**
Products: **live fish 115.4 tons**
fish products

197 PENDZHIKENT MEAT PROCESSING PLANT and DAIRY

Ownership: *state*
Industry: *Food & food processing*
Number of Employees: *86.00*
CEO: **Atkhamdzhon Razykov**
Address: 735500, Republic Tadjikistan, Leninabad Reg., Pendzhikent, Tereshkova St., 28

Phone: **(37775) 2-34-44, 2-37-73**
Products: **meat, incl. edible offal 184.8 tons**
sausages 25.7 tons
fat

198 PLANT "ALMOS"

Ownership: *state*
Industry: *Radio-electronic industry*
Number of Employees: *485.00*
CEO: **Abdulakhat L.Kadyrov**
Address: 735708, Republic Tadjikistan, Leninabad Reg., Khudzhand, K.Khudzhandi St., 8

Phone: **(37922) 4-00-74**
Products: **crystal vibrators 1,000 ths pcs**
quartz filters 19 ths pcs
television receivers

199 PLANT "ETALON"

Ownership: *state*
Industry: *Medical equipment industry*
Number of Employees: *177.00*
CEO: **Yury V.Gritsaev**
Address: 735716, Republic Tadjikistan, Leninabad Reg., Khudzhand, Syrdarya St., 13-a

Phone: **(37922) 5-67-55, 2-16-74, 2-18-83**
Products: **instruments and apparatus**
repair of instrumentation

200 PLANT "LENINABADSELMASH"

Ownership: *state*
Industry: *Machine building industry*
Number of Employees: *616.00*
CEO: **Maikham Dodobaev**
Address: 735830, Republic Tadjikistan, Leninabad Reg., pos. Nau, Zavodskaya St., 66

Phone: **2-26-28, 2-26-29, 2-25-28**
Products: **agricultural machines**

201 PLANT "TADZHIKKHIMSELKHOZMASH"

Ownership: *state*
Industry: *Machine building industry*
Number of Employees: *470.00*
CEO: **Rustam M.Khakimov**
Address: 735830, Republic Tadjikistan, Leninabad Reg., Kanibadam Dist., pos. Makhram, Leninabadskaya St., 10

Phone: **2-22-64**
Products: **agricultural equipment**

202 PRINT-SHOP

Ownership: *joint-stock*
Industry: *Publishing & printing*
Number of Employees: *32.00*
CEO: **Khalik I.Ibragimov**
Address: 734027, Republic Tadjikistan, Dushanbe, Karamov St., 205

Phone: **(3772) 36-22-37**
Products: **printed matter**

203 PRINTING PRODUCTION COMPANY COMPANY

Ownership: *state*
Industry: *Publishing & printing*
Number of Employees:
CEO: President
Address: 735360, Repiblic Tadjikistan, Khatlon Reg., Kulyab, Dzhumaev St., 26

Dushanbe,
Phone: no data
Products: **newspapers 2,400 ths copies**
business forms 1,263 ths copies

1,293

204 PROCUREMENT PRODUCTION

"TADZHIKVTORTSVETMET"

Ownership: *state*
Industry: *Scrap & waste processing industry*
Number of Employees: *21.00*
CEO: **Akhat Akramov**
Address: 734060, Republic Tadjikistan,

Dzh.Rasulov Ave., 8

Phone: **(3772) 31-14-31, 31-14-01**
Products: **non-ferrous waste and scrap**

tons

205 PRODUCTION COMPANY "KHODZHENTATLAS"

Ownership: *state*
Industry: *Textile industry*
Number of Employees: *1,259.00*
CEO: **Gafar Mukhamedov**
Dushanbe,
Address: 735700, Republic Tadjikistan, Leninabad Reg., Khudzhand-17, Kosmonavtov St., 93

Phone: **(37922) 6-30-31, 2-65-75**
Products: **fabrics of silk 838.9 ths m**
fabrics of man-made filaments
fabrics of cotton

206 PRODUCTION COMPANY "PAMIR"

Ownership: *state*
Industry: *Machine building industry*
Number of Employees: *822.00*
CEO: **Vladimir G.Lesin**
Address: 734036, Republic Tadjikistan,

40 let Oktyabrya St., 343

Phone: **(3772) 31-26-27, 31-22-87, 31-06-23**
Products: **refrigerators 61 ths pcs**
spare parts for refrigerators
refrigerating plants

207 PRODUCTION COMPANY "PAMIRKVARTSSAMOTSVETY"

Ownership: *state*
Industry: *Mining industry (building mateirlas)*
Number of Employees: *679.00*
CEO: **Zurmakhmad Erov**
Dushanbe,
Address: 734013, Republic Tadjikistan, Dushanbe, Lakhuti St., 16

Phone: **(3772) 27-23-69, 27-24-59**
Products: **consumer goods**
semi-precious stones
blocks of marble

208 PRODUCTION COMPANY "TADZHIKENERGOLEGPROM"

Ownership: *state*
Industry: *Machine building industry*
Number of Employees: *27.00*
CEO: **Mikhail S.Zubko**
Address: 734013, Republic Tadjikistan,

P.Lumumba St., 41

Phone: **(3772) 22-56-72**
Products: **repair of equipment**

209 PRODUCTION COMPANY "TADZHIKGIDROAGREGAT"

Ownership: *state*
Industry: *Machine building industry*
Number of Employees: *2,478.00*
CEO: **Akbar M.Fayazov**
Address: 734013, Republic Tadjikistan, Dushanbe, Druzhby narodov Ave., 47

Phone: **(3772) 27-16-23, 23-08-04**
Products: **hydraulic drives and automated devices**
Products:

cast articles of pig iron

210 PRODUCTION COMPANY "TADZHIKKHIMPROM"

Ownership: *state*
Industry: *Chemical, pharmaceutical & micribiology industry*
Number of Employees:
CEO: **M.S.Umedov**
Address: 735310, Repiblic Tadjikistan, Khatlon Reg., pos. Yavan, pos. Planernyi

Phone: **(37741) 4-16-71, 2-26-54**
spare parts for hydraulic drives
liquid chlorine 16 ths tons
caustic soda 16 ths tons
calcium chloride

211 PRODUCTION COMPANY "TADZHIKNEFT"

Ownership: *state*
Industry: *Oil & gas industry*
Number of Employees: *1,131.00*
CEO: **Nabi Malikov**
Address: 734018, Republic Tadjikistan, Dushanbe, Mushfiki St., 77
Dushanbe,

Phone: **(3772) 33-60-96**
Products: **crude petroleum oils 56.6 ths tons**
gas condensate 4.8 ths tons
gaseous hydrocarbons
conv.

asbestos-cement

212 PRODUCTION COMPANY "TADZHIKTSEMENT"

Ownership: *state*
Industry: *Building materials industry*
Number of Employees: *845.00*
CEO: **Boris I.Sevastyanov**
Address: 734008, Republic Tadjikistan,

Rudaki Ave., 205

Phone: **(3772) 24-24-58, 24-23-01**
Products: **cement 446.8 ths tons**
pipes of asbestos-cement 1,097.7

km corrugated sheets of

213 PRODUCTION COMPANY "TADZHIKZOLOTO"

Ownership: *state*
Industry: *Ore mining industry*
Number of Employees: *1,564.00*
CEO: **Abdunumon A.Abdurazakov**
Address: 734018, Republic Tadjikistan, Dushanbe,
Dushanbe,
Mushfiki St., 77

Phone: **(3772) 33-57-53, 33-44-19, 33-43-56**
Products: **gold**

214 PRODUCTION COOPERATIVE "PISHCHEVIK"

Ownership: *state*
Industry: *Food & food processing*
Number of Employees: *285.00*
CEO: **Orif Raupov**
Address: 734024, Republic Tadjikistan,

Akhmadi Donish St., 55

Phone: **(3772) 23-06-61**
Products: **bakers' wares**
ground rusks 16 tons
corn sticks

215 PROLETARSK CENTRAL ELECTROMECHANICAL WORKSHOP

Ownership: ***state***
Industry: ***Machine building industry***
Number of Employees: ***249.00***
CEO: **Boris B.Kiyamov**
Address: 735820, Republic Tadjikistan, Leninabad Reg., pos. Proletarsk, Zavodskaya St., 11

Phone: **2-13-54, 2-25-85, 2-13-10**
Products: **cast articles of steel 280 tons**
cast articles of pig iron
spare parts

216 PROLETARSK GINNERY

Ownership: ***state***
Industry: ***Textile industry***
Number of Employees: ***572.00***
CEO: **Khaimamad Yarmatov**
Address: 735820, Republic Tadjikistan, Leninabad Reg., pos. Proletarsk, Yubileinaya St., 39

Phone: **2-13-47, 2-20-40**
Products: **cotton 15,985 tons**
lint 2,198 tons
seeds

217 PROLETARSK ORE CONCENTRATING MILL

Ownership: ***state***
Industry: ***Building materials industry***
Number of Employees: ***839.00***
CEO: **Khodzha Khaitov**
Address: 735820, Republic Tadjikistan, Leninabad Reg., pos. Proletarsk, Sovetskaya St., 1

Phone: **2-25-41, 2-19-34**
Products: **concentrated sand 226 ths tons**
ceramic wall tiles 268 sq m
building bricks

218 PROSTHETIC and ORTHOPAEDIC APPLIANCES PLANT

Ownership: ***state***
Industry: ***Medical equipment industry***
Number of Employees: ***63.00***
CEO: **President**
Address: 734029, Republic Tadjikistan, Dushanbe, Karateginskaya St., 1

Phone: **(3772) 25-04-21**
Products: **orthopaedic footwear**
prosthetic appliances

219 PUBLISHING HOUSE

Ownership: ***state***
Industry: ***Publishing & printing***
Number of Employees: ***353.00***
CEO: **Vakhid A.Ibragimov**
Address: 734018, Republic Tadjikistan, Dushanbe, Pravdy Ave., 16

Phone: **(3772) 33-32-88, 33-24-16**
Products: **newspapers 78 mln copies**
magazines 18 mln sheets

220 PYANDZH GINNERY

Ownership: ***state***
Industry: ***Textile industry***
Number of Employees:
CEO: **Zokir Sharipov**
Address: 735330, Repiblic Tadjikistan, Khatlon Reg., Vose Dist., pos. Pyandzh, 50 let Pogranvoisk St., 36

Phone: **25-85, 28-89**
Products: **cotton**

221 SHAARTUZ CREAMERY

Ownership: ***state***
Industry: ***Food & food processing***
Number of Employees:
CEO: **Yusuf Abdusamadov**
Address: 735180, Repiblic Tadjikistan, Khatlon Reg., Shaartuz Dist., pos. Gidrostroitelei

Phone: **2-29-12**
Products: **milk and dairy products**

222 SHAARTUZ GINNERY

Ownership: ***state***
Industry: ***Textile industry***
Number of Employees: ***20.00***
CEO: **Abdulmadchid Kakhorov**
Address: 735180, Repiblic Tadjikistan, Khatlon Reg., pos. Shaartuz, Kirov St., 7

Phone: **2-18-61, 2-28-48**
Products: **cotton**

223 SHAKHRISTAN CREAMERY

Ownership: ***state***
Industry: ***Food & food processing***
Number of Employees: ***27.00***
CEO: **Karim Gaibullaev**
Address: 735700, Republic Tadjikistan, Leninabad Khudzhand, pos. Shakhristan St., 5

Phone: **(37922) 2-62-31**
Products: **butter 205.4 tons**
milk and dairy products

224 SHURAB MECHANICAL WORKS "FILIZ"

Ownership: ***state***
Industry: ***Metal-working industry***
Number of Employees: ***173.00***
CEO: **Subkhon N.Narziev**
Address: 735930, Republic Tadjikistan, Reg., Isfara Dist., pos. Shurab, Mira

Phone: **2-45-01**
Products: **table and kitchen articles of aluminium 238.2 ths pcs**

225 SMALL ENTERPRISE "BETON"

Ownership: ***joint-stock***
Industry: ***Building materials industry***
Number of Employees:
CEO: **Khudzhali Khusravov**
Address: 736000, Republic Tadjikistan, Gorno-Badakhshan Autonomous Region, Khorog, Michurin St., 58

Phone: **(377910) 29-03**
Products: **pre-cast ferroconcrete**

226 SOUTHERN ELECTRIC POWER TRANSMISSION NETWORK

Ownership: ***state***
Industry: ***Power industry***
Number of Employees: ***940.00***
CEO: **U. Ubaidulaev**
Address: 735140, Repiblic Tadjikistan, Khatlon Reg., Kurgan-Tyube, Aini St., 80

Phone: **(37744) 2-35-74**
Products: **electric power supply**

227 STATE FARM-PLANT "EFIRONOS"

Ownership: *state*
Industry: *Chemical, pharmaceutical & micribiology industry*
Number of Employees: *20.00*
CEO: **I.Khatamov**
Address: 735000, Republic Tadjikistan, Dushanbe,
Tursunzade, kolkhoz XX parts'ezda

Phone: **4-63**
Products: **geranium oil kWh**
peppermint

228 STATE JOINT-STOCK HOLDING COMPANY "BARKI TOCHIK"

Ownership: *state*
Industry: *Power industry*
Number of Employees:
CEO: **Bakhrom Sirozhev**
Address: 734026, Republic Tadjikistan,

Samoni St., 64

Phone: **(3772) 35-87-38, 24-53-16**
Products: **electric power supply 16,805 mln**

heating 3,648 ths Gcal

229 TADJIK ALUMINIUM WORKS

Ownership: *state*
Industry: *Metallurgy*
Number of Employees: *20.00*
CEO: **Mikhail F.Sinani**
Address: 735014, Republic Tadjikistan,
Tursunzade, p/o Seshanbe
Leninabad

Phone: **(37730) 2-23-86, 2-23-92**
Products: **primary aluminium 345 ths tons**
anode blocks 240 ths tons
non-standard machinery and equipment 64.5 tons

230 TADJIK PRODUCTION COMPANY "SVETOTEKHNIKA"

Ownership: *state*
Industry: *Electrical engineering*
Number of Employees: *1,308.00*
CEO: **Dzhabar Rasulov**
Address: 735926, Republic Tadjikistan,

Reg., Isfara Dist., pos. Kim

Phone: **3-34-28, 2-20-92**
Products: **lighting engineering equipment**
lighting fixtures 1,185 ths pcs
low-voltage apparatus

231 TAKOB FLUORSPAR WORKS

Ownership: *state*
Industry: *Mining industry (building mateirlas)*
Number of Employees: *414.00*
CEO: **Seilkhon M.Barikov**
Address: 734046, Republic Tadjikistan, Dushanbe, Dushanbe,
pos. Takob

Phone: **24-96, 1-27**
Products: **fluorspar**

232 TRAINING and PRODUCTION WORKS n1

Ownership: *joint-stock*
Industry: *Consumer goods, furniture, household & cultural goods*
Number of Employees: *273.00*
CEO: **President**
Address: 734036, Republic Tadjikistan,

40 let Oktyabrya St., 349

Phone: **(3772) 31-08-13**
Products: **bed-linen 82 ths pcs**
articles of feather and down

233 TRAINING and PRODUCTION WORKS n3

Ownership: *joint-stock*
Industry: *Consumer goods, furniture, household & cultural goods*
Number of Employees: *148.00*
CEO: **President**
Address: 734013, Republic Tadjikistan, Dushanbe, Druzhby narodov Ave., 72

Phone: **(3772) 27-17-54, 27-17-56**
Products: **anodized articles**
saddlery and harness articles
textile haberdashery

234 TRAINING and PRODUCTION WORKS n4

Ownership: *joint-stock*
Industry: *Consumer goods, furniture, household & cultural goods*
Number of Employees: *624.00*
CEO: **Tolib Dodobaev**
Address: 735690, Republic Tadjikistan, Leninabad Reg., Khodzhent Dist., Gafurov, F.Akhmedov St., 8

Phone: **4-25-32**
Products: **pile carpets 10,810 sq m**
floor coverings of cotton
fabrics of silk

235 TRAINING and PRODUCTION WORKS n5

Ownership: *joint-stock*
Industry: *Consumer goods, furniture, household & cultural goods*
Number of Employees: *115.00*
CEO: **President**
Address: 734029, Republic Tadjikistan, Dushanbe, Aini Shosse, 5-i km

Phone: **(3772) 25-29-67**
Products: **wadding 2,166 tons**
apparel wadding 49 tons

236 TURSUNZADE GINNERY

Ownership: *state*
Industry: *Textile industry*
Number of Employees: *700.00*
CEO: **Khasan Manonov**
Address: 735000, Republic Tadjikistan, Tursunzade, Khlopkovaya St., 1

Phone: **(37730) 2-26-79**
Products: **cotton 16,011 tons**
seeds 29,388 tons
lint 2,833 tons

237 TURSUNZADE PORCELAIN WORKS

Ownership: *state*
Industry: *Building materials industry*
Number of Employees: *30.00*
CEO: **Sh. M.Abdusattorov**
Address: 735003, Republic Tadjikistan, Tursunzade, Lomonosov St.

Phone: **(37730) 2-32-32, 2-21-79, 2-15-34**
Products: **tableware of porcelain**

238 TURSUNZADE PRINT-SHOP

Ownership: *state*
Industry: *Publishing & printing*
Number of Employees: *30.00*
CEO: **President**
Address: 735000, Republic Tadjikistan, Tursunzade, Lomonosov St., 140

Phone: **no data**
Products: **newspapers**
business forms

239 URA-TYUBE BAKERY

Ownership: ***state***
Industry: ***Food & food processing***
Number of Employees: ***189.00***
CEO: **Kuli M.Marufov**
Address: 735610, Republic Tadjikistan, Leninabad Leninabad Reg., Ura-Tyube, Pushkin St., 13

Phone: **2-19-35**
Products: **bakers' wares 3,920 tons**

240 URA-TYUBE BRICK YARD

Ownership: ***state***
Industry: ***Building materials industry***
Number of Employees: ***170.00***
CEO: **Kamil Ayubov**
Address: 735610, Republic Tadjikistan, Reg., Ura-Tyube

Phone: **2-24-67**
Products: **building bricks 10,360 ths pcs**

241 URA-TYUBE CANNERY

Ownership: ***state***
Industry: ***Food & food processing***
Number of Employees: ***236.00***
CEO: **Nabidzhon Naimov**
Address: 735610, Republic Tadjikistan, Leninabad Leninabad Reg., Ura-Tyube Dist., pos. Yakkaton, 8

Phone: **2-32-35, 2-51-04**
Products: **apple puree**
peach puree 69 ths tins
tomato paste

242 URA-TYUBE CREAMERY

Ownership: ***state***
Industry: ***Food & food processing***
Number of Employees: ***94.00***
CEO: **Khabibullo Kh.Abdulloyev**
Address: 735610, Republic Tadjikistan, Reg., Ura-Tyube, Lenin St., 271

Phone: **2-62-31, 2-15-53, 2-35-00**
Products: **butter 408 tons**
milk and dairy products
milk products

243 URA-TYUBE FACTORY "NEKSOZ"

Ownership: ***joint-stock***
Industry: ***Consumer goods, furniture, household & cultural goods***
Number of Employees: ***721.00***
CEO: **Inom Khatamov**
Address: 735610, Republic Tadjikistan, Leninabad Leninabad Reg., Ura-Tyube, Gagarin St., 38

Phone: **2-12-11**
Products: **articles of plastics**
baby linen
pile carpets

244 URA-TYUBE KNITTED OUTERWEAR FACTORY

Ownership: ***joint-stock***
Industry: ***Textile industry***
Number of Employees: ***2,558.00***
CEO: **Uidzhiboi Obidov**
Address: 735610, Republic Tadjikistan, Reg., Ura-Tyube, Fabrichnaya St., 1

Phone: **2-22-72, 2-23-22**
Products: **knitwear**

245 URA-TYUBE TRAINING and PRODUCTION ENTERPRISE

Ownership: *joint-stock*
Industry: *Consumer goods, furniture, household & cultural goods*
Number of Employees:
Leninabad
CEO: **A. M.Kasymov**
Address: 735610, Republic Tadjikistan, Leninabad Reg., Ura-Tyube

Phone: no data
Products: **floor coverings of cotton73.7 ths sq m**

lids

246 URA-TYUBE WINE PLANT

Ownership: *state*
Industry: *Food & food processing*
Number of Employees: *136.00*
CEO: **Abduvakhkhob K.Kayumov**
Address: 735610, Republic Tadjikistan,

Reg., Ura-Tyube, Lenin St., 22

Phone: **2-22-82, 2-32-46, 2-10-15**
Products: **wine 322 ths dal**
crude alcohol 1,369.4 dal
carpets grape must

247 UYALP GINNERY

Ownership: *state*
Industry: *Textile industry*
Number of Employees:
CEO: **E. A.Gulov**
Address: 735130, Repiblic Tadjikistan, Khatlon Reg., Iliychevsky Dist., pos. Uyalp

Phone: **2-12-84, 2-12-87**
Products: **cotton**

248 VAKHSH HYDROELECTRIC STATION CASCADE

Ownership: *state*
Industry: *Power industry*
Number of Employees: *150.00*
CEO: **T.Sabirov**
Address: 735147, Repiblic Tadjikistan, Khatlon Reg., Kalininabad

Phone: **(37744) 7-32-50, 2-23-92, 2-23-58**
Products: **electric power supply**

249 VAKHSH NITROGENOUS FERTILIZER PLANT

Ownership: *state*
Industry: *Chemical, pharmaceutical & micribiology industry*
Number of Employees: *1,345.00*
CEO: **A. Ganiev**
Address: 735147, Repiblic Tadjikistan, Khatlon Reg., Kalininabad

Phone: **(37744) 2-35-14, 2-35-84**
Products: **nitrogenous fertilizers 53 ths tons**
urea 114 ths tons
ammonia

250 VOSE GINNERY

Ownership: *state*
Industry: *Textile industry*
Number of Employees: *300.00*
CEO: **Samardin Fazlitdyainov**
Address: 735330, Repiblic Tadjikistan, Khatlon Reg., pos. Vose, O.Khaiyam St., 18

Phone: **2-31-47, 2-23-02**
Products: **cotton 5,304 tons**
seeds 9,649 tons
lint 506 tons

251 VOSE SALT WORKS

Ownership: *state*
Industry: *Mining industry (building mateirlas)*
Number of Employees: *100.00*
CEO: **A. Samadov**
Address: 735330, Repiblic Tadjikistan, Khatlon
Shakhrinau

252 WINE PLANT "SHAKHRINAU" (LEASING-BASED ì

Ownership: *state*
Industry: *Food & food processing*
Number of Employees: *300.00*
CEO: **P. Karimov**
Address: 735020, Republic Tadjikistan,

Reg., pos. Vose, Amirshoev St., 8

Phone: 2-23-87, 2-20-58
Products: salt 14,916 tons

Dist., i

Phone: 3-32-18
Products: wine 302 ths dal
vodka 110 ths dal
sparkling wine

253 WOOLEN SHAWL FACTORY "ZARBOF"

Ownership: ***state***
Industry: ***Textile industry***
Number of Employees: ***1,008.00***
CEO: Abdullodzhon Khoshimov
Address: 735702, Republic Tadjikistan, Leninabad Reg., Khudzhand, Lenin St., 234-a

Phone: (37922) 4-37-52, 6-47-91, 6-43-85
Products: yarn of mixed wool 370 tons
fabrics

254 YAVAN ELECTROCHEMICAL WORKS

Ownership: ***state***
Industry: ***Machine building industry***
Number of Employees:
CEO: President
Address: 735310, Repiblic Tadjikistan, Khatlon Reg., Yavan Dist., pos. Pionernyi

Phone: (37741) 4-15-94, 4-16-63
Products: cast articles of steel 629 tons
electrical-sheet steel 905 tons
chemical machinery

255 YAVAN LIME WORKS (JOINT-STOCK COMPANY)

Ownership: ***joint-stock***
Industry: ***Mining industry (building mateirlas)***
Number of Employees:
CEO: Kh. Tilloev
Address: 735310, Repiblic Tadjikistan, Khatlon Reg., Yavan Dist., kishlak Darash

Phone: (37741) 2-12-57
parts
Products: burnt lime 31 ths tons
packed lime
cement blocks

256 YAVAN MECHANICAL REPAIR WORKS

Ownership: ***state***
Industry: ***Machine building industry***
Number of Employees:
CEO: President
Address: 735310, Repiblic Tadjikistan, Khatlon Reg., pos. Yavan

Phone: (37741) 3-41
Products: cast articles of steel 629 tons
chemical machinery and spare

equipment of stainless steel

TADJIKISTAN INDUSTRY: LARGEST COMPANIES BY INDUSTRY

	COMPANY	INDUSTRY	Number in Alphabetical Section
1	KHUDZHAND AUTOMOBILE REPAIR WORKS n4	*Automobile industry*	129
2	KULYAB BRICK YARD	*Building materials industry*	150
3	ISFARA FERROCONCRETE STRUCTURES and BUILDING ARTICLES PLANT n5	*Building materials industry*	97
4	KAIRAKKUM SUBSIDIARY ENTERPRISE	*Building materials industry*	111
5	KALININABAD FERROCONCRETE STRUCTURES PLANT n1	*Building materials industry*	112
6	KALININABAD FERROCONCRETE STRUCTURES PLANT n8	*Building materials industry*	113
7	KANIBADAM FERROCONCRETE STRUCTURES PLANT n2	*Building materials industry*	119
8	TURSUNZADE PORCELAIN WORKS	*Building materials industry*	237
9	SMALL ENTERPRISE "BETON"	*Building materials industry*	225
10	JOINT-STOCK ENTERPRISE "LACHP"	*Building materials industry*	106
11	LENINSKY NON-METALLIFEROUS MATERIALS PLANT	*Building materials industry*	176
12	MATCHINSKY RURAL CONSTRUCTION PLANT	*Building materials industry*	177
13	PROLETARSK ORE CONCENTRATING	*Building materials industry*	217

26	GAFUROV FERROCONCRETE STRUCTURES PLANT n7	*Building materials industry*	74
27	GANCHI BRICK YARD	*Building materials industry*	77
28	URA-TYUBE BRICK YARD	*Building materials industry*	240
29	ISFARA BUILDING MATERIALS PLANT	*Building materials industry*	92
30	PRODUCTION COMPANY "TADZHIKKHIMPROM"	*Chemical, pharmaceutical & micribiology industry*	210
31	DUSHANBE PAINTS and VARNISHES PLANT "RANGINKAMON"	*Chemical, pharmaceutical & micribiology industry*	44
32	ISFARA CHEMICALS PLANT	*Chemical, pharmaceutical & micribiology industry*	94
33	ISFARA MINERAL PAINTS PLANT "NILUFOR"	*Chemical, pharmaceutical & micribiology industry*	102
34	ISFARA MEDICAL PREPARATIONS and FEED PROTEIN PLANT	*Chemical, pharmaceutical & micribiology industry*	101
35	VAKHSH NITROGENOUS FERTILIZER PLANT	*Chemical, pharmaceutical & micribiology industry*	249
36	STATE FARM-PLANT "EFIRONOS"	*Chemical, pharmaceutical & micribiology industry*	227
37	CLOTHING FACTORY "FIRUZA"	*Clothing industry*	12
38	DUSHANBE CLOTHING PRODUCTION COMPANY "CHEVAR"	*Clothing industry*	22
39	CLOTHING FIRM "GULISTAN"	*Clothing industry*	13
40	NUREK CLOTHING FACTORY	*Clothing industry*	189
41	DUSHANBE COMPANY "GULDAST"	*Clothing industry*	23

42	KURGAN-TYUBE EXPERIMENTAL FURSKIN FACTORY "MUINNA"	*Clothing industry*	164
43	KURGAN-TYUBE CLOTHING FACTORY	*Clothing industry*	161
44	KHOROG CLOTHING FACTORY n3 "KHAIET"	*Clothing industry*	127
45	KANIBADAM CLOTHING PRODUCTION COMPANY "KHUSNORO"	*Clothing industry*	118
46	KHUDZHAND CLOTHING PRODUCTION and TRADE COMPANY NAMED AFTER N.K.KRUPSKAYA	*Clothing industry*	132
47	MINE "FAN-YAGNOB"	*Coal mining & peat industry*	179
48	MINING ENTERPRISE "TADZHIKSKOYE"	*Coal mining & peat industry*	180
49	KANIBADAM TRAINING and PRODUCTION ENTERPRISE	*Consumer goods, furniture, household & cultural goods*	123
50	TRAINING and PRODUCTION WORKS n4	*Consumer goods, furniture, household & cultural goods*	234
51	ISFARA FURNITURE PLANT	*Consumer goods, furniture, household & cultural goods*	98
52	KHUDZHAND FURNITURE PLANT	*Consumer goods, furniture, household & cultural goods*	136
53	INDUSTRIAL and COMMERCIAL FIRM "ISMAIL"	*Consumer goods, furniture, household & cultural goods*	89
54	TRAINING and PRODUCTION WORKS n1	*Consumer goods, furniture, household & cultural goods*	232
55	KULYAB TRAINING and PRODUCTION ENTERPRISE	*Consumer goods, furniture, household & cultural goods*	158
56	URA-TYUBE TRAINING and PRODUCTION	*Consumer goods, furniture,*	245

	ENTERPRISE	*household & cultural goods*	
57	TRAINING and PRODUCTION WORKS n5	*Consumer goods, furniture, household & cultural goods*	235
58	TRAINING and PRODUCTION WORKS n3	*Consumer goods, furniture, household & cultural goods*	233
59	URA-TYUBE FACTORY "NEKSOZ"	*Consumer goods, furniture, household & cultural goods*	243
60	DUSHANBE JEWELLERY PLANT	*Consumer goods, furniture, household & cultural goods*	38
61	KHUDZHAND CONTAINER REPAIR WORKS	*Consumer goods, furniture, household & cultural goods*	133
62	DUSHANBE FURNITURE PLANT	*Consumer goods, furniture, household & cultural goods*	36
63	DUSHANBE SOUVENIR FACTORY "ARMUGON"	*Consumer goods, furniture, household & cultural goods*	54
64	KOFARNIKHON TRAINING and PRODUCTION ENTERPRISE	*Consumer goods, furniture, household & cultural goods*	147
65	KHUDZHAND TRAINING and PRODUCTION WORKS n2	*Consumer goods, furniture, household & cultural goods*	143
66	KHUDZHAND TRAINING and PRODUCTION ENTERPRISE	*Consumer goods, furniture, household & cultural goods*	142
67	DUSHANBE CABLE PLANT "TADZHIKKABEL"	*Electrical engineering*	20
68	TADJIK PRODUCTION COMPANY "SVETOTEKHNIKA"	*Electrical engineering*	230
69	ENTERPRISE "TADZHIKENERGOREMONT"	*Electrical engineering*	66

	FACTORY "LAZZAT"		
123	KULYAB DAIRY	*Food & food processing*	152
124	KULYAB CREAMERY	*Food & food processing*	151
125	KURGAN-TYUBE OILERY	*Food & food processing*	171
126	KURGAN-TYUBE BAKERY	*Food & food processing*	159
127	LEASING-BASED ENTERPRISE "SHARBAT"	*Food & food processing*	174
128	SHAARTUZ CREAMERY	*Food & food processing*	221
129	KOLKHOZABAD GRAIN PROCESSING PLANT	*Food & food processing*	148
130	KOFARNIKHON RICE PLANT	*Food & food processing*	146
131	DUSHANBE AGRARIAN PRODUCTION COMPANY "NONPAZ"	*Food & food processing*	17
132	PENDZHIKENT MEAT PROCESSING PLANT and DAIRY	*Food & food processing*	197
133	NAU GRAIN PROCESSING PLANT	*Food & food processing*	185
134	BAKERY "NONPAZ"	*Food & food processing*	8
135	AGROINDUSTRIAL GRAIN PROCESSING PRODUCTION COMPANY	*Food & food processing*	3
136	NON-ALCOHOLIC BEVERAGES and MINERAL WATER PLANT	*Food & food processing*	188
137	PRODUCTION COOPERATIVE "PISHCHEVIK"	*Food & food processing*	214

138	DUSHANBE LEATHER HABERDASHERY FACTORY "CHARMDUZ"	*Footwer & tanning industry*	41
139	DUSHANBE JOINT-STOCK LEATHER FOOTWEAR COMPANY "RAFIK"	*Footwer & tanning industry*	39
140	KHUDZHAND SHOE FACTORY n2	*Footwer & tanning industry*	140
141	INDUSTRIAL and TRADING FIRM "SIMO"	*Footwer & tanning industry*	90
142	DUSHANBE WOOD-WORKING PLANT	*Forestry & timber processing industry*	61
143	DUSHANBE WOOD-WORKING PLANT	*Forestry & timber processing industry*	62
144	DUSHANBE WOOD-WORKING PLANT	*Forestry & timber processing industry*	60
145	COMPUTING APPARATUS REPAIR WORKS	*High-tech products, PC, research & design services*	14
146	PLANT "LENINABADSELMASH"	*Machine building industry*	200
147	PLANT "TADZHIKKHIMSELKHOZMASH"	*Machine building industry*	201
148	KURGAN-TYUBE MECHANICAL REPAIR WORKS	*Machine building industry*	168
149	MECHANICAL WORKS "KHLOPKOZAPCHAST"	*Machine building industry*	178
150	DUSHANBE SPECIALIZED ENGINEERING DESIGN BUREAU	*Machine building industry*	55
151	NUREK EXPERIMENTAL MECHANICAL WORKS	*Machine building industry*	190
152	PRODUCTION COMPANY "TADZHIKENERGOLEGPROM"	*Machine building industry*	208

153	DUSHANBE PLANT "TADZHIKTEKSTILMASH"	*Machine building industry*	49
154	DUSHANBE PLANT "STROMMASH"	*Machine building industry*	48
155	PROLETARSK CENTRAL ELECTROMECHANICAL WORKSHOP	*Machine building industry*	215
156	KHUDZHAND GAS EQUIPMENT ENGINEERING WORKS	*Machine building industry*	137
157	DUSHANBE PILOT-PRODUCTION and EXPERIMENTAL PLANT "SELEKTSIONNAYA TEKHNIKA"	*Machine building industry*	46
158	PRODUCTION COMPANY "TADZHIKGIDROAGREGAT"	*Machine building industry*	209
159	KOFARNIKHON MECHANICAL REPAIR WORKS	*Machine building industry*	144
160	YAVAN ELECTROCHEMICAL WORKS	*Machine building industry*	254
161	PRODUCTION COMPANY "PAMIR"	*Machine building industry*	206
162	YAVAN MECHANICAL REPAIR WORKS	*Machine building industry*	256
163	DUSHANBE PLANT "TORGMASH"	*Machine building industry*	50
164	DUSHANBE EXPERIMENTAL PLANT "SISTEMAVTOMATIKA"	*Medical equipment industry*	28
165	PLANT "ETALON"	*Medical equipment industry*	199
166	PROSTHETIC and ORTHOPAEDIC APPLIANCES PLANT	*Medical equipment industry*	218
167	LENINABAD RARE METALS PLANT	*Metallurgy*	175
168	TADJIK ALUMINIUM WORKS	*Metallurgy*	229

184	YAVAN LIME WORKS (JOINT-STOCK COMPANY)	*Mining industry (building mateirlas)*	255
185	KALININABAD GRAVEL SIZING MILL	*Mining industry (building mateirlas)*	114
186	TAKOB FLUORSPAR WORKS	*Mining industry (building mateirlas)*	231
187	VOSE SALT WORKS	*Mining industry (building mateirlas)*	251
188	PRODUCTION COMPANY "TADZHIKNEFT"	*Oil & gas industry*	211
189	NEFTEABAD OILFIELD	*Oil & gas industry*	187
190	KURGAN-TYUBE OIL EXTRACTING ENTERPRISE n1	*Oil & gas industry*	170
191	KULYAB OIL EXTRACTING ENTERPRISE n2	*Oil & gas industry*	157
192	OIL ASPHALT PLANT	*Oil refining & gas processing*	192
193	GISSAR COMPANY "GIDROSTROIMATERIALY"	*Oil refining & gas processing*	79
194	PRODUCTION COMPANY "TADZHIKZOLOTO"	*Ore mining industry*	213
195	ADRASMAN LEAD and ZINC WORKS	*Ore mining industry*	1
196	KAIRAKKUM MINE	*Ore mining industry*	110
197	ANZOBSKY ORE CONCENTRATING MILL	*Ore mining industry*	5
198	VAKHSH HYDROELECTRIC STATION CASCADE	*Power industry*	248

199	CENTRAL ELECTRIC POWER TRANSMISSION NETWORK	*Power industry*	10
200	BAIRAZA HYDROELECTRIC STATION	*Power industry*	7
201	SOUTHERN ELECTRIC POWER TRANSMISSION NETWORK	*Power industry*	226
202	GORNO-BADAKHSHAN ELECTRIC POWER TRANSMISSION NETWORK	*Power industry*	84
203	DUSHANBE TOWN ELECTRIC POWER TRANSMISSION NETWORK	*Power industry*	58
204	NUREK HYDROELECTRIC STATION	*Power industry*	191
205	STATE JOINT-STOCK HOLDING COMPANY "BARKI TOCHIK"	*Power industry*	228
206	DUSHANBE THERMOELECTRIC STATION	*Power industry*	56
207	KHUDZHAND ELECTRIC POWER TRANSMISSION NETWORK ENTERPRISE	*Power industry*	135
208	DUSHANBE PRINTING WORKS	*Publishing & printing*	52
209	DUSHANBE PRINT-SHOP n18	*Publishing & printing*	51
210	TURSUNZADE PRINT-SHOP	*Publishing & printing*	238
211	PUBLISHING HOUSE	*Publishing & printing*	219
212	PRINTING PRODUCTION COMPANY	*Publishing & printing*	203
213	PRINT-SHOP	*Publishing & printing*	202
214	FIRM "BORCHOMA"	*Pulp & paper industry*	70
215	PLANT "ALMOS"	*Radio-electronic industry*	198

216	FIRM "DOVUD"	*Scrap & waste processing industry*	71
217	PROCUREMENT PRODUCTION COMPANY "TADZHIKVTORTSVETMET"	*Scrap & waste processing industry*	204
218	WOOLEN SHAWL FACTORY "ZARBOF"	*Textile industry*	253
219	UYALP GINNERY	*Textile industry*	247
220	CLOSED JOINT-STOCK COMPANY "BOFANDA"	*Textile industry*	11
221	BUSTON GINNERY	*Textile industry*	9
222	AINI GINNERY	*Textile industry*	4
223	DUSHANBE COMPANY "TADZHIKATLAS"	*Textile industry*	24
224	VOSE GINNERY	*Textile industry*	250
225	KANIBADAM GINNERY	*Textile industry*	120
226	PRODUCTION COMPANY "KHODZHENTATLAS"	*Textile industry*	205
227	OKTYABRSKY COTTON PROCESSING MILL	*Textile industry*	193
228	NAU GINNERY	*Textile industry*	184
229	MOSKOVSKY GINNERY	*Textile industry*	182
230	PROLETARSK GINNERY	*Textile industry*	216
231	KURGAN-TYUBE GINNERY	*Textile industry*	166
232	KURGAN-TYUBE FOLK DECORATIVE HANDICRAFT FACTORY	*Textile industry*	165

233	PYANDZH GINNERY	*Textile industry*	220
234	KURGAN-TYUBE COTTON SPINNING MILL	*Textile industry*	163
235	KULYAB GINNERY	*Textile industry*	154
236	SHAARTUZ GINNERY	*Textile industry*	222
237	KHUDZHAND SILK MILL	*Textile industry*	141
238	JOINT-STOCK COMPANY "FAIZ"	*Textile industry*	104
239	KANIBADAM SPINNING and WEAVING MILL	*Textile industry*	122
240	FIRM "NAFISA"	*Textile industry*	72
241	DUSHANBE KNITTING MILL	*Textile industry*	40
242	URA-TYUBE KNITTED OUTERWEAR FACTORY	*Textile industry*	244
243	DUSHANBE SILK MILL	*Textile industry*	53
244	FACTORY "ZARDUZ"	*Textile industry*	67
245	KHODZHENT GINNERY	*Textile industry*	125
246	FARKHOR GINNERY	*Textile industry*	68
247	DUSHANBE FOLK DECORATIVE HANDICRAFT COMPANY "DILOROM"	*Textile industry*	34
248	GANCHI CLOTHING and KNITWEAR FACTORY	*Textile industry*	78
249	GISSAR GINNERY	*Textile industry*	80

TADJIKISTAN INDUSTRY: LARGEST COMPANIES BY INDUSTRY

	COMPANY	INDUSTRY	PERSONNEL	Number in Alphabetical Section
1	KHUDZHAND SILK MILL	*Textile industry*	8960	141
2	JOINT-STOCK COMPANY "KOLINKHO"	*Textile industry*	5429	105
3	DUSHANBE JOINT-STOCK LEATHER FOOTWEAR COMPANY "RAFIK"	*Footwer & tanning industry*	3928	39
4	KHUDZHAND CLOTHING PRODUCTION and TRADE COMPANY NAMED AFTER N.K.KRUPSKAYA	*Clothing industry*	2650	132
5	URA-TYUBE KNITTED OUTERWEAR FACTORY	*Textile industry*	2558	244
6	PRODUCTION COMPANY "TADZHIKGIDROAGREGAT"	*Machine building industry*	2478	209
7	JOINT-STOCK COMPANY "BOFANDA"	*Textile industry*	2281	103
8	DUSHANBE SILK MILL	*Textile industry*	1986	53
9	KHUDZHAND SHOE FACTORY n2	*Footwer & tanning industry*	1835	140
10	KANIBADAM CLOTHING PRODUCTION COMPANY "KHUSNORO"	*Clothing industry*	1791	118
11	KANIBADAM SPINNING and WEAVING MILL	*Textile industry*	1722	122
12	FIRM "NAFISA"	*Textile industry*	1702	72
13	KANIBADAM BRAKE EQUIPMENT PLANT	*Metal-working industry*	1682	116
14	CLOTHING FIRM "GULISTAN"	*Clothing industry*	1668	13
15	ISFARA CHEMICALS PLANT	*Chemical, pharmaceutical & micribiology industry*	1609	94

16	PRODUCTION COMPANY "TADZHIKZOLOTO"	*Ore mining industry*	1564	213
17	DUSHANBE PLANT "TADZHIKTEKSTILMASH"	*Machine building industry*	1400	49
18	VAKHSH NITROGENOUS FERTILIZER PLANT	*Chemical, pharmaceutical & micribiology industry*	1345	249
19	DUSHANBE PIPE APPLIANCES PLANT NAMED AFTER ORDZHONIKIDZE	*Metal-working industry*	1328	47
20	TADJIK PRODUCTION COMPANY "SVETOTEKHNIKA"	*Electrical engineering*	1308	230
21	PRODUCTION COMPANY "KHODZHENTATLAS"	*Textile industry*	1259	205
22	CENTRAL ELECTRIC POWER TRANSMISSION NETWORK	*Power industry*	1237	10
23	DUSHANBE CLOTHING PRODUCTION COMPANY "CHEVAR"	*Clothing industry*	1196	22
24	DUSHANBE AGRARIAN PRODUCTION COMPANY "NONPAZ"	*Food & food processing*	1146	17
25	PRODUCTION COMPANY "TADZHIKNEFT"	*Oil & gas industry*	1131	211
26	KURGAN-TYUBE CLOTHING FACTORY	*Clothing industry*	1100	161
27	JOINT-STOCK COMPANY "FAIZ"	*Textile industry*	1055	104
28	WOOLEN SHAWL FACTORY "ZARBOF"	*Textile industry*	1008	253
29	ANZOBSKY ORE CONCENTRATING MILL	*Ore mining industry*	985	5
30	DUSHANBE COMPANY "TADZHIKATLAS"	*Textile industry*	958	24
31	KANIBADAM GINNERY	*Textile industry*	951	120
32	ISFARA CANNERY	*Food & food processing*	941	93
33	SOUTHERN ELECTRIC POWER TRANSMISSION NETWORK	*Power industry*	940	226

34	DUSHANBE FOLK DECORATIVE HANDICRAFT COMPANY "DILOROM"	*Textile industry*	938	34
35	DUSHANBE OILERY and FAT PLANT	*Food & food processing*	917	43
36	KHUDZHAND ELECTRIC POWER TRANSMISSION NETWORK ENTERPRISE	*Power industry*	900	135
37	KOFARNIKHON MECHANICAL REPAIR WORKS	*Machine building industry*	870	144
38	PRODUCTION COMPANY "TADZHIKTSEMENT"	*Building materials industry*	845	212
39	PROLETARSK ORE CONCENTRATING MILL	*Building materials industry*	839	217
40	KHUDZHAND CANNERY	*Food & food processing*	824	131
41	PRODUCTION COMPANY "PAMIR"	*Machine building industry*	822	206
42	KHUDZHAND PLANT "TORGMASH"	*Metal-working industry*	812	139
43	GISSAR COMPANY "GIDROSTROIMATERIALY"	*Oil refining & gas processing*	800	79
44	DUSHANBE THERMOELECTRIC STATION	*Power industry*	748	56
45	DUSHANBE KNITTING MILL	*Textile industry*	743	40
46	KANIBADAM CANNERY	*Food & food processing*	730	117
47	URA-TYUBE FACTORY "NEKSOZ"	*Consumer goods, furniture, household & cultural goods*	721	243
48	LENINABAD RARE METALS PLANT	*Metallurgy*	720	175
49	KOFARNIKHON TRAINING and PRODUCTION ENTERPRISE	*Consumer goods, furniture, household & cultural goods*	700	147
50	TURSUNZADE GINNERY	*Textile industry*	700	236
51	PRODUCTION COMPANY "PAMIRKVARTSSAMOTSVETY"	*Mining industry (building mateirlas)*	679	207
52	AINI GINNERY	*Textile industry*	650	4
53	CONFECTIONERY FACTORY "SHIRIN"	*Food & food processing*	644	16

54	TRAINING and PRODUCTION WORKS n4	*Consumer goods, furniture, household & cultural goods*	624	234
55	PLANT "LENINABADSELMASH"	*Machine building industry*	616	200
56	KHUDZHAND FURNITURE PLANT	*Consumer goods, furniture, household & cultural goods*	600	136
57	KHODZHENT GINNERY	*Textile industry*	586	125
58	KURGAN-TYUBE TRANSFORMER PLANT	*Electrical engineering*	583	172
59	PROLETARSK GINNERY	*Textile industry*	572	216
60	GORNO-BADAKHSHAN ELECTRIC POWER TRANSMISSION NETWORK	*Power industry*	570	84
61	DUSHANBE MEAT PROCESSING PLANT	*Food & food processing*	562	42
62	KULYAB GINNERY	*Textile industry*	558	154
63	CLOTHING FACTORY "FIRUZA"	*Clothing industry*	550	12
64	KHOROG CLOTHING FACTORY n3 "KHAIET"	*Clothing industry*	545	127
65	DUSHANBE FURNITURE PLANT	*Consumer goods, furniture, household & cultural goods*	537	36
66	ADRASMAN LOW-VOLTAGE ELECTRIC EQUIPMENT WORKS	*Electrical engineering*	529	2
67	GRAIN PROCESSING PLANT	*Food & food processing*	513	87
68	ISFARA BUILDING MATERIALS PLANT	*Building materials industry*	508	92
69	PENDZHIKENT FERMENTED TOBACCO PLANT	*Tobacco industry*	500	195
70	NAU GRAIN PROCESSING PLANT	*Food & food processing*	498	185
71	JOINT-STOCK ENTERPRISE "LACHP"	*Building materials industry*	495	106
72	DUSHANBE PLANT "TORGMASH"	*Machine building industry*	493	50
73	PLANT "ALMOS"	*Radio-electronic industry*	485	198
74	KHUDZHAND LEASING-BASED ENTERPRISE	*Metal-working industry*	484	138

	"EMALIROVSHCHIK"			
75	CLOSED JOINT-STOCK COMPANY "BOFANDA"	*Textile industry*	480	11
76	GANCHI CLOTHING and KNITWEAR FACTORY	*Textile industry*	471	78
77	PLANT "TADZHIKKHIMSELKHOZMASH"	*Machine building industry*	470	201
78	DUSHANBE FERROCONCRETE STRUCTURES and PRE-CAST PARTS PLANT	*Building materials industry*	467	33
79	FACTORY "ZARDUZ"	*Textile industry*	462	67
80	MOSKOVSKY GINNERY	*Textile industry*	460	182
81	KAIRAKKUM AGROINDUSTRIAL PRODUCTION COMPANY	*Food & food processing*	442	107
82	DUSHANBE DAIRY	*Food & food processing*	439	26
83	DUSHANBE COMPANY "GULDAST"	*Clothing industry*	426	23
84	TAKOB FLUORSPAR WORKS	*Mining industry (building mateirlas)*	414	231
85	DUSHANBE JEWELLERY PLANT	*Consumer goods, furniture, household & cultural goods*	401	38
86	KAIRAKKUM SUBSIDIARY ENTERPRISE	*Building materials industry*	397	111
87	GAFUROV MEAT PROCESSING PLANT	*Food & food processing*	390	75
88	KOFARNIKHON MECHANICAL WORKS "ZARFSOZ"	*Metal-working industry*	390	145
89	KULYAB EXPERIMENTAL MACHINING ATTACHMENTS PLANT	*Metal-working industry*	389	153
90	NAU GINNERY	*Textile industry*	387	184
91	BUSTON GINNERY	*Textile industry*	383	9
92	DUSHANBE PRINTING WORKS	*Publishing & printing*	382	52
93	DUSHANBE TOWN ELECTRIC POWER TRANSMISSION	*Power industry*	380	58

	NETWORK			
94	KHUDZHAND GAS EQUIPMENT ENGINEERING WORKS	*Machine building industry*	367	137
95	NEFTEABAD OILFIELD	*Oil & gas industry*	362	187
96	PUBLISHING HOUSE	*Publishing & printing*	353	219
97	KHUDZHAND BAKERY	*Food & food processing*	344	130
98	LEASING-BASED ENTERPRISE "SHARBAT"	*Food & food processing*	339	174
99	KULYAB BRICK YARD	*Building materials industry*	320	150
100	ISFARA FERROCONCRETE STRUCTURES and BUILDING ARTICLES PLANT n5	*Building materials industry*	310	97
101	DUSHANBE BRICK YARD PRODUCTION COMPANY	*Building materials industry*	300	19
102	WINE PLANT "SHAKHRINAU" (LEASING-BASED ì	*Food & food processing*	300	252
103	VOSE GINNERY	*Textile industry*	300	250
104	DUSHANBE FOOD PROCESSING ENTERPRISE	*Food & food processing*	300	35
105	DUSHANBE WOOD-WORKING PLANT	*Forestry & timber processing industry*	294	61
106	KURGAN-TYUBE CANNERY	*Food & food processing*	290	160
107	DUSHANBE PAINTS and VARNISHES PLANT "RANGINKAMON"	*Chemical, pharmaceutical & micribiology industry*	290	44
108	DUSHANBE FERROCONCRETE STRUCTURES and BUILDING ARTICLES PLANT n1	*Building materials industry*	288	29
109	PRODUCTION COOPERATIVE "PISHCHEVIK"	*Food & food processing*	285	214
110	DUSHANBE AGROINDUSTRIAL PRODUCTION COMPANY	*Food & food processing*	275	18
111	TRAINING and PRODUCTION WORKS n1	*Consumer goods, furniture, household & cultural goods*	273	232
112	DUSHANBE CABLE PLANT	*Electrical engineering*	271	20

	"TADZHIKKABEL"			
113	ENTERPRISE "TADZHIKENERGOREMONT"	*Electrical engineering*	268	66
114	INDUSTRIAL and TRADING FIRM "SIMO"	*Footwer & tanning industry*	262	90
115	DUSHANBE WINE PLANT	*Food & food processing*	260	59
116	PROLETARSK CENTRAL ELECTROMECHANICAL WORKSHOP	*Machine building industry*	249	215
117	ISFARA MINERAL PAINTS PLANT "NILUFOR"	*Chemical, pharmaceutical & micribiology industry*	244	102
118	DUSHANBE GRAIN PROCESSING PLANT	*Food & food processing*	243	37
119	GANCHI BRICK YARD	*Building materials industry*	240	77
120	URA-TYUBE CANNERY	*Food & food processing*	236	241
121	DUSHANBE TOBACCO FACTORY	*Tobacco industry*	235	57
122	KHUDZHAND TRAINING and PRODUCTION WORKS n2	*Consumer goods, furniture, household & cultural goods*	234	143
123	KHUDZHAND DAIRY	*Food & food processing*	225	134
124	DUSHANBEPRESSURE PIPES and FERROCONCRETE ARTICLES PLANT	*Building materials industry*	221	63
125	KURGAN-TYUBE OILERY	*Food & food processing*	220	171
126	DUSHANBE FERROCONCRETE STRUCTURES and BUILDING ARTICLES PLANT n3	*Building materials industry*	216	31
127	KULYAB TRAINING and PRODUCTION ENTERPRISE	*Consumer goods, furniture, household & cultural goods*	202	158
128	KALININABAD FERROCONCRETE STRUCTURES PLANT n1	*Building materials industry*	202	112
129	ASHTI SALT WORKS n2	*Mining industry (building mateirlas)*	190	6
130	URA-TYUBE BAKERY	*Food & food processing*	189	239
131	DUSHANBE FERROCONCRETE STRUCTURES and BUILDING ARTICLES PLANT n6	*Building materials industry*	178	32

132	BAKERY "NONPAZ"	*Food & food processing*	178	8
133	PLANT "ETALON"	*Medical equipment industry*	177	199
134	DUSHANBE SPECIALIZED ENGINEERING DESIGN BUREAU	*Machine building industry*	174	55
135	SHURAB MECHANICAL WORKS "FILIZ"	*Metal-working industry*	173	224
136	URA-TYUBE BRICK YARD	*Building materials industry*	170	240
137	KULYAB MEAT PROCESSING PLANT	*Food & food processing*	170	156
138	GAFUROV FERROCONCRETE STRUCTURES PLANT n7	*Building materials industry*	164	74
139	KULYAB DAIRY	*Food & food processing*	160	152
140	KANIBADAM BAKERY	*Food & food processing*	159	115
141	KURGAN-TYUBE MEAT PROCESSING PLANT and DAIRY	*Food & food processing*	156	167
142	VAKHSH HYDROELECTRIC STATION CASCADE	*Power industry*	150	248
143	OIL ASPHALT PLANT	*Oil refining & gas processing*	150	192
144	KALININABAD FERROCONCRETE STRUCTURES PLANT n8	*Building materials industry*	150	113
145	TRAINING and PRODUCTION WORKS n3	*Consumer goods, furniture, household & cultural goods*	148	233
146	DUSHANBE LEATHER HABERDASHERY FACTORY "CHARMDUZ"	*Footwer & tanning industry*	143	41
147	DUSHANBE PILOT-PRODUCTION and EXPERIMENTAL PLANT "REMSTROIDORMASH"	*Metal-working industry*	141	45
148	URA-TYUBE WINE PLANT	*Food & food processing*	136	246
149	PENDZHIKENT BRICK YARD	*Building materials industry*	133	194
150	FIRM "BORCHOMA"	*Pulp & paper industry*	133	70
151	DUSHANBE FERROCONCRETE STRUCTURES and BUILDING ARTICLES PLANT n2	*Building materials industry*	132	30

152	COMPUTING APPARATUS REPAIR WORKS	*High-tech products, PC, research & design services*	132	14
153	LEASE-HOLDER COLLECTIVE "VREMYA"	*Mining industry (building mateirlas)*	130	173
154	KUIBYSHEVSK FISHING FARM	*Fishing & fish processing*	130	149
155	GRAIN INTAKE PLANT	*Food & food processing*	126	85
156	KHUDZHAND CONTAINER REPAIR WORKS	*Consumer goods, furniture, household & cultural goods*	125	133
157	ISFARA BAKERY	*Food & food processing*	125	91
158	ISFARA MEDICAL PREPARATIONS and FEED PROTEIN PLANT	*Chemical, pharmaceutical & micribiology industry*	125	101
159	ISFARA MEAT PROCESSING PLANT	*Food & food processing*	122	100
160	DUSHANBE WOOD-WORKING PLANT	*Forestry & timber processing industry*	121	60
161	KULYAB GRAIN PROCESSING PLANT	*Food & food processing*	118	155
162	TRAINING and PRODUCTION WORKS n5	*Consumer goods, furniture, household & cultural goods*	115	235
163	MATCHINSKY RURAL CONSTRUCTION PLANT	*Building materials industry*	113	177
164	ISFARA CONFECTIONERY FACTORY	*Food & food processing*	106	95
165	NON-ALCOHOLIC BEVERAGES and MINERAL WATER PLANT	*Food & food processing*	102	188
166	KURGAN-TYUBE EXPERIMENTAL FURSKIN FACTORY "MUINNA"	*Clothing industry*	102	164
167	KANIBADAM FERROCONCRETE STRUCTURES PLANT n2	*Building materials industry*	100	119
168	KURGAN-TYUBE NON-ALCOHOLIC BEVERAGES and MINERAL WATER PLANT	*Food & food processing*	100	169
169	KULYAB CREAMERY	*Food & food processing*	100	151
170	VOSE SALT WORKS	*Mining industry (building mateirlas)*	100	251

171	DUSHANBE PLANT "STROMMASH"	*Machine building industry*	98	48
172	FIRM "DOVUD"	*Scrap & waste processing industry*	96	71
173	DUSHANBE SOUVENIR FACTORY "ARMUGON"	*Consumer goods, furniture, household & cultural goods*	96	54
174	URA-TYUBE CREAMERY	*Food & food processing*	94	242
175	DUSHANBE CHEESE PLANT	*Food & food processing*	93	21
176	NAU MECHANIZED QUARRY	*Mining industry (building mateirlas)*	92	186
177	DZHILIKUL FISHING FARM	*Fishing & fish processing*	90	64
178	DZHILIKUL FISHING FARM	*Fishing & fish processing*	89	65
179	PENDZHIKENT MEAT PROCESSING PLANT and DAIRY	*Food & food processing*	86	197
180	KHUDZHAND AUTOMOBILE REPAIR WORKS n4	*Automobile industry*	86	129
181	FERMENTED TOBACCO PLANT	*Tobacco industry*	85	69
182	DUSHANBE EXCAVATOR REPAIR WORKS	*Metal-working industry*	82	27
183	CONFECTIONERY FACTORY "MAISHAT"	*Food & food processing*	80	15
184	FISHING FARM "CHUBEK"	*Fishing & fish processing*	80	73
185	ISFARA CREAMERY	*Food & food processing*	79	96
186	KANSAI NON-METALLIFEROUS and FACING MATERIALS PLANT	*Building materials industry*	78	124
187	DUSHANBE WOOD-WORKING PLANT	*Forestry & timber processing industry*	74	62
188	DUSHANBE EXPERIMENTAL PLANT "SISTEMAVTOMATIKA"	*Medical equipment industry*	65	28
189	KOFARNIKHON RICE PLANT	*Food & food processing*	65	146
190	GISSAR GRAIN INTAKE PLANT	*Food & food processing*	64	81
191	PROSTHETIC and ORTHOPAEDIC APPLIANCES PLANT	*Medical equipment industry*	63	218
192	KURGAN-TYUBE MECHANICAL REPAIR WORKS	*Machine building industry*	60	168

193	KAIRAKKUM MECHANICAL REPAIR WORKSHOP	*Metal-working industry*	60	109
194	DUSHANBE CONFECTIONERY FACTORY "LAZZAT" (JOINT-STOCK COMPANY)	*Food & food processing*	52	25
195	ISFARA FURNITURE PLANT	*Consumer goods, furniture, household & cultural goods*	52	98
196	KALININABAD GRAVEL SIZING MILL	*Mining industry (building mateirlas)*	50	114
197	KURGAN-TYUBE CONFECTIONERY FACTORY "LAZZAT"	*Food & food processing*	40	162
198	ILIYCHEVSKY FEED MILL	*Food & food processing*	37	88
199	PRINT-SHOP	*Publishing & printing*	32	202
200	PENDZHIKENT FISH PROCESSING PLANT	*Fishing & fish processing*	32	196
201	TURSUNZADE PRINT-SHOP	*Publishing & printing*	30	238
202	TURSUNZADE PORCELAIN WORKS	*Building materials industry*	30	237
203	PRODUCTION COMPANY "TADZHIKENERGOLEGPROM"	*Machine building industry*	27	208
204	SHAKHRISTAN CREAMERY	*Food & food processing*	27	223
205	PROCUREMENT PRODUCTION COMPANY "TADZHIKVTORTSVETMET"	*Scrap & waste processing industry*	21	204
206	SHAARTUZ GINNERY	*Textile industry*	20	222
207	TADJIK ALUMINIUM WORKS	*Metallurgy*	20	229
208	NUREK CLOTHING FACTORY	*Clothing industry*	20	189
209	STATE FARM-PLANT "EFIRONOS"	*Chemical, pharmaceutical & micribiology industry*	20	227
210	GISSAR TEXTILE MILL	*Textile industry*	20	82
211	GRAIN INTAKE YARD	*Food & food processing*	20	86
212	MINING ENTERPRISE "TADZHIKSKOYE"	*Coal mining & peat industry*	10	180
213	GISSAR GINNERY	*Textile industry*	10	80
214	INDUSTRIAL and COMMERCIAL FIRM "ISMAIL"	*Consumer goods, furniture, household & cultural goods*	10	89

215	DUSHANBE PILOT-PRODUCTION and EXPERIMENTAL PLANT "SELEKTSIONNAYA TEKHNIKA"	*Machine building industry*	10	46
216	NUREK EXPERIMENTAL MECHANICAL WORKS	*Machine building industry*	10	190
217	BAIRAZA HYDROELECTRIC STATION	*Power industry*	10	7
218	LENINSKY NON-METALLIFEROUS MATERIALS PLANT	*Building materials industry*	10	176
219	ISFARA HYDROMETALLURGICAL PLANT	*Metallurgy*	10	99
220	PRINTING PRODUCTION COMPANY	*Publishing & printing*		203
221	PRODUCTION COMPANY "TADZHIKKHIMPROM"	*Chemical, pharmaceutical & micribiology industry*		210
222	PYANDZH GINNERY	*Textile industry*		220
223	SHAARTUZ CREAMERY	*Food & food processing*		221
224	STATE JOINT-STOCK HOLDING COMPANY "BARKI TOCHIK"	*Power industry*		228
225	URA-TYUBE TRAINING and PRODUCTION ENTERPRISE	*Consumer goods, furniture, household & cultural goods*		245
226	UYALP GINNERY	*Textile industry*		247
227	YAVAN ELECTROCHEMICAL WORKS	*Machine building industry*		254
228	AGROINDUSTRIAL GRAIN PROCESSING PRODUCTION COMPANY	*Food & food processing*		3
229	YAVAN LIME WORKS (JOINT-STOCK COMPANY)	*Mining industry (building mateirlas)*		255
230	SMALL ENTERPRISE "BETON"	*Building materials industry*		225
231	KOLKHOZABAD GRAIN PROCESSING PLANT	*Food & food processing*		148
232	GAFUROV WINE PLANT	*Food & food processing*		76
233	GISSAR TRAINING and	*Food & food processing*		83

PRODUCTION WORKS

TADJIKISTAN INDUSTRY: BY PRODUCTS

	PRODUCTS	COMPANU	Number in Alphabetical Section
1	**agricultural equipment**	PLANT "TADZHIKKHIMSELKHOZMASH"	201
2	**agricultural machines**	PLANT "LENINABADSELMASH"	200
3	**alloys**	LENINABAD RARE METALS PLANT	175
4	**anodized articles** saddlery and harness articles textile haberdashery	TRAINING and PRODUCTION WORKS n3	233
5	**antimony concentrate** mercury concentrate	ANZOBSKY ORE CONCENTRATING MILL	5
6	**apple puree** peach puree 69 ths tins tomato paste	URA-TYUBE CANNERY	241
7	**appliances for pipes, boilers, etc** gate valves of steel cast articles of pig iron	DUSHANBE PIPE APPLIANCES PLANT NAMED AFTER ORDZHONIKIDZE	47
8	**articles of apparel** hosiery 2.4 ths pcs knitwear articles	KURGAN-TYUBE FOLK DECORATIVE HANDICRAFT FACTORY	165
9	**articles of apparel and clothing accessories** trousers for children bed-linen	CLOTHING FACTORY "FIRUZA"	12

10	**articles of apparel and clothing accessories** fabrics of cotton fabrics of silk	DUSHANBE FOLK DECORATIVE HANDICRAFT COMPANY "DILOROM"	34
11	**articles of apparel and clothing accessories**	KHOROG CLOTHING FACTORY n3 "KHAIET"	127
12	**articles of jewellery** metal haberdashery fittings	DUSHANBE JEWELLERY PLANT	38
13	**articles of plastics** packing containers of paperboard articles of polyethylene and cellophane	FIRM "BORCHOMA"	70
14	**articles of plastics** baby linen pile carpets	URA-TYUBE FACTORY "NEKSOZ"	243
15	**auxiliary mechanized devices** electric cranes 344 pcs spare parts for road building machines	KOFARNIKHON MECHANICAL REPAIR WORKS	144
16	**bakers' wares**	KURGAN-TYUBE BAKERY	159
17	**bakers' wares** confectionery pasta	KHUDZHAND BAKERY	130
18	**bakers' wares**	KHOROG BAKERY	126
19	**bakers' wares** pasta	DUSHANBE AGRARIAN PRODUCTION COMPANY "NONPAZ"	17
20	**bakers' wares** ground rusks 16 tons corn sticks	PRODUCTION COOPERATIVE "PISHCHEVIK"	214
21	**bakers' wares**	ISFARA BAKERY	91

22	**bakers' wares**	**KANIBADAM BAKERY**	**115**
23	**bakers' wares 6,415 tons** confectionery 362 tons corn sticks	**BAKERY "NONPAZ"**	**8**
24	**bakers' wares 3,920 tons**	**URA-TYUBE BAKERY**	**239**
25	**bakers' wares 7,038 tons**	**DUSHANBE AGROINDUSTRIAL PRODUCTION COMPANY**	**18**
26	**barium metal 9,812 kg** chemical products 6,555 tons precious metals	**ISFARA HYDROMETALLURGICAL PLANT**	**99**
27	**bathrobes 0.3 ths pcs** suits 317.7 ths pcs	**CLOTHING FIRM "GULISTAN"**	**13**
28	**bed-linen 82 ths pcs** articles of feather and down	**TRAINING and PRODUCTION WORKS n1**	**232**
29	**beer 1,082 ths dal** non-alcoholic beverages 216 ths dal mineral waters	**DUSHANBE FOOD PROCESSING ENTERPRISE**	**35**
30	**beer 120 ths dal** non-alcoholic beverages 46 ths dal mineral waters	**NON-ALCOHOLIC BEVERAGES and MINERAL WATER PLANT**	**188**

31	**building bricks 10,360 ths pcs**	URA-TYUBE BRICK YARD	240
32	**building bricks 15,844 ths pcs**	GANCHI BRICK YARD	77
33	**building bricks 17,801 ths pcs**	DUSHANBE BRICK YARD PRODUCTION COMPANY	19
34	**building bricks 7,886 ths pcs**	KULYAB BRICK YARD	150
35	**burnt lime 31 ths tons** packed lime cement blocks	YAVAN LIME WORKS (JOINT-STOCK COMPANY)	255
36	**butter 124 tons** cheese 692 tons milk and dairy products	DUSHANBE CHEESE PLANT	21
37	**butter 205.4 tons** milk and dairy products	SHAKHRISTAN CREAMERY	223
38	**butter 226 tons** cheese 29 tons milk and dairy products	DUSHANBE DAIRY	26
39	**butter 408 tons** milk and dairy products milk products	URA-TYUBE CREAMERY	242
40	**butter 465.4 tons** milk 2,138.6 tons fermented milk products	ISFARA CREAMERY	96
41	**butter 494 tons** milk and dairy products fermented milk products	KULYAB DAIRY	152

42	**butter 613 tons** milk and dairy products cheese of sheep's milk	**KHUDZHAND DAIRY**	**134**
43	**cables**	**DUSHANBE CABLE PLANT "TADZHIKKABEL"**	**20**
44	**cans 100 mln pcs** bottles 8,000 ths pcs paperboard boxes	**JOINT-STOCK ENTERPRISE "LACHP"**	**106**
45	**caramel**	**ISFARA CONFECTIONERY FACTORY**	**95**
46	**carpets 54 ths sq m** floor coverings vests	**CLOSED JOINT-STOCK COMPANY "BOFANDA"**	**11**
47	**carpets and other textile floor coverings 8,297.5 ths sq m** twisted yarn 4,014.5 tons yarn in skeins	**JOINT-STOCK COMPANY "KOLINKHO"**	**105**
48	**cast articles of steel 280 tons** cast articles of pig iron spare parts	**PROLETARSK CENTRAL ELECTROMECHANICAL WORKSHOP**	**215**
49	**cast articles of steel 629 tons** chemical machinery and spare parts equipment of stainless steel	**YAVAN MECHANICAL REPAIR WORKS**	**256**
50	**cast articles of steel 629 tons** electrical-sheet steel 905 tons chemical machinery	**YAVAN ELECTROCHEMICAL WORKS**	**254**
51	**cement 446.8 ths tons** pipes of asbestos-cement 1,097.7 conv. km corrugated sheets of asbestos-cement	**PRODUCTION COMPANY "TADZHIKTSEMENT"**	**212**

52	**cereal meal 4,974 tons** rice meal 947 tons	**GRAIN INTAKE YARD**	**86**
53	**cigarettes 2,607 mln pcs**	**DUSHANBE TOBACCO FACTORY**	**57**
54	**coal 177.7 ths tons**	**MINING ENTERPRISE "TADZHIKSKOYE"**	**180**
55	**coal 29 ths tons**	**MINE "FAN-YAGNOB"**	**179**
56	**concentrated sand 226 ths tons** ceramic wall tiles 268 sq m building bricks	**PROLETARSK ORE CONCENTRATING MILL**	**217**
57	**confectionery 1,223 tons**	**KURGAN-TYUBE CONFECTIONERY FACTORY "LAZZAT"**	**162**
58	**confectionery 1,430 tons** preserved fruit 100 ths tins milk and dairy products	**CONFECTIONERY FACTORY "MAISHAT"**	**15**
59	**consumer goods** gaseous hydrocarbons	**KHUDZHAND GAS EQUIPMENT ENGINEERING WORKS**	**137**
60	**consumer goods** semi-precious stones blocks of marble	**PRODUCTION COMPANY "PAMIRKVARTSSAMOTSVETY"**	**207**
61	**cotton**	**KURGAN-TYUBE GINNERY**	**166**

62	cotton	SHAARTUZ GINNERY	222
63	cotton	PYANDZH GINNERY	220
64	cotton	UYALP GINNERY	247
65	cotton	OKTYABRSKY COTTON PROCESSING MILL	193
66	**cotton 1,035 tons** seeds 1,831 tons lint	GISSAR GINNERY	80
67	**cotton 10,289 tons** seeds 18,670 tons lint 1,747 tons	NAU GINNERY	184
68	**cotton 11,439 tons** seeds 19,391 tons lint 2,081 tons	KHODZHENT GINNERY	125
69	**cotton 15,985 tons** lint 2,198 tons seeds	PROLETARSK GINNERY	216
70	**cotton 16,011 tons** seeds 29,388 tons lint 2,833 tons	TURSUNZADE GINNERY	236
71	**cotton 17,499 tons** seeds 32,492 tons lint 2,641 tons	KANIBADAM GINNERY	120
72	**cotton 4,433 tons** seeds 8,184 tons lint 853 tons	MOSKOVSKY GINNERY	182

73	**cotton 5,304 tons** seeds 9,649 tons lint 506 tons	VOSE GINNERY	250
74	**cotton 6,048 tons** seeds 10,361 tons lint	FARKHOR GINNERY	68
75	**cotton 6,055 tons** seeds 10,537 tons lint 889 tons	KULYAB GINNERY	154
76	**cotton 7,320 tons** seeds 13,626 tons lint	BUSTON GINNERY	9
77	**cotton 7,514 tons** seeds 14,291 tons lint 1,859 tons	AINI GINNERY	4
78	**cotton oil 10,657 tons**	KURGAN-TYUBE OILERY	171
79	**cotton seed oil 2,738 tons** oil-cake 12,735 tons hulls	KULYAB CREAMERY	151
80	**crude alcohol 286.7 ths dal**	ISFARA MEDICAL PREPARATIONS and FEED PROTEIN PLANT	101
81	**crude petroleum oils 19 ths tons** gaseous hydrocarbons 1 mln cu m	KURGAN-TYUBE OIL EXTRACTING ENTERPRISE n1	170
82	**crude petroleum oils 38 ths tons** gas condensate gaseous hydrocarbons	NEFTEABAD OILFIELD	187
83	**crude petroleum oils 56.6 ths tons** gas condensate 4.8 ths tons gaseous hydrocarbons	PRODUCTION COMPANY "TADZHIKNEFT"	211

84	**crude petroleum oils 7 ths tons** gas condensate gaseous hydrocarbons	**KULYAB OIL EXTRACTING ENTERPRISE n2**	**157**
85	**crushed stone 22.2 ths cu m** natural sands 12.8 ths cu m	**KALININABAD GRAVEL SIZING MILL**	**114**
86	**crushed stone 186 ths cu m** natural sands 156 ths cu m blocks of stone	**LEASE-HOLDER COLLECTIVE "VREMYA"**	**173**
87	**crushed stone 34 ths cu m** gravel 32.3 ths cu m natural sands	**NAU MECHANIZED QUARRY**	**186**
88	**crushed stone 80 ths cu m** natural sands 84.6 ths cu m ferroconcrete articles 868 cu m	**LENINSKY NON-METALLIFEROUS MATERIALS PLANT**	**176**
89	**crystal vibrators 1,000 ths pcs** quartz filters 19 ths pcs television receivers	**PLANT "ALMOS"**	**198**
90	**designing** non-standard machinery and equipment	**DUSHANBE SPECIALIZED ENGINEERING DESIGN BUREAU**	**55**
91	**dresses 41.1 ths pcs** dresses of silk 24.8 ths pcs	**DUSHANBE COMPANY "GULDAST"**	**23**
92	**dresses, bathrobes 638.2 ths pcs**	**KHUDZHAND CLOTHING PRODUCTION and TRADE COMPANY NAMED AFTER N.K.KRUPSKAYA**	**132**
93	**dry ochre 5,980 tons** silicate paints paints and varnishes	**ISFARA MINERAL PAINTS PLANT "NILUFOR"**	**102**

94	**electric cookers 13,459 pcs** spoons	**KHUDZHAND PLANT "TORGMASH"**	**139**
95	**electric power supply**	**DUSHANBE TOWN ELECTRIC POWER TRANSMISSION NETWORK**	**58**
96	**electric power supply**	**SOUTHERN ELECTRIC POWER TRANSMISSION NETWORK**	**226**
97	**electric power supply**	**VAKHSH HYDROELECTRIC STATION CASCADE**	**248**
98	**electric power supply 680 mln kWh** heating 3,245 ths Gcal	**DUSHANBE THERMOELECTRIC STATION**	**56**
99	**electric power supply 11,541 mln kWh**	**NUREK HYDROELECTRIC STATION**	**191**
100	**electric power supply 16,805 mln kWh** heating 3,648 ths Gcal	**STATE JOINT-STOCK HOLDING COMPANY "BARKI TOCHIK"**	**228**
101	**electric power supply 2,289 mln kWh**	**BAIRAZA HYDROELECTRIC STATION**	**7**
102	**electric power supply 692 mln kWh**	**KHUDZHAND ELECTRIC POWER TRANSMISSION NETWORK ENTERPRISE**	**135**
103	**electric power supply 93,500 ths kwh**	**GORNO-BADAKHSHAN ELECTRIC POWER TRANSMISSION NETWORK**	**84**
104	**electric power supply 96 mln kWh**	**CENTRAL ELECTRIC POWER TRANSMISSION NETWORK**	**10**

105	**fabrics of silk 3,064.8 ths m** twisted threads of silk 38.2 ths m folk handicraft articles	**DUSHANBE COMPANY "TADZHIKATLAS"**	**24**
106	**fabrics of silk 838.9 ths m** fabrics of man-made filaments fabrics of cotton	**PRODUCTION COMPANY "KHODZHENTATLAS"**	**205**
107	**fabrics, unbleached 3,207 ths m**	**GISSAR TEXTILE MILL**	**82**
108	**facing tiles 19.5 ths sq m**	**KANSAI NON-METALLIFEROUS and FACING MATERIALS PLANT**	**124**
109	**fermented tobacco 1,186 tons**	**FERMENTED TOBACCO PLANT**	**69**
110	**fish**	**DZHILIKUL FISHING FARM**	**65**
111	**fish 497 tons** live fish 298 tons smoked fish	**KAIRAKKUM FISHING INDUSTRY ENTERPRISE**	**108**
112	**floor coverings of cotton 134 ths sq m** carpets1.2 ths sq m mattresses	**KANIBADAM TRAINING and PRODUCTION ENTERPRISE**	**123**
113	**floor coverings of cotton 32 ths sq m** carpets 1,051 ths pcs ropes of cotton	**KOFARNIKHON TRAINING and PRODUCTION ENTERPRISE**	**147**
114	**floor coverings of cotton 35.9 ths sq m** lids 13 mln pcs	**KHUDZHAND TRAINING and PRODUCTION ENTERPRISE**	**142**

115	**floor coverings of cotton 54 ths sq m** pile carpets ropes of cotton	**KULYAB TRAINING and PRODUCTION ENTERPRISE**	**158**
116	**floor coverings of cotton73.7 ths sq m** carpets lids	**URA-TYUBE TRAINING and PRODUCTION ENTERPRISE**	**245**
117	**flour 60 ths tons** bran 13 ths tons mixed fodder	**KULYAB GRAIN PROCESSING PLANT**	**155**
118	**flour, mixed fodder**	**AGROINDUSTRIAL GRAIN PROCESSING PRODUCTION COMPANY**	**3**
119	**flour, mixed fodder**	**KOLKHOZABAD GRAIN PROCESSING PLANT**	**148**
120	**fluorspar**	**TAKOB FLUORSPAR WORKS**	**231**
121	**folk handicraft articles**	**DUSHANBE SOUVENIR FACTORY "ARMUGON"**	**54**
122	**footwear**	**KHUDZHAND SHOE FACTORY n2**	**140**
123	**footwear 2,005 ths pairs**	**DUSHANBE JOINT-STOCK LEATHER FOOTWEAR COMPANY "RAFIK"**	**39**
124	**footwear 500 ths pairs**	**INDUSTRIAL and TRADING FIRM "SIMO"**	**90**

125	**furniture**	**DUSHANBE FURNITURE PLANT**	**36**
126	**furniture**	**KHUDZHAND FURNITURE PLANT**	**136**
127	**furniture** tables beds	**ISFARA FURNITURE PLANT**	**98**
128	**geranium oil** peppermint	**STATE FARM-PLANT "EFIRONOS"**	**227**
129	**gold**	**PRODUCTION COMPANY "TADZHIKZOLOTO"**	**213**
130	**gypsum, building bricks**	**ISFARA BUILDING MATERIALS PLANT**	**92**
131	**hides** meat 2,657 tons sausages	**GAFUROV MEAT PROCESSING PLANT**	**75**
132	**high-voltage apparatus 1,705 pcs** electric transformers 45 ths pcs power transformers 489 ths kWh	**KURGAN-TYUBE TRANSFORMER PLANT**	**172**
133	**household chemicals** paints and varnishes mineral fertilizers	**ISFARA CHEMICALS PLANT**	**94**
134	**hydraulic drives and automated devices** spare parts for hydraulic drives cast articles of pig iron	**PRODUCTION COMPANY "TADZHIKGIDROAGREGAT"**	**209**

135	**industrial clothing** suits 256 ths pcs	DUSHANBE CLOTHING PRODUCTION COMPANY "CHEVAR"	22
136	**industrial clothing** dresses, bathrobes 696.7 ths pcs	KANIBADAM CLOTHING PRODUCTION COMPANY "KHUSNORO"	118
137	**instruments and apparatus** repair of instrumentation	PLANT "ETALON"	199
138	**instruments and apparatus** maintenance of instruments and automated equipment	DUSHANBE EXPERIMENTAL PLANT "SISTEMAVTOMATIKA"	28
139	**jam 6,379 ths rbls 202 ths tins** fruit juices grape juice	LEASING-BASED ENTERPRISE "SHARBAT"	174
140	**kitchen furniture** stools 86.6 ths rbls 865 pcs dinner-tables	INDUSTRIAL and COMMERCIAL FIRM "ISMAIL"	89
141	**knitted linen**	DUSHANBE KNITTING MILL	40
142	**knitted outerwear 687 ths pcs**	GANCHI CLOTHING and KNITWEAR FACTORY	78
143	**knitwear**	URA-TYUBE KNITTED OUTERWEAR FACTORY	244
144	**lids for preserves 15,801 ths pcs** crown corks 3,724 ths pcs folders	GISSAR TRAINING and PRODUCTION WORKS	83

145	**lighting engineering equipment** lighting fixtures 1,185 ths pcs low-voltage apparatus	**TADJIK PRODUCTION COMPANY "SVETOTEKHNIKA"**	**230**
146	**linoleum 355.6 ths sq m** roll roofing materials 1,811 ths sq m building bricks	**GISSAR COMPANY "GIDROSTROIMATERIALY"**	**79**
147	**liquid chlorine 16 ths tons** caustic soda 16 ths tons calcium chloride	**PRODUCTION COMPANY "TADZHIKKHIMPROM"**	**210**
148	**live fish 1,116 tons** smoked fish 19 tons	**KUIBYSHEVSK FISHING FARM**	**149**
149	**live fish 115.4 tons** fish products	**PENDZHIKENT FISH PROCESSING PLANT**	**196**
150	**live fish 600 tons** smoked fish 190 tons	**DZHILIKUL FISHING FARM**	**64**
151	**live fish 90 tons** chilled fish 8 tons	**FISHING FARM "CHUBEK"**	**73**
152	**low-voltage apparatus**	**ADRASMAN LOW-VOLTAGE ELECTRIC EQUIPMENT WORKS**	**2**
153	**meal of rice 14 ths tons**	**KOFARNIKHON RICE PLANT**	**146**
154	**meat** butter milk and dairy products	**KHOROG MEAT PROCESSING PLANT and DAIRY**	**128**

155	**meat 2,558 tons**	**DUSHANBE MEAT PROCESSING PLANT**	**42**
156	**meat 545.5 tons**	**ISFARA MEAT PROCESSING PLANT**	**100**
157	**meat, incl. edible offal** sausages 90 tons semi-prepared products	**KURGAN-TYUBE MEAT PROCESSING PLANT and DAIRY**	**167**
158	**meat, incl. edible offal 1,304 tons** sausages 2,110 ths rbls 70.9 tons fat	**KULYAB MEAT PROCESSING PLANT**	**156**
159	**meat, incl. edible offal 184.8 tons** sausages 25.7 tons fat	**PENDZHIKENT MEAT PROCESSING PLANT and DAIRY**	**197**
160	**metal structures** repair and maintenance of road building machinery and spare parts ucts of ferrous metals	**KURGAN-TYUBE MECHANICAL REPAIR WORKS**	**168**
161	**metal-working tools** machining attachments consumer goods	**KANIBADAM BRAKE EQUIPMENT PLANT**	**116**
162	**metal-working tools** consumer goods parts of agricultural machines	**KULYAB EXPERIMENTAL MACHINING ATTACHMENTS PLANT**	**153**
163	**milk and dairy products**	**SHAARTUZ CREAMERY**	**221**
164	**mineral waters 19 ths bottles** beer wine	**KURGAN-TYUBE NON-ALCOHOLIC BEVERAGES and MINERAL WATER PLANT**	**169**

165	**mixed fodder**	**ILIYCHEVSKY FEED MILL**	**88**
166	**mixed fodder 31 ths tons**	**GRAIN INTAKE PLANT**	**85**
167	**newspapers** business forms	**TURSUNZADE PRINT-SHOP**	**238**
168	**newspapers 2,400 ths copies** business forms 1,263 ths copies	**PRINTING PRODUCTION COMPANY**	**203**
169	**newspapers 78 mln copies** magazines 18 mln sheets	**PUBLISHING HOUSE**	**219**
170	**nitrogenous fertilizers 53 ths tons** urea 114 ths tons ammonia	**VAKHSH NITROGENOUS FERTILIZER PLANT**	**249**
171	**non-ferrous waste and scrap 1,293 tons**	**PROCUREMENT PRODUCTION COMPANY "TADZHIKVTORTSVETMET"**	**204**
172	**oil asphalt**	**OIL ASPHALT PLANT**	**192**
173	**orthopaedic footwear** prosthetic appliances	**PROSTHETIC and ORTHOPAEDIC APPLIANCES PLANT**	**218**
174	**oxygen 61 ths cu m** non-standard machinery and equipment 343.7 tons	**DUSHANBE PLANT "STROMMASH"**	**48**

175	**paints and varnishes 996 tons** floor oil paints pottery articles	**DUSHANBE PAINTS and VARNISHES PLANT "RANGINKAMON"**	**44**
176	**pile carpets 10,810 sq m** floor coverings of cotton fabrics of silk	**TRAINING and PRODUCTION WORKS n4**	**234**
177	**pre-cast ferroconcrete** articles of concrete, not reinforced concrete	**DUSHANBE FERROCONCRETE STRUCTURES and BUILDING ARTICLES PLANT n2**	**30**
178	**pre-cast ferroconcrete**	**MATCHINSKY RURAL CONSTRUCTION PLANT**	**177**
179	**pre-cast ferroconcrete** structural components for house construction crushed stone	**MOSKOVSKY FERROCONCRETE STRUCTURES PLANT n1**	**181**
180	**pre-cast ferroconcrete** chutes power transmission line supports	**DUSHANBEPRESSURE PIPES and FERROCONCRETE ARTICLES PLANT**	**63**
181	**pre-cast ferroconcrete** structural components for house construction 3.3 ths sq m supports for power transmission lines	**ISFARA FERROCONCRETE STRUCTURES and BUILDING ARTICLES PLANT n5**	**97**
182	**pre-cast ferroconcrete**	**KAIRAKKUM SUBSIDIARY ENTERPRISE**	**111**
183	**pre-cast ferroconcrete** crushed stone 34.2 ths cu m natural sands	**NAU BUILDING MATERIALS and STRUCTURES PLANT**	**183**

184	**pre-cast ferroconcrete**	**KALININABAD FERROCONCRETE STRUCTURES PLANT n1**	**112**
185	**pre-cast ferroconcrete** wall panels	**DUSHANBE FERROCONCRETE STRUCTURES and BUILDING ARTICLES PLANT n3**	**31**
186	**pre-cast ferroconcrete**	**SMALL ENTERPRISE "BETON"**	**225**
187	**pre-cast ferroconcrete 26,763 cu m** concrete 1,331 cu m	**GAFUROV FERROCONCRETE STRUCTURES PLANT n7**	**74**
188	**pre-cast ferroconcrete 7.7 ths cu m** welded metal structures 639 tons bars and rods for use in construction	**KALININABAD FERROCONCRETE STRUCTURES PLANT n8**	**113**
189	**pre-cast ferroconcrete 16.8 ths cu m** articles of concrete, not reinforced concrete	**DUSHANBE FERROCONCRETE STRUCTURES and PRE-CAST PARTS PLANT**	**33**
190	**pre-cast ferroconcrete 25.2 ths cu m** pipes concrete	**DUSHANBE FERROCONCRETE STRUCTURES and BUILDING ARTICLES PLANT n1**	**29**
191	**pre-cast ferroconcrete 4.3 ths cu m** ferroconcrete articles concrete	**KANIBADAM FERROCONCRETE STRUCTURES PLANT n2**	**119**
192	**pre-cast ferroconcrete 6.2 ths cu m**	**DUSHANBE FERROCONCRETE STRUCTURES and BUILDING ARTICLES PLANT n6**	**32**
193	**precious metals**	**KAIRAKKUM MINE**	**110**

194	**preserved fruit and vegetables 2,566 ths tins**	KURGAN-TYUBE CANNERY	160
195	**preserved fruit and vegetables 39,085 ths tins**	KHUDZHAND CANNERY	131
196	**preserved vegetables 6,657 ths tins**	ISFARA CANNERY	93
197	**preserved vegetables 4,232 ths tins** preserved fruit 13,501 ths tins	KANIBADAM CANNERY	117
198	**primary aluminium 345 ths tons** anode blocks 240 ths tons non-standard machinery and equipment 64.5 tons	TADJIK ALUMINIUM WORKS	229
199	**printed matter**	PRINT-SHOP	202
200	**printed matter**	DUSHANBE PRINTING WORKS	52
201	**printed matter**	DUSHANBE PRINT-SHOP n18	51
202	**processing of metal scrap 40,234 tons**	FIRM "DOVUD"	71
203	**refrigerators 61 ths pcs** spare parts for refrigerators refrigerating plants	PRODUCTION COMPANY "PAMIR"	206
204	**repair of automatic data processing machines**	COMPUTING APPARATUS REPAIR WORKS	14

205	**repair of containers**	**KHUDZHAND CONTAINER REPAIR WORKS**	**133**
206	**repair of equipment**	**PRODUCTION COMPANY "TADZHIKENERGOLEGPROM"**	**208**
207	**repair of motor vehicles**	**KHUDZHAND AUTOMOBILE REPAIR WORKS n4**	**129**
208	**repair of power equipment** spare parts for power machinery	**ENTERPRISE "TADZHIKENERGOREMONT"**	**66**
209	**salt 14,916 tons**	**VOSE SALT WORKS**	**251**
210	**salt 28,454 tons**	**ASHTI SALT WORKS n2**	**6**
211	**sheepskins 843 ths sq dm** men's anoraks 2,230 pcs short coats	**KURGAN-TYUBE EXPERIMENTAL FURSKIN FACTORY "MUINNA"**	**164**
212	**shirts of cotton 633.3 ths pcs**	**NUREK CLOTHING FACTORY**	**189**
213	**silk yarn 683.1 tons** twisted articles fabrics of silk, unbleached	**KHUDZHAND SILK MILL**	**141**
214	**socks for men 7 ths pairs** socks for children panty hoses for children	**JOINT-STOCK COMPANY "FAIZ"**	**104**

215	**spare parts for road building machines** metal structures for use in construction 194 tons non-standard machinery and equipment	**NUREK EXPERIMENTAL MECHANICAL WORKS**	**190**
216	**steel enamelled tableware 946.3 ths pcs**	**KHUDZHAND LEASING-BASED ENTERPRISE "EMALIROVSHCHIK"**	**138**
217	**stockings 4,260 ths pairs** panty hoses socks	**FIRM "NAFISA"**	**72**
218	**structural aluminium 172 tons** welded metal structures 6.7 tons	**DUSHANBE PILOT-PRODUCTION and EXPERIMENTAL PLANT "REMSTROIDORMASH"**	**45**
219	**sugar confectionery**	**CONFECTIONERY FACTORY "SHIRIN"**	**16**
220	**sugar confectionery 112.7 tons**	**DUSHANBE CONFECTIONERY FACTORY "LAZZAT" (JOINT-STOCK COMPANY)**	**25**
221	**suitcases 7.5 ths pcs** satchels 18.9 ths pcs bags 118.6 ths pcs	**DUSHANBE LEATHER HABERDASHERY FACTORY "CHARMDUZ"**	**41**
222	**table and kitchen articles of aluminium 238.2 ths pcs**	**SHURAB MECHANICAL WORKS "FILIZ"**	**224**
223	**table and kitchen articles of aluminium 620 tons** trays of aluminium articles of alloys	**KOFARNIKHON MECHANICAL WORKS "ZARFSOZ"**	**145**
224	**tableware of porcelain**	**TURSUNZADE PORCELAIN WORKS**	**237**

225	**textile haberdashery 240 mln pcs** articles of apparel and clothing accessories 100 mln pcs	**FACTORY "ZARDUZ"**	**67**
226	**threads of silk, unbleached 70 tons** fabrics of silk twisted threads of silk	**DUSHANBE SILK MILL**	**53**
227	**trade equipment and spare parts** electric ovens 23,911 pcs electric cabinets	**DUSHANBE PLANT "TORGMASH"**	**50**
228	**trousers** skirts shorts	**KURGAN-TYUBE CLOTHING FACTORY**	**161**
229	**unmanufactured tobacco 6,559 tons**	**PENDZHIKENT FERMENTED TOBACCO PLANT**	**195**
230	**unwrought lead 3,800 tons** silver 27.2 tons	**ADRASMAN LEAD and ZINC WORKS**	**1**
231	**vegetable oil 11.2 ths tons** hydrogenated fat 3.5 ths tons household soap 5 ths tons	**DUSHANBE OILERY and FAT PLANT**	**43**
232	**vegetable oil 18,457 tons**	**KANIBADAM OILERY and FAT PLANT**	**121**
233	**vodka 258 ths dal** wine 110 ths dal brandy	**DUSHANBE WINE PLANT**	**59**
234	**wadding 2,166 tons** apparel wadding 49 tons	**TRAINING and PRODUCTION WORKS n5**	**235**
235	**wadding of cotton 1,916 tons** articles of apparel and clothing accessories	**KHUDZHAND TRAINING and PRODUCTION WORKS n2**	**143**

236	**wall materials 7,720 ths pcs**	PENDZHIKENT BRICK YARD	194
237	**warehousing equipment**	DUSHANBE PILOT-PRODUCTION and EXPERIMENTAL PLANT "SELEKTSIONNAYA TEKHNIKA"	46
238	**welded metal structures 447 tons** repair of building machinery	KAIRAKKUM MECHANICAL REPAIR WORKSHOP	109
239	**welded metal structures 898 tons** repair of motor vehicles	DUSHANBE EXCAVATOR REPAIR WORKS	27
240	**wheat flour 93,206 tons** pasta 7,701 tons bran	KAIRAKKUM AGROINDUSTRIAL PRODUCTION COMPANY	107
241	**wheat flour 110,390 tons**	DUSHANBE GRAIN PROCESSING PLANT	37
242	**wheat flour 132 ths tons** bran 35 ths tons mixed fodder	NAU GRAIN PROCESSING PLANT	185
243	**wheat flour 142 ths tons** bran 40 ths tons semolina	GRAIN PROCESSING PLANT	87
244	**wheat flour 44 ths tons** bran 11 ths tons	GISSAR GRAIN INTAKE PLANT	81
245	**winding machinery and spare parts 200 pcs** textile spinning machines 152 pcs trade equipment	DUSHANBE PLANT "TADZHIKTEKSTILMASH"	49

246	**window assemblies 25.5 ths sq m** door assemblies 14.7 ths sq m wood sawn lengthwise	**DUSHANBE WOOD-WORKING PLANT**	**61**
247	**window assemblies 4.9 ths sq m** door assemblies 1.9 ths sq m PVC pipes	**DUSHANBE WOOD-WORKING PLANT**	**62**
248	**window assemblies 9.4 ths sq m** door assemblies 3.5 ths sq m floor panels	**DUSHANBE WOOD-WORKING PLANT**	**60**
249	**wine 302 ths dal** vodka 110 ths dal sparkling wine	**WINE PLANT "SHAKHRINAU" (LEASING-BASED ì**	**252**
250	**wine 322 ths dal** crude alcohol 1,369.4 dal grape must	**URA-TYUBE WINE PLANT**	**246**
251	**wine of fresh grapes 368.1 ths dal** vodka	**GAFUROV WINE PLANT**	**76**
252	**wire 991 tons** repair of electric motors non-standard machinery and equipment	**MECHANICAL WORKS "KHLOPKOZAPCHAST"**	**178**
253	**yarn of cotton**	**KURGAN-TYUBE COTTON SPINNING MILL**	**163**
254	**yarn of cotton 4,473 tons** unbleached fabrics of cotton 3,840 tons finished fabrics of cotton	**KANIBADAM SPINNING and WEAVING MILL**	**122**
255	**yarn of cotton 6,371 tons**	**JOINT-STOCK COMPANY "BOFANDA"**	**103**
256	**yarn of mixed wool 370 tons** fabrics	**WOOLEN SHAWL FACTORY "ZARBOF"**	**253**

SELECTED EXPORTERS AND IMPORTERS

FOOD AND LIGHT INDUSTRY

Company or firm	Information
Production corporation "TAJIKTEXTILE" Adress: 6 Sherozi ave., Dushanbe, Tajikistan, 735042 phone: 21-36-73 fax: 21-33-55	• Established: in 1942. • Pattern of ownership: collective. • Number of the workers: 4490 persons. • The industrial areas: 6000 sq. m. • The join makes deep processing cotton of a fiber. • Subject of the basic activity: production of a cotton yarn. Rough and ready cotton fabrics. • Volume of demand: 90 millions meters annually. • The name of the project: " Modernisation of the basic production ". • The purpose of the project: modernizing of operating productive capacities of join on the basis of modern foreign equipment and issue of competitive products • Direction of usage of the investments: purchase of the equipment and enforcement of circulating assets. • Cost of the project: 178,7 millions USD. • Necessary volume of the investments: 155,85 millions USD. • Payback time: 5 years. • Realization of production: a home market 45 %, export to countries of CIS 30 % in other countries 25 %. • The warranty of realization of production: the agreements, and also designed measures on the extension of a seller's market. • Beginning of return of the investments in 24 months. • Final payment in 60 months. • Security of return of the investments: the state warranty. • The solutions on support of state organs is present. • Enterprise manager Anvar Kurbanov
Joint venture "ASIA LTD" Address: 1, Krasnoarmeiskay str., Leninabad area, Chkalovsk, 735737 phone.: (37771) 5-46-35 fax 6-53-51	• Patterns of ownership: joint ventures. • Established: in 1997. The founders: republics a Tajikistan and Switzerland. • The basic activity: production of cooling drinks and mineral water. • Productive capacities: a line on issue of water and drinks (Italy), productivity 2500 litres / hours per polyethylene capacities in volume 1,5 l.; a line on a blowing of capacities (Francium) of volume 1,5, productivity 5 thousand units/hour. They have completely automized the production. • Number of the workers: 90 persons.

	• Realization of production: On territory of a Tajikistan (up to 80%), is exported to countries of CIS, Central Asia (15 - 20%). • The charter capital: 2,5 million's USD. • The investment projects: "Factory on issue of oil ". • The purpose of the project: construction of a factory on issue of oil in polyethylene capacities in volume 1,0 l. • Now construction is completed, but investments for the investments for the investments for the investments for investments • Total cost of the project: 900 thousand $. • Necessary volume of the investments: 500 thousand $. • Payback time of the project: 3 years. • Beginning of return of the investments in 24 months. • The warranty of return of the investments the lien of own assets. • Enterprise manager Rahim Ismoilov
Joint Stock company "ABRESHIM" Address: 238, Lenin St., Khudjand city,Republic of Tajikistan 725702 phone: 6-34-20	• Established: in 1992 on the base of Leninabad's silk factory. S.C. Abreshim is one of the largest enterprises in its branches in the North of Tajikistan. • Type of property: - Stock 51.2 percent, states 48.8 % • Main activities: production & realization of heat network, cotton & silk fabrics as well as sewing items. • Number of Workers: 3280 people • Facilities/Assets: good communications including auto & railway access as well as great production premises. • Name of Project: "Spinning factory". • Project's purpose: construct cotton-spinning factory. • Overall value of the project: USD 6.7 million. • Required volume of investments: USD 6.7 million. • Use of investments: to buy equipment. • Payback period: 2.5 years. • Beginning of return on investments: in 30 months. • Final payment: in 60 months. • On the base of marketing, sales market the volume of demand for realization defined. • Product realization planned to be carried out on the territory of Tajikistan 2,5 percent, åxport to CIS countries - 75 %. Warranties to products sale are presence of agreements on delivery. • Guarantee: At present, S.C. Abreshim prepared pilot model to ensure returns on investments (i. e. defined by state warranties as well as guarantee of S.C. Assets). • There is a decision of state & regional bodies to support the investment project. • Project Manager Tohir Babaev

Joint venture "JAVONI" Address: 1, Javoni Str., Khujand, 735400 phone: 4-02-95 fax 4-08-61	• Established: 1993. • Number of the workers: more than 1000 persons. • Own assets: about 39 million's USD. • The basic activity: deep processing cotton of a fiber from modern technique, production and sale of a cotton yarn, fabrics, sewing articles of a broad assortment (ready man's, female and children's clothes) consumer goods. • Operating productions: spinning, weavers', sewing and plot on furnish velvet of a fabric. The civil works on shops of furnish and they carry on colour of production that will allow the enterprise to begin export of finish products and will increase volumes in money terms. • The name of the project: "Extension of a finishing shop of spinning production ". • Total cost of the project: 5 millions USD. • Necessary volume: 3 million's USD. • The warranty of return of the investments - liens of own assets. • Enterprise manager Sharif Kalandarov
Joint venture "KABOOL TAJIK TEXTILE" Address: 238, Lenin Str., Khujand city, 735702 phone: (37922) 4-32-28, 6-68-77 fax: (3772) 51-00-80	• Established: 1994. • The basic activity: production of a yarn, cotton, severe fabrics and finished products. • The charter capital: 10 million's USD, Korean side - 56 %, Tajik sides - 44%. • Number of the workers: more than 2000 persons. Annual design volume of sale of production 30 million's USD. • Annual productive capacity: 12 thousand tons of a clap - fiber and issue of a cotton yarn of 10 500 tons, cotton fabric 22 million's m, jeans' fabric 6 million's m., ready sewing articles 158000 thousand pieces annually. • Based on more deep processing of a clap - fiber, issue of fabrics and sewing articles, increases of production and realization of production, they ensure the seizure working and receipt in a republic of convertible currency. • The joint venture is ready for mutually advantageous cooperation to the foreign investors in matter of overgrowth issue of competitive production. • Enterprise manager Keun Woo Lim
Joint Stock company of close type "KOLOS LTD" Address: 69 Chehova Str., Leninabad region	• Established: 1930. • In they transform 1997 in a JSCCT. • The basic activity: processing of a grain wheat and its processing. • Number of the workers: 45 persons

phone: 3-28-79, 3-29-45	• Productivity: 70 tons / day. • The basic production assets: 104 thousand USD. • The common area: 130 hectares. • The industrial areas 1,90 hectares; under the sowing area 94 hectares. • Names project: "Modernisation of a mill". The purpose of the project: increase of volume of processing of a grain about 100 tons / day. • Total cost of the project: 350 thousand USD. • Necessities in the investments 250 thousand USD. • Period of return: 2 years, beginning of return in 6 months. • The warranty of return of the investments: the lien of own assets, insurance. • Enterprise manager Nazar Kasimov
Production corporation "KULOB" Address:36, Lenin St. , Kulob, Khatlon area, 35360 phone: 2-32-30, 2-55-38	• Established: 1993. • Type of prorety: collective • Main activities: remaking of cotton and production of competitive products: production and sale of sewn wares. • Facilities/ Assets: The construction of sewing and looms, for paper production, sock/stocking and carpet production, and juice production. The corporation has a comfortable hotel in the city of Kulob. • Authorized capital stock USD 200,000. • Value of immovable assets: USD 3200 thousand. Established: 1993. • Type of property: Collective. • Main activities: remaking of cotton and production of competitive products: production and sale of sewn wares. • Number of workers: 60 people. • Facilities/Assets: The construction of sewing factory on the project of American specialists was begun by the approval of Government of the Republic of Tajikistan in 1993. At present the construction of complex of buildings realized on 80%. The power substation (4000 kWh/h) and 5 km of electro-transmission line built and delivered into complex. Has a sewing workshop, which has Japanese machinery (30). Yet to be constructed: Total area of 6240 sq.m: Production area (4320 sq.m.); Storage (880 sq.m.), Offices: (1200 sq.m.). • Available power: electric: 4000 kW/h, water consumption: 24 liters/sec. Output can be used to operate different equipment: • Total area of production premises 6240 sq. m. • Name of project: "Sewing-knitted fabric".

	• Project's purpose: complete construction of sewing factory, issue and sale of products. • Total value of project: USD 8000 thousand. • Necessary volume of investments: USD 6000 thousand. • Payback period: 3 years. • Main use of investments: buying of equipment. • The realization of commodity output: 10%, export to CIS countries: 90%. • Guarantee: state warranties. • There is decision from state and local bodies supporting the enterprise. • Enterprise manager: Zafar Mirzoev
Joint Stock company of openning type "NONPAZ" Address: 28, T.Pulodi St., Dushanbe, Republic of Tajikistan, 743013 phone: 21-87-66	• Established: in 1938. • Type of property: State • Main activity: production of bread and lacer's articles. Formally the enterprise produced bread, macaroni, spaghetti, confectionery articles, and caramel. Enterprise productivity - 120 tons of bread a day. Number of workers: 182 people • Facilities/Assets: Authorized capital: USD 187,000. Cost of fixed and turnover means: USD 193,000. Immovable property (as assessed in 1998): USD 540,000. Production areas: more than 8,000 sq.m. • Name of project: "Re-equiping and stockholding of corporation Nonpaz." • Project's purpose: technical modernization and reequiping of production to increase quantity and improve quality of products. The project passed through complex examination. Business plan is elaborated. Use of investments: purchase of complecting articles and materials, issue of shares for joint stock corporation. • Overall value of the project: USD 300,000. Necessary volume of investments: USD 200,000. Payback period: 2 years. • Guarantee: bank guarantees and insurance. Beginning of return on investments: in 12 months Final payment: in 24 months. • There is a decision of state and local bodies supporting the enterprise. • Enterprise manager Abdurasul Mukhidov
Joint Stock company "POIAFZOL" Address: 14 Rudaki str., Dushanbe, 734012 phone: 23-24-23	• Established: in 1999. • They created the factory in 1938. • Subject of the basic activity is having sewed children's and school footwear. • Medial-list numbers working - 50 persons. A production area of the plant - 8450 sq. m.

	• Investment's project "Reconstruction of a shop on production of footwear". • Purpose - modernisation and retrofit of acting productive capacities, for a quality improvement of commodities. • A direction of investments usage - acquisition of knowledge, purchasing of machinery and furnishing articles, replenishment of current assets. • Overall value of the project: 1,5 million. USD. • Necessary volume of investments: 1 million. USD. • Payback time: 3 years. • Beginning of returning: in 12 months. • Final repayment: 36 months. • Guarantee: liens of own assets. • Enterprise manager Rahmatjon Davlatov

Company or firm	Information
State enterprise "RESMON" Adress: 45, Hoji Sodik St., Kanibadam 735900 phone/fax: 2-23-03	• Established: in 1962. • Form of property: state. Main activities: production of cotton yarn and fabric. Number of workers: 1,330. Facilities/Assets: 23,873 sq. m. Regulations capital of the enterprise: 1,401,000 $ US. • Cost of the major and turnover facilities: 7,884,000 $ US. • Name of Project: "Technical re-equipment of enterprise or creation of joint venture". • Project's purpose: installing new technological lines for processing fiber. Increasing production of cotton yarn and fabric, meeting international standards. • Use of investments: purchase of equipment and materials, plenishement of the turnover facilities. Total value of project: USD 35,000.Demand volume: 6,000 tons of cotton yarn fabric, 910 mln. of ready-made fabric. Payback period: 5 years. • There is adecision of the regional bodies on supporting of the project. • Enterprise manager Abdumadjid Kahharov
Stock company of opened type "SAMAR" Address: 13 Omar Khayam str., Khatlon area, Voge region, The	• SCOT "Samar" was founded on 01/01/96 on the bas of Vose cotton enterprise. • Which was created in 1982 on the bas of Vose storing cotton. • After the SCOT "Samar" was formed. much enerav and

Republic of Tajikistan	means were spent on it's reconstruction, expansion and creation of the modern technological lines. • The main for today form of the activity of SCOT "Samar" processing of raw cotton, commodity output of consumer goods and productive-technological goods. • The assortment of SCOT "Samar" includes 88 names. • The cost of main funds 2146 thousand $ • The cost of equipment 1062, 3 thousand $ • The total area of production premises 13604 sq. m. • The cost of the project of enterprise (three shifts work) 1466511 thousands rubles. • The capital of SCOT "Samar" is 500,4 $ • Besides the processing of raw cotton SCOT "Samar" has: o oil factory output of oil o textile factory (spinning yarn, weaving mill) o factory for the output of socks o production of Knitting articles o mini tinned factory (tomato-paste, compotes and etc.) o assembling telephone set uses o sewing factory and etc. • Enterprise manager Samaridin Phazliddinov
Stock company of opened type "SUMAN" Address: 78, International str., Dushanbe city, 734001. phone: 24 86 81.	• Established: in 1992. • Main activity production of sewing manufactured articles consumer & artistic handicraft goods. At Present schedule number of employees 142 people. • Production area of enterprise 5372 sq. m. more than 100 sewing makers work there. • They produce national quilted blankets “Kuurpa” & “kurpachi”, pillows, mattresses & lots of other items. • Name of project “Expansion & reconst-ruction of sewing produc-tion & products of consu-mer and artistic handicraft goods”. • Project's purpose is increasing of volume & assortment of sewing production & creation of a shop on production of people's artistic handicraft items. It allows to revive & save ancient people's handicrafts, as well as organizing

	of skilled workmen from talented youth number. • Direction of using investments buying equipment, construction of a shop, raw material purchase overall value of investments 3,5 mln USD. • Necessary volume of investments 3 mln USD. • Pay-back period 6 years. Beginning of returning investments in 36 months. • At present series of products production is carrying on. • Ensuring investments returning is a transmission of rights on property, insurance. • There is a Decision of regional bodies on supporting. • The project allows enlarging a volume & assortment of sewing production & people artistic handicraft trade will attract workman in order to use their talent largely. • Enterprise manager Fajizimo Ibragimova
State enterprise "SHIRIN" Address: 10, Djabar Rasulov str., Dushanbe city, 734049 phone/fax: 35-82-83.	• The form of property - collective. • They formed the factory in 1964 and considered being the first large confectioner's factories in Tajikistan, fully satisfying population demand in confectionery. Production capacities allowed to produce broad assortments of articles (caramel, biscuits, zephyrs, sweets, etc.) right now demand for products compose 10 thousands tons per annum. • Production areas of premises 3442 sq. m., including shops, refrigerator chambers, etc. • Right now schedule number of employees 489 persons. • Project's name is “Reconstruction and introduction of modern techniques”. • Project's aim is acquisition of new techniques and world standard technology. • Overall value of project and necessary volume of investments compose 6000 thousands USD investments are to be used on equipment acquisition and supplement of turnover means. Taking into consideration own production there is an idea of the project, and scientific technological documentation is elaborated, as well as prepared active models, collaborate technico-economic ground. • Principal sale market domestic market (100%). • Ensuring investments returning are assets pledge.

	There is a decision of local bodies on supporting. • Beginning of investments returning in 2003 year ultimate payment in 2000 year. • Enterprise manager Mustafo Davlatov

INDUSTRY

Enterprises or facility	Information
Stock Company of opening type "CHEMICAL PLANT" Address: Navobod Str., Isfara, 735920 phone:2-21-90 fax: 2-29-46	• Established: in 1965. • In 1997 is transformed in joint-stock company. The basic activity: production of industrial explosives. Number of the workers 1100 persons. The issue of complex fertilizers for needs of an agriculture is organized on the basis of usage of local raw resources in volume 50 thousand MTA. • The basic activity: production of explosives granulits an AC - 4, AC - 8, AC - 4B, AC - 8B, C - 6M gramonits 30/70, 79/21, 82/18, intended for open and underground operations, except for operations dangerous on gas and dust. There is sorting railway a station. Cost of a fixed capital 2.380 millions rublov. The charter capital 1.108 millions rublov. Names project ¹ 1: " Construction of a line of a factory on production of ammoniacal niter ". Productivity 50 thousand ton / year on the basis of local raw material. Total cost of the project 10,2 million. USD. • The required investments 6 million. USD. • The project ¹ 2: "Architecture of production of automobile storage batteries ", productivity 300 thousand pieces /year. A total cost 3,1 million. USD. • The required investments 1,5 million. USD. The purpose of engaging of the investments: acquisition of the process equipment. • There is a warranty of Government. • Enterprise manager Ilias Aslamov
State enterprise "TRANSFORMER PLANT" Address: #1 Gafurov str., Kurgan-Tube, Republic of Tajikistan phone: 2-37-53.	• Established: in 1937. • Emitted production was exported to many foreign countries. • Number of the workers: 140 persons. • The charter capital: 545 million's rublov. • Own assets: 464 million's rublov. • Names project: "Completion of construction of 2 queues of Kurgan - Tyube of a transformer factory ". • Projects purpose: issue of power transformers TM-63 Kwa and TM-10000 Kwa. Modernisation and

	modernizing of operating productive capacities. Usage of the investments: purchase of furnishing articles and materials; construction; enforcement of circulating assets. • Realization of production: republics a Tajikistan - 80%, country of CIS - 20% from total amounts. • Cost of the project: 26 million. USD. • Payback time: 5 years. • Attractiveness of the project: absence of a similar factory and productions of transformers in Central Asia, vast sellers' market. • Security of return of the investments: the lien of assets, cession of rights on permanent assets. • Enterprise manager Nurali Kukiev
State enterprise "PORCELAIN PLANT" Address: # 28 Lomonosova str., Tursun-zade, Republic of Tajikistan.	• Established: in 1980. • Number of the workers: 1255 persons. • Productive capacities: 5750 thousand pieces of articles annually. • The basic activity: production of ware. • Assortments of emitted production: porcelain ware, piala, teapots, the trays, are oblique, dishes and other. • Production of a factory is in demand not only in republics, but also abroad. • Names project: " Mastering of new aspects of production ". • The basic purposes: production of new aspects of production and improvement of the quality manufactured production. • Total cost: 700 thousand USD. • Indispensable volume of the investments 500 thousand USD. • Use of investments: purchase of materials, equipment, dye markers. • Payback time: 1,5 years. • Beginning of return of the investments in 12 months. • Security of return of the investments the state warranties. • There is a solution on support of state organs.
State enterprise "TAJIK ALUMINIUM PLANT" Address: Tursun-zade, 735014, Republic of Tajikistan phone: 2-23-86,2-32-87 fax: 2-23-86.	• Established: in 1975. • Number of the workers: 15000 persons. • The basic activity: production of aluminum and articles from him. • Productive capacity: 340 thousand tons of aluminum annually. • Names project: "Reconstruction of production calcination of anodes, overhauls of electrolytic baths ".

	• Projects purpose: restoring of productive capacities, reconstruction of production Calcination of anodes, overhauls of electrolytic baths, modernisation and modernizing of operating productive capacities. • Total cost of the project: 150 million. USD. • Indispensable volume of the investments: 120 million. USD. • Payback time: 5 years. • Usage of the investments: purchase of the equipment and materials. • Security of return of the investments - state warranties and granting of the rights on acquisition up to 49 % of the shares of the enterprise. • Beginning of return of the investments - in 3 years. • The solution on support of state organs - is present. • Enterprise manager Abdukadyr Ermatov
Production corporation "TAJIKTEXTILEMACH" Address: #7, Nazarhoev str., Dushanbe, 734042, Republic of Tajikistan phone: 23 27 - 88 fax: 21-65 - 83.	• Established: in 1944. • Main activity production of textile & equipment, spare parts for cotton purify industry, consumption goods. • Schedule number of employees 810 persons . • Production area of undertaking 190000 m2. • Authorized capital 720 thousands USD. • Cost of main circulating assets 1427 thousands USD. • Project's name "Gas counter of consumer mark CGB 6". • Project's purpose arrangement of production of consumer instruments ensuring Supervision & account of consumption of natural gas. • Realization of project allows significantly shorten consumption of natural gas. • Direction of using investments buying completing products. • Overall value of project 4 years. • Beginning of returning investments in 12 months; Ultimate payments in 36 months. • Ensuring of returning investments a guarantee of assets, insurance. • There is a decision on supporting of state bodies. Volume of supply & demand 200 thousands pieces of CGB-6. • Enterprise manager Hamid Abdulloev
Srock company Dushanbe refrigerator plant "PAMIR" Adress: # 343, R.Nabiev str.. Dushnbe. Republicof	• They formed SCDRP "Pamir" in 1964. • The plant exported its production to 15 countries of the world. • Main activities mass production of a powerful being engine (refrigerators).

Tajikistan, 734036 phone: 31-05-47 fax: 31-07-97	• Schedule number of employees 578 persons. • Authorized capital of the enterprise 254,1 thousands USD. • The cost of fixed and turnover means 615,9 thousands USD. • Immovable property 460,6 thousands USD.(1.01.1998) • Production premises 17044 sq. m. • The plant possesses auto and railway excess ways. They arrange stable contacts with the plants of CIS countries. • Accountings above mentioned material SCDRP "Pamir" elaborated business-plan and investment project "Mastering production of new models of refrigerators". • Projects' aim is to produce two-chambered refrigerators at the level of world standards at the expense of foreign investments and at the expense of own production, (purchase of completing articles, materials). • Market investments determine demand which form 92 thousands refrigerators per annum. • Sale markets: domestic 20 percent, export to CIS countries 60 percent, export to the other countries 20 percent. • Guarantee of realization presence of agreements, determination of a sale market. Now SCDRP "Pamir" is ready to transfers into production two-chambered refrigerators. Investment projects supported either local and sated bodies. Overall cost of the project 1000 thousands USD. Necessary volume of investments 500 thousands USD. Payback period three years. • Beginning of investments returning 12 months. • Enterprise manager Ibodullo Mirov
State enterprise "SANGTUDINSK Hudroelectric Station" Address: # 64, I.Somoni str., Dushanbe, Republic of Tajikistan, 734026 phone: 35-06-82 fax: 35-86-92.	• Established: in 1957. • Type of property: state, joint-stock, including percentage of the state - 1 %. • Main activity: production and distribution of electrical power. • Number of workers: 11 thousand people. • The exploitation of existing hydro-electric stations permits cheap electrical power to keep factories operating and to provide the population with electric power. • Name of project: "Sangtudin HES", elaborated by "Tajikhydroenergyproject".

	• Project's purpose: construction of a complex irrigation-power hydronode; production of electrical power as well as regulation of the drainage of Vakhsh river. Bulk of supply and demands - 2,7 milliards Kw/hour; electrical power realized: in Tajikistan 50%; in CIS countries - 25%; in other countries 25%. • Total cost of project: USD 360,9 million. • Necessary volume of investments: 265,9 million USD. • Payback period: 4 years. • Guarantee: state warranties. • There is a decision of state and regional bodies supporting the project. • Enterprise Manager Bahrom Sirojev
Joint-stock company "ROGUNGESSTROI" Address: 734026 Dushanbe, I. Somony str., 64. Tel.: 35-06-82, 35-86-92.	• Rogun the hydro power node is largest on p. Vakhsh. With lead it in maintenance, probably, practically completely to run in a water-energy potential of all rivers, and for to regulate a drain of Amu Darya. Alongside with it, the common development of the electric power on will be increased Vakhsh on 0,7 milliards. kw. Hour. Not the smaller value has and water-economic effect of reservoir Rogun HYDROELECTRIC POWER STATION, in a part of regulation of a drain and water of distribution. • The charter capital - 150 million. USD. • The name of the project "Rogun HYDROELECTRIC POWER STATION ". The purpose of the given project: construction of a complex irrigation-power hydro node. • Usage of the investments: construction, purchase of the equipment. Manufactured production - electric power, at volume of demand - 10 milliards. kw. Hour. • Realization of production: republics a Tajikistan - 50%; export to countries of CIS - 25%; export to other countries - 25%. A total cost: 1250 million. USD. • Payback time of the project - 6 years. Attractiveness of the project: economically net production of the cheap electric power for all locales. • Security of return of the investments: the state warranty. • Enterprise manager S. Siyamardov
Joint-stock company "ISFARA FBM" Address: village Honobod, Isfara, Leninabad area, Republic of Tajikistan, 735920 phone: 2- 32 04	• Established: in 1973, they share the Isfara Combine of building materials " in 1998 in joint-stock company". • The basic activity: production of building materials based on local raw material. The annual power of the enterprise is issue in volume 102 thousand ò. Gypsum, 26 thousand tons' Inform, 750 thousand ò. Fossil rock and 42 million. Pieces of bricks. Number of

fax 2-31-03	the workers: 550 persons. The charter capital: 200 thousand USD. • Fixed capital: 1,25 million. USD. Cumulative assets: 2,8 million. USD. Names project "Architecture and construction a small of a cemented factory". • Projects purpose: mastering issue of cement with annual volume 60 thousand tons. Overgrowth of power of industry of building materials based on local raw material. Total cost of the project: 3,5 millions USD • Necessities in the investments: 2,1 millions USD • Period of return of the investments: 3 years • Beginning of return in 12 months • Enterprise manager Nematullo Muhamadov

Enterprises or facility	Information
StocStock enterprise of closed type "LAHL" Address: #262, Lenin str., Khujand, Leninabad oblast, 735702 phone: 6-45-94 telex: 275235 "Soda"	• JSCOT "Lahl" is founded in 1999 on the basis glass of a tare factory grounded in 1943. • The majors revalue of a factory, and nowadays joint-stock company "Lahl" was and there is a production of a glass container for needs of an industry. • The Leninabad area is rich by gardens, grapes, plantations of vegetables etc. On territory of area many of canning and other refining factories. The normal operation of these factories wholly depends on availability of empties. Therefore a main role of a JSCOT "Lahl" - solution of a problem, bound with empties not only for needs of area, but also other locales of a Tajikistan. • The basic line of business of a JSCOT is: production and delivery of empties for an industry making a wine, canning and lactic factories. • The manufacturing floor spaces of a JSCOT "Lahl" compound 3,16 hectares. 350 persons here work. • The charter capital of the plant - 15 million. USD. The installed power of the plant compounds 182 million. The conditional jars annually. • Now on a JSCOT "Lahl" the investment design is prepared "Modernisation flown down productions". The given design is designed TASIS and favoured by Worldwide Bank. • Overall costs of the design - 6 million. USD (Installment financing). • The own facilities, put in this design, compound 2,0 million. USD.Payback time of the design - 3 years. A beginning of returning of the investments - in 18 months. • Warranties of returning of the investments own assets.

	• Enterprise manager Mirzohalim Mirzokarimov
State enterprise "ADRASMAN ORE-MINING AND PROCESSING ENTERPRISE " Address: #72, Ganchbakhsh str., Adrasman, Kairakkum, 735780 phone: 2-23-13, ext. 2-12	• Established: 1943. • The basic activity: production of leaden silver ores and leaden concentrate. • Number of staff: 1128 persons. • The industrial areas of 8820 sq. m. • The charter capital: 980 thousand USD. • Own assets: 1047 thousand USD. • Names project: " Architecture of an ore mining, production of a leaden - silvered concentrate ". • The purpose of the project: increase of productive capacity of an ore mine up to 600 thousand ò of ore annually on the basis Adrasman enterprise, extension of development of a field Eastern Kanimansur at the expense of padding commissioning of three refining blocks, implicating(involving) in handling stores of a part Large Kanimansur. Construction of a complex of buildings and buildings for a service of an ore mine. Usage of the investments: purchase of the equipment, acquisition of gears of materials, construction. Indispensable volume: 7,2 million. USD. Payback time: till 5 years, after a termination of construction. Security of return of the investments: the state guarantees. There is a solution on support of state and regional organs. • Enterprise manager Rahimdjan Nurmatov
State enterprise "ANZOB AND PROCESSING ENTERPRISE" Address: Zeravshan, Aini district, Sogd oblast, 735522 phone: 24-21	• Established: in 1954. • Source of raw materials: a field "Djijikrud", (90 % of known reserves). The field is rich by different minerals (antimony, quicksilver, gold, argentum, taxes etc.). • Number workers: 920 persons. • Industrial plants: a underground ore mine, dressing-works, central, repair-mechanical, transport shop and etc. • Names project "Reconstruction of productive capacities of combine ", • Projects purpose: o increase of power on production and processing of ore up to 700 thousand ò. Annually; o commissioning of padding powers on dressing-works; o construction of a mercury factory on demercury of a concentrate on furnaces of a boiling bed ; o construction surma of a factory for deriving finish products. • Indispensable volume: 102 million. USD. • Payback time of the project 8, 6 years.

	• After a realization of the first stage - creation of metallurgical powers and engaging to processing ores containing precious metals, the sum of effect from the investments will be significant and, accordingly, payback time will make 3-4 years. • The creation of joint ventures or other forms of co-operation on mutually advantageous conditions is possible. • Enterprise manager Holnazar Halikov
Joint-stock company "BODOM" Address: #257, Lenin str., Khudgand, region Kanibadam, Republic of Tajikistan phone:(37968)2-77-90 fax:(37967)2-42-07	• Established: in 1939. • Since 1992. Joint-stock company of "Bodom". • The enterprise emits: automobiles spare, back bridges, boxes of a change of transmissions, cylinders of the principles brake, forward and back brakes, rudder control, differentials, brake drums and other details, for automobiles of the mark "GAS". They run in the issue: bicycles, bicycle shops and bicycle trailers. • Divisions: a bicycle factory, power 6000 articles annually; mechanical assembly shop ¹ 1 and other. • Cost of annual production: 2 milliards. 380 million. Rbl. • Names project: "Modernizing bicycles of production". Projects purpose: improvement of the quality and competitive strengths of bicycles, overgrowth of production. • Total cost of the project: 14 million. US dollars. • Indispensable volume of the investments: 9 million. US dollars. Period of return: 5 years. A beginning of return in 12 months. • The warranty of return: government of a RT - 15% and lien of own assets - 85%. • Enterprise manager Yusuf Ahmedov
State enterprise "VOSTOKREDMET" Address: #10, A.Oplanchuk str., Leninabad region, Chkalovsk, 735730 teletype:27-51-35, 27-51-89 "Seagulls". fax:5-09-45. phone:(37771)5-24-51, 5-53-70	• Established: 1945. The Tajikistan is in immediate subparameter of Government of Republic. • In composition of join consist: a metal works; Chkalovsk machine works; joint venture a Khudjand - ÇÈË (Tajikistan - Russia); research-and-production Center "Know-how"; research-and-production Center "ELTA"; the manufacturing - collective plant " an ore Mine of opened mining operations "; control of a central heating and delivery of energy; control of a motor-vehicle transport; Center of economical studies; pioneer camp - Preventive sanatorium "Orlenok"; the house of rest "Kairakkum"; state farm "Palass". • The main commodity and aspects of services: the monoxide - Protoxide of uranium, efinirovan of gold and silver, jeweller and souvenired articles(workpieces),

	signs of the state awards, dressing tungsten of inclusive concentrates, buses "Tajikistan", parts and clusters to minihydroelectric power station, sprinkling systems, mining equipment and other machine-building commodity, facing tile from a natural rock, assembly of electronic package, agricultural commodity, service in the field of programming, link, is warm energy of procurement, motor transportation carriages, technological minings, civil and erection works etc. • The design #1. The indispensable investments: the uranium design - "Creation of joint venture on a mining of ores" - 15 million. US dollars. Period of returning of the investments - 5 years. • The design #2. "Assembly both implementation computer and consumer electronics" - 500 thousand USD. A beginning of returning of the investments - during 2 years (there are manufacturing floor spaces and trained staff); • The design #3. "Fabrication of a facing tile" - 200 thousand USD. A beginning of returning of the investments - in 2 years (there are 2 open casts of pink marble and gabbro, rock cut shop, grinding lines. The carved machinery is necessary a modern rock. Warranty of returning - lien of own assets. • Enterprise manager Zafar Razykov

TELECOMMUNICATION

Company or firm	Information
Internet service provider "TELECOMM TECHNOLOGY" Adress: 734001, Republic of Tajikistan, Dushanbe city, Bokhtar street 35/1 phone/fax: 21-14-22, 51-01-44	• Established: in 1994. • Type of property: private. • Main activity: telecommunications services and computer technology. Number of workers: 25 people. • Facilities/Assets: Premises with total area 40 sq.m. • Name of project: "Integrated satellite communication". Project's purpose: creation of developed telecommunications satellite network on the basis of VSAT technology and presentation telecommunication services to Bank Stock exchanges and population. Guarantee of the project's realization is considered to be the presence of agreements as well as determination of demand channels realization and services. Company has elaborated scientific-technological and constructive documentation, and prepared experimental sample. Realization of its services and technology: in Tajikistan 75-85%: rest to be exported to other countries. Business

	plan prepared by company. • ATK "Telecomm Technology Ltd." is first Internet service provider in Tajikistan. Since January 1999 the company has begun submission of services on network access to Internet to users in Tajikistan. The company plans by 2000 to supply access of all regions of Tajikistan to services of the world web Internet. Total cost of the project: USD 5,500,000. • Necessary volume of investments: USD 2,800,000. • Use of investments: acquisition of technology and equipment purchase. Payback period: 2-3 years. • Beginning of return on investments: in 24 months • Final payment: in 48 months. • Guarantee: insurance, ownership part of the share of enterprises. There is a decision of the state bodies supporting this enterprise. • Enterprise Manager Shavkat Khalilov

COMMERCIAL STRUCTURES

Company or firm	Information
Private firm "RASULIEN" Address: 735718, Leninabad area, Khudjand, 18 microregions. phone.: (37922) 2-62-09; 2-84-93; 2-56-37. fax: 6-06-30.	• Established: in 1998. • Main activity: processing of agricultural production, drying of vegetables and fruit. • The corporation is arranged with unique drying aggregates. The soft process drying high density finites infrared, allows completely (about 90%) to save vitamins, flavouring qualities, erasing thus, parasitic micro flora. For drying the ecological net vegetables and fruit are used. • Manufactured production: 900 tons / years. • The industrial areas: 1,5 thousand's sq.m. • Productive capacity: 800 MTA. • The charter capital 240 million. USD. • Number of the workers: 350 persons. • Names project: "Project of a line of sorting and prepacking of production in small-sized packaging ". • Return of investments: in 7 years. • Beginning of return: in 12 months. • The warranty of return: own assets. • Enterprise manager Abdugaffor Rasulov
State enterprise "TAJIK RAILWAY" Address: 734012, Dushanbe 35.	• Established: in 1994 on the basis of Tajik section of the Middle Asian railway, which they built in 1929. • Facilities/Assets: Authorized capital stock USD 1.335.814.000; principles sum and turnover means

Academician Nazarshoev St. phone.: 23-35-29 fax: 21-57-91	USD 2,139,933,000 (as of 1996) • Project #1: "Electrification Tajik railway road in Leninabad regions". • Project's purpose: The creation of an electrification railway road the northern parts of Tajik railways. The construction began, but because of the lack of the means is frozen. • Total cost of the project: USD 10,700,000 • Necessary volume of investments: USD 35,000,000 • Payback period: 5 years. • Beginning of the return on investments: in 24 months. • Final payment: in 96 months. • Guarantee: state and banking warrants. • There is a decision of state bodies supporting this project. • Project #2: "The construction of new railway line Kurgan-Tjube Yavan". • Project's purpose: Construction of an iron line for improvement of a transport service of a southeast part of a Tajikistan. An expansion: 116 km. The realization of services: in Tajikistan - 12%; in CIS - 88%. Total cost of the project: USD 270,000,000 Necessary volume of investment: USD 112,000,000. • Payback period: 5 years. • Beginning of return on investments: in 24 months. • Final payment: in 96 months. • Guarantee: state and banking warrants. • There is a decision of state bodies supporting this project. • Project #3: "Construction of new railway Vakhsh-Yavan". • Project's purpose: The reestablishment of the section rail road Termez-Yavan by the clay torrents Termez - Yavan. • Project period: 5 years. The realization of services: in Tajikistan: 15%; in CIS: 85%. • Total cost of the project: USD 200,000,000. • Necessary volume of investments: USD 195,000,000. • Payback period: 8 years. • Beginning of the return on investments: in 24 months. • Final payment: in 96 months. • Guarantee: state and banking warrants. • There is a decision of state bodies supporting this project. • Chief of the Enterprise Muhamad Habibov
Jointstock company of opened type "LADA -	• Established: in 1994 • Patterns of ownership mixed.

HULBUK" Address: Khatlon area, Vose region collective farm M. Mahmadaliev, Site "Aral" phone: 2-28-56 (switchboards) 3-42 phone in in Dushanbe: 31-73-73, 31-88-89	• The basic activity: rendering of services to the citizens, enterprises, architectures in maintenance service and repair of cars, them before selling preparation and realization; leasing, and also buying up, restoring both realization of the supported automobiles and renewals; manufacture of new renewals both other own production and their realization. • Number of the workers: 25 persons. • Own assets: 120 thousand US dollars. • Cost of the real estate: 240 thousand US dollars. • Industrial locations: more than 1000 sq. ì. • The common area: 1,2 hectares. The building HUNDRED is included by a one-storeyed industrial location, and also double stored administrative body. The building HUNDRED modular - block, production of the "engineering Design" corporation (Poland, Warsaw) also is in good condition. • Throughput: 1500 automobiles. • Cost a HUNDRED as of 1986 about 1 million. roubles. • A HUNDRED is supplied with automobiles electrical engineering supply. • Names project "Car-service centres". • Project purposes: reconstruction of powers for rendering all aspects of services, including services in the foreign marks. • Total cost: 300 thousand US $. Own means (location, equipment and etc.) constitute 100 thousand US $. • Indispensable volume of the investments 200 thousand US $. • Beginning of return of the investments in 18 months, termination in 36 months. • Security of return of the investments a property as security, insurance. • The solution of local organs on support is present. • Enterprise manager Shodi Musoev
Joint-stock company "NURI-NAV" Address: 734044, Dushanbe, Chorteppa, 44 phone: 35-75-01	• The fruit of vegetable facilities of a republic is established on March 3, 1989 on the basis of abandoned Ministry. • Number of the workers: 2800 persons. • Circulating assets: 15% of the budgets of republics, 70% of the agricultural enterprises - had the agreement with the corporation "Nuri Nav". Assist 8 children's houses (1500 children). • In 1997 is constructed: a polyethylene factory, productivity 700 MTA (film for lemons, hothouses); 2

	canning plants, productivity 10 million. The conditional jars; a factory on issue of cooling drinks (stage of surrender in maintenance). • In 1990 the joint venture "Indium - Tajikistan - Germanium " is created. • In 1997 the joint venture " Railway a RT " on construction of petroleum refineries, productivity 400 thousand tons of processed oil annually are created. • The basic activity: preform, storage, processing of agricultural production (more than 100 names), production of cooling drinks. • The industrial areas: 12 hectares. • Cost of the equipment: 5 million. USD. • Own assets: 1,6 million. USD. • Names project: " Issue of cooling drinks ". • Total cost: 18 million. USD. • The own means put in the project constitute 7 million. $. • Indispensable volume of the investments: 11 million. $. • Sellers' market: Russia, Arabian countries, Europe, Central Asia, Tajikistan. • Payback time: 2 years. • Enterprise manager R. Abdurahmanov
Stock company "INTOURIST - TAJIKISTAN" Address: 734001, Republic of Tajikistan, Dushanbe city, Shotemur str.22 phone: 21-62-62 fax: 21-52-37 e-mail: ashurov@intoun.td.silk.org	• The form of property collective (70 % preliminary payment, 30 % sate). • SC Intourist Tajikistan was formed in 1991 on the base of Tajik corporation on foreign tourism Tajik intourist founded in 1956. • Main activity organization of reception and provision of cultural and living facilities of foreign tourists and other visitors of the country, renderings informational, mediators, advertisement and other services. • SC Intourist Tajikistan organized material-technical supply of hotel complex by means of resources acquisition at domestic and foreign market and services directly from producers in wholesale trade, including fairs and auctions. All above mentioned activity is carrying out on the base of market conjuncture publishing and possibilities of potential partners. • Schedule number of employees 268 persons. • Authorized capital 119,8 thousands USD. • The cost of fixed and turnover means 722,7 thousands USD. The cost of immovable property 438,6 thousands USD (24.03.1996). • In order to perfect services SC Intourist Tajikistan

	elaborated business-plan and prepared investment project "Reconstruction and modernization of hotel complex".
	• Project's aim is Reconstruction accounting requiThe form of property collective (70 percent preliminary payment, 30 percent sate).
	• SC Intourist Tajikistan was formed in 1991 on the base of Tajik corporation on foreign tourism Tajik intourist founded in 1956.
	• Main activity organization of reception and provision of cultural and living facilities of foreign tourists and other visitors of the country, rendering informational, mediator, advertisement and other services.
	• SC Intourist Tajikistan organizes material-technical supply of hotel rements of hotels 3 stars.
	• Overall value of the project - 10100 thousands USD.
	• Necessary volume of investments construction,
	• Purchase of uncompleted articles, materials and equipment.
	• Payback period 6 years.
	• Sale market:
	  o - republic of Tajikistan, Dushanbe 95 percent
	  o - export 5 percent
	• Guarantee of project realization to determine sale markets of their services.
	• Ensuring investments returning assets pledge.
	• Beginning of investments returning 12 months.
	• Enterprise manager Inoajtullo Ashurov

BANKING SYSTEM AND BANKS IN TAJIKISTAN

The reform of the banking system in Tajikistan started in 1994 with the financial assistance of the World Bank, IMF, EBRD and technical assistance of companies such as "Arthur Andersen" (U.S.) and "IDP" (Italy.) The new Law "On Banks and Banking Activities" became a logical step in reforming Tajikistan's banking system. Reforms of the system will improve after the promulgation of the following normative acts:

- On the Qualification Committee of the National Bank;
- On Forming Procedures of the Statutory Capital;
- Procedures for Starting and Terminating Commercial Banks'Activities;
- Procedure for Issuing and Recalling Licenses for Banking Activities' Auditing;
- Procedures for Establishing Non-Banking Financial Organizations;
- On Banks' Bankruptcy.

These legislative acts are aimed at regulating both banks' and non-banking financial organizations activities. Non-banking financial organizations are legal entities which may execute some banking operations and provide some financial services for individuals and companies after they get a license of the National Bank. According to Mr Valiev, such financial organizations in the future will be reorganized into loan companies, clearing houses, etc. Right now the experiences of other NIS countries are being examined to develop appropriate laws for Tajikistan.

At the beginning of 1998, 27 commercial and private banks were officially registered in the country. Before January 1, 1998, $300,000 was sufficient to establish a bank. According to Tajikistan's National bank decision, since January 1, 1998 the statutory minimum capital requirement of already existing and newly established joint-stock, commercial, and private banks is to be $1,000,000. After all those restrictions were introduced, only 19 banks with their branches have survived. Three banks such as Bahtovar, Toribank, and Ziroat failed
to reach the required capital requirement and were closed down. Two other banks, Ilhom and Rishta, which also failed to meet the necessary capital requirement, were transformed into branches of Agroinvestbank. As the Deputy National Bank Navruz Valiev said, after the National Bank raised the minimum capital requirement, they have received no application for getting licenses for banking activities and opening any new banks.

The National Bank also introduced a minimal working capital amounting to $500,000 by January 1, 1998. By July, 1, 1999 it will have to be $750,000 and by January 1, 2000 $1,000,000. The increase of the minimum capital requirement and of the working capital level is supposed to help settle the problem with banks' liquidity.

For registering a bank and issuing a license for banking activities the National Bank charges 0.5% of the announced capital requirement. A license provides a right for banking operations for the entire period of its activity.

In implementation of the Memorandum on Restructuring the Banking System in Tajikistan signed between the National Bank and the World Bank, the National Bank signed agreements with the four biggest commercial banks Agroinvestbank, Tajikbankbusiness, Sberbank, and Vnesheconombank on their reorganization. According to this document, by November 30, 1998 these four banks are to increase their statutory capital, reduce expenditures, try harder to collect earlier issued loans and to reimburse overdue loans, and liquidate unprofitable branches. Another important requirement of the agreement is the implementation of International Accounting Standards by local banks.

Mr Valiev is of the opinion that the future of the banking system in Tajikistan will depend on strict observance of the adopted laws and regulations.

BANKS IN DUSHANBE

1. National Bank of the Republic of Tajikistan

Murodali Alimardonov
Chairman

23/2, Rudaqi Ave.
734025 Dushanbe, Tajikistan
Tel: 7(3772) 21 26 28
Fax: 7(3772) 21 25 02
Telex: 201 129

2. Joint Stock Commercial Agroindustrial Investment Bank Agroinvestbank (Agroinvestbank)

Maqsud Kodirov
Chairman
31, Sherozi Ave.
734018 Dushanbe, Tajikistan
Tel: 7(3772) 33 31 04, 36 79 89
Fax: 7(3772) 901 50 16
Telex: 201 221

3. Joint Stock Commercial Industrial and Construction Bank Orionbank (Orionbank)

Gaffor Idiev
Chairman
95/1, Rudaqi Ave.
734025 Dushanbe, Tajikistan
Tel: 7(3772) 21 09 20
Fax: 7(3772) 21 16 62
Telex: 201 136

4. Tajik Joint Stock Commercial Bank of Social and Economic Development Tajikbankbusiness (Tajikbankbusiness)

Kayum Kavmiddinov
Chairman
29, Shotemur Street
734025 Dushanbe, Tajikistan
Tel: 7(3772) 21 05 03, 21 06 34
Fax: 7(3772) 23 44 17, 21 06 21, 21 08 46
Telex: 201 113

5. State-Commercial Bank for Foreign Economic Affairs of the Republic of Tajikistan Vnesheconombank (Vnesheconombank)

Izatullo Lalbekov
Chairman
4, Husrav Dehlavi Street
734012 Dushanbe, Tajikistan
Tel: 7(3772) 23 35 61

Fax: 7(3772) 21 47 38
Telex: 201 121

SAVINGS BANK OF THE REPUBLIC OF TAJIKISTAN (TAJIKSBERBANK)

Kurbonali Juraev, Chairman
67, Rudaqi Ave.
734025 Dushanbe, Tajikistan
Tel: 7(3772) 21 70 81
Fax: 7(3772) 23 14 53

7. Joint-Stock Commercial Industrial Bank of Reconstruction and Development Tajprombank (Tajprombank)

Jamshed Zeyeyev
Chairman
12/3, Dehlavi (Ostrovskogo) Str
734025 Dushanbe, Tajikistan
Tel: 7(3772) 21 27 20, 21 26 42
Fax: 7(3772) 21 27 96
Telex: 201 197

8. Joint-Stock Investment Commercial Bank Tajbank
59/1, Somoni Ave.
Dushanbe, Tajikistan
Tel: 7(3772) 24 53 15

9. Commercial Bank Somonbank

N Kalandarov, Chairman
3, 1y Proezd Tursun-Zadeh Str
734003 Dushanbe, Tajikistan
Tel: 7(3772) 21 78 13
Fax: 7(3772) 21 78 13, 21 86 02

10. Commercial Bank Fonon

Tatyana Dedurova, Chairman
113/1, Lomonosov Str
734025 Dushanbe, Tajikistan
Tel: 7(3772) 35 27 03, 35 28 83
Fax: 7(3772) 35 27 13

11. Commercial Bank Texinvestbank

Atobullo Babaev
Acting Chairman
35/1, Bohtar Str
Tel: 7(3772) 21 79 52
Tel/fax: 7(3772) 21 80 00
734011 Dushanbe, Tajikistan

12. Commercial Bank Dushanbe

Goib Davlaytov
Chairman
24, Aini Str
Dushanbe, Tajikistan
Tel: 7(3772) 23 46 76
Tel/fax: 7(3772) 21 36 24

13. Commercial Bank Kafolat

Davlatahmad Gadoev
Chairman
4/1, Kuibishev Str.
Tel: 7(3772) 21 59 13, 21 76 22
Fax: 7(3772) 21 88 61

BANKS IN KHOJAND AND LENINABAD REGION

14. Commercial Joint-Stock Bank Akbarbank

Shahodat Mahmajonova, Chairman
1B, Pushkin Str
735730 Chkalovsk
Leninobod Region, Tajikistan
Tel: 7(271)5 39 41
Fax: 7(271)5 44 24

15. Commercial Joint-Stock Bank Ganjina

Valentina Zdunyuk
Chairman
Chief Post Office, Post Box 26
735700 Khojand, Tajikistan
Tel: 7(37922) 2 54 41
Tlx: 201 150

16. Commercial Bank Khojand

Ahmajon Shukurov, Chairman
5, Kvartal 120
Gafurov, Khojand District
Leninabad Region, Tajikistan
Tel: 7(37942) 3 15 33, 3 19 09
Fax: 7(37942) 3 25 52

17. Commercial Bank Eskhata

Khurshed Nosirov, Chairman
40, Lenin Str
735700 Khojand, Tajikistan
Tel: 7(37922) 4 39 45
Fax: 7(37922) 6 74 10

18. Joint-Stock Commercial Bank Ayem in Kanghurt, Sovetsky District, Khatlon Region

Contact information is not available.

19. State Bank on Rehabilitation and Development of Executive Committee of Khatlon Regional Council of People's Deputies
Khatlonbank

FOREIGN BANKS

1. Central Asian Bank (Tajik-Cyprus Joint Venture)

Alisher Tajiev
Chairman
42, Negmat Karabaev Str
734018 Dushanbe, Tajikistan
Tel: 7(3772) 33 36 15, 33 59 79
Fax: 7(3772) 33-33-33, 33-33-57
Tlx: 201 164

2. Joint-Stock Commercial Bank "East Credit Bank" (Tajik-Luxemburg Joint Venture), (East Credit Bank)

Serj Chernousan
Chairman
91, Rudaki Ave.
734001 Dushanbe, Tajikistan
Tel: 7(3772) 21 74 84, 21 81 86
Fax: 7(3772) 24 14 24

3. Branch of Commercial Bank "Tijorat" (Iran), (Tijorat)

Hushang Razmhoh
Chairman
70, Rudaki Ave.
734001 Dushanbe, Tajikistan
Tel: 7(3772) 21 14 76

IMPORTANT LAWS AND REGULATIONS AFFECTING BUSINESS

LAW ON PROPERTY IN THE REPUBLIC OF TAJIKISTAN

DIVISION I COMMON REGULATIONS

Article 1. The right of ownership

1.1 The right of ownership in the Republic of Tajikistan is recognized and protected by law.
1.2 An owner possesses, enjoys and disposes of his property. An owner has the right to take any allowable actions relating to his property provided the rights of co-owners are not violated. The owner may use his property for any economic activity or other activities not prohibited by law.
1.3 An owner is responsible to preserve his property from deterioration or accidental damage in case it is not already provided for by law or contract.
1.4 In certain cases, under the terms of the law, an owner may be obliged to allow a limited use of his property by other persons.
1.5 An owner may alienate his property, and also give it into the possession of other persons for their enjoyment and disposition without alienation.
1.6 An owner has the right under the terms of the law of the Republic of Tajikistan to conclude contracts with physical persons in order to use their labor while exercising his rights.

Article 2. Enforcement of the right of ownership
2.1 Enforcement of the right of ownership must not harm the environment and the health of citizens nor must it breach the rights and lawful interests of citizens, enterprises, organizations and the State.
2.2 Enforcement of the right of ownership on historical and cultural artifacts is regulated by the legislation of the Republic of Tajikistan.

Article 3. Legislation of the Republic of Tajikistan on property
3.1 Legislation of the Republic of Tajikistan on property is based on the Constitution of the Republic of Tajikistan and comprises the present law, other legislative documents adopted in accordance with the constitution and the present law, international legal documents recognized by Tajikistan as well as international agreements and interstate treaties signed and accepted by the Republic of Tajikistan.
3.2 The state guarantees and protects property rights and non-property author rights on discoveries, inventions, and scientific achievements. Property rights connected with the

creation and enjoyment of achievements of science, literature and art, discoveries, inventions of manufacture models, electronic programming devices and other objects of intellectual property are regulated by copyrights and other legislation of the Republic of Tajikistan as well as international agreements and interstate treaties signed and approved by the Republic of Tajikistan.

Article 4. Objects falling under ownership rights
4.1 Objects falling under the right of ownership may be enterprises, the ground and its resources, water, flora, fauna, tracts of mountains, buildings, constructions, equipment, raw materials, food products, money, securities, industrial consumer goods, social and cultural articles and the produce, income and profits on economic and other intellectual and creative activities of the owner.
4.2 Objects of intellectual property include scientific achievements, works of literature, artistic creations and other activities involving discoveries, inventions, production models, electronic programming devices, sources of education, testing systems, know-how, commercial secrets, consumer indexes, company trademarks, and service indexes.

Article 5. Those entitled to the right of ownership
5.1 Those entitled to the right of ownership in the Republic of Tajikistan are physical and legal persons, public and religious organizations, other unions of citizens and collectives, local state authorities and the self governing authorities of towns and villages, the State, foreign States, foreign citizens, persons without citizenship and foreign legal persons.
5.2 The Republic of Tajikistan guarantees the inviolability of property and the possibility of exercising the right of ownership for every owner.

Article 6. Forms of property
6.1 The state guarantees equal rights and protects the rights of all forms of ownership including private ownership.
6.2 Ownership in the Republic of Tajikistan can be either private, collective or public.
6.3 Ownership by other states, international organizations, foreign citizens, persons without citizenship and foreign legal persons is allowed in the Republic of Tajikistan.
6.4 Joint property of citizens, legal persons and the State may be established under mixed forms of ownership including ownership of joint enterprises with the participation of foreign citizens, persons without citizenship and foreign legal persons.
6.5 Property, regardless of the form of ownership, may be simultaneously owned by several owners by having each owner's share defined (joint stock ownership) or not defined (joint ownership).
6.6 Ownership, use, and disposal of joint property is carried out with the permission of all the owners; in case of absence of an agreement, the case is settled by a court according to the actions of each owner.
6.7 The state prohibits the establishment of limitations or preferences in the enforcement of property rights related with the form of ownership.

Article 7. Ownership of land and other natural resources
7.1 Land and all it contains, water, air, fauna, flora and other natural resources are the inherent property of the State which also guarantees their productive usage in peoples favor. Tracts of land according to the land code and other legislation of the Republic of Tajikistan may be granted for possession and exploitation to physical and legal persons according to the law of the Republic of Tajikistan.

7.3 Tracts of mountains for the exploitation and extraction of minerals are owned by the State and may be granted for possession and exploitation to physical and legal persons according to the law of the Republic of Tajikistan.
7.4 Alienation and unification of tracts of land and mountains is provided for by the law of the Republic of Tajikistan.

Article 8. Acquisition and loss of ownership rights
8.1 If not otherwise specified by law or contract, a citizen or other person has the right of ownership on legally acquired property, on raw materials created or fully reproduced by him or her, on his or her output, its profit and other income earned through the exploitation of his or her property, natural resources or other property under his or her responsibility for the latter purposes even if it doesn't belong to him.
8.2 If not otherwise specified by law or contract, a buyer of property acquires ownership rights on the object of the purchase as soon as the payment is settled and the object of the purchase is remitted.
8.3 Breaking ownership rights without the owner's will is prohibited except for cases when the owner is forfeited for debt in accordance with the law of the Republic of Tajikistan and in cases when property is legally confiscated.
8.4 In cases of natural disasters, accidents, epidemics, loss of cattle and other circumstances of extra-ordinary nature, property may be confiscated in the interest of society according to the law of the Republic of Tajikistan with compensation for the value (according to current market prices) of the property.
8.5 In cases determined for by the law of the Republic of Tajikistan, property may be confiscated by a decision of court or other authorities as a sanction for committing a crime or for having violated the law.
8.6 If private property, property of associations, and public property, involves property that according to the law cannot belong to the owner, it must be alienated from the owner for a period of one year should another duration fixed by law not specify otherwise. In case the owner has not been alienated from the property within the fixed period, the property must be alienated by a court's decision with a compensation for the cost of the property and a deduction including alienating expenses.

Article 9. Exaction of forfeiture from the owner's property
9.1 An owner is not responsible for the obligations of legal persons created by him and these legal persons are not responsible for the owner's obligations, barring cases defined by law, legislative documents, or documents establishing the status of legal persons.
9.2 According to the obligations of a legal person, forfeiture is exacted from every property owned by him or her, or under his or her full right of disposal.
9.3 Legal persons are responsible for their financial obligations and in case these obligations can not be met, the owner concerned takes the responsibility for the financial obligations on himself.
9.4 Compulsory forfeiture by the state for debts related to the owner including sums due to the State, is allowed according to the law of the Republic of Tajikistan. In case of disagreement with forfeiture, the owner has the right to appeal to court.

Article 10. The responsibilities of an owner
10.1 Should other terms not be specified by law or contract, the owner is responsible for the obligations concerning his or her property.

10.2 A list of the property of a physical person which is not forfeit to the claims of creditors is fixed by the laws of the Republic of Tajikistan.

DIVISION II PRIVATE PROPERTY

Article 11. Common regulations on private property
11.1 The amount and value of the property of a citizen is created and increased by virtue of his or her income from participation in production and other realizations related to his or her hard working capabilities, from entrepreneurial activity, from profits on credit, shares and other securities, from inheriting property, and from other sources not prohibited by the law of the Republic of Tajikistan.
11.2 A citizen with the owner's permission has the right to make pecuniary or other investments in property of enterprises, other economic organizations, farms or other businesses, functioning according to their contract, and may take part in the distribution of the income of the enterprise in proportion to his investment or as defined by an agreement.
11.3 The right of inheritance of a citizen's property is recognized, accepted and protected by the Constitution of the Republic of Tajikistan, the Civil Code, other laws of the Republic, and international legislation approved by Tajikistan.

Article 12. Objects of private property covered by law
12.1 The followings objects of private property are covered by law:
a) Dwelling premises including houses, flats and datchas, garages, housekeeping and personal material;
b) Pecuniary investments, shares, loans and other securities;
c) Mass media equipment;
d) Enterprises, complexes producing consumer goods and providing living facilities, complexes involved in trade and other spheres of entrepreneurial activity, buildings, constructions, equipment, transport vehicles, and other means of production.
e) Any sort of property meant for industrial, consumer, social, cultural, and other purposes except for specific types of property that cannot belong to citizens for state security and social motives as well as international obligations, defined by legislation of the Republic of Tajikistan.
12.2 The structure, quantity and value of property acquired by a citizen according to law or contract is unlimited.
12.3 The terms and conditions of privatization of enterprises or means of production belonging to the State are fixed by the law of the Republic of Tajikistan.

Article 13 Joint ownership
13.1 Private property jointly owned for the benefit of a business may include several families, members of families and other persons, workshops, enterprises producing consumer goods or providing living facilities, dealing in trade, public nutrition and other spheres of economic activity, dwelling premises, office buildings, machinery, equipment, transport means, raw material and other property necessary for the business.
13.2 The property of business including its produced output and income is jointly owned by the members of the family and other persons participating in the business unless an agreement between themselves provides for other conditions.

Article 14 Property of farms and personal farming entities

14.1 The ownership of farms consists of dwelling premises, farm buildings, plantations, cattle, poultry farms, agricultural implements, vehicles- and other property necessary for independent farming, production and realization of output.
14.2 Produced output and the earned income belongs to the farm and may be disposed of as the owner wishes as long as the Law does not specify otherwise.
14.3 The property of the farm belongs to its members jointly if the Law and other legislation of the Republic of Tajikistan does not specify otherwise.
14.4 The rules of this article also apply to personal farming entities.

Article 15 Property rights of citizens conducting entrepreneurial activity
15.1 A citizen may use his private property for commercial activity.
15.2 Property of members of family and other citizens, which is jointly used for entrepreneurial activity and its output and income belong to them under the status of joint ownership unless a contract among themselves provides for other terms.
15.3 A citizen may use his property as a form of company share or contribution to the associations, cooperatives, collective and other enterprises, other unions of citizens and legal persons, necessary for his entrepreneurial activity.

Article 16. The right of disposal and exploitation of land plots
16.1 In order to encourage agricultural production, promote construction of dwelling premises, and develop kitchen gardening, a citizen may be granted a right of exploitation and inheritance on land plots.
16.2 Products and income of these land plots are property of the citizen and can be disposed of as he wishes.

Article 17 The citizen's property right
17.1 A citizen owning private property, may dispose of the property as he or she wishes.

DIVISION III COLLECTIVE PROPERTY

Article 18. Common regulations on collective property
18.1 Collective property consists of property of leased enterprises, collective enterprises, cooperatives, collective farms, joint-stock companies, profit societies and associations, public and religious organizations, ownership of the mahalla (neighborhood) and other associations possessing a legal identity.
18.2 The creation and increase of the amount and value of collective property is ensured by the leasing of state enterprises, by providing working collectives the possibility of using earned income for purchase of state property, by the transformation of state enterprises into joint companies, and by voluntary unification of the property of citizens and legal persons for the creation of cooperatives, joint-stock companies, and other productive societies and associations.
18.3 The list of enterprises and production facilities which may not be transferred into collective ownership is defined by the law of the Republic of Tajikistan.
Article 19 Property of a collective enterprise
19.1 Property of a collective enterprise is created by transferring all the property of state enterprises to the ownership of a working collective, by purchase of leased property, or by other legal means of property acquisition.

19.2 The collective enterprise's property, including the output and income earned from the property is for the common benefit of the collective.
19.3 The property share of the workers of a collective enterprise should be defined. This share includes the sum of each worker's contribution to the state or leased property on which the collective enterprise has been created as well as each worker's contribution to increase the amount and value of property in question after creation of the enterprise.
19.4 The measuring of a worker's contribution to increasing the amount and value of the property is defined according to his participation in the enterprise's activities. Workers contributions to the collective enterprise are mandatory and paid according to a percentage reflecting the results of the economic activities of the enterprise and rules defined by the working collective. A worker who is no longer employed by an enterprise or an inheritor of a dead worker must be paid the value of the worker's contribution.
19.5 In case of liquidation of the collective enterprise, the value of each worker's contribution is paid to the worker or his inheritor from the remaining properties after settling due payments to the state budget, banks and other creditors of the enterprise.
Article 20. Property of a leased enterprises
20.1 Leasing property does not give ownership right on the property. The output and income from the activities on the leased property belongs to the lessee. Material values excluded from the leased property and legally acquired by a lessee, belong to the lessee.
20.2 The terms of participation of the members of the working collective of the leased enterprise in the management of its activities and distribution of its income is regulated by the law of the Republic of Tajikistan on "Leasing in the Republic of Tajikistan".
Article 21. Property of a cooperative
21.1 The property of a cooperative is formed by money and property contributions of its members, the output of the cooperative, its income, sale proceeds and activities provided for in the charter of the cooperative and by the law of the Republic of Tajikistan.
21.2 In case of liquidation of a cooperative, remaining property, after settling due payments to the State Budget, banks and other creditors, is distributed among the members of the cooperative.
Article 22. Property of companies and the property of businesses
22.1 Property of companies and the property of businesses which is constituted into a legal identity, is formed by participant's contributions and property acquired as a result of economic activity and other legal means.
22.2 Share contributions of participants into business or public funds may include ordinary circulating funds, capital, securities and the right of enjoyment of property.
22.3 Participants in a business or company may be enterprises, institutions, organizations, the Government and citizens unless their participation is prohibited by the laws of the Republic of Tajikistan.
Article 23. Property of joint-stock companies
23.1 A joint-stock company owns property created by the sale of shares related to its economic activities, and other legal means.
23.2 Legal and physical persons may be shareholders unless otherwise prescribed by Law or the company's charter.
23.3 Upon joint decision of the working collective and the state authority, a state enterprise may be reorganized into a joint-stock company by distributing shares reflecting the value of the enterprise. Revenue obtained from the sale of shares, after settling the debts of the state enterprise, is deposited in the company's new budget.
Article 24. Property of business associations

24.1 A business association of enterprises or organizations has the right to own property that has been acquired as a result of its economic activities.
24.2 A business association does not have the right to own the property of its constituent enterprises and organizations.
24.3 Property remaining after the disbanding of a business association is distributed among its constituent enterprises and organizations.
Article 25. Property of public associations and funds
25.1 Public associations and funds, including charities, may own buildings construction, housing funds, the means of production, equipment, stock, property for cultural, educational and health purposes, money, shares, and other securities and properties, required for their activities which are defined by their own charter. Enterprises serving economic, industrial or social purposes, created by investments of public funds or associations according to the charter of the enterprise, may be property of public funds or associations.
25.2 Property of public associations or public funds is formed by initial contributions, should this be required by their charter, by voluntary contributions, income earned from lotteries and other activities, by income from production, income from publications and other legal activities. Legislation of the Republic of Tajikistan may determine types of property that may not be owned by public associations.
25.3 In cases where a member of a public association leaves the association, he does not have the right to have his contributions, whether in payments or property, be returned to him unless provided for otherwise by the law of the Republic of Tajikistan.-
25.4 Property remaining after liquidation of a public association after settling due payments to the State Budget, banks and other creditors is invested according to the charter of the association.
Article 26. Property of the mahalla (neighborhood)
26.1 A mahalla may own buildings; construction; equipment; warehouses; plantations;-property serving cultural, educational and public health purposes; money; and other property necessary for the well-being of the mahalla provided the property does not belong to other public associations.
26.2 The property of the mahalla is formed by the voluntary payments and contributions of it's inhabitants as long as the donations are legal.
Article 27. Property of religious organizations
27.1 The following may be owned by religious organizations: buildings, objects of worship serving industrial, social and charitable purposes, money and other property that is necessary for the functioning of religious organizations.
27.2 Religious organizations have the right to own to property acquired or created by contributions of its members- or ac-quired by- other means fixed by law.
27.3 Problems related to the use of a religious organization's property after quitting its religious activities, are solved by the administrative staff of the association or the higher authority of the religious organization in coordination with State Religious Authorities.
27.4 After ending its religious activities, property of a religious organization that had been granted to it by state organizations, public associations and/or citizens must be returned to its former owner.
27.5 Forfeit on a religious organization may be exacted in cash or from its property. Forfeit or demands of creditors may however not be exacted from property related to objects of worship.
STATE PROPERTY
Article 28. Common regulations on state property

28.1 The State of Republic of Tajikistan enjoys exclusive ownership rights on its property, and can dispose of it according to its discretion.
28.2 State property in the Republic of Tajikistan includes: property of the Republic of Tajikistan (Republican Property), property of the Autonomous Mountainous Region of Badakhshan, and property of Local Assemblies of People's Representatives (Communal Property).
28.3 Disposal and administration of state property are carried out by:
a) A Representative for the administration of state property, appointed by a State Authority in the name of the State to deal with Republic Property.
b) A Representative appointed by a Local Assembly to deal with Communal Property.
28.4 Property created or acquired at the expense of public funds from the State Budget or other means of the Republic of Tajikistan, the Autonomous Mountainous Region of Badakhshan, Local Assemblies of People's Representatives, or State owned enterprises, organizations, and institutions, belongs to either the Republic of Tajikistan, the Autonomous Mountainous Region of Badakhshan or Local Assemblies of People's Representatives.
28.5 The Republic of Tajikistan, the Autonomous Mountainous Region of Badakhshan, Local Assemblies of People's Representatives, Town and Village Authorities and other entities entitled to the right of ownership, are not responsible for mutual obligations arising from the exploitation and disposal of their property, except for cases stipulated by the law of the Republic of Tajikistan.
Article 29. Property of the Republic of Tajikistan
29.1 The Republic of Tajikistan owns the land within its borders, its resources, water, air, flora, fauna, and other natural resources, the State Budget, the banks of the Republic, including currency reserves and state property granted to joint stock companies, enterprises and compounds serving the needs of the national economy, insurance and welfare funds, state schools of higher education, property of State Administrative Authorities, cultural and historical heritage of the Republic of Tajikistan, objects of social and -cultural value, and other property acquired by the Republic of Tajikistan or gifted to it by foreign countries, legal entities or citizens including persons without citizenship in order to ensure- the sovereignty and economic independence and development of the Republic of Tajikistan.
Article 30. Property of the Autonomous Mountainous Region of Badakhshan
30.1 The Autonomous Mountainous Region of Badakhshan owns the property of its Local Assemblies of People's Representatives (entities of Republican Property and Communal Property), the Regional State Budget, other state funds, state engineering infrastructure, and other entities, enterprises, association, institutes of public education, public health and welfare insurance, cultural and scientific organizations, acquired through the Regional State Budget or other means of the Autonomous Mountainous Region of Badakhshan including contributions or other sources like securities and financial assets gifted to Local Assemblies of People's Representatives.
Article 31 Property of Local Assemblies of People's Representatives
31.1 Regions, towns and districts own Local State Budgets, housing funds, the Municipal Housing Fund of Local Assemblies of People's Representatives, industrial enterprises specialized in the production of raw materials for the benefit of the region, town or district, constructions-, trans-portation vehicles, commercial goods, agricultural enterprises, daily services, educational institutes, public health and cultural institutes and other necessary property for the social and economic development of regions, towns or districts, including securities and financial assets.

Article 32. Property of Local Self-Managed State Authorities
32.1 Objects serving public and social purposes including objects constructed or purchased by Local Self-Managed State Authorities or objects legally granted to them; transportation vehicles, commercial goods, including money and other material means allotted by Municipal and District Assemblies of People's Representatives to Local Self-Managed State Authorities, voluntary donations of citizens and working collectives, and contributions from charitable funds and other legal sources are all property of Local Self-Managed State Authorities.
Article 33. Property of state enterprises
33.1 State property granted for the use of a state institution operating on the account of the State Budget is directly controlled by the institution. State enterprises have the right to fully dispose and enjoy property owned by the state and granted for use to state enterprises.
33.2 A state enterprise enjoys full property rights while implementing its right of disposal and enjoyment on state property granted to it within the limits of the law of the Republic of Tajikistan and the enterprise's objectives. Regulations concerning ownership rights and related to the right of full property disposal are applied only if legislation of the Republic of Tajikistan has not provided for any other terms.
33.3 State Authorities having the right to manage state property, may decide matters related to the creation of state enterprises, the definition of its aims, and the reorganization or liquidation of state enterprises, they may also control the effective use and preservation of state property entrusted to state enterprises and accomplish obligations stipulated by the law of the Republic of Tajikistan.
33.3 In case a state authority entrusted with the administration of state property decides to reorganize or liquidate a state enterprise for reasons excluding bankruptcy, the working collective may legally request to lease the enterprise or have the enterprise be reorganized on a basis of collective ownership. Disputes between the State and the employees of a state enterprise are arbitrated in court.

Article 34. Property of state institutions
34.1 State property granted for use to a state institution operating on the account of the State Budget is under the direct control of the state institution.
34.2 State institutions functioning at the expense of the State Budget, and being able to legally undertake entrepreneurial activities, obtain the right to freely dispose of incomes related to these activities and the property acquired at the expense of the latter income.
34.3 State institutions must meet their pecuniary obligations. In case such obligations can not fully be met by the state institution, they should be met by the owner of the property of the state institution.

DIVISION V PROPERTY OF JOINT VENTURES, FOREIGN STATES, ORGANIZATIONS AND CITIZENS

Article 35. Property of joint ventures
35.1 Joint ventures with the participation of legal persons of the Republic of Tajikistan and foreign legal persons and citizens created within the Republic of Tajikistan or abroad in the form of joint-stock companies and associations, and other legal forms, may own any property necessary for the activities listed in the company's charter.

Article 36. Property of foreign states and international organizations

36.1 Foreign states and international organizations have the right to own property necessary for diplomatic, consular, social, cultural and other activities within the Republic of Tajikistan according to the terms of international legal treaties approved by the Republic of Tajikistan.

Article 37. Property of foreign legal entities
37.1 Foreign legal entities may own industrial enterprises and other companies, buildings, constructions, and other property necessary for their economic activities in accordance with the legislation of the Republic of Tajikistan.

Article 38 Property of foreign citizens and persons without citizenship
38.1 Regulations of this law valid for Tajik citizens except for cases stipulated by the law of the Republic of Tajikistan, may also be applied for foreign citizens and persons without citizenship.

DIVISION VI GUARANTEES AND PROTECTION OF PROPERTY RIGHTS

Article 39. Guarantees of property rights
39.1 The Republic of Tajikistan guarantees the order of ownership relations fixed by this law.
39.2 Nobody has the right to confiscate the owner's property, except for cases defined by the law of the Republic of Tajikistan.
39.3 Nobody has the right to deprive or limit any citizen of his property rights.
39.4 The State fosters conditions for the free development of different forms of property and the increase of their value and ensures their protection equally.
39.5 In case the Republic of Tajikistan approves legislation depriving owners of their rights, resulting damages are compensate for by the State upon approval of a court.

Article 40. Protection of property rights
40.1 The Republic of Tajikistan ensures equal protection of property rights for all owners. Nobody has the right to deprive or limit the rights of an owner.
40.2 In accordance with the Civil Code of the Republic of Tajikistan, an owner has the right to demand his property from a person illegally exploiting it.
40.3 An owner has the right to demand the settling of all kinds of feuds involving the breaching of his rights even if these violations are not connected with the deprivation of his property rights.
40.4 Property rights are protected by State Courts.
40.5 Rights provided for by this article also apply for persons who are not owners but have been granted full disposal rights, the right of disposal for a lifetime, or other disposal rights provided for by law or contract. Such persons have the right to defend their property rights even from the actual owner.

Article 41. Protection of an owner's interests upon legal expiry of his rights
41.1 The right of ownership may terminate upon decision to expropriate a plot of land where a house, building, construction, or plantations belonging to the owner is situated; or upon approval of the decision of another State Authority that is not directly in charge with the expropriation of the owner's property. Such an expropriation may only take place under circumstances determined by the law of the Republic of Tajikistan and in cases where resulting damages are fully compensated for.

41.2 When an owner disagrees, the resolution to expropriate his or her property may not be implemented until the issue is not settled by a State Court or the High Economic Court. During the settling of this dispute, the matter of paying compensation for damages to the owner has to be solved.

Article 42. Invalidation of acts which infract on the right of ownership
42.1 In case the Government or a Local State Authority approves an Act which contradicts the law and the rights of an owner and other persons having full right of disposal of the property, the Act should be challenged as invalid on request of the owner or the person who's rights have been violated.
42.3 Resulting damages are compensated to concerned citizens, organizations, and other persons at the expense of the corresponding Local State Authority.
42.4 Material and moral damages caused to a person as a result of the illegal action of a State Authority are compensated for at the State Authority's expense according to the law.

The President of
The Republic of Tajikistan, Mr. I. Rahmonov
Dushanbe, December 14, 1996

LAW ON CONCESSIONS

THE PRESENT LAW DEFINES THE MAIN PRINCIPLES OF AN CONCESSION ACTIVITY ON THE TERRITORY OF THE REPUBLIC OF TAJIKISTAN AND DETERMINES LEGAL, ECONOMIC, AND OTHER PROPERTY RELATIONS CONNECTED WITH THIS ACTIVITY.

I. COMMON REGULATIONS

ARTICLE 1. CONCEPTS OF TERMS USED IN THIS LAW
CONCESSION (YIELDING) - AN AGREEMENT ON PASSING TO A FOREIGN INVESTOR FOR TEMPORARY EXPLOITATION ON CERTAIN CONDITIONS OF ENTERPRISES (ASSOCIATIONS) BELONGING TO STATE, LAND WITH THE RIGHT TO EXTRACT MINERALS, CONSTRUCTION SITES, WATER RESOURCES, WATER AND AIR SPACE, FLORA AND FAUNA, AND OTHER NATURAL RESOURCES NOT PROHIBITED BY LEGISLATION OF THE REPUBLIC OF TAJIKISTAN.

CONCESSION AGREEMENT - AN AGREEMENT ON PASSING BY AN AUTHORIZED STATE BODY OR A LOCAL STATE BODY WITHIN THEIR COMMISSION TO A FOREIGN INVESTOR FOR A TEMPORARY USE OF LAND, OTHER NATURAL RESOURCES, ENTERPRISES (ASSOCIATIONS), AND OTHER STATE PROPERTY, NOT PROHIBITED BY LEGISLATION OF THE REPUBLIC OF TAJIKISTAN.
FOREIGN INVESTOR - A LEGAL ENTITY OR AN INDIVIDUAL PERFORMING LONG-TERM INVESTMENT INTO ECONOMY OF ANOTHER COUNTRY.
CONCESSIONAIRE - A FOREIGN INVESTOR WITH WHOM A CONCESSION AGREEMENT IS CONCLUDED.

OBJECTS OF CONCESSION - TYPES OF ECONOMIC ACTIVITIES CONNECTED WITH TEMPORARY YIELDING TO A FOREIGN INVESTOR OF PROPERTY, LAND, AND OTHER NATURAL RESOURCES ALLOWED BY LEGISLATION OF THE REPUBLIC OF TAJIKISTAN.

SUBJECTS OF CONCESSION - SIDES PARTICIPATING IN CONCESSION RELATIONS.

CONCESSION BODIES ARE BODIES AUTHORIZED BY THE GOVERNMENT OF THE REPUBLIC OF TAJIKISTAN OR LOCAL GOVERNMENT BODIES WHICH ARE AUTHORIZED TO BE ENGAGED IN THE ESTABLISHED ORDER IN THE CONCESSIONS ISSUES.

ARTICLE 2. LEGAL REGULATING OF CONCESSION ACTIVITY

LEGAL RELATIONS IN THE PROCESS OF THE CONCESSION ACTIVITY ARE REGULATED BY THIS LAW AND OTHER LEGISLATIVE ACTS OF THE REPUBLIC OF TAJIKISTAN.

ARTICLE 3. BASIS OF CONCESSION ACTIVITY

THE CONCESSION ACTIVITY IN THE REPUBLIC OF TAJIKISTAN IS IMPLEMENTED ON THE BASIS OF:

- MUTUAL BENEFIT;
- CHOOSING A CONCESSIONAIRE IS TO BE COMPETITIVE AND THROUGH AUCTIONS;
- NON-INTERFERENCE INTO THE CONCESSIONAIRE'S ECONOMIC ACTIVITY PERFORMED IN ACCORDANCE WITH LEGISLATION OF THE REPUBLIC OF TAJIKISTAN;
- OBSERVING LEGISLATION OF THE REPUBLIC OF TAJIKISTAN ON PROTECTION OF LAND AND MINERAL WEALTH, LABOR SAFETY, NATURE AND WATER RESOURCES USE, ENVIRONMENTAL PROTECTION, ECOLOGICAL AND SANITARY-HYGIENIC SAFETY, SOCIAL INSURANCE AND PROVISION;
- MANUFACTURING PRODUCTS WHICH ARE ECOLOGICALLY SAFE AND WHICH MEET STANDARDS AND NORMATIVE DOCUMENTS OF THE REPUBLIC OF TAJIKISTAN, IF OTHERWISE NOT STIPULATED BY INTERNATIONAL AGREEMENTS OR AGREEMENTS WITH PARTICIPATION OF THE REPUBLIC OF TAJIKISTAN.

ARTICLE 4. PROPERTY RELATIONS IN CONCESSION ACTIVITY

PASSING OBJECTS IN CONCESSION DOES NOT MEAN TRANSFER OF THE RIGHT FOR THESE OBJECTS TO THE CONCESSIONAIRE OR GRANTING HIM THE UNLIMITED RIGHT TO PERFORM SOME SPECIFIC RIGHTS OF STATE. PRODUCTS AND PROFITS, OBTAINED BY THE CONCESSIONAIRE IN THE RESULT OF THE CONCESSION ACTIVITY, ARE HIS PROPERTY IN THE LIMITS STIPULATED BY THE CONCESSION AGREEMENT.

THE REPUBLIC OF TAJIKISTAN HAS A PRIMARY RIGHT FOR PURCHASE OF PRODUCTS FROM THE CONCESSIONAIRE.

COMPETENCE OF STATE BODIES IN REGULATING CONCESSION RELATIONS

ARTICLE 5. STATE REGULATING OF CONCESSION RELATIONS
THE STATE REGULATING OF CONCESSION RELATIONS IS IMPLEMENTED BY THE GOVERNMENT OF THE REPUBLIC OF TAJIKISTAN OR BY AN AUTHORIZED STATE MANAGEMENT BODY, AND ALSO BY LOCAL STATE MANAGEMENT BODIES.

ARTICLE 6. COMPETENCE OF GOVERNMENT OF TAJIKISTAN
THE GOVERNMENT OF THE REPUBLIC OF TAJIKISTAN IS ENTITLED:

- TO DEVELOP THE PROGRAM OF PRIORITIES IN THE CONCESSION ACTIVITY;
- TO ESTABLISH THE STATE EXPERTISE PROCEDURE OF CONCESSION PROJECTS AND PROGRAMS;
- TO ESTABLISH THE REGISTRATION PROCEDURE OF CONCESSION AGREEMENTS AND TO CONTROL THEIR OBSERVANCE;
- TO PROVIDE THE LIST OF OBJECTS WHICH ARE NOT SUBJECT TO CONCESSION OR LIMITED TRANSFER;
- TO CONCLUDE CONCESSION AGREEMENTS FOR USING MINERAL RESOURCES;
- TO SETTLE OTHER ISSUES RELATED TO CONCESSION RELATIONS IN ACCORDING WITH LEGISLATION.

ARTICLE 7. COMPETENCE OF AUTHORIZED STATE MANAGEMENT BODY
THE AUTHORIZED STATE MANAGEMENT BODY IS ENTITLED:
- TO CONDUCT CONTESTS AND AUCTIONS;
- TO CONCLUDE CONCESSION AGREEMENTS WITHIN GRANTED AUTHORITIES;
- TO CONTROL CONDITIONS' OBSERVANCE OF CONCESSION AGREEMENTS;
- TO SETTLE OTHER ISSUES IN ACCORDANCE WITH LEGISLATION OF THE REPUBLIC OF TAJIKISTAN.

ARTICLE 8. COMPETENCE OF LOCAL STATE BODIES
LOCAL STATE BODIES ARE ENTITLED:
- TO CHARACTERIZE OBJECTS CONTROLLED BY LOCAL STATE BODIES WHICH MAY BE CONCLUDED IN CONCESSION AGREEMENTS;
- TO CONDUCT CONTESTS AND AUCTIONS ON OBJECTS BELONGING TO THEM;
- TO CONCLUDE CONCESSION AGREEMENTS WITHIN THEIR AUTHORITY AND TO CONFORM CONDITIONS OF OTHER CONCESSION AGREEMENTS ON OBJECTS LOCATED ON THEIR TERRITORY;
- TO SETTLE OTHER ISSUES IN ACCORDANCE WITH LEGISLATION OF THE REPUBLIC OF TAJIKISTAN.

III. PROCEDURE AND CONDITIONS FOR GRANTING CONCESSIONS

ARTICLE 9. PREPARATION OF CONCESSION OFFERS

PREPARATION OF CONCESSION OFFERS IS IMPLEMENTED BY CONCESSION BODIES TAKING INTO CONSIDERATION THEIR PRIORITY AND ECONOMIC EXPEDIENCY FOR THE REPUBLIC OF TAJIKISTAN AND IT INCLUDES DEFINING THE TYPE OF ACTIVITY AND THE LIST OF PROPERTY PASSED IN CONCESSION.

ARTICLE 10. PROCEDURE OF GRANTING CONCESSIONS

GRANTING CONCESSIONS IS IMPLEMENTED THROUGH TENDERS. IN EXCEPTIONAL CASES, IN ACCORDANCE WITH DISCRETION OF THE GOVERNMENT OF THE REPUBLIC OF TAJIKISTAN, GRANTING CONCESSIONS IS PERFORMED THROUGH DIRECT NEGOTIATIONS BETWEEN CONCESSION BODIES AND POTENTIAL INVESTORS.

CHOOSING THE WAY OF GRANTING CONCESSIONS THROUGH CONTESTS OR AUCTIONS IS MADE BY THE CONCESSION BODY.

PROCEDURES AND CONDITIONS FOR CONDUCTING CONTESTS AND AUCTIONS ARE DETERMINED BY THE GOVERNMENT OF THE REPUBLIC OF TAJIKISTAN.

BIDS FOR PARTICIPATING IN CONTESTS AND AUCTIONS ARE FORWARDED BY POTENTIAL CONCESSIONAIRES TO THE CONCESSION BODY.
THE BID SHOULD INCLUDE:

A) DATA OF THE CONCESSIONAIRE, INCLUDING HIS MAIN JOB AND HIS RELATIONS WITH FINANCIAL AND BUSINESS PARTNERS;
B) DATA OF FINANCIAL POSITION OF THE CONCESSIONAIRE WHICH DEMONSTRATE HIS ABILITY TO FULFILL PLANNED WORKS;
C) DATA OF TECHNICAL AND TECHNOLOGY POTENTIAL OF THE CONCESSIONAIRE AND OTHER COMPANIES ACTING AS CONTRACTORS;
D) INFORMATION ON FORTHCOMING PROJECTS OF THE BIDDER-CONCESSIONAIRE, INCLUDING THE LIST OF COUNTRIES OF HIS BUSINESS IN THE LAST FIVE YEARS;
E) THE BIDDER'S PLANS ON USING CONCESSIONS, INCLUDING THE WORK PLAN AND ESTIMATE OF EXPENSES;
F) THE PERIOD OF CONCESSION;
THE CONCESSION BID FOR EXTRACTING MINERAL RESOURCES SHOULD ALSO INCLUDE:
G) CONCESSION DATA ON PROSPECTING AND THE CONCESSION RESULTS IF ANY;
H) THE PLANNED CAPACITY AND STARTING DATE OF EXTRACTING MINERAL RESOURCES;

INFORMATION ON CONCESSION CONTESTS AND AUCTIONS IS PUBLISHED IN MASS MEDIA IN FIXED PERIODS WITH INDICATION OF THEIR TERMS, PLACE, AND DEADLINE.
T
HE CONTEST OR AUCTION BID MAY BE REFUSED IN THE FOLLOWING CASES:
- THE BID HAS BEEN SUBMITTED BEYOND FIXED PERIODS;

- THE BIDDER HAS SUBMITTED FALSE INFORMATION ON HIS FINANCIAL AND TECHNICAL CAPABILITY.

ARTICLE 11. CONCLUDING CONCESSION AGREEMENT AND ITS CONTENT
THE CONCESSION AGREEMENT IS CONCLUDED BETWEEN THE FOREIGN INVESTOR AND THE GOVERNMENT OF THE REPUBLIC OF TAJIKISTAN OR BY APPROPRIATE CONCESSION BODY. THE AGREEMENT BECOMES EFFECTIVE FROM MOMENT OF ITS REGISTRATION.
THE CONCESSION AGREEMENT SHOULD INCLUDE:
- SUBJECT OF THE AGREEMENT, NAMES AND COST OF PROPERTY PASSED IN CONCESSION;
- SPACE BORDERS OF LAND, MINERAL WEALTH, WATER, AND AIR;
- TERMS OF THE CONCESSION AGREEMENT AND THE STARTING DATE OF WORKS;
- RIGHTS AND RESPONSIBILITIES OF SIDES;
- AMOUNTS, PROCEDURES, AND TERMS OF TAX AND OTHER PAYMENTS ACCORDING TO LEGISLATION OF THE REPUBLIC OF TAJIKISTAN;
- PRODUCTION SHARES AND NET PROFITS OF THE CONCESSIONAIRE AND THE CONCESSION BODY;
- FIXED AMOUNTS AND TERMS OF YEARLY INVESTMENT AND THE PRODUCTION VOLUME STIPULATED IN THE BUSINESS PLAN;
- REQUIREMENTS ON ENVIRONMENTAL PROTECTION, PROTECTION OF MINERAL RESOURCES, AND WORKS SAFETY;
- RESUME OF STATE ECOLOGICAL EXPERTISE;
- RIGHT OF SIDES FOR INFORMATION RECEIVED IN THE PROCESS OF THE CONCESSION ACTIVITY;
- CONDITIONS OF HIRING, TRAINING, INSURING, AND SOCIAL PROTECTION OF EMPLOYEES NOT CONTRADICTING TO LEGISLATION OF THE REPUBLIC OF TAJIKISTAN;
- PROCEDURES, CONDITIONS, AND TERMS OF BY-STEP RETURN OF THE AGREEMENT SUBJECT, LAND, AND MINERAL WEALTH FOR THEIR REHABILITATION OR RE-CULTIVATION;
- LEGAL, ECONOMIC, AND ORGANIZATIONAL CONSEQUENCES UNDER FORCE MAJEURE;
- PROCEDURES FOR SETTLING DISPUTES AND RESPONSIBILITIES OF SIDES WHEN BREACHING AGREEMENT CONDITIONS;
- FINANCIAL GUARANTEES OF SIDES, JURIDICAL ADDRESSES, AND BANKS' DATA;
- AMENDMENTS AND CANCELLATION CONDITIONS OF THE CONCESSION AGREEMENT.
THE CONCESSION AGREEMENT MAY INCLUDE OTHER CONDITIONS WHICH DO NOT CONTRADICT TO THE CURRENT LEGISLATION OF THE REPUBLIC OF TAJIKISTAN.

ARTICLE 12. CONCESSIONAIRE'S PAYMENTS
THE CONCESSIONAIRE IS COMMISSIONED TO PAY:
- FEE FOR STATE REGISTRATION OF THE CONCESSION AGREEMENT;
- FEE FOR CONCESSION IN THE ORDER ESTABLISHED BY THE AGREEMENT;

- TAXES AND OTHER PAYMENTS STIPULATED BY LEGISLATION OF THE REPUBLIC OF TAJIKISTAN.

ARTICLE 13. PERIOD OF CONCESSION PERIOD
THE CONCESSION AGREEMENT MAY BE CONCLUDED FOR A PERIOD NOR EXCEEDING 50 YEARS, DEPENDING ON TECHNICAL-ECONOMIC CHARACTERISTICS OF CONCESSION OBJECTS. EXCEPTIONAL ARE DEPOSITS OF MINERAL RESOURCES DEMANDING MAJOR INVESTMENT AND KNOWN FOR A LONG-TERM REPAY PERIOD. DURATION OF THE CONCESSION AGREEMENT MAY LAST AS LONG AS IT IS NECESSARY TO FULLY EXPLOIT THE DEPOSIT BUT NOT LONGER THAN 99 YEARS:

- WHEN THE CONCESSION AGREEMENT EXPIRES, THE CONCESSIONAIRE WHO HAS CONSCIENTIOUSLY FULFILLED THE AGREEMENT CONDITIONS, HAS A PRINCIPAL RIGHT TO PROLONG A SHORT AND MEDIUM-TERM AGREEMENT.

ARTICLE 14. AMENDING AND CANCELING CONCESSION AGREEMENTS
CONDITIONS OF CONCESSION AGREEMENTS MAY BE AMENDED IN THE ORDER STIPULATED BY THE AGREEMENT OR BY SIDES' CONSENT.

IF ONE OF THE SIDES BREAKS THE AGREEMENT CONDITIONS, THE CONCESSION AGREEMENT MAY BE CANCELED AT MUTUAL CONSENT OF SIDES, BY COURT'S DECISION, OR BY THE CONCESSION BODY IF THE CONCESSIONAIRE HAS PROVIDED FALSE INFORMATION WHEN CONCLUDING THE CONTRACT.

THE CONCESSION AGREEMENT IS CANCELED FROM THE MOMENT OF ITS EXCLUDING FROM THE STATE REGISTER.

ARTICLE 15. TRANSFER OF RIGHTS AND RESPONSIBILITIES ON CONCESSION AGREEMENTS
IN CASE OF REORGANIZATION OF ONE OF THE SIDES OF THE CONCESSION AGREEMENT, HIS RIGHTS AND RESPONSIBILITIES GO TO THEIR LEGAL LEGATEES, IF OTHERWISE NOT STIPULATED BY LEGISLATION OF THE REPUBLIC OF TAJIKISTAN.
FULL OR PARTIAL YIELDING OF THE CONCESSIONAIRE'S RIGHTS ON THE CONCESSION OBJECT TO THIRD PERSONS IS NOT ALLOWED.

ARTICLE 16. INSURANCE

THE CONCESSIONAIRE INDEPENDENTLY INSURES RISKS OF CONCESSION AGREEMENTS, THE CONCESSION ACTIVITY, AND EMPLOYEES.

IV. CONCESSIONAIRE'S RIGHTS AND RESPONSIBILITIES

ARTICLE 17. CONCESSIONAIRE'S RIGHTS
THE CONCESSIONAIRE IS ENTITLED:
- IN ACCORDANCE WITH LEGISLATION OF THE REPUBLIC OF TAJIKISTAN AND THE CONCESSION AGREEMENT, TO USE THE AGREEMENT SUBJECT, TO BUILD

ON USED TERRITORY
PREMISES, ACCESS ROADS, HIGHWAYS, AND COMMUNICATIONS INFRASTRUCTURE;
- IN ACCORDANCE WITH THE CONCESSION BODY AND, IF THE POSITIVE ECOLOGICAL EXPERTISE IS AVAILABLE, TO AMEND THE PROPERTY STOCK, TO RENOVATE, TO EXPAND, AND TO TECHNICALLY MODERNIZE IT RESULTING IN PROPERTY COST INCREASE;
- TO BRING IN HIS OWN PROPERTY AND NECESSARY MATERIALS FOR OWN PRODUCTION NEEDS AND PERSONAL NEEDS OF EMPLOYEES;
- TO BRING OUT HIS PROPERTY AND PRODUCED PRODUCTS;
- TO APPEAL IN COURT ILLEGAL ACTIONS OF STATE BODIES, THEIR OFFICIALS, COOPERATIVE, PUBLIC ORGANIZATIONS, AND INDIVIDUALS OF THE REPUBLIC OF TAJIKISTAN.

ARTICLE 18. CONCESSIONAIRE'S RESPONSIBILITIES
THE CONCESSIONAIRE IS RESPONSIBLE:
- TO OBSERVE THE CONCESSION AGREEMENT CONDITIONS;
- TO PERFORM AN ECONOMIC ACTIVITY IN STRICT ACCORDANCE WITH LEGISLATION OF THE REPUBLIC OF TAJIKISTAN AND THE CONCESSION AGREEMENT;
- TO KEEP RECORDS IN THE ORDER ESTABLISHED BY LEGISLATION OF THE REPUBLIC OF TAJIKISTAN;
- TO RETURN TO CONCESSION BODIES THE PROPERTY AND OBJECTS PASSED TO HIM IN ACCORDANCE WITH THE AGREEMENT, AND ALSO TO TAKE CARE OF HIS OWN PROPERTY IN A TWO-MONTH PERIOD FROM THE DAY OF THE CONCESSION AGREEMENT'S EXPIRATION OR CANCELLATION;
- TO FULFILL OTHER RESPONSIBILITIES STIPULATED BY LEGISLATION OF THE REPUBLIC OF TAJIKISTAN.

ARTICLE 19. CONCESSIONAIRE'S PROFITS
THE CONCESSIONAIRE'S PROFITS LEFT AFTER PAYMENT OF TAXES AND OTHER FEES, REMAINS AT HIS FULL DISPOSAL.

V. FINAL REGULATIONS

ARTICLE 20. PROCEDURE FOR CONSIDERING DISPUTES
DISPUTES BETWEEN THE CONCESSIONAIRE AND CONCESSIONAIRE BODY ARE SUBJECT TO CONSIDERATION IN ECONOMIC COURTS OF THE REPUBLIC OF TAJIKISTAN, IF OTHERWISE NOT STIPULATED BY INTERNATIONAL AGREEMENTS AND TREATIES OF THE REPUBLIC OF TAJIKISTAN.
DISPUTES OF CONCESSIONAIRES WITH STATE ENTERPRISES, PUBLIC ASSOCIATIONS, OTHER LEGAL ENTITIES, AND INDIVIDUALS OF THE REPUBLIC OF TAJIKISTAN, AS WELL AS DISPUTES AMONG CONCESSIONAIRES ON ISSUES CONNECTED WITH THEIR ACTIVITY, ARE SUBJECT TO CONSIDERATION IN COURTS OF THE REPUBLIC OF TAJIKISTAN AND, IF AGREED WITH SIDES, IN ECONOMIC COURT OR ARBITRATION ABROAD.

ARTICLE 21. RESPONSIBILITIES OF CONCESSION RELATIONS SUBJECTS

THE SIDES WHICH HAVE CONCLUDED THE CONCESSION AGREEMENT ARE RESPONSIBLE FOR ITS NON-FULFILLMENT OR IMPROPER FULFILLMENT IN THE ORDER ESTABLISHED BY LEGISLATION OF THE REPUBLIC OF TAJIKISTAN.

NOTE: THIS LAW IS THE MAIN DOCUMENT FOR U.S. MINING COMPANIES WHICH WOULD LIKE TO ENTER TAJIKISTAN'S MINERAL WEALTH MARKET. MINING, EQUALLY WITH HYDRO POWER ENERGY AND COTTON GINNING ARE PRIORITY SECTORS IN THE COUNTRY'S ECONOMIC REFORM PROGRAM TILL 2000. TAJIKISTAN HAS CONSIDERABLE MINERAL RESERVES WITH MORE THAT 400 OF DIFFERENT DEPOSITS, INCLUDING THOSE OF PRECIOUS AND NON-PRECIOUS METALS. HOWEVER, DUE TO THE WEAK COUNTRY'S CAPACITY TO DEVELOP THESE DEPOSITS, THE MINING SEGMENT IN TAJIKISTAN'S TOTAL INDUSTRIAL OUTPUT IS LOW (LESS THAN FIVE PERCENT.)

THE FLOW OF FOREIGN INVESTMENT TO THE MINING INDUSTRY STARTED AFTER 1992. IT IS KNOWN THAT DEPOSITS' DEVELOPMENT REQUIRES THE CONCESSION OF A CERTAIN TERRITORY FOR A LONG PERIOD OF TIME WITH THE RIGHT TO EXTRACT MINERALS. HOWEVER, THE PAST LEGISLATION AND LEGAL LEXICON IN THE COUNTRY DID NOT PROVIDE EVEN THE CONCEPT CHARACTERIZING THESE LEGAL RELATIONS. THE CONCEPT OF "CONCESSION" IN THE LOCAL LEGISLATURE DID NOT EXIST AND THE PUBLIC'S ATTITUDE TO IT WAS RELATIVELY NEGATIVE. IN ORDER TO REMOVE THE LEGAL SHORTAGES AFFECTING THE FLOW OF FOREIGN INVESTMENT TO MINING AS WELL AS OTHER INDUSTRIES AND GIVE MORE GUARANTEES TO INVESTORS, THE PARLIAMENT OF TAJIKISTAN (MAJLISI OLI) AT ITS MAY SESSION IN 1997 ADOPTED THIS LAW ON CONCESSIONS.

ACCORDING TO THE LAW, CONCESSION IS AN AGREEMENT PROVIDING FOREIGN INVESTORS WITH A PASS FOR A TEMPORARY EXPLOITATION OF LAND, WATER, AND AIR SPACE WITH THE RIGHT TO EXTRACT MINERALS, EXPLOIT FLORA AND FAUNA, AND OTHER NATURAL RESOURCES NOT PROHIBITED BY THE LEGISLATION OF TAJIKISTAN. THE TERM OF CONCESSION AGREEMENT IS 50 YEARS. IN CASE OF LONG COMPENSATED DEPOSITS REQUIRING CONSIDERABLE INVESTMENT, THE TERM OF THE AGREEMENT MAY BE PROLONGED UP TO 99 YEARS. PRODUCTS AND PROFITS RECEIVED BY THE CONCESSIONAIRE BELONG TO HIM IN THE AMOUNT DETERMINED BY THE CONCESSION AGREEMENT. THE STATE MANAGEMENT OF CONCESSIONS IS EXECUTED BY THE GOVERNMENT OF TAJIKISTAN OR OTHER AUTHORIZED AUTHORITY, OR BY LOCAL STATE ENTITIES.

CONCESSIONS ARE GRANTED ON A TENDER OR AUCTION BASIS. IN SOME CASES, IN ACCORDANCE WITH THE GOTI DECISION, CONCESSION MAY BE GRANTED ON THE BASIS OF DIRECT NEGOTIATION BETWEEN THE CONCESSION BODIES AND THE INVESTOR. LOCAL AUTHORITIES MAY INITIATE TENDERS AND AUCTIONS ON THE SITES WHICH BELONG TO THEM.
BIDS FOR ACTIONS AND TENDERS SHOULD BE SENT BY THE INVESTOR TO THE CONCESSION ORGAN. THE TENDER OR AUCTION WINNER SIGNS THE CONCESSION AGREEMENT WITH THE GOTI OR OTHER AUTHORIZED CONCESSION ENTITY. THE CONCESSIONAIRE MUST PAY A FEE FOR

REGISTRATION OF THE AGREEMENT, A CONCESSION FEE, AND TAXES PROVIDED BY LOCAL LEGISLATION. PROFITS LEFT AFTER PAYMENT OF TAXES AND OTHER PAYMENTS ARE AT FULL DISPOSAL OF THE CONCESSIONAIRE. DISPUTES BETWEEN THE CONCESSIONAIRE AND THE CONCESSION ENTITY ARE SUBJECT TO CONSIDERATION OF ECONOMIC COURTS OF TAJIKISTAN, IF OTHER NOT PROVIDED BY INTERNATIONAL AGREEMENTS SIGHED BY TAJIKISTAN.

REGISTRATION OF FOREIGN LEGAL ENTITIES BY NOTARIES IN TAJIKISTAN

In accordance with the 15 May 1997 Law of the Republic of Tajikistan "On State Notary", all enterprises, regardless of forms of property (including private, collective, state, joint ventures, branches, and filials) are acknowledged as a legal entity from the moment's of state registration at
state notaries on the territory where the legal entity is located. The state registration procedure is determined by the above mentioned law.

The enterprise is registered by the state notary in the period of not later than five days from the moment when the registration application with all necessary documents attached is presented.

The registration certificate is issued to the registered enterprise afterwards.
Applying to the state notary, the enterprise founders (legal entities and individuals) are to submit the following documents:

-- registration application - one copy
-- constituent documents (charter) - two copies
-- resolution of constituent documents issued by the Justice Ministry of the Republic of Tajikistan
-- statistical classification code
-- certificate stating the enterprise's location
-- receipt on state fees payment
-- for joint ventures - feasibility study and financial resolution issued by Finance Ministry
The Charter of the enterprise should meet the following requirements:
-- name of enterprise and its organizational-legal form
-- enterprise's location
-- activity's subject and aims
-- bodies of management and control and their competence
-- established order to form property and distribute profits
-- conditions of re-organization and cancellation of activity.
The legislation stipulates the cases when the legal entity is refused in registration:
-- violation of the established order of setting up the enterprise (for instance, lack of the necessary
number of enterprise founders)
-- non-conformity of constituent documents to legislation requirements.

The enterprise location may be confirmed by several ways:

a) rental of premises. The charter should be attached by a letter of guarantee issued by the enterprise-landlord to the new enterprise-tenant confirming a lease of premises and its address.

b) any enterprise is entitled to provide the new enterprise with its legal address so that the new enterprise could use it as its own legal address. In this case, the copy of the agreement granting the legal address or an appropriate letter from the legal entity are provided to the notary.

The new Housing Code adopted on December 12, 1997 prohibited using houses, apartments, and residences for non-housing residences. Using of private apartments and houses of citizens for establish various enterprises is allowed only if district governments permit this.

The state fee for enterprise registration excluding joint ventures is 100,000 Tajik rubles (USD 125). For registration of joint ventures is 500,000 Tajik rubles (USD 620). To register amendments to constituent documents and to re-register enterprises, regardless of their forms of property, is charged 50% of the previuosly imposed sum for registration.

LAW OF THE REPUBLIC OF TAJIKISTAN ON PRIVATIZATION OF STATE PROPERTY IN THE REPUBLIC OF TAJIKISTAN

ARTICLE 1. GENERAL PROVISIONS

The present Law regulates relations between the State and its authorized bodies and legal and natural persons in the process of privatization of state property.

ARTICLE 2. DEFINITION OF PRIVATIZATION

Privatization shall be defined as actions of the state to transfer the rights in state property to natural and legal persons in the manner prescribed by laws and other legal and regulatory acts.

ARTICLE 3. LAWS OF THE REPUBLIC OF TAJIKISTAN ON PRIVATIZATION

The laws of the Republic of Tajikistan on privatization shall consist of the Constitution and laws of the Republic of Tajikistan, this Law, legal acts of the President and the Government of the Republic of Tajikistan, and legal acts of local governments.
The privatization of property of the Republic of Tajikistan located outside its borders shall be regulated by this Law, unless otherwise provided by international legal acts recognized by the Republic of Tajikistan.

ARTICLE 4. BASIC PRINCIPLES OF PRIVATIZATION

Privatization shall be conducted according to the following basic principles:

- legality;

- transparency;
- equal rights of citizens;
- competition;
- succession.

ARTICLE 5. AUTHORIZED BODIES IN PRIVATIZATION

Decisions on the privatization of objects of Republican property shall be made by the Government of the Republic of Tajikistan.
Decisions on the privatization of communal property of Gorno-Badakhshan Autonomous Oblast, oblasts, cities and districts shall be made by the corresponding Majlisi of People's Deputies of GBAO, oblasts, cities and districts, and, within the limits of their authority, chairmen of GBAO, oblasts, cities and regions.

ARTICLE 6. POWERS OF GOVERNMENT AGENCIES IN THE AREA OF PRIVATIZATION

The Government of the Republic of Tajikistan, within the limits of its competence, shall:

Top

- manage the process of privatization of state property in the Republic of Tajikistan;
- approve programs for the privatization of state property;
- establish the order and methods of valuation for objects, subject to privatization
- make other decisions on privatization issues.

The Government of the Republic of Tajikistan may, in the manner established by law, delegate a portion of its powers to the agency for the management of state property in the Republic of Tajikistan.

ARTICLE 7. AUTHORITY OF LOCAL BODIES IN PRIVATIZATION

The authority of the local Majlisi' Oli of people's deputies, GBAO, oblasts, cities and regional chairmen in privatization arising from Article 5 of this Law shall be regulated by the Constitution and other laws of the Republic of Tajikistan.

ARTICLE 8. OBJECTS OF PRIVATIZATION

Objects of privatization shall be:

- property of state enterprises which is used in executing their activity, the land tenure rights of the property on which the enterprise rests, state enterprises as property complexes, which shall consist of all types of property used for its activity, including buildings, facilities, equipment, inventory, raw materials, goods produced, rights of use in the parcels of land on which they are located, receivable, debts, and all exclusive rights belonging to the enterprise as a legal entity;
- production and non-production subdivisions and structural units of a state enterprise as a property complex, the privatization of which will not violate the closed technological cycle;
- the property of state enterprises;
- shares in enterprises and organizations belonging to the state.

State property became the object for privatization when decision on privatization is made by the authorized body in the Article 5 of this Law.

ARTICLE 9. OBJECTS EXCLUDED FROM PRIVATIZATION

Property belonging to the state shall be subject to privatization, with the exception of objects that are the exclusive property of the state under Article 13 of the Constitution of the Republic of Tajikistan, objects of historical value and national heritage, defense enterprises, enterprises engaged in the disposal of radioactive wastes, and administrative buildings and facilities.
Privatization of objects providing the support for the infrastructure of the cities and regions : electrical energy, water supplying buildings, railway and auto way communications, communications, objects of health protection and education is implemented after the decision of the government.
The list of objects not subject to privatization shall be approved by the Government of the Republic of Tajikistan.

ARTICLE 10. PARTICIPANTS IN PRIVATIZATION

Subjects of privatization shall be natural and legal persons.
Legal persons in which the state owns greater than a 25% share shall not be participants in privatization.
Foreign natural and legal persons shall participate in the privatization of state property on terms determined by the laws of the Republic of Tajikistan.

ARTICLE 11. FORMS OF PRIVATIZATION

Privatization is conducted through the following mechanisms:

a. Sale
b. Case by case privatization on tender basis

The forms and conditions of privatization, order of organizing the sale or case by case privatization shall be determined by the Government of the Republic of Tajikistan.

ARTICLE 12. SALE OF OBJECTS OF PRIVATIZATION

Sales are conducted as tenders or auctions.
Prior to sale, the seller is to prepare complete information on the object of privatization.

ARTICLE 13. CASE BY CASE PRIVATIZATION

Large and unique objects, the list of which is approved by the Government of the Republic of Tajikistan, are subject to case by case privatization.
Case by case privatization consists of:

a. Analysis of the activity and competitiveness of the object;
b. Valuation of the property complex
c. Decision on the percentage of the shares to be sold ;
d. Decision on the technological and organizational changes which may be proposed;
e. Decision on the form of privatization.

Top

Execution of case by case privatization shall be executed by the body approved by the Government of the Republic of Tajikistan.

ARTICLE 14. PRIVATIZATION SECURITIES

In order to create equal starting conditions for participation in privatization, to attract broad participation by the population in the acquisition of state property, and to guarantee social justice, privatization securities may by used in the privatization of state property, which shall give their owners the right to a share in freely distributed state property.
The terms of the issuance and the manner of circulation and use of privatization securities shall be established by the Government of the Republic of Tajikistan.

ARTICLE 15. TRANSFER OF PROPERTY RIGHTS IN OBJECTS OF PRIVATIZATION

The right of property in objects of privatization shall arise from the moment of state registration of the right of acquisition of property in the manner established by law.

ARTICLE 16. FUNDS RECEIVED FROM PRIVATIZATION

Funds received from privatization shall be deposited in the state budget of the Republic of Tajikistan.

ARTICLE 17. PROTECTION OF LEGAL RIGHTS IN PRIVATIZATION

The legal rights of subjects of privatization shall be protected in the manner established by the laws of the Republic of Tajikistan.

REGULATION ON PROCEDURE FOR THE SALE OF OBJECTS OF PRIVATIZATION AT AUCTIONS AND TENDERS

I. GENERAL PROVIZION

The Regulation is developed in accordance with the law of the Republic of Tajikistan of May 16, 1997 “On privatization of state property”, and it established the general procedure and terms for sale of objects of privatization of the republican and communal property at auctions and tenders.

1. Words and expressions of the Regulation, as they are further defined, will have the following meaning unless otherwise foreseen by the context:

a. “Auction” - advertised bidding for sale of objects of privatization when fulfillment of any terms in relation to the object being privatized is not required;
b. “Tender” - closed bidding for sale of objects of privatization when fulfillment of some definite terms is required;
c. “Object of privatization” - a state owned enterprise or organization as a property complex; segmented production and non-production subdivisions and structural units of the enterprise which do not infringe technological cycle; separate property of a state owned enterprise; the state shares of enterprises and organizations;

d. "Object for sale" - an object of privatization on which the decision of selling it at auction or tender is taken by an authorized body;
e. "Seller" - a body authorized by the Government of the Republic of Tajikistan to implement privatization process in relation to the objects of the republican property, and appropriate Majlisis Oli of people's deputies in relation to the property of GBAO, oblasts, cities and regions;
f. "Organizer" - a seller or any other legal person selected by the seller on the competitive basis who organizes and holds an auction to sell objects of privatization;
g. "Bidder" - a legal or natural person being registered in the established order to bid in the auction or tender;
h. "Commercial tender" - bidding between the bidders who agreed to fulfill the terms of the tender when the highest bidder is considers to be the winner by the tender commission;
i. "Investment tender" - bidding when the tender commission considers the bidder offering the best program which meets the tender requirements to be the winner;
j. "Lot" - an object of privatization offered for tender. In case shares are sold, lot is a whole number of shares of a concrete joint stock company offered for bidding
k. "Bidding" - sale of lots at auction or tenders;
l. "Lot bidder" - a bidder who agrees to the announced price of the lot by rising his number;
m. "English method" - an auction method when the starting price is increased by previously announced step up to the moment when there is one highest bidder;
n. "Dutch method" - an auction method when the starting price is reduced by announced step up to the moment when one of the bidders agrees to buy the lot at the announced price;
o. "Starting price of the lot" - the price with which auction on every lot begins;
p. "Minimum price of the lot" - the price below which the lot cannot be sold;
q. "Price of sale" - the final price of the lot ascertained in the result of auction;
r. "Winner" - a highest bidder at auction or commercial tender, or a bidder presenting the most effective business plan;
s. "Purchaser" - the winner who made the purchase and sale contract on the object of privatization with the seller;
t. "Auctioneer" - a natural person appointed or hired by the Organizer to auction objects of privatizatin.

2. Specifically important and significant objects of privatization affecting environment and infringing upon economic interests of the Republic of Tajikistan, and objects of unfinished construction being of great importance for the economy of the republic are subject to sale at tender. The list of objects of privatization subject to sale at tender is approved by the Government of the Republic of Tajikistan.

Seller makes a decision on the term of putting the object of privatization for tender. Sale of the object at first three auctions is executed by English method. If the object is not sold at the English auction, the seller has the right in agreement with the Government of the Republic of Tajikistan as for the republican property, and with the Madjlisis Oli of people's deputies and in the limits of competence of the chairmen of

GBAO, oblasts, the city of Dushanbe, cities and towns, and regions as for the republican property to continue English auction or use the Dutch auctions.

3. If the object of privatization is a state shareholding of a joint stock company, the seller takes a decision to put it up for auction or tender as a whole, or divides the shareholding into lots, the number of shares in each lot must be whole.
4. The state shareholdings in the joint stock companies which have already registered their prospectus in the order established by the Ministry of Finance of the Republic of Tajikistan are put up for auctions and tenders .
5. Seller sells the state shareholdings in the procedure prescribed by the present Regulation.
6. Functions of the Seller are:

a. distribution of objects of privatization to be sold at specific auctions and tenders, setting their term and location;
b. division the shares into lots;
c. definition of the starting price of the lot;
d. creation of the auction and tender commission;
e. receipt of guaranteed fees;
f. making contracts with the Organizers to organize and conduct auctions;
g. carrying out control over the course of organization and conducting auctions and tenders;
h. making purchase and sale contracts with the Winner and control over their implementation;
i. effecting settlements with the Bidders, Purchasers and Organizers.

7. The Seller organizes and conducts the auction by himself, or in exclusive cases with the Republic of Tajikistan Government's consent he can make a contract with the Organizer on organization and conducting one or several auctions on sale the objects of privatization.
8. Contract on organization and conducting one auction for sale of objects of privatization is made in writing between the Seller and the Organizer and is to contain:
   - list of objects for sale;
   - deadline for conducting auctions;
   - number of shares put up for auction; number of lots, number of shares in each lot, face value of shares;
   - auction method for sale of each lot;
   - starting and minimum prices of each lot;
   - powers the Seller gives to the Organizer to organize and conduct the auction;
   - size of the guaranteed fees and procedure of its payment;
   - list of documents on each object for sale to be transferred to the Organizer;
   - periodicity and the Organizer's form of reporting on preparation and conducting the auction;
   - size and remuneration for the Organizer and procedure of mutual settlements with the Seller;
   - mutual obligations and property liabilities;

  - term of the contract and provisions for cancellation of the contract.

Contract on organization and conducting several auctions for sale of objects of privatization is made in writing between the Seller and the Organizer and it is to contain:

- powers the Seller gives to the Organizer to organize and conduct the auction;
- periodicity and the Seller's form of information about the coming auction is to contain: list of objects for sale put up for the auction; deadline for conducting auctions; number of shares put up for auction; number of lots, number of shares in each lot, face value of shares; the auction method for sale of each lot; starting and minimum prices of each lot; size of the guaranteed fees and procedure of its payment;
- periodicity and the Organizer's form of reporting on the process of preparation and conducting the auction;
- size and remuneration for the Organizer and procedure of mutual settlements with the Seller;
- mutual obligations and property liabilities;
- term of the contract and provisions for cancellation of the contract.

The seller does not have the right to transfer to the Organizer the contractual functions prescribed Paragraph 6 of the present Regulation except sub-points a, b, c, d, f, and g.

9. Natural and legal persons including foreigners, who have been registered in the procedure defined by Paragraph 32 of the present Regulation, with the exception of those persons indicated in Paragraph 10, are admitted to take part in auction.

Participation of foreign natural and legal persons in auctions and tenders is regulated by a specific Law of the Republic of Tajikistan.

10. Bidders at auction and tenders cannot be:
    - Legal entities of the republic of Tajikistan whose state share in the charter fund exceeds 25 %;
    - The Organizer of the auction and members of the auction commission;
    - The Organizer of the tender and members of the tender commission;
    - The Winners of the previous auctions who did not fulfill obligations prescribed by the present Regulation are deprived the right to participate in the subsequent auctions and tenders within 6 months.

II. CREPARATION FOR AUCTION AND TENDER

11. The Seller of the auction creates an auction commission to execute control over the organization and conducting the auction. Staff, competence and organization of the auction commission activity is defined by the 'Regulation on auction commission' to be approved by the Seller.
12. To prepare and conduct the tender, the Seller creates a tender commission which consists of representatives of the Seller, the Ministry of finance of the

Republic of Tajikistan, the Ministry of economy and external economic relations of the Republic of Tajikistan, the Ministry of justice of the Republic of Tajikistan, the higher ministry or department of the republican object being privatized, and the representatives of financial, economic, banking bodies, the Khukumat, other bodies of local government, the higher body of the communal object being privatized. The commission should consist of not less than 5 persons, the number of the members of the commission should be odd. The chairman of the commission is the representative of the Seller.

The tender commission is to:

- independently develop and approve the rules of the work;
- define and approve the terms and conditions of the tender;
- make a decision on the publication of official announcement;
- conduct the tender;
- announce the winner of the tender.

13. Decisions of the auction or tender commission is taken by a simple majority of votes of the total number of the members of the commission. In case of equality of votes, the chairman's vote is decisive.
14. Preparation for auction or tender is cried out in the following procedure:
    - lots are formed;
    - lots are distributed for specific auctions or tenders;
    - term for conducting auctions is set;
    - starting prices of the lots are determined;
    - procedure of the guaranteed fee payment is defined;
    - in case of need a tender for the right of making contract to organize and conduct auction for sale of objects of privatization is held;
    - sale prospectus, auction cards and schedules for visiting objects are made;
    - official announcement of auction or tender is published and other advertisement is carried out;
    - guaranteed fees received;
    - participants are registered.

15. With the purpose of complex study of the structure of expenses for financing the object, state of the object, valuation of the object of privatization, studying of the tender terms, the Seller has the right to involve independent consulting firms or an auditor during the period of preparation for tender.
16. The tender commission determines the terms of tender. The terms of tender can be:
    - determination of a certain level of volumes of production, nomenclature of the manufacture produced or the services rendered in the term set by the tender commission;
    - delivery of production to the certain consumers within the term set by the tender commission;
    - preserving, cutting down of not more than on the size established by the tender commission or creating of working spaces in term set by the tender commission;

- obligations on the indicated volume, type and term of investments into the objects of privatization;
- redemption of wage arrears in the term set by the tender commission;
- redemption of the accounts payable in the term set by the tender commission;
- restriction on fulfillment of the bargains (resale, pledge, transfer to management, lease out) in the term set by the tender commission;
- ecological requirements.

17. The starting price of the object of privatization put up for auction or tender is calculated in accordance with Instruction on valuation of objects of privatization approved by the Government Resolution of May 4, 1997, # 181.
18. When selling the object by Dutch method, the starting (primary) price is defined by multiplying the starting price by increasing coefficient. The coefficient is established by the Seller, but it cannot be lower then 5.
19. While putting up the object for the Dutch auction, the floor price of the lot is established in the identical size for all objects at the level of minimal wages multiplied by 100.
20. Guaranteed fee is to ensure the fulfillment of the following obligations of the participant:
    - signing the record of the auction results in case he becomes a winner;
    - making a purchase and sale contract in accordance with the record of auction results.

21. The guaranteed fee to participate in the auction or tender is established in the identical size for all lots being out up for auction or tender, and is equal to the size which is equivalent to US$ 200 and is entered in the national currency of the Republic of Tajikistan.
22. The participant has the right to pay any of guaranteed fees, but one guaranteed fee gives the right to purchase one lot.
23. The guaranteed fee is paid in the procedure established in the official announcement. The recipient of the guaranteed fee is the Seller.
24. The Guaranteed fee of the Winner who made a purchase and sale contract is included due to the payments on the purchase and sale contract.
25. The guaranteed fee is not returned to the participant in case of:
    - refusal to participate in the auction or tender less than three days before they are conducted;
    - refusal of the Winner to sign the record of the auction results, or to make purchase and sale contract;
    - non-performance or improper performance of the purchase and sale contractual obligations;
    - participant's violation of the present Regulation.

In all other cases the guaranteed fees are returned within 10 banking days after the auction or tender is closed; if the money is entered into the Seller's account after the auction or tender is closed then - within ten banking days after the money is entered.

26. Official announcement to sell the objects of the republican property by auction or tender should be published in the state and Russian languages in the republican

mass media and the objects of the communal property - in local newspapers not less than 30 days before auction .

27. Official announcement should contain:
    - date, place and time of the auction or tender;
    - name, location and major characteristics (type of activity, square of the site and the characteristic of the buildings located on the site, square of the object /general and industrial/, average number of employees) of the object for sale;
    - size of the accounts payable;
    - size of lots put up for sale (in percentage of the charter fund) from each joint stock company;
    - starting prices of the lots put up for sale;
    - size of the commission collected by the Seller;
    - size of the guaranteed fee defined by Paragraph 21 of this Regulation, procedure of its payment, recipient's settlement account in case of - the fee transfer;
    - place and term of submitting applications;
    - telephone numbers and addresses where at the indicated time one can get prospectus of sale, auction and tender regulations;
    - terms and conditions of tender;
    - criterion to define the Winner;
    - other additional information on the Seller's decision.

28. Before the publication of the official announcement there must be prepared:

    a) the prospectus on every object for sale containing the data on the object and consisting of:

    - at selling state owned enterprises as a property complex, production and non-production subdivisions and structural units:
        - copies of the legal persons' founder documents;
        - copies of the balance sheet (separate balance sheet) with attachments for the recent accounting period before the decision to put up an object of privatization for auction or tender is taken by the Seller;
        - acts of valuation;

- - at selling shares of joint stock companies:
    - copies of prospectus of emission and certificate of registration;
    - acts of valuation of the object of privatization;
- - at selling a property unit of the enterprise:
    - technical certificate of a property unit to be the object for sale, or any other document characterizing technical condition of the object;
    - acts of valuation.

The prospectus can also contain other additional data (staff of the bodies of management of the object of privatization, analysis of investment risk, data on possible variants of technical re-equipment, settlements of the enterprise's profits after the re-equipment, estimation of necessary investments for production, valuation of perspective of the production manufactured at the world and domestic markets);

a. Auction card contains the list of lots, indicated in the official announcement, put up for auction which is given to every BIdder at the moment of registration.
b. Objects' visiting schedule

29. After publication of the official announcement, the Seller must ensure free access to study the objects for sale for all interested parties, including visiting and examination of the object, and regulations of the auction and tender.
30. Other kinds of advertisement may be done in any form to attract as many participants as possible.
31. Registration of the of the Bidders is started on the day of the official announcement publication in the republican press and is over one hour before the auction or tender begins.
32. For registration as the Bidder it is necessary to submit:
    - two copies of application form for participation in auction or tender without the indication in it the object of sale which the Bidder is going to purchase (Attachment # 1-4). One copy of the application with the indication of the date it is received, certified and stamped by the Organizer is at once returned to the Bidder as the document certifying the application is received and the guaranteed fee is paid;
    - passport or any other identification card;
    - original and a copy of the payment agreement confirming that the guaranteed fee is paid in the size equivalent to US$ 200;
    - notarized document certifying the representative's authority of the legal and natural person.

Legal persons additionally submit:

- - notarized copies of the charter and legal person's registration certificates.

Joint stock companies additionally submit the extract from the stockholders' list with the information of the state share in the charter fund of the company to be signed and stamped by the first chairman.
In case of conducting a commercial tender, the Bidder additionally submits five copies of his agreement to fulfill the condition (conditions) of the tender in the stamped envelope where should be indicated:

- the name of the object of sale;
- agreement to fulfill the condition (conditions) of the tender with the indication of the condition (conditions) published in the official announcement on auction;
- suggestion on the purchasing price of the object of sale;
- information about the Bidder;
- signature of the Bidder.

The Investment bidder additionally submits a business plan (Attachment # 5) on the above mentioned object of sale.

33. The Seller and Organizer have no right:

- to demand that the Bidder should provide them with the information of his intentions to purchase this or that lot from those put up for auction or tender;
- to divulge the information dealing with the Bidders or interfering the course of bidding during the whole period of preparation for auction or tender and the time of their conducting. A person bears responsibility for divulging the above mentioned information in accordance with law of the Republic of Tajikistan;
- to demand that additional documents should be submitted for the Bidder's registration besides those enumerated in Paragraph 32 of the present Regulation.

34. The Organizer or tender commission carries out registration of Bidders separately for each auction or tender in a special paginated register in the order the documents are received.

In case the auction is held, the Bidder's number of registration should coincide with the number of registration in the register.

35. The documents of the registered Bidders are kept in a separate safe until the day of auction or tender.
36. The person, who has got registration, gets an auction number on the day of auction when he shows the second copy of the application. Use of the auction number by other person is forbidden.
37. On the day of auction, the envelopes are transferred to the tender commission in accordance with the attached Record (Attachment #5) on receiving Bidders' applications, signed by the person responsible for receiving the applications.

III. CONDUCTING AUCTIONS

38. Auctioneer conducts Auction. Auction is started with the explanations of the auction regulations.

Decision of sequence to put out lots to tender is taken by the Auctioneer. This procedure may differ from the procedure established in the auction card.
The process of auction is watched by the auction commission, representatives of the Organizer (provided his participation in organization of auction). Representatives of mass media and international organizations have the right to attend the auction.
The Bidders and the persons present who try to influence the course of auction or breaking its regulations, are removed from the hall.
Auctioneer begins the auction on every lot with the announcement of the object of sale, its brief characteristics, auction method starting price and the step of changing the price. Auctioneer has the right to change the step in the course of auction, announcing it. The step of changing is established in the limits between 5 - 10 % of the current price of the lot.

39. Auction is held by one of the two methods described below:
    - English method:

The Auctioneer announces a starting price of the lot and the step of increasing the price. By rising their numbers, the lot bidders increase the starting price for the step announced. The Auctioneer announces auction numbers of the bidders on the lot, fixes the price and suggests to increase it. Auctions of the lot continue until the maximum price is proposed. The lot bidder who has offered the highest price for the lot is announced by the Auctioneer. The Auctioneer repeats the last price of the lot three times, and if there are not any other numbers raised, he declares by banging the gavel that the lot is sold.
Auction of the lot is considered to have gone through if there are not less than two lot bidders.
Dutch method:

1. The Auctioneer announces a starting price of the lot and reduces it with the step declared, announcing a new price. The Auctioneer calls the number of the lot bidder who is the first to raise the auction number when the price is announced, and he declares the bidder to be the winner of the given lot. If not a single bidder desires to purchase the given lot when the Auctioneer announces the minimum price, the lot is removed from auction.
2. If two or more numbers are raised simultaneously, it is up to the Auction Commission to take decision who is the first, and the bidders have no right to dispute the decision. In some exclusive cases the Auction Commission has the right to decide by random drawing.

40. The result of auction on every lot are recorded and the record is signed by the Organizer, the Auction Commission and the Winner at the end of auction on every lot (Attachment # 6). The Auctioneer has the right to declare a break to sign the record. The record is made in three copies, one copy for each - for the Seller, the Purchaser and the Auction Commission. The Auction Commission must hand a copy of the record on the auction results to the Seller on the day not later than the next day after the auction if conducted.
41. The record on the auction results is a document which fixes the auction results and obligations of the Winner and the Seller to make a purchase and sale contract on the object of privatization at the price of sale. The Winner has the right to make a purchase and sale contract within not more than 5 banking days after signing the record, at the expiration of the term this right is lost.
42. If the lot is not sold by Dutch method after having been put up for auction several times, the Seller takes the decision to use the procedures on restructurization and liquidation in relation to the object of privatization.

IV. CONDUCTING TENDERS

43. The sittings of the tender commission are closed and are conducted if one or more envelope with the offer of the price have been received.

44. The envelopes are opened by the commission during the tender. All the members of the commission have to study and compare the Bidders' suggestions.
45. During the commercial tender, the tender commission announces the Bidder, who bids up and if his bid meets the requirements of the tender, to be the Winner of the tender.
46. During the investment tender, the bidders' business plans are considered by the tender commission. The Winner of the investment tender is defined by the tender commission proceed from the criteria established by the commission.

The tender commission announces the Bidder of the investment tender , whose business plan is more effective and meets the requirements of the tender, to be the Winner of the tender.

47. If the bids of two or more Bidders at the commercial tender contain one and the same price, or business plans of two or more Bidders at the investment tender contain adequate proposals on the investments and other factors, the person who has registered first is considered the Winner.
48. In case of registration of one Bidder of the tender on sale of an object of privatization, the tender commission announces him the Winner under condition he offers the price higher than the starting one.
49. The record is drawn up on the results of every lot (Attachment # 7) with the indication of:
    - the staff of the commission;
    - terms and conditions of the tender;
    - number of the Bidders and their registration numbers in accordance with those indicated in the envelopes;
    - the list of prices offered in accordance with the Bidders' registration numbers;
    - the Winner, his registration number, his offered price;
    - the selling price of the object of privatization.

In case of adequate prices, the date of receiving the application is additionally indicated in the record.
In case of the investment tender, the number of Bidder's balls gained is indicated the record, and also the best proposal in accordance with the business plan submitted.

50. The record is signed by all the tender commission members. Any member of the commission has the right express his own point of view in writing and attach it to the record.
51. The record is made in three copies, one copy for each - for the Seller, the Winner and the tender commission. Two copies of the record are handed to the Seller who must inform the Bidders of the tender results not later than the next day after the tender.
52. The record on the tender results is a document which fixes the tender results and obligations of the Winner and the Seller to make a purchase and sale contract within not more than 10 banking days after signing the record, at the expiration of the term this right is lost.

53. In case of non-conclusion the Winner does not make a purchase and sale contract , the Seller suggests that the other Bidders conclude the purchase and sale contract on the base of the tender commission's record with taking into account the price offered by them.
54. The rest of the Bidders are informed of the number of Bidders on the object declared by them and the list of prices offered by them not later than the next day after the tender. In case of adequate prices, the date of applications is indicated.
55. In case the applications for the commercial and investment tenders on sale of the object of privatization are not submitted, on the day of conducting the tender the commission has to take the decision:
    - either to conduct the second tender on sale of the above mentioned object of privatization changing the conditions of tender in the term of not later than one month after the first tender. Commercial tenders cannot be but two;
    - or to transfer the Seller the above mentioned object of privatization to be put up for the next auction in the term not later than one month after the tender.

V. PROCEDURE OF EFFECTING ETTLEMENTS WITH PURCHASERE AND REGISTERING OWNERSHIP

56. The Winner enters the commission to the Seller's account, the size of which should not exceed 2 % of the selling price of each lot, which after entering into the budget of the Republic of Tajikistan is spent for organization and realization of auctions and tenders.
57. The purchase and sale contract of the object of privatization between the Seller and the Purchaser is made in the written form and it should have reference to the record on auction or tender results (Attachments # 8 and #9).
58. Settlements on the purchase and sale contract are executed between the Seller and the Purchaser, for all this the Seller executes settlement in the following procedure:

    a. advance payment is made in the size of not less than 15 % of 10 banking days after the purchase and sale contract is signed. The guaranteed fee is included into the advance payment.
    b. the remained sum should be made not later than 30 banking days after the purchase and sale contract is signed.

59. Privatization securities can be used to pay for the object of privatization (privatization checks until their expiration term). The terms and procedure to use privatization securities are defined by the Government of the Republic of Tajikistan.
60. In case the final payment is delayed for more than 10 banking days, the Seller has the right to cancel the contract in the unilateral manner and claim to indemnify for real losses not covered by the guaranteed fee.
61. After full payment of the object of privatization, the Seller and the Purchaser should sign the act of transfer the object within three days (Attachment # 10).

62. The Purchaser has got ownership of the object of privatization after the state registration in the order prescribed by the law and full payment of the price indicated in the purchase and sale contract.
63. The ownership certificate is the document certifying ownership being given by the state notary offices at the place of the sold object's location.
64. Auction or tender results can be protested within 30 calendar days after the auction or tender.
65. In case the terms and obligation of the tender prescribed by the purchase and sale contract are not fulfilled , legal consequences prescribed by the purchase and sale contract come into force.

VI. MONEY RECEIVED FROM SALE OF OBJECTS OF PRIVATIZATION

66. Money received from sale of objects of privatization is entered to the state budget.
67. The remuneration due to the Organizer is included in the charges of the Seller on preparation and conducting the auction.

SUPPLEMENTS

REPRESENTATIVES OF THE REPUBLIC OF TAJIKISTAN ABROAD

Country	Ambassador's name	Telephone	Fax	Mailing address
Austria e-mail: tajikembassy@teleri ng.at g.at	Zaripov Khamrohon	(43-1) 409 826 611 650 505 55 00	(43-1) 409 826 614	1090 Vienna Universitats Strasse
Islamic Republic of Iran ??? e-mail: tajiribem@apanda.c om	Nazirov Toshmad Radzhabovich	(98-21) 2299584	(98-21) 229 16 07 229 70 39	Майдю Ниёваон Хиеб Шахид Зинали кю3,б10
China	Karimov Dzhamshedeд Khilolovich	(86-10) 6532 30 39 6532 25 98	(86-10) 6532 30 39 6416 82 12	100 600, Pekin Ta Uan, д,4 / office1 Кв, 31
Pakistan	Khodzhiev Bobodzhon	(92-51) 229 46 75	(92-51) 229 97 10	Islamabad
	Bobokalonov Yusyf T.	(92-021) 583 82 45	(92-021) 583 74 22	Karachi
USA	Alimov Rashid Kutbudinovich	(1-212) 744 21 96	(1-212) 472 76 45	136 East 67th Str.NY USA
Turkey	Dododzhonov Rustam Nachmiddin I.	(90-312) 446 16 02 0535-232 18 02	(90-312) 446 36 21	M. Gandhi Str. 06700 Ankara, Turkey
Germany	Mirzoev Akbar	(49-30) 347 93 00 05364 7289-1576	(49-30) 3479 30 29 3479 30 18	Otto-Suhr-Allee 84 10585 Berlin

REPRESENTATIVES OF THE REPUBLIC OF TAJIKISTAN IN CIS COUNTRIES

Country	Ambassador's name	Telephone	Fax	Mailing address
Republic of Byelorussia	Rakhimov Olim Sabirovich	8-10 (37517) 226 19 44	8-10 (37517) 227 76 13	Minsk, Kirova Str.17
Republic of Kazakhstan	Iskandarov Akbarsho	8-10 (7-3272) 54 28 69	8-10 (7-3272) 54 28 69	Almaty Dzhandosova Str. 58
Russian Federation	Mirzoev Rhamazan Zariphovich	8-10 (7-095) 290 41 86 290 38 46 290 57 36	8-10 (7-095) 291 89 98	Moscow Granatniy pereulok 13
	Mirzoev Komil	8-10 (7-095)	290 57 36	
Republic of Turkmenistan	Mardonov Tadzhiddin Nuriddinovich	8-10 (998-712) 35 56 96 39 34 31	8-10 (993-12) 39 31 74	Ashgabat Turkmenbashy Str. 13
Republic of Uzbekistan	Amirzaev Kulyamzhan Amirzaevich	8-10 (998-712) 54 99 66 185 75 16 (сот.)	8-10 (998-712) 54 89 69	Tashkent M. Torobi Square 19
CIS Secretariat Minsk			(37517) 227 23 39	Minsk Kirova Str.17
Central Asia Association on Economics Bishkek	Sobirov Makhmud Nosirovich	(996-312) 22 12 36 66 13 51	(996-312) 22 74 57	Bishkek
Integration Committee			62 48 97	Almaty
ЭКО ???	Mirshakarov Mirafzad		283 17 32	Teheran
Mardonov T.N.		43 47 46		Tashkent
Spinerov D.N.	23 61 15	26 96 18 (home)		Almaty

INTERNATIONAL ORGANIZATIONS

AAN (Action Against Hunger) (8 Firdausi St.)
Head of Mission Philippe Mougin 24-14-09
Administrator Mahina Safarmamadova 21-51-73
Assistant Firuz tel/fax: 901-50-43

ABA (American Bar Association)/CEELI (Central East European Law Initiative) (72 Tolstoy St.)
Liaison to Tajikistan 24-15-05
Legislative Specialist/Rule of Law Liaison Bernard Ryan 21-15-02
Office Manager Zarona Ismailova 24-68-62
Translator Larisa Petrosyan fax: 24-26-80

ACCELS /American Center (American Council for Collaboration in Education and Language Study)
(105 Rudaki Ave. Apart. 13-14)
Deputy Director Matluba Mamadjanova tel/fax: 21-17-95
Program Assistant Yelena Lodde tel/fax: 21-21-03
Program Assistamt Zarrina Muhiddinova
oseas@amc.tajik.net

ACTED (Agency for Technical Cooperation and Development) (15 Academicians Rajabovs Ave.)
Regional Coordinator Frederic Roussel 21-92-89
Country Director Stephan Nicolas 24-65-83
Administrative Assistant Mavluda Kamalova fax: 51-01-12
Secretary Anna

ADB (Asian Development Bank)
(3 Academicians Rajabovs St., Bldg. of the Ministry of Finance, 3rd fl., Room 30)
Liasion Officer Oxana Nazmiyeva 27-24-97
Office Manager Muhabbat Salimova fax: 901-50-51 mobile: 901-05-15

ADRA (Adventist Development and Relief Agency) (43 Schors St.)
Country Director Vladimir Kononkov 21-47-05 Office Manager Svetlana Babanina 34-69-95
fax: 21-47-06

AED /Global Project (Academy for Educational Development) (40 Rudaki Ave., Rooms 300-303)
Director Shamsiddin Karimov 21-06-00
Senior Training Specialist Savriniso Rasulova 21-08-44
Admin. & Finance Manager Mahmadsodiq Tolibov 21-82-49

American Business Resource Center
Manager Faridun Kamoliddinov 21-05-22
Assistant Savriniso Qurbonbekova 21-05-26
tel/fax: 21-05-18
fax: 51-01-02

AKDN (Aga Khan Development Network) (6 Hamza Hakimzoda St.)
Resident Representative Hakim Feerasta 24-65-00 *(Secretary Latofat)* 21-71-94
Assistant Finance Manager Firuz Vatanshoyev tel/fax: 21-70-87
AKFED Project Manager Mathew Scanlon 24-65-65
Executive Aid Mahina tel/fax: 51-00-66
Assistant Amina 21-56-63
21-87-48

AKF (Aga Khan Foundation) (10 Hamza Hakimzoda St.)
Chief Executive Officer Mirzo Jahani 21-84-06 Executive Assistant Yevgeniya Mordenskaya 21-84-06 *Receptionist Nargis* 24-34-42

AKHPCA (The Aga Khan Humanities Program for Central Asia) (75 Tolstoi St.)
Director Rafique Keshavjee 24-58-23
Deputy Firuza Tursunzade 24-07-02
Secretary Dilorom 24-52-97

ARD/CHECCHI/USAID (Commercial Law Project) (4 Govorov St.)
Director Garland Boyette 21-17-79
Deputy Akbar Muratov 24-22-84
Attorney/Office Manager Suhrob Jabborov 24-03-52
tel/fax: 21-26-50

CAAEF (Central Asian-American Enterprise Fund) (31 Kirov St., Apart. 1)
Vice President Benjamin Ryan 21-50-14 Office Manager Nazar Nabiyev 21-60-13
Secretary Gulchin 21-56-01
tel/fax: 51-00-88
Khujand Office (1 Lenin St.)
Office Manager 4-35-32; 6-53-48
fax: 6-00-73

CAD (Children's Aid Direct)
(9 Samad Gani St.)
Country Representative Dr. Julian Paul Edward 21-66-05
Administrator Zuhra Irgasheva tel/fax: 24-83-27

CADA (Central Asian Development Agency)
(40 Rudaki Ave., Room 307)
Director David Lovett 21-22-10
(Secretary Shukufa) res: 24-62-64
Deputy Tim Austin 21-21-75
Nigina 21-71-59
fax: 51-00-52

CARANA Corporation (44 Rudaki Ave., Room 159)
Project Manager Julian Simidjiyski 21-75-50
Office Manager Tatiana Khairova fax: 21-88-87

CARE International (Coordination for American Relief Everywhere) (25 Behzod St. 1st & 2nd fl.)
Country Director Jenevieve Abel 21-17-83
res: 24-06-46
Food Program Coordinator Benoy B. Saha 21-00-91
Health Sector Advisor Paula Boogart 21-75-42 21-78-71
Admin. Assistant Gulchin 24-43-06
fax: 21-17-78 fax: 51-00-36

Counterpart Consortium (20 Huseinzoda *(Kirov)* St.)
Country Director tel/fax: 21-75-59
Deputy Farhod Boqiyev tel/fax: 21-65-14
tel/fax: 21-82-65
Office Manager Adiba Ansori
Secretary Shoira tel/fax: 51-01-31
jbarbee@counterpart-tj.org

DEXTER Construction Corporation
President Yakov Krivoruk tel/fax: 34-88-96
Vice-President Vitaly Basteyev

EBRD (European Bank for Reconstruction and Development) (38 Shotemur St., Rooms ## 36, 38) **Assistant/Mission Coordinator** Nasiba Ahrorova tel/fax: 21-07-63
Mission Advisor Muzaffar Usmanov mobile: 901-00-78

ECHO (European Community Humanitarian Office)
(25 M. Tursunzoda St., 3rd fl.)

ECHO Correspondent Peter Burgess tel/fax: 21-60-83
Administrator Sitora Ahrori tel/fax: 23-16-15 Operations Officer Zafar Teshayev
Information Officer Azamat Khasanov

EF (Eurasia Foundation) (18 Rudaki Ave. 2nd fl.)
Regional Director Elizabeth Coll (Tashkent)
Country Representative Tatyana Falko tel/fax: 21-69-86
res: 21-52-98

FOCUS USA (Disaster Preparedness and Mitigation Project) - affiliate of AKDN
(15 Mamadali Qurbonov St.)
Program Director Goulsara Pulatova tel/fax: 21-98-30
Program Assistant Vladimir Kuimov tel/fax: 21-96-11
tel/fax: 23-02-20

GAA (German Agro - Action) (20/1 Behzod St.,)
Project Coordinator Beate Schoreit 21-54-79
21-33-68
fax: 21-21-68

Global Partners (184 Zainabbibi St.)

Country Director Greg Gamble 21-07-95
fax: 51-00-37

GTZ (German Technical Assistance Agency)
(21 Rudaki Ave.)
Head of Office Karlfried Metzler 21-71-26
Assistant Lyuba Frolova tel/fax: 51-00-37

ICRC (International Committee of Red Cross) (14/3 Aini St.)
Head of Delegation Elizabeth Knecht 21-68-23
21-73-37
Assistant Madina 21-86-60
fax: 51-00-53

IFES (International Foundation for Election Systems) (25 Behzod St., 3rd fl.)
Project Manager Philip Griffin (*Zumrad*) 21-80-52
Assistant Mouqim Mallayev 21-70-98
Finance Coordinator Farangis fax: 21-25-80

IFRC (International Federation of the Red Cross) (120 Omar Khayam St., 3rd fl.)
Head of Delegation Charlotta Relander 24-59-81
Secretary Shahlo Rajabova 24-42-96
24-00-33
tel/fax: 24-85-20

IMF (International Monetary Fund) (23/2 Rudaki Ave. #34, National Bank)
Resident Representative Henri Lorie 21-24-80
Assistant/Interpreter Munira Soliyeva tel/fax: 51-01-21
"Internews" (92 Rudaki Ave., 4th fl., Apart. 24)
Country Director Roshan Khadiri tel/fax: 21-43-12
mobile: 901-50-32
Director Bahodur Qosymov tel/fax: 24-54-83
Administrator *Roziya Jalilova*

IOM (International Organization of Migration) (5 Zakariyoi Rozi St.)
Chief of Mission Igor Bosc tel/fax: 24-71-96
Administrator Natalia Karpova tel/fax: 21-03-02
Assistant/Interpreter Mavsuma Valiyeva sat.fax: 51-00-62
MCI (Mercy Corps International) (1 Firdausi St., behind "Saodat" tea-house)
Country Director Kurt Gibson 24-00-16
24-06-89
Admin/Finance/Food Aid Shah Jalal Bhyian 21-08-60/64/79
Assistant Janat 21-36-21
tel/fax: 51-01-33

MERLIN (Medical Emergency Relief International) (8 Karamov St.)
Program Coordinator Paul Handley 24-45-89
Administrator Parvina Sadiyeva 21-47-64 tel/fax: 51-01-20

MSDSP (Mountain Societies Development Support Program) (2nd Proyezd,14 Azizbekov St.)
General Manager Mahmadamin Mahmadaminov 21-87-48
Secretary Nisso 21-56-63
fax: 21-38-93

MSF (Medecins Sans Frontiers/Holland) (21 Guliston St.)
Country Manager Ton Koene 21-44-25
Medical Coordinator Marie Skinnider 24-34-49
Admin. & Financial Coordinator Ms. Jose Hulsenbek 24-52-34
24-75-40
tel/fax: 51-00-71

ORA (Orphans, Refugees & Aid/Germany) International (17 Academicians Rajabovs St, Apart. 11)
Director Jeffrey Paulsen 27-46-10
Assistant Mamlakat res: 24-40-77
tel/fax: 21-64-42
OSCE (Organization for Security & Cooperation in Europe) (12 Zikrullo Khojayev/Mendeleyev/ St.)
Ambassador/Head of Mission Marc Gilbert 21-40-63
Deputy Head of Mission Jan Malekzade 24-58-79
Finance/Admin. Officer Mathieu Goodstein
Mission Assistant Dilorom (901-05-98) tel/fax: 24-91-59

OSI (Open Society Institute/ Soros Foundation) (65 Tolstoy St.)
Executive Director Zuhra Halimova tel/fax: 21-19-58
Grants Manager Sirojiddin Nasriddinov 21-32-60
Assistant 24-22-41
tel/fax: 51-01-42

English Language Center (Bldg. of the Firdausi Library, 2nd fl.)
Director Valentina Sobko 21-48-73
PSF CI(Pharmaciens Sans Frontiers Comite International) (122 Proletarsky St.)
General Coordinator Bruno Clary 24-64-33
Administrator Nicolas Molle 24-34-40
tel/fax: 51-01-32

Swiss Cooperation Office (20 Pavlov St.)
Coordinator Luigy De Martino 24-38-97
National Program Officer Sayora Dodikhudoyeva 24-73-16
tel/fax: 901-50-40

SCF/UK (Save the Children Fund/UK) (1st Proyezd, 14 Shota Rustaveli St.)
Program Manager Mandal Urtnasan 21-81-57
Information/Admin. Assistant 21-40-23
21-70-84
27-54-47
fax: 51-00-75

SC/US (Save the Children Fund/US) (53 Ibn Sino St.)
Field Office Director A. K. M. Jamaluddin 21-07-71
Deputy Director/Admin. & Finance Rashid Massaud 24-02-06
Secretary Tahmina 24-33-88
Victoria (Telephone Directory) tel/fax: 51-00-79
SNI (Shelter Now International) (5 Lutfi St.)
Country Director Randall B. Olson 21-48-35
Secretary Malika res: 24-57-97
Deputy Mark Baltzer 21-51-98
mobile: 901-06-08

Swedish Committee for Afghanistan (9 Lutfi St.)
24-65-62
UMCOR (United Methodist Committee on Relief) (108 Lohuti St. 2nd floor)
Head of Mission Eileen Ihrig 21-42-39
Office Manager Rasul Sharipov 21-70-48
fax: 51-01-60

UNDP (United Nations Development Program) (39 Aini St.)
Resident Representative/UN Resident 901-01-83
Coordinator Matthew Kahane *(Dilbar)* 21-06-79
res: 24-53-24
Deputy Akbar Usmani (*Nargis*) 21-06-85 *Receptionist Aishe Muratova* 21-06-70/80
21-06-86/94

UNHCR (United Nations High Commissioner for Refugees) (106 Druzhba Narodov St.)
Program Officer Taslimur Rahman (*Secretary Galiya)* 901-02-39
res: 24-10-86
NGO Coordinator/NRG Mahmoud Naderi 21-74-24
Radio Operator Malika 21-83-78
21-44-06
24-62-65
24-61-84
tel/fax: 51-00-39

UNICEF (14/1 H. Hakimzoda St.)
Assistant Representative Branislav Jekic 21-82-61
Assistant Project Officer Sobir Qurbonov 24-72-61
Secretary/Translator Marina Zhukova 24-91-08
fax: 24-19-05

UNIFEM (UN Development Fund for Women) (25 Behzod St., Room 7)
Program Coordinator Nushin Yovari D'Hellencourt 21-70-31
Program Officer Shuhrat Rajabov 23-09-61 Program Assistant Jahongir Munzim
Training Center (270 Huvaidulloyev St., former bldg. of the Ministry of Social Welfare)
Manager Khiromon 35-36-86
35-05-38

UNOCHA (OCHA Office in Tajikistan) (39 Aini St.)
Head of Office Valentin Gatzinski 21-78-27
Program Assistant Marziya Nazarova 21-06-08
21-06-86

UN ODCCP (UN Office for Drug Control and Crime Prevention) (25 Said Nosyrov St.)
Acting Program Coordinator Timur Aziz Ahmad tel/fax: 21-33-67
Senior Technical Advisor Sergei Ratushnyy tel/fax: 24-00-96
24-66-08
24-86-60

UNOPS (UN Office for Project Services) (25 Behzod St.)
Acting Program Manager Jan Harfst 21-06-82
21-08-96
Senior Admin. Assistant Natalia Azizova 21-03-89
Admin. Assistant Viktoriya 23-09-16
21-09-34
Social Sector Rehabilitation Project (SSRP) (2nd Proyezd, 28 Telman St.)
International Team Leader Janny Bosscher 24-55-94
res: 21-09-79
National Director Mahmadsharif Nozimov mobile: 901-06-62
Assistant Rukhshona

UNTOP (UN Tajikistan Office of Peace-Building) (7 Tehron St.)
Head of Mission/RSG Ivo Petrov 21-01-25
(Personal Secretary Marlene Keffer) res: 24-31-31
Assistant Saifiddin
Deputy Head of Mission Hiroshi Takahashi
Political Affairs Officer Waldemar Rokoszewski
Political Affairs Officer Ms. Gisela Nauk
Human Rights Officer Lilia Zaharieva
Administrative Officer Fermino Balangtaa
Communications Officer David Padi
Switch-board operator 21-01-10/27/47

USAID (US Agency for International Development) (10 Pavlov St.)
Country Program Officer Michael Harvey 7(3272) 50-76-12/17
7(3272) 63-28-80
fax: 7(3272) 69-64-90
fax: 7(3272) 50-76-36
Project Management Specialist Abdurahim Muhidov 21-03-48/50/52/54
Admin. Assistant Sayora Halimova

VI (Vision International Healthcare) (15 Lutfi St.)
Project Director Dorothy Finlay 24-64-47
Deputy Dr. Zarina Musayeva

World Bank/IBRD (International Bank for Reconstruction and Development) (105 Rudaki Ave.)
Country Manager Mustafa Rouis 21-07-56
Assistant Saodat Ibragimova 21-67-43
Receptionist Dilshod 21-03-81
21-15-18
fax: 51-00-42

WFP (UN World Food Program) (13 Pushkin St.)
Representative/Country Director Bouchan Hadj-Chikh 21-09-07
Emergency Officer Romein Sirois 21-09-19 21-57-15
Receptionist Malika 24-39-50
23-38-75

tel/fax: 51-00-87
WHO (UN World Health Organization) (106 Druzhba Narodov St.)
Head of Office Prof. Lyubomir Ivanov 21-01-08 Liaison Officer Nazira Artykova 21-48-71 *Secretary/Accountant Dilafruz Tursunova* tel/fax: 21-48-71

BUSINESS AND GOVERNMENT CONTACTS FOR TAJIKISTAN

U.S. Embassy Dushanbe c/o U.S. Embassy Almaty
Ambassador - The Honorable Robert Finn
Political/Economic Officer - Arlene Ferrill
Furmanova Street 99/97
Almaty 480091
Tel: +7-(3272)-63-39-21
Fax: +7-(3272)-63-38-83

Agency for International Development
Richard Fraenkel
105 Rudaki, Apt 3
734025 Dushanbe
Tel: 7-3772-21-00-77; Fax: 21-01-71
E-mail: dushanbe@usaid.gov

Tajikistan Embassy in the U.S.
[Tajikistan does not yet have an embassy in Washington]

Tajikistan Mission to the United Nations
Ambassador Rashid Alimov
136 East 67th Street
New York, NY 10021
Tel: (212) 744-2196; Fax: (212) 472-7645

United States - Tajikistan Chamber of Commerce
Sadriddin Akramov, Executive Director

1250 24th Street, NW, Suite 350
Washington, D.C. 20037-1124
Tel.: (202) 776-7779; Fax: 9202) 776-7765
Email: ustajcc@aol.com

Central Asian-American Enterprise Fund
Dushanbe
Daniel R. Dougherty, Vice President
14 Pushkin Street
Dushanbe, Tajikistan
Tel: 7 (3772) 21-56-01, 21-60-13
Fax: 7 (3772) 51-00-88
E-mail: daniel@aclc.khj.td.silk.org

Washington
Brian Mercer, Chief Financial Officer and Senior Vice President
Frederic B. Francke, Chief Investment Officer
1634 Eye Street, NW Suite 200
Washington, DC 20006
Tel: (202) 737-7000
Fax: (202) 737-7077
E-mail: us@caeef.com
Web: http://www.caaef.com

European Bank for Reconstruction and Development (EBRD)

Kazuya Murakami, Director
Central Asia Team
Banking department
EBRD
One Exchange Square
London EC2A 2JN
United Kingdom
Tel.: (44-171) 338-6617
Fax: (44-171) 338-7590

Ken Tanimura
Senior Banker
Central Asia Team
Tel.: (44-171) 338-6658
Fax: (44-171) 338-7590

Muzaffar Usmanov
Mission Adviser
Naciba Ahrorova
Mission Assistant
EBRD Dushanbe Office
Room 38, 29 Shotemur Street

734025 Dushanbe
Tajikistan
Tel./Fax: (7-3772) 21-07-63
E-mail: naciba@ebrd.td.silk.org

SELECTED TAJIKISTAN GOVERNMENT CONTACTS

President
Emomali Rakhmonov
80 Rudaki Street
Dushanbe 734023
Tel: 7-3772-21-29-14

Chairman, National Assembly (Majlisi Oli)
Safarali Rajabov

Prime Minister
Yakhyo Azimov
80 Rudaki Street
Dushanbe 734023
Tel: 7-3772-21-19-47

Ministry of Agriculture
1 Rudaki Prospekt
Dushanbe
Tel: 7-3772-21-10-94 or 21-71-18

Ministry of Economy and External Economic Affairs
42 Rudaki Street
Dushanbe 734025
Tel: 7-3772-21-64-00 or 21-30-24
Fax: 7-3772-21-69-14 or 21-38-54

Ministry of Finance
3 Academic Rajabov Street
Dushanbe
Tel: 7-3772-27-39-41 or 21-6-37 or 21-38-04
Fax: 7-3772-21-33-29

Ministry of Foreign Affairs
40 Rudaki Prospekt
734025 Dushanbe
Tel: 7-3772-21-19-87 or 21-18-08 or 21-39-21
Fax: 7-3772-21-02-59
E-mail: dushanbe@mfaumo.td.silk.org

Chairman, National Bank
Murodali Alimardonov

23/2 Rudaki Prospekt
734025 Dushanbe
Tel.: (7-3772) 21-26-19 or 21-54-51
Fax: (7-3772) 21-25-02 or 21-77-92
E-mail: root@natban.tajikistan.su

State Customs Committee
49 Negmat Karabaev Street
Dushanbe 734018
Tel: 7-3772-33-01-33 or 33-92-08; Fax: 7-3772-34-87-19

State Statistical Agency
17 Bokhtar Street
Dushanbe 734025
Tel: 7-3772-27-63-31
Fax: 7-3772-27-54-08

KEY PHONE NUMBERS IN TAJIKISTAN

OFFICE OF THE PRESIDENT (80 RUDAKI)

President		
Emomali Rahmonov		**21-29-11**
President's Administration		
Chief Mamadnazar Salihov	**1-22**	**21-68-00**
1st Deputy Chief Hasan Khudoyorov	**3-45**	**21-06-25**
President's Secretariat		
Chief Saimurod Fattoev	**3-14**	**21-04-18**
Security Council (80 Rudaki)		
Secretary Amirqul Azimov	**5-87**	**21-46-33**
Consultant Murod Shoimov	**4-02**	**21-31-24**
State Advisors to the President		
State Advisor on International Affairs		
Karim Yuldoshev	**4-29 fax: 21-69-71**	
State Advisor on Defense		
Mizrob Kabirov	**9-67**	**21-39-13**
Senior Advisor Zafar Ikromov	**1-85**	**21-76-82**
State Advisor on National Economy		
Gulom Babaev	**9-49**	**21-34-46**

State Advisor on Parliamentary and Legislative Affairs
Khalifabobo Homidov 3-86 21-04-19

State Advisor on Personnel Policy
Amirsho Miraliev 2-81 21-70-26

State Advisor on Contacts with Public Organizations and Interethnic Relations
Davlatali Davlatov 4-82 21-25-22

State Advisor on Science, Culture and Social Affairs
Niyoz Safarov 3-27 21-65-00

Press-Secretary
Zafar Saidov 5-00 21-25-20
Turanboy Tuychiev 21-26-69

PRESIDIUM OF THE GOVERNMENT RT

(80 Rudaki)

Prime Minister
Yahyo Azimov 3-77 21-18-71
Reception 4-89 21-26-36
21-06-24
fax 21-51-10
First Deputy Prime Minister
3-22 21-59-56
21-26-36
Deputy Prime Minister
Abdurahmon Raupovich Azimov 6-36 23-32-43
Asst Uktam Ergashevich Toshmatov 8-84 23-35-84
Deputy Prime Minister
4-00 21-30-83
Deputy Prime Minister
Bozgul Dodkhudoeva 6-44 21-37-74
Deputy Prime Minister
Jamoliddin Mansurov 1-55 21-43-34
Deputy Prime Minister
6-65 21-66-81
Deputy Prime Minister
Ismat Eshmirzoev 6-48 21-86-01

Prime Minister's Secretariat
Chief Valijon Musaev 1-11 21-40-42
res 23-22-75

Foreign Economic Relations Department
Chief Faizali Musovirov 4-60 21-41-49
Deputy Ikrom Burkhan Rahimov 21-47-36
Chief Specialist Mansur Oripov 3-20 21-70-66

Strategic Research Center at the President RT
Director Nuriddin Kayumov 1-98 21-16-90
21-17-47
Deputy Mirmahmad Nurmahmadov 21-08-26

President's Guards Office
General Ghaffor Rahmonovich Mirzoev 1-92 31-16-97
res 34-46-21
Deputy Col Ubaid Narzulloev 0-57 31-12-07
Chief of Unit Davlat Karimov 31-09-93

CNR (Commission on National Reconciliation) (Hotel Vakhsh)
Chairman Said Abdullo Nuri 21-07-32
Deputy Abdumajid Dostiev (Majlisi Oli) 21-59-12
Ibrohim Usmonov 21-06-40
Otakhon Latifi 21-01-98
Shukurjon Zukhurov 21-05-10
Habib Sanginov 21-02-89
pocket telephone 21-00-96

MAJLISI OLI (PARLIAMENT) OF THE REPUBLIC OF TAJIKISTAN

(42 Rudaki)
Chairman
Safarali Rajabov 1-61 21-22-53
Assistant Abdufatoh Sharipov 21-62-51

First Deputy Chairman
Abdumajid Dostiev 7-35 21-59-12
21-32-97
Through: Usmon Sabzov, Chief of Dept 3-83 21-33-44
21-14-54
Deputy Chairman
Qozidavlat Qoimdodov 5-63 21-22-54

Deputy Chairman
Gulafzo Savriddinova 6-22 21-53-42

Majlisi Oli Committees

Economics and Budget Cmt		
Chairman Safar Safarov	6-37	21-11-10
Legislation and Human Rights Cmt		
Chairman Safarali Kenjaev	0-69	21-78-93
Law, Order, Defense and Security Cmt		
Chairman Muzaffar Ashurov	6-19	21-63-44
State Construction Cmt		
Chairman Rafika Musoeva	4-44	21-11-22
Int'l Affairs, Interethnic Relations and Culture Cmt		
Chairman Ibrohim Usmonov	0-73	21-11-21
	fax 21-18-16	
Agricultural Policy, Foodstuffs and Employment Cmt		
Chairman Karimjon Faqirov	2-23	21-76-21
Science, Education and Youth Policy Cmt		
Chairman Mahmadsho Ilolov	6-80	21-24-65
Women's Affairs, Health, Social Protection and Ecology Cmt		
Chairman Khujiahmad Khidiraliev	1-09	21-79-95
Deputy's Ethics and Privileges Cmt		
Chairman Mehmon Bakhti		24-57-71
Central Elections and Referendums Commission		
Mirzoali Boltaev	9-91	21-13-75
Inter-Parliamentary Relations Dept		
Chief Saadi Aminov	0-78	21-01-41
CONSTITUTIONAL COURT /42 Rudaki		
Chairman Faizullo Abdulloev	0-49	21-60-96
Deputy Chairman Zarif Aliev	3-43	21-39-08
SUPREME COURT /17 Karabaev St.		
Chairman Ubaidullo Davlatov	4-53	33-48-21
1st Dep. Ch. Shuhrat Mustafakulov	7-30	33-49-72
Deputy Chairman Sabzali Rahmonov	1-39	33-52-62
SUPREME ECONOMIC COURT /37 Foteh Niyazi St.		
Chairman Bakhtiyor Khudoyorov	5-56	23-28-52

REPUBLICAN PROSECUTOR'S OFFICE /12 Profsoyuz St.

Prosecutor General Salomiddin Sharopov	5-45	36-77-53
1st Deputy Bobojon Bobokhonov	0-29	36-04-45
Deputy	9-83	36-99-97
Deputy Sharif Rajabov	4-01	36-27-23
Department Chief Mamadjon Khairullaev		36-96-79

MINISTRIES

Ministry of Security /8 Gorky St./

Minister Saidamir Zuhurov	0-11	21-23-12
1st Dep. Minister Anatoly Kouptsov	7-23	21-32-38
Deputy Minister Davlat Mamadruzibekov	2-87	21-39-54
Department Chief COL Ahtam Pirov		21-05-97
Duty Officer	5-52	21-37-37
Drug Enforcement Section		
Nazirkhon Zoirov	21-11-59	
Press Center		
Zafar Zakirov	1-46	27-86-53
Educational Center Farhod Sharipov		21-13-93

Ministry of Internal Affairs /29 Gorky St.

Minister Humdin Sharipov	4-66	21-10-71
Advisor LTC Emomali Azimov	8-12	21-83-44
		27-83-34
First Deputy Minister Nikolay Majar	6-31	21-10-60
	21-06-52	
Deputy Minister Abdusattor Rajabov	9-57	
Deputy Minister Abdumannon Gaziev	9-42	21-09-94
Deputy Minister Davlat Bulbulshoev	8-46	21-25-50
Duty Officer	0-92	21-08-30
Antinarcotics Department		
Chief Turaboy Komilov		21-04-87
Department to combat organized crime		
Col Tohir Nurmatov		21-32-64

State Commission on Drug Control (3 Parvina St.)

Chairman Rustam Nazarov	8-01	24-92-27
Office	24-79-84, 24-91-10	
	fax 24-68-79	

Ministry of Health /69 Shevchenko St.

Minister Alamkhon Ahmadov	8-44	21-30-64
First Deputy Minister Ismoil Usmonov	0-17	21-12-48
Deputy Minister Nasrullo Abdujabborov	1-26	21-04-63
Deputy Minister Zuhra Mirzoeva	1-04	21-10-74

Deputy Minister Muzaffar Mamadnazarov	5-29	21-17-03
Diagnostic Center Chief Nurullo Shukurov	34-92-00	
Ministry of Foreign Affairs /42 Rudaki St.		
Minister Talbak Nazarov	4-61	21-18-08
1st Dep. Minister Erkin Rahmatullaev	4-80	21-19-87
Asst to 1st Dep. Minister Hisrav Goibov	21-15-03	
Deputy Minister	2-54	21-39-21
Deputy Minister Gulomjon Mirzoev	6-49	21-15-34
Personnel and special information Dept		
Davlamad Gulmadov, Chief	7-58	21-01-17
Bilateral and Multilateral links Dept		
Abdullo Yuldoshev, Chief	6-42	21-15-46
Analysis and Strategic Researches Dept		
Alijon Salibaev, Chief	4-49	21-10-93
Information Dept (Press-Center)		
Chief Igor Sattarov (Olga)	8-87	21-43-53
Deputy Chief Davlatali Nazriev	21-01-26	
Sulaimon Rashidov	fax 21-43-69	
International Organizations Dept (Room 28)		
Chief Erkin Kasimov	4-13	21-15-08
State Protocol Dept		
Chief Zubaidullo Zubaidov (Nigora)	0-12	21-15-62
Deputy Chief Mirafzal Mirshakar	4-25	21-61-05
Muhamad Surkhov		21-61-05
Rahimjon Nosyrov	4-25	21-09-14
Yatimshoh Musofirov		21-09-14
Komil Mirzoev		21-09-14
Consular Dept		
Chief Garibsho Shabozov	1-24	21-15-60
Deputy Nurullo Sharipov (visa for foreigners)		21-04-70
Deputy Chief Sharifa Azamovna Yakubova		21-04-70
Deputy Lyubov Kulikova (visa for Tajik citizens)		21-10-51
Deputy Chief Isamatov		21-10-51
Administrative Dept		
Chief Saidjafar Safarov	1-06	21-10-40
Dep. Chief, Head of Dip. Corp Services Section		
Masaid Komilov		21-17-37
Financial Dept		
Chief Zebinisso Vasiyeva	4-52	21-08-41
Ministry of Agriculture (44 Rudaki)		
Minister Muso Barotov	1-88	21-15-96
		21-64-61
Deputy Minister Aziz Sharipov	9-69	21-10-94

Deputy Minister Ikhtiyor Ashurov	4-69	21-71-18
Ministry of Culture (34 Rudaki St.)		
Minister Bobokhon Mahmadov	0-33	21-03-05
		23-43-77
First Deputy Minister Akbar Juraev	8-77	21-34-01
Deputy Minister Jamshed Ismoilov	3-73	21-36-30
Deputy Minister Olimjon Salimzoda	1-93	21-53-34
Dep. Minister(Econ/Fin) Guljon Mirzoeva	3-21	21-04-06
Cultural & International Ties Department		
Chief Buston Shukurov		21-53-07
Ministry of Melioration and Water Management (78 Rudaki)		
Minister Davlatbek Makhsudov	9-52	21-10-12
First Deputy Minister Nurullo Ashurov	5-08	27-39-96
Ministry of Defense (59 Bokhtar St.)		
Minister Sherali Khairullaev	3-09	21-18-09
Aide Major Tagaimurod Menglibaev		21-69-83
1st Dep. Min. Abdullo Habibov	2-00	21-22-78
Dep.Min./Chief of Staff Sodiq Bobojonov	8-15	21-23-69
Deputy Min. COL Latif Faiziev		
Deputy Min. COL A. Abulasanov		
Aide to Bobojonov Ltnt Avaz Timurov		
Asst to the Minister Ltnt-Capt Abdullaev		21-32-47
Asst on Special Orders Capt Andrey Kovalenko		23-17-83
Chief of Admin Dept LtntCol Qodyr Teshaev		23-16-57
Int'l Dept Major Maaruf Hasanov	0-94	23-43-02
extension		1-86
Duty Officer	9-11	21-18-53
Telephone operator		21-50-18
Military College		32-18-10
Khairullo Khaidarov		32-18-06
Ministry of Education (13 Chekhov St.)		
Minister Munira Inoyatova	6-33	23-33-92
1st Dep. Minister Abdulbashir Rashidov	8-59	27-43-74
Dep. Ismoil Davlatov		
Dep. Minister Kurbonmamad Goibnazarov	8-29	23-37-66
Foreign Relations Department		
Kadir Berdiev		23-23-73
Printing House (7 Kuibyshev St.)		
Director Nabi Rabievich Tohirov		21-73-58

Ministry of Environmental Protection (12 Bokhtar St.)

Minister	2-66	23-28-78
1st Dep. Minister Negmatullo Safarov	6-81	21-42-71
Science Department		
Chief Sirojiddin Aslov		22-30-39

Ministry of Communications (57 Rudaki)

Minister Nuriddin Muhiddinov	4-32	21-22-84
First Deputy Ibrohim Usmonov	5-88	21-23-84
Deputy Minister Tukhtaboy Kayumov	4-55	23-28-63
Administration Chief Mavluda Rustamova		21-60-18

Republican Center for International Accounts

Director Saodat Niyazova		
Deputy Director Yelena Zenkova		21-49-86
Specialist Maruf Muhamedov		21-71-79
		fax: 21-47-39

State Department "Pochtai Tojik" (Tajik Post Office)(42/2 Ibn-Sino St.)

Director General Shukurullo Komilov	2-64	35-07-41

Joint-stock Company "Tojiktelecom" (Mezhgorsvyaz) (53 Rudaki)

Director General Farhat Shukurov	6-24	23-44-44

Ministry of Social Welfare (61 Borbad St.)

Minister Abdusattor Jabborov	7-00	31-37-57
First Deputy Minister Navruz Afzalov	3-02	31-56-56

Ministry of Transport and Roads (14 Aini St.)

Minister Faridun Muhiddinov	2-11	21-17-13
First Deputy Minister Narzullo Dustov 2	-94	21-25-93

Ministry of Labor and Employment (5/2 A. Navoi St.)

Minister Khudoiberdy Kholiqnazarov	1-65	36-18-37
1st Dep. Minister Beg Kurbonov	8-22	36-24-15
Deputy Minister Alisher Yarbabaev	9-19	36-25-21

Ministry of Finance (3 Academicians Rajabovs St.)

Minister Anvarsho Muzafarov	5-66	27-39-41
First Deputy Sharif Mulloev	6-27	21-62-37
	21-57-06	
"Tajikinvest" (1 Proyezd Lohuti #6)	27-08-98	
	6-33	27-09-00

Ministry of Economics and Foreign Economic Relations/44 Rudaki

Minister Davlat Usmon	2-45	21-69-14
		21-64-00
1st Dep. Minister Isroil Makhmudov	3-88	21-30-24
Deputy Minister	1-33	21-62-09
Deputy Minister Victor Boltov	3-16 fax	21-37-54
Deputy Amonullo Ashurov		21-30-26

Ministry of Justice (25 Rudaki)

Minister Shavkat Ismailov	6-11	21-44-05
		23-22-50
1st Dep. Minister Shermahmad Shoev	7-07	21-87-97
Deputy Minister Larisa Smeyanova	7-08	21-36-96
		21-87-97

STATE COMMITTEES OF THE REPUBLIC OF TAJIKISTAN

State Committee for Administration of State Property (44 Rudaki)

Matlubkhon Davlatov	3-91	21-86-59
First Deputy Chairman Asror Rashidov	5-49	21-81-50

State Committee for Industry (22 Rudaki)

Chairman Rajabali Kadyrov	3-49	21-69-97
First Deputy Chairman	1-34	21-88-89

State Committee for Contracts and Trade (37 Bokhtar St.)

Chairman Hakim Soliev	0-22	27-34-34
First Deputy Chairman Akbar Akhmedov	1-50	27-12-51

GOVERNMENT COMMITTEES AND DEPARTMENTS

State Statistical Agency /Gosstatagentstvo/ (17 Bokhtar St.)

Director Habib Gaibullaev	2-88	27-63-31
First Deputy Director Shamsidin Saifov	2-37	27-34-29
Deputy Director Barot Turaev	8-27	27-56-28

Committee for Precious Metals (Tajikdragmetsamotsvety) (77 Mushfiki)

Chairman Saidullo Khairulloev	7-51	33-44-19
		33-43-56
First Deputy Azim Jangiev		33-41-41

Committee for Precious Stones and Semi-precious Raw Materials

(6 Rudaki)		
Chairman Jahongir Ruziev	7-17	21-44-24
Asst Avaz Kurbonov		21-84-19

Customs Committee /Tajiktamozhnya/ (40? Bukhoro St.)

Chairman Rahim Karimov	6-07	21-16-92
First Deputy Chairman Kenja Hasanov		5-91
Deputy Chief Abdujalilov		1-84
Foreign Department Chief Tohir Oripov		7-72
Telephone operator		23-27-26

Tax Committee (155 Kirov St.)

Chief Sulton Quvvatov	4-11	21-31-74
First Deputy Chief Hairullo Alimadov	9-05	27-12-82
Deputy Aslidin Sohibnazarov	6-02	21-35-88
Tax Police: Chief Sanginmurod Abdullaev		21-63-47
		21-34-54

Committee for Extraordinary Situations and Civil Defense (59 Bokhtar)

Chairman		
Husanboy Achilov	2-77	23-17-78
1st Dep. Chairman Ziyoratsho Ashurov	5-17	21-13-31

Committee for Meat and Milk Industry /Tajikmyasomolprom (35 Kaharov)

Chairman Habibullo Tabarov	5-84	21-77-46
First Deputy Chairman Bahtiyor Gadoev	7-56	21-78-22

Committee for Physical Culture and Sports (31 Shotemur St.)

Chairman Saimumin Rahimov	5-85	23-16-24
1st Dep. Chairman Sulaimon Abdulvahidov	0-47	23-39-16

Committee for Women and Family Affairs (44 Rudaki)

Chairman Latofat Nasriddinova	6-57	21-34-71
Deputy Mukarramhon Buzurukova		21-86-97

Committee for Religious Affairs (80 Rudaki)

Chairman Said Akhmedov	2-61	23-33-66
		21-60-05
Deputy Ikromiddin Nematov	1-68	21-40-65

Committee for Architecrure and Construction (11/6 Valamatzoda)

Chairman Bahovadin Zuhurdinov	1-44	23-18-82
First Deputy Chairman Yuri Potekhin	8-05	23-26-57

Committee for Oil and Gas /Tajikneftegas/ (77 Mushfiki St.)
Chairman 9-61 33-36-51
1st Deputy Chairman Saidjon Saidrahmonov 33-41-82

Committee for Food and Processing Industry /Tajikpishcheprom
("Tojikmatlubot", 5 Floor)
Chairman Faizullo Quvvatov 7-77 21-15-91
First Deputy Chairman Ismonkul Bilolov 2-33 21-17-80

Industry and Mining Security State Control Cmt /Gosgortekhnadzor
(63 Karabaeva)
Chairman Ayub Aliev 7-47 34-87-30
1st Dep. Chairman Vyacheslav Kuznetsov 3-30 34-87-10

Special Property Providing Committee
Chairman Hukmat Odinaev 4-77

Committee for Land Resources (Giprozem)
Chairman Bakhtiyor Kabilov 31-16-83

Tajik State Center for Standartization and Metrology
(42/2 Karabaev)
Director Amir Kataev 4-20 33-68-69

Chief Department for Cotton-Cleaning Industry /"Pakhtai Tojik"
(44 Rudaki)
Chief Gulom Boyakov 1-66 21-32-22
First Deputy Chief Bayon Davlatov 21-77-66

Chief Department for Archives /Glavarkhiv/ (38/1 Karabaev St.)
Chief Zafar Dustmuhamedov 3-41 33-95-71
Deputy Chief Dilovar Komilov 33-63-52

Defense Industry Committee
Chairman Ghafforkhon Muhitdinov

Border Guarding Committee
COL Rustam Akramov 0-14
Duty officer 21-81-21

Chief Dept for Geology /Tajikglavgeologiya/ (27 Tursunzade St.)
Chief Ayubjon Orifov 8-00 27-27-29
Deputy Chief Alexander Akhmedov 1-05 27-27-49

TV and Radio Committee (Dom Radio)		
Chief Saif Rahimov	**3-69**	
Chief Department for Geodezy and Cartography /Tajikglavgeodeziya/ (4/1 Abai St.)		
Chief Muzaffar Ishanov		**31-24-23**
Deputy Chief Gul Oimahmadov		**31-35-41**
Tajik Information Agency "Hovar" ((37 Rudaki)		
Director Nabijon Karimov	**3-19**	**21-33-13**
UNION OF CONSUMERS SOCIETY (Tajikmatlubot)(137 Rudaki)		
Chairman Yatim Mirzoev	**4-83**	**21-00-35**
First Deputy Chairman Sharif Saidov	**0-59**	**24-87-04**
GBAO Representation at the Government of RT (40 Rudaki)		
Representative Plenipotentiary		
Shodavlat Shodavlatov		**27-85-97**

HUKUMAT (DUSHANBE CITY COUNCIL)

Mayor Mahmadsaid Ubaidullaev	**7-33**	**21-27-04**
		21-27-39
First Deputy Akbar Mirzoevich Fayazov	**3-82**	**21-02-85**
Deputy Mayor Muslima Valieva	**4-65**	**21-20-60**
Deputy Mayor Husnoro Mirzoeva	**7-28**	**21-46-67**
International Department		
Chief	**6-52**	**21-45-14**
		21-27-43
Secretary Tamara Alekseevna		**21-45-14**
Interpreter Ibragim Murodov		**23-18-31**
Inquiry office		**21-26-95**

EDUCATIONAL INSTITUTIONS

Tajik State University	
Rector Habib Safarov	**21-62-25**
Pro-Rector for Foreign Relations Nazir Jumaev	**21-76-71**
Tajik State Medical University	
Rector Hamdam Rofiev	**24-45-83**
Pro-Rector Karim Gafarov	**24-89-65**

Dushanbe State Pedagogical University

Rector Kurbon Rasulov		24-78-09
		24-83-13
Pro-Rector for Foreign Relations Mavjuda Abdulloeva		24-16-82

Tajik Agricultural University

Rector Yusuf Nasirov	24-72-07

Tajik Technical University (in Dushanbe)

Rector Khisrav Sadikov	23-43-42
Deputy Ikram Negmatov	22-36-87
Foreign Students Dept Dean Sharofiddin Nuriddinov	27-37-81

(In Khojand: Rector 7(37922)6-04-54/6-18-42)

Tajik Institute of Physical Culture/Natinal Olympic Cmt

Rector Burikhon Jobirov	24-14-61

Tajik Technological University (63/3 Karabaev Str.)

Rector Pulat Pulatov	5-19	34-79-87
	fax 34-79-88	
	res 37-05-43	
Personnel Office	34-59-10	

e-mail: pulatov@tecnol.td.silk.glas.apc.org.

Tajik Institute of Languages

Rector Mavluda Abdullaeva	32-95-15
Head of Foreign Languages Chair Holida Astanova	35-87-01
	32-95-17

Tajik Institute of Services and Enterpreneuship

Rector Khabibullo Umarov	34-88-30
Head of Foreign Languages Chair Normat Khaibatov	34-88-26

Tajik Commercial Institute

Rector Olim Boboev	34-86-22
Head of Foreign Languages Chair Ganijon Rahmonov	34-85-80

Tajik Institute of Fine Arts

Rector Rajabahmad Amirov	31-18-27
Deputy Said Shamsov	31-45-45
Deputy Abdurahim Rahimov	31-13-51

Slavic University (34 Tursunzade St.)

Rector Abdujabbor Sattorov	27-99-93
Pro-Rector Svetlana Balkhova	27-42-27
Dean of Humanities Dept Khusrav Shambezoda	27-78-93

CENTRAL INSTITUTIONS AND ORGANIZATIONS

ACADEMY OF SCIENCES (33 Rudaki)			
President Ulmas Mirsaidov	8-55	21-50-85	
Vice-President Muso Dinorshoev	6-01	21-37-63	
Institute of Philosophy and Law		21-77-96	
Central Scientific Library of the Academy of Sciences			
Director		off 27-55-46	
Institute of Chemistry			
Director Ulmas Mirsaidov		25-26-04	
Institute of Gastroenterology			
Director Hamid Mansurov		23-36-09	
		21-72-40	
		24-81-47	
Institute of Seismology			
Director Sobit Negmatullaev		25-06-69	
		25-11-93	
Institute of World Economics & International Relations			
Director Rashid Rahimov		23-27-32	
ACADEMY OF AGRICULTURAL SCIENCES (25 Rudaki)			
President Bobo Sanginov		4-78	23-18-32
Vice-President Abdurahim Khojibaev		1-70	21-70-04
Botanical Garden			
Director Abdullo Asrakulovich Madaminov			24-71-88
Dep. Dir. Muhabbat Mirzotash. Sharipova			24-43-57
Firdavsi State Library			
Director Sohib Goibnazarov			27-47-26
Law and Democracy Center: Elena Degtyareva			21-44-07
			21-49-64

BANKS

Tajik National Bank (23/2 Rudaki)		
Chairman Murodali Alimardonov	4-91	21-26-28
		21-26-79
First Deputy Chairman Sharif Rahimov	7-25	21-54-51
Foreign Economic Relations Department	21-78-50	

Tajikagroprombank "Sharq" (97 Rudaki)		
Chairman Maqsud Kadyrov	2-08	21-10-14
1st Deputy Chairman Mirzo Sharipov	1-95	21-10-77
Tajikvnesheconombank (4 Khisrav Dehlavi St.)		
Chairman Izatullo Lalbekov	8-14	23-35-61
Orionbank (95/1 Rudaki)		
President Abdumutalib Abdusattorov	4-36	21-09-20
		21-19-69
Foreign Econ. Relations Dept Chief Alisher Babajanov		21-16-62
		21-16-42
Tajikbankbusiness (29 Shotemur St.)		
President Kayum Kavmiddinov	9-07	21-05-03
1st Vice-President Murodjon Vafaev	9-56	21-06-34
Savings Bank /Tajiksberbank/ (67 Rudaki)		
Chairman Kurbonali Juraev	0-13	21-70-81
Tajbank (59/1 Somoni St.) President	1-42	24-53-15
Fononbank Chairman Tatyana Dedurova		35-27-13
		35-27-03
Interbank Currency Exchange		
Director Negmatullo Rahimov		21-11-89

CONCERNS, COMPANIES, ASSOCIATIONS

State Concern "Tajikcommunservice" (31 Shotemur St.)		
Chairman Aziz Inoyatov	3-66	27-99-10
Tajik State-Cooperative Concern "TAJIKSELSTROY"(Village building) (50 Dehoti St.)		
President Rahimjon Gafurov	0-50	34-79-77
Tajik State Concern "MADAD" on Technical Service and Support of Agricultural Complexes (27 Rudaki)		
President Abdujalol Salimov	8-81	21-81-07
Tajik Republican Concern "KHIZMAT" /Service/ (14 Lohuti St.)		
President Abdulahat Normatov	4-88	21-43-98

Tajik State Concern "Furuzon" (734060, PB 889)
President Tukhtasin Teshabaev 5-98 35-85-76

State Building Company "TAJIKSTROY" (36 Khuseinzoda St.)
Chairman Abdumalik Azimov 6-29 21-61-43

State Joint-Stock Holding Company "Barqi Tojik" (Tajik Power)
(64 Ismoili Somoni St.)
President Bahrom Sirojev 7-11 35-87-66
29-56-50

State Company "Tajiknefteproduct" (Tajik Oil Product)
(14 Khuseinzoda St.)
Chairman Amonullo Hukumov 5-64 21-59-37

State Company for Building Power Units "Tajikhydroenergostroy"
(39a Kakharov St.)
President Vladimir Shichkin 7-22 23-38-87

Joint-Stock Company "Intourist-Tojikiston" (22 Shotemur St.)
President Murtazo Ostanaev 1-28 21-62-62

National Tourism Company "Tajiktourism" (14 Pushkin St.)
President Qosym Abdusalomovich Gafarov off 23-14-01
res 24-14-06

Tajik State Aviation Company "TOJIKISTON" (32/1 Titov St.)

General Director Mirzo Mastangulov	0-77	21-21-45
Reception		29-82-01
		21-32-83
		51-01-10
		fax 21-86-85
		fax 51-00-41
First Deputy Vilsuor Avidzba	5-58	27-85-76
Airport Director Rustam Rustamov	9-33	21-09-52
		21-03-48
Chief Dispatcher Alisher Rustamov		21-09-62
Dispatcher/Inquiry Desk		23-26-31
		29-85-31
Airport Tower		29-86-10
Aeroflot Intourist Cashier		21-79-19
VIP Waiting Room		29-82-39
Intourist Waiting Room		29-87-51
Intn'l Dpt, Firuz Ishankulov	5-66	21-22-47
		29-85-45
		fax 21-22-47

Telephone operator		21-32-28
Commercial Warehouse		29-82-71
Airport Garage		29-82-09
Aeroflot Agency		
Galina Gonchar		29-83-30
		27-74-02
Inquiry desk		21-65-89
Airtickets dispatcher Komil / Natasha		21-70-78

Tajik Republican Commercial-Industrial Company "Tajikles" (Tajik Wood)(31 Shotemur St.)		
Director General Gaibullo Fazylov	9-25	27-68-88
		27-98-79
State Joint-Stock Company "Umron" (build. materials industry) (3-a Rudaki)		
President Kim Nazirov	1-77	21-88-13
State Corporation "Tajikmontazhspetsstroy" (3 Tursunzade St.)		
President Sirojiddin Saidov	5-03	21-87-65
Tajik State Insurance Company "Tajikgosstrakh" (3 Academikov Rajabovykh St.)		
Director General Mansur Ochildiev	7-01	27-58-49
Forestry Industrial Association "Tajikles" (22 Sh. Rustaveli St.)		
Director General Gaibullo Avzalov	7-55	23-19-92
Republican Industrial Association "Mohiparvar"(Fishing industry) (44 Rudaki St.)		
Director General Nazir Mullojanov	5-24	21-40-49
Tajik Railway (35 Shapkin St.)		
Chief Muhammad Khabibov	5-96	21-88-54
		27-37-90
Republican Industrial Association "Tajikselkhozkhimiya" (Tajik Agricultural Chemistry) (21-a Rudaki)		
Chairman Vahob Vahidov	8-10	27-98-40
Joint-Stock Industrial-Investment Corporation "Somoniyon" (48 Rudaki)		
President Abdurahmon Mukhtashov	5-05	23-29-03

Republican Association "Tojikboghbunyod"(Tajik Gardens)(126 Aini)
Chief Aslan Anvarov 6-40 25-16-59

Republican Association "Tajikvneshtrans"(3 Yuzhno-Obkhodnaya St.)
President Alamhon Kurbanov 31-56-17

Joint-Stock Industrial Commercial Firm "Pamir-Lada"(125 Karabaev)
President Yusufali Khudoikulov 31-94-63

Tajik Republican Association "Automotoservice"(1 October 40 let)
Director General Farhod Ashurov 31-09-36

State Holding Company "Ghalla" (5/1 Shamsi St.)

Chairman Bekmurod Uroqov	2-55	32-14-36
First Deputy Chairman Manaim Kasimov	3-65	32-15-22
Deputy Chairman Urunboy Isakov	4-30	32-19-69
Deputy Chairman Inom Turaboev	5-36	32-16-14
32-18-65		
Asst to Chairman Bahodur Mahmudov		32-18-28

COMMERCIAL STRUCTURES

Foreign Economic Company "IMPEX"
General Director Ahad Abdulkholov 27-58-11

Chamber of Commerce
President Kamol Sufiev 9-41 27-95-19

Tajik-American Joint Venture "Interfur"(40 Let Tajikistana, N141)
General Director Raf Yadgarov 34-92-92
34-92-78

Tajik-Lebanese Joint Venture "Tolib"
General Director Mamadnazar Karimov 33-97-75

"Guliston": Commercial Manager Bakhtiyor Makhkamov 27-15-93

"Russia-Tojikiston"
President Mahbuba Kosimi 24-89-38
24-18-92

"Shukur" President Kakhor Mahkamov 27-71-93

RT Corporation "Hima" (21 Pavlova Str.)
President Ismatullo Izzatulloevich Khayoev 24-81-36

UNIONS

Union of Architects (1 Behzod St.)

Chairman Rustam Karimov	6-10	27-18-71
Union of Artists (89 Rudaki)		
Chairman Suhrob Kurbonov	0-15	24-15-71
Union of Cinematographers (43 Bukhoro St.)		
Chairman Anvar Turaev	1-90	21-75-09
Union of Composers (1 Tehron St.)		
Chairman Damir Dustmuhamedov	7-15	27-62-33
Creative Union		
General Director Abdugaffor Abdujaborov		27-33-87
Union of Cooperators and Businessmen		
Chairman S. Komilov		27-63-58
Union of Designers		
Chairman Anatoly Zanevsky		34-47-19
	Res 33-80-19	
Union of Journalists (31 Bukhoro St.)		
Chairman Khayot Davlatov	8-09	21-75-23
Union of Photo Journalists (18 Rudaki)		
Chairman Gennady Ratushenko		27-75-37
	res 32-94-48	
Commercial Creative Union "Romish"		
Chairman Botur Karimov		22-79-51
Scientific Industrial Union of Tajikistan (6 Rudaki)		
Chairman Abdurahmon Dadabaev	4-76	27-23-29
Union of Theater Workers (107 Rudaki)		
Chairman Ato Muhamadjonov	24-29-68	
Deputy Nurullo Abdulloev	24-50-07	
Deputy Abdugaffor Abdujaborov	24-89-38	
Union of War and Labor Veterans (3 Tehron St.)		
Chairman Rauf Dadabaev	7-92	27-13-42
Union of Afghan War Veterans		
Chairman Suhrob Alimov		21-06-91
Union of Writers (8 Somoni St.)		
Chairman Askar Hakim	8-98	24-57-37

Deputy Chairman Abdurahmon Abdumanonov	7-97	24-57-67
Deputy Chairman Abdulhomid Samadov		24-57-46
Trade-Unions Federation (20 Rudaki)		
Chairman Murodali Salikhov	8-66	23-35-16
Deputy Chairman Shakir Kashaev	8-22	21-88-63
Central Soviet of the Youth Union (42 Rudaki)		
Chairman Ibod Rahimov	3-42	21-63-14
		23-05-41
Association of University Women RT		
President Guljahon Bobosadykova		21-17-50
	fax	21-05-55

SOCIETIES

Tajik Society of Friendship and Cultural Relations with Foreign Countries (7 Gorky St.)		
Chairman Maisara Kalonova	9-01	27-74-94
Reception		21-01-84
Tajik Center of Civic Education (NGO)		
Director Gulchehra Nosirova		27-73-69
	fax	21-70-33
	res	33-98-66
"Paivand" (17 Bokhtar St.)		
Chairman Kamol Aini	8-36	27-77-39
1st Deputy Chairman Uktam Kholikov		27-77-39
Deputy Chairman Nuriddin Kurbanov		27-04-23
Red Crescent Society (120 Omar Khayam)		
President Jura Inomzoda	5-46	24-03-74
Vice-President Davron Muhamadiev		24-44-86
Society of the Deaf (270 Khuvaidulloev St.)		
Chairman Galina Malisheva	36-71-21	
Society of the Invalids (4 Telman St.)		
Chairman Hakim Khaknazarov	21-15-74	
Society of the Blind (205 Karamov St.)		
Chairman Turabek Davlatov	37-32-31	
"Znaniye":	23-26-73	
	27-84-70	

HOTELS

"Oktyabrskaya"

Director Marhamat Akramova	21-12-70
Reception	21-12-80
Chief Accountant	21-12-86
Chief Engineer	21-12-16
Restaurant Director Rizvon Rahmonov	21-12-29

"Tajikistan"

Director General Samijon Sadyev	21-70-00
Reception	21-82-28
	21-62-62
	21-33-56
Restaurant Manager Rustam Muradov	21-70-77

MUSEUMS

Ethnographic Museum

Director Zebo Kavrakova	res 21-07-64

Republican Museum

Director Sangin Khafizov	23-15-44
	23-08-72

Shahidi Museum of Musical Culture (108 K. Marx/Shahidi St.)

Director Munira Shahidi	24-23-42
	Res 27-08-66

Museum of National Musical Instruments

Director Gurminj Zavkibekov	res 23-42-29
Deputy Director Tamara Pavlovna	

THEATERSOpera & Ballet Theater

Director Nariman Karimov	0-90	21-80-47
		21-62-91

Russian Drama Theatre

Director Suhrob Mirzoev	21-36-22
Chief Conductor Anatoly Mamaev	21-73-73

Lohuti Tajik Drama Theater

Director Iso Abdurashidov	21-78-43
	21-43-76

Vohidov Youth Theater

Manager Mahamdnazar Kholov	23-08-74
Deputy Manager Makhkam Hojikulov	33-34-36

Experimental Miniature Theater "Oina"

Chief Director Ubaidullo Rajabov 25-04-97

Puppet Theater
Manager Rustam Ahmadov 23-15-83
23-15-93

State Dance Ensemble "Lola"
Manager Radif Yafaev 21-12-13

State Dance Ensemble "Zebo"
Art Director Zarrina Yadgarova 34-56-44

Theater-Studio "Akhorun"
Chief Director Farrukh Kosimov 27-09-68

MASS MEDIA

"Biznes i Politika"
Editor-in-Chief Nina Pak 3-46 33-32-26
Correspondent Ilhom 33-43-96

"Golos Tajikistana"
Editor-in-Chief Inom Musaev 33-76-27

"Khalq Ovozi" (Uzbek) (16 Sherozi St.)
Editor-in-Chief Ismoil Mukhsinov 6-21 33-12-27

"Jumhuriyat" (16 Sherozi St.)
Editor-in-Chief 4-93 33-08-11
33-05-64

"Narodnaya Gazeta" (16 Sherozi St.)
Editor-in-Chief Vladimir Vorobyev 8-24 33-08-25
Deputy Editor-in-Chief Tatyana Karatygina

"Navruzi Vatan"
Editor-in-Chief Muhammadjon Mirzoshoyev 33-57-05

"Sadoi Mardum"
Editor-in-Chief Mirzomahmud Mirbobev 2-43 33-10-77

"Vecherny Kuryer"
Editor-in-Chief Javohir Kabilov 33-55-59
33-13-16, 33-24-13

"Payomi Dushanbe"
Editor-in-Chief Ibod Fayzullaev 6-14

"Asia Plus", "Komsomolskaya Pravda"
Editor Umed Babakhanov off 21-78-63

res 21-21-93

"Naqsuz"
Habibullo Boturov 21-38-33

"Stolichnaya Gazeta" (36 Karabaev)
Victor Kim 33-44-17

CORRESPONDENT POINTS

"Ostankino" (ORT) (72/1 Somoni St.) 2-24 36-43-21
Correspondent Tatiana Lagunova 1-29 36-42-21

"Vesti" (26 Tehron): Zarina Baranova 21-62-11
21-50-48

"ITAR-TASS" (55 Rudaki)
Galina Gridneva 8-21 21-30-97

RIA "Novosti" (18 Rudaki)
Najmiddin Azizov 5-72 23-49-06
Yevgeny Ratushenko 27-75-37

"Interfax": Surayo Sobirova 9-46 fax 21-42-96

TV Company "MIR" (55 Rudaki)
Negmat Mirsaidov 9-35 21-16-53
Tolib Shahidi 21-15-67
fax 27-23-22

BBC Monica Witlock 21-00-81
Mardoni Muhammad 24-16-73

INTERNATIONAL ORGANIZATIONS AND COMPANIES

ACCELS/ACTR (American Center) /Freedom Support Act/
(Firdavsi Library, 1st floor)
Laura Meenk off 21-17-95
res 24-73-09
Matluba Mamadjanova 27-45-41
Lena Logge, Zarrina Muhiddinova
Ilhom Kadyrov 27-45-41

ACTED (Agency for Technical Cooperation and Development)
(66 Tolstoy Str.)
Technical Director Dean Harvey 24-70-58

ADRA (Adventist Development and Relief Agency) (43 Schorsa Str.)
Tajikistan Director Conrad Vine 33-15-70

AED/Globe Project (Academy for Educational Development)
(40 Rudaki, Room 301)
Country Repres. Tamara Lashbrook off 21-06-00
Program Specialist Niso Rasulova 21-08-44
Gulru Azamova 21-82-49
fax 21-05-18

American Business Center
Manager Faridun Kamoliddinov 21-05-22
Asst to Manager Savriniso Kurbonbekova 21-05-26
Turkish line: 51-01-02

AKF (Aga Khan Foundation)/AKDN (Aga Khan Development Network)
(6 Hamza Hakimzade)
Chief Executive Officer Hakim Feerasta 21-51-18
Asst Natasha Avakova 24-65-00
Firuz Vatanshoev fax 21-70-87
Admin. Asst 24-19-42
Turkish line: 51-00-66
mob tlx: 583-492-282-520
E-mail for internet users: akftjk@atge.automail.com

Pamir Relief and Development Program/Khorog Office
tel: 27-19, 26-99, 67-99, 60-37, 65-99
AKDN/ Khorog tel: 25-99, 43-45

Project Office
Project Director Rafique Keshavjie off 24-58-23
res 23-09-44
27-69-35

ABA (American Bar Association) (44 Shevchenko St., Apt. 37)
Chief Jack Martin off 21-18-67
fax 21-17-86

BASICS/PROJECT USAID/CCCID (20/1 Behzod Str., 7)
Chief Ibod Sharifi res 24-34-43
off 21-83-12
21-46-91

CAAEF (Central Asian-American Enterprise Fund) (35 Kirov Str.)
Vice-President Dan Dougherty (in Khojand) 21-50-14
Consultant Bakhtiyor Umarov 21-56-01

CADA (Central Asian Development Agency)(40 Rudaki Av., Room 307)

Chief David Lovett off 21-21-75
res 24-62-64, 24-51-77

Acting Director Teh Seng Chuan (till March 22)
Susan Layman off 21-08-80
res 24-51-11
Doctor Beverley Ankerman res 24-58-93
office address: 64 Rudaki, Apt 37

Administration (Sitora) fax 21-22-10
Administrator/Interpreter 21-11-27
E-mail: cada@cada.silk.glas.asc.org 21-01-56

CARANA (44 Rudaki, Room 159)
Project Manager Mathew Scanlon 21-88-87
Joseph Sean Morris 21-75-50

CARE (4 Mendeleyev St.)
Country Representative Peter Goossens off 21-17-83
res 24-06-46
Food Project Advisor Golam Azam 21-00-91
Project Manager (agriculture) Anthony Johnson 24-04-89
Admin. Manager Gulchin Sarkorova (Munira, adiba) 24-70-39
fax 21-17-78
Turkish line 51-00-36

CARITAS Switzerland (20/2 Ahmadi Donish Str., Apt.13-14)

Chief Lutz Leichtfuss 23-05-44
Prof. Abdumumin Sharifov (TTU) 21-62-27

Counterpart Consortium (20 Kirova St., Apt. 7)
Country Director John Barbee 21-82-65
21-65-14

EBRD (29 Shotemur Str., Apt. 19)
Mission Asst Nasiba Ahrorova 21-07-63

ECHO (European Community Humanitarian Office) (European Union)
(25 Tursunzade St., 3rd Floor)
Representative Janny Bosscher 23-24-86

EF (Eurasia Foundation) (18 Rudaki)
Regional Director Daniel Bliss (Tashkent)
Coordinator Alla Kuvvatova off 21-69-86

GAA (German Agro Action) (Sharq Str., 3rd proyezd, h. 14)

Project Coordinator 24-74-11
21-23-48

GTZ (German Agency for Technical Development) (14 Aini)
Project Manager Karlfried Metzler 21-71-26
21-74-51
fax 51-00-37

ICRC (International Committee of the Red Cross) (14/3 Aini St.)
Head of Mission Mark Hofstetter 21-68-23
Deputy Denis Berthoud 21-82-14
Admin. Coordinator Irene Zuend 21-73-37
Fax 21-86-60

IFRC (International Federation of the Red Cross)
(120 Omar Khayam St., 3rd Floor)
Head of Delegation George Heron 24-59-81
Admin. Asst Aishe Muratova 24-42-96
Operator Victoriya fax 24-85-20

IMF (International Monetary Fund) (23/2 Rudaki)
Chief 9-95 21-24-80

"Internews" (92 Rudaki, Apt. 24)
Jennifer Minor off 24-54-83
fax 21-43-12
res 24-16-32

IOM (International Organization for Migration)(30 Sino St.)
HOM Raynald Blouin 24-71-96
Program Asst Jamilla Babaeva fax 21-03-02
fax 51-00-62

MCI (Mercy Corps International) (12 Tehron St.)
Head of Mission 21-08-60
Michael Allen 27-61-13
Koryun Alaverdian fax 21-08-64

MERLIN (Medical Emergency Relief Int'l)
(1 Proyezd Shota Rustaveli Str., h. 16)
Head of Mission Ms. Taz Khaliq 21-47-64
Medical Coordinator 51-01-20

MSF (Holland) (166 Zainab-bibi Str.)
Kurian Bos off 24-67-93
Paul McPhun

ORA International (Orphans, Refugees and Aid (Germany)
(17 Kuibishev Av., Apt. 11)

Chief Jeffrey Paulsen	27-46-10 21-64-42 res 24-40-77
Rich Berghan	res 24-08-78
Vince Simmonds	res 24-63-68

OSCE (Organization for Security & Cooperation in Europe)(53 Sino)

Head of Mission Dimitri Manjavidze	off 24-42-01
DCM William Ferrell	
Lara Griffith	
Oinihol Bobonazarova	24-91-59

Vladimir Nickolaevich Chernyakov

Thomas Bolinger (Shaartuz)

OSI (Open Society Institute) Soros Foundation (Presidium of Academy of Sciences, 3rd Floor)

Resident Represent.	off 21-19-58 23-22-05

PSF (Pharmaciens sans Frontieres) (35/1 Bokhtar St., Room 703)

Chief Geoffroy de Vaulgrenant	21-09-67
Technical Administrator Andre Olivier	fax: 27-70-69

RI (Relief International) (70 Rudaki, 4th Fl., Apt 76)

Acting Country Director	fax: 21-86-53 21-07-17

Save the Children Fund (UK) (2 Proyezd Ozodi Zanon, House 17)

Bronwen Lewis (Program Manager)	24-03-39
Consultant Joanna Raikes	
Nicole Hurtubise (Khatlon)	
Turkish line:	51-00-75
e-mail:office@scfuk.td.silk.glas.apc.org	

Save the Children (US) (18 Turdiyev St.)

Director Bharat Devkota	off 21-07-71
Program Manager Rob Kaufman	res 24-75-40 21-18-86
Turkish line:	51-00-79
e-mail: scdush@glas.apc.org	
satphone:	(873) 153-6374/5

Shelter Now International (54 Zainab-Bibi Str.)

Country Director Kumar Periasamy	21-51-98
res 24-01-55	

Deputy Director Brad Rust	24-70-29
Regional Program Director Harry J.R. Van Burik	
Liaison Officer Glen Taylor	
Craig Simonian	
Joachim Jackle	

TACIS (Ministry of Agriculture, 46 Rudaki, 2nd floor)

Coordination Unit (room 104)	
Acting Director Rahmat Yusupov. Haqqulov	21-26-09
(comes to the office periodically)	21-02-26
	21-82-94

UNDP (United Nations Development Program)(25 Bekhzod St.)

Res. Repres. Paolo Lembo	21-06-70
Dep. Res. Repr. Blanche de Bonneval	21-06-85
Program Adviser Pamela Khussein	23-08-51
Junior Professional Officer Shoko Noda	21-06-79
OPS Program Manager Basil Comnas (Gulya)	21-06-82
res 24-03-73	
Secretary Gulnora Burkhanova	23-05-96
Senior Program Asst Tatiana Falco	23-06-12
Community Development Coordinator Sukumar Mishra	23-07-71
Peace Building Project Coordinator Prosper Bani	23-07-71
ACU Director Bahrom Alizade	fax 21-41-81
Janna Yusupjanova	fax 21-50-25
	fax 51-00-43
DHA Chief Jamie McGoldrick	fax 21-03-89
NGO Liasion Officer Guissou Jahangiri-Jeannot	
FAO (Food and Agriculture Org-n) Pavel Chernogorsky	23-05-53
Junior Professional Officer Luigi de Marfino	23-07-81
Emergency Specialist Greg Sanchez	21-06-79
Program Officer Abdukahor Nurov	21-06-80
Administrator Matlyuba Turayeva	21-06-88
Finance Assistant	21-06-86
Muna Khamidova	21-06-94
Secretary Dilbar Jalolova	21-06-79

UNESCO (MFA building)

Guljahon Bobosadykova	21-17-50
Munzifa Bobojanova	fax 23-29-64
	tlx 201137 PAMIR SU

UNICEF (14/1 H. Hakimzade St.)

Head of Mission Johan Fagerskiold	off 21-82-61

John Conteh		24-72-61 fax 24-19-05

UNHCR (United Nations High Commissioner for Refugees)
(25 Said Nosirov St.)

Res. Coordinator for CA John McCallin		21-74-24
Head of Office Gang Li (Asst. Dilrabo)		
Regional Workshop Manager Silas Itiveh		
Program Officer George Labor		
Sudang Kaentrakool		
Senior Legal Officer Annika Linden		
Gulnora Ibragimova		24-61-84
Aziza, Muhabbat		24-62-65
Radio Operators	Turkish line:	51-00-40

UNMOT (United Nations Mission of Observers to Tajikistan)
(7 Gorky St.)

Head of Mission, SGSR Gerd Dietrich Merrem	21-01-25
Chief Military Observer Gen Boleslav Izydorczyk	21-02-51
Deputy Chief Military Observer COL Jan Andersen	21-01-27
Head of Civil Affairs Yogesh Saksena	21-01-03
Senior Civil Affairs Officer Wlodek Cibor	21-01-05
Civil Affairs Officer Hasmik Egian	21-33-80
Security Officer Kenrick Cato	21-01-29
Chief Admin. Officer Marcellin Savard (Zarina)	21-01-10
Chief General Services/Procurement Officer	21-34-43
24-Hour Duty Officer	21-01-47

USAID (Agency for International Development)(US Embassy)

Christine Sheckler	ext 102	off 21-03-56 res 24-74-63
Turkish line/fax		51-00-49
Admin. Asst. Olga Krylova	ext 126	fax 21-01-71
Progr. Asst Abdurahim Muhidov	ext 126	fax 21-04-29

VI (Vision International-U.K.) 24-64-47

WFP (World Food Program) (51 Turdiyev Str.)

Country Director Gerard Viguie	21-09-07
Abu Sayod Saifuzzaman	21-09-07
Duty Officer	24-39-50
Turkish line/fax	51-00-87

WHO (World Health Organization) (8 Chapaev Str.) 21-48-71

World Bank (95/1 Rudaki, "Orion Bank", 7th Floor)	
Field Office Repres. Mustafa Rouis	**21-15-18**
Operations Officer Muzaffar Usmonov	**21-14-03**
Secretary Saodat	**21-27-10**
Tohir Mirzoev	**21-16-00**

INTERNATIONAL BUSINESS ORGANIZATIONS

Commonwealth & British Minerals (CBM)(27 Tursunzade, 3rd Floor)	
Craig Brown	**21-29-64**
	23-17-84
	fax 21-30-25
DHL Dushanbe (8 Somoni St.)	
Mahbuba Jumankulova	**24-62-79**
Parviz	**21-02-80**
Arthur Andersen Company of Lawyers (National Bank building)	
Chief Wilfredo Alvarez	**off 21-25-81**

INTERNATIONAL SCHOOLS

Dushanbe International School (2 Bofanda Str.)	
Eric Prost	**off 21-77-91**
	23-85-04
Quality School International (8 Sharq Str.)	**24-53-49**

THE NATIONAL ASSOCIATION OF SMALL BUSINESSES OF TAJIKISTAN

The National Association of Small and Medium Sized-Businesses of Tajikistan (NASMB) is a non-governmental organization set to assist small and medium-sized firms in Tajikistan. It was established in September 1993 after the Government issued the regulation "On Support of Enterpreneurial Structures within the General Strategy Developing the Private Sector of Tajikistan's Economy." The main goal of the Association is to assist the development of small and medium-sized businesses, of the market infrastructures, and to coordinate the activities of Tajik entrepreneurs.

The NASMB Board members are businessmen, bankers, business associations, business consulting centers, etc. The Government of Tajikistan granted the NASMB with a legislative initiative right.

Due to objective reasons, the NASMB activities were temporarily stopped in 1994-1996. After April, 1996 the NASMB resumed its operations:
-- at present the NASMB has more than 500 members;
-- the NASMB has regional offices in Khojand, Kulyab, the Khatlon Region, and Gorny Badakhshan. Businessmen from districts of the republican subordination, such as Leninsky, Hissar, Garm, Faizabad also expressed an interest to join the NASMB;
-- the NASMB conducts regular educational seminars for its members at the Dushanbe American Business Center;
-- more than ten NASMB members improved their qualification abroad through the U.S. NET Program funded by the Academy through Educational Development (AED);
-- since 1994 the NASMB started cooperation with the EBRD on opening the EBRD credit lines for small and medium businesses in Tajikistan;
-- in August, 1996 the NASMB jointly with the EBRD conducted research on lending possibilities for the private sector in Tajikistan and opening of Business Consulting Centers in Dushanbe and Khojand;
-- since April, 1996 the NASMB established a close cooperation with Dushanbe TACIS office and participated in the TACIS program "Europartenariat" (5 NASMB members took part in the Partenariat session in Italy, 16 companies - in the Partenariat session in CIS, 3 companies - in Partenariat Greece, 6 companies - in Partenariat France) and the TACIS Project on Spread of Technical Assistance;
-- the MASMB established cooperation with various entrepreneurial associations in CIS and all around the world;
-- since 1995 the NASMB members participated in the SABIT Experts Program funded by USDOC;
-- the NASMB represents its members' interests in Dushanbe-cited international and financial organizations as Mercy Corp., the Central Asia America Enterprise Fund, Carana Corporation, Counterpart Consortium, etc.
-- the NASMB actively participated in conducting the 1st Economic Forum in Dushanbe in November, 1996 under the aegis of the UNDP, OSCE, and the Government of Tajikistan;
-- the NASMB jointly with the German Society of Technical Assistance GZT arranged training workshops for local entrepreneurs;
-- the NASMB established close contacts with local NGOs, such as the Tajik Center for Entrepreneurship and Management in Khojand, Women in Development, etc.

Note: For U.S. companies looking for business partners in Tajikistan the NASMB can be the right entity to contact.

Contact: Matljuba Uljabaeva
Chairman
9, Bofanda Str. Dushanbe Tajikistan
Tel: 7(3772)27 79 78

RESTAURANTS IN DUSHANBE

EUROPEAN/TAJIK CUISINE

Restaurant Elite

Varied selection of European and Tajik dishes with Elite specials. Any dish by preliminary order. Full desert table and wide bar selection. Soft music and nice Western interior. No credit cards accepted. The most expensive restaurant in Dushanbe. Cash only.
$25-40 per person.
Location: Chapaev Street (opposite Radio House)
Tel: {7}(3772) 21-25-12
Hours: 11 a.m.-11 p.m.

Bar-Restaurant Polonaise

Exquisite European and Tajik cuisine (red and black caviar, sturgeon, trout, mushrooms, beef, lamb, smoked meat, and chicken.) Any course by preliminary order. Natural juices. Wide bar collection. Exclusively nice design. Cash only.
$5-20 per person.
Location: 2nd floor, 35/1 Bohtar Street (in building of Avtotranstechnika)
Tel: {7}(3772)21-25-26
Hours: 9 a.m.-11 a.m.

Restaurant Continent

Mostly European cuisine with Continent specials. Delicious desert. Wide range of Moldovan, Bulgarian, licensed French and Italian wines. Any dish on preliminary order. Nice indoor and outdoor seating. Cash only.
$5-20 per person
Location: 32, Buhoro Street
Tel: [7](3772)21-44-98
Hours: 12 p.m.-till last client

Bar/Restaurant Intourist-Tojikiston

Two bars, four indoor (purely Tajik, European, and mixed design) and outdoor seating. European and Tajik dishes with restaurant's specials. Any dish by preliminary morning order. Wide bar selection including Tajik, Georgian, and Moldovan wines. Cash only.
Breakfast - $4-5 per person
Lunch - $5-6 per person
Dinner - $7-10 per person
Location: 22, Shotemur Street
Tel: [7](3772)21-70-77, 21-33-52
Fax: [7](3772)21-64-26

Cafe Shahrom

European cuisine only (meat and vegetable salads, mushrooms, shrimps, clear and cabbage soups, fish, chicken, fried meat, and natural juices. Alcohol beverages are temporarily not available. Cash only.
Location: 16, Kirov (Husein-Zoda) Street
Hours: 12 p.m.-23 p.m. daily except Sunday.

Bar Manhattan

Excellent selection of poultry: chicken, duck, turkey, partridge. Rabbit, fish, and meat courses are also available. Anything by preliminary order. Private rooms available. Wide bar selection. Cash only.
$7-15 per person.
Location: 32, Shotemur Street, Dushanbe
Hours: 9 a.m.-9 p.m.daily except Sunday

Bar Vostochny

Tajik food mostly and some European. Nice indoor and outdoor seating. Private cabins for 8/6/4/2 persons are available. Various alcoholic beverages. Ice-cream. Cash only.
$5 per person without alcohol, $6-7 with strong beverages.
Location: 56, Rudaki Avenue (along the main street of Dushanbe)
Hours: 11 a.m.-till last client daily except Sunday

Cafe Romashka

Snack and beer. Oudoor ground. No credit cards. Cash only.
$5-10 per person
Location: 33, Rudaki Avenue (along the main street of Dushanbe)
Hours: daily except Sunday

Restaurant Kapris

Standard European (salads, chicken, beefsteak, sausages) and Tajik food. Wide selection of Georgian wines, champagne, and liqueurs. No vodka. Indoor and outdoor seating. Western interior and private cabins available.
$10-12.5 per person.
Location: 32, Ghafurov Street, 82-y mikrorayon
Tel: [7](3772)37-94-50
Hours: 9 a.m.-9 p.m. daily

U.S. TAJIKISTAN EXPORT AND IMPORT STATISTICS

U.S. Exports to Tajikistan

CALENDAR YEAR

HS Description	Millions of U.S. Dollars 1996	1997	1998	% Share 1996	1997	1998	% Change 98/97
Tajikistan	17	19	12	0.00	0.00	0.00	-34.59
10 CEREALS	6.529	5.004	4.939	37.92	26.93	40.64	-1.28
11 MILLING;MALT;STARCH	2.850	6.709	2.967	16.56	36.11	24.42	-55.77
98 SPECIAL OTHER	0.785	0.266	1.215	4.56	1.43	10.00	356.82
04 DAIRY,EGGS, HONEY,ETC	0.000	0.426	1.165	0.00	2.29	9.59	173.40
15 FATS AND OILS	1.469	2.905	0.648	8.53	15.63	5.33	-77.69
84 MACHINERY	2.098	0.837	0.409	12.18	4.51	3.36	-51.19
49 BOOK+NEWSPAPR; MANUSCRPT	0.000	0.228	0.220	0.00	1.22	1.81	-3.30
85 ELECTRICAL MACHINERY	0.799	0.045	0.125	4.64	0.24	1.03	176.47
20 PRESERVED FOOD	0.000	0.000	0.058	0.00	0.00	0.47	###.##
88 AIRCRAFT, SPACECRAFT	0.000	0.000	0.054	0.00	0.00	0.44	###.##
28 INORG CHEM;RARE ERTH MT	0.266	0.406	0.051	1.54	2.19	0.42	-87.32
69 CERAMIC P RODUCTS	0.000	0.000	0.050	0.00	0.00	0.41	###.##
70 GLASS AND GLASSWARE	0.000	0.113	0.046	0.00	0.61	0.38	-58.81
29 ORGANIC CHEMICALS	0.000	0.000	0.039	0.00	0.00	0.32	###.##
39 PLASTIC	0.723	0.309	0.033	4.20	1.66	0.27	-89.17
22 BEVERAGES	0.575	0.300	0.033	3.34	1.62	0.27	-89.03
71 PRECIOUS STONES, METALS	0.000	0.000	0.031	0.00	0.00	0.25	###.##
82 TOOL,CUTLRY, OF BASE MTL	0.000	0.000	0.024	0.00	0.00	0.20	###.##
21 MISCELLANEOUS FOOD	0.024	0.088	0.019	0.14	0.47	0.16	-77.89
63 MISC TEXTILE ARTICLES	0.000	0.000	0.010	0.00	0.00	0.08	
35 ALBUMINS;MOD STRCH;GLUE	0.000	0.010	0.006	0.00	0.05	0.05	-43.03
30 PHARMACEUTICAL PRODUCTS	0.000	0.000	0.005	0.00	0.00	0.04	
48 PAPER,PAPERBOARD	0.004	0.000	0.005	0.02	0.00	0.04	
61 KNIT APPAREL	0.003	0.000	0.000	0.02	0.00	0.00	0.00
68 STONE,PLASTR, CEMENT,ETC	0.000	0.000	0.000	0.00	0.00	0.00	0.00
87 VEHICLES, NOT RAILWAY	0.224	0.497	0.000	1.30	2.68	0.00	0.00
90 OPTIC,NT 8544;MED INSTR	0.000	0.008	0.000	0.00	0.04	0.00	0.00

94 FURNITURE AND BEDDING	0.000	0.000	0.000	0.00	0.00	0.00	0.00
32 TANNING,DYE,PAINT,PUTTY	0.042	0.000	0.000	0.24	0.00	0.00	0.00
37 PHOTOGRAPHIC/ CINEMATOGR	0.012	0.000	0.000	0.07	0.00	0.00	0.00
41 HIDES AND SKINS	0.134	0.000	0.000	0.78	0.00	0.00	0.00
07 VEGETABLES	0.680	0.423	0.000	3.95	2.28	0.00	0.00
12 MISC GRAIN,SEED,FRUIT	0.000	0.006	0.000	0.00	0.03	0.00	0.00

Source of Data: U.S. Dept of Commerce, Bureau of the Census

U.S. IMPORTS FROM TAJIKISTAN

CALENDAR YEAR

	Millions of U.S. Dollars			% Share			% Change
HS Description	1996	1997	1998	1996	1997	1998	98/97
Tajikistan	33	9	33	0.00	0.00	0.00	281.69
76 ALUMINUM	27.386	5.544	29.912	83.48	64.89	91.73	439.56
52 COTTON FABRIC	3.311	2.840	2.034	10.09	33.24	6.24	-28.38
62 WOVEN APPAREL	0.000	0.000	0.225	0.00	0.00	0.69	###.##
84 MACHINERY	0.002	0.000	0.215	0.01	0.00	0.66	###.##
10 CEREALS	0.000	0.000	0.113	0.00	0.00	0.35	###.##
99 O SPECL IMPR	0.095	0.018	0.096	0.29	0.21	0.30	437.49
98 SPECIAL OTHER	0.113	0.000	0.010	0.34	0.00	0.03	
49 BOOK+NEWSPAPR; MANUSCRPT	0.002	0.000	0.002	0.01	0.00	0.01	###.##
61 KNIT APPAREL	0.015	0.000	0.000	0.04	0.00	0.00	0.00
64 FOOTWEAR	0.012	0.000	0.000	0.04	0.00	0.00	0.00
03 FISH AND SEAFOOD	0.020	0.000	0.000	0.06	0.00	0.00	0.00
21 MISCELLANEOUS FOOD	0.017	0.000	0.000	0.05	0.00	0.00	0.00
28 INORG CHEM;R.ERTH MT	1.117	0.000	0.000	3.41	0.00	0.00	0.00
39 PLASTIC	0.001	0.000	0.000	0.00	0.00	0.00	0.00
43 FURSKIN+ARTIFICIAL FUR	0.001	0.000	0.000	0.00	0.00	0.00	0.00
85 ELECTRICAL MACHINERY	0.041	0.000	0.000	0.12	0.00	0.00	0.00
87 VEHICLES, NOT RAILWAY	0.022	0.000	0.000	0.07	0.00	0.00	0.00
97 ART AND ANTIQUES	0.000	0.103	0.000	0.00	1.20	0.00	0.00
71 PRECIOUS STONES,METALS	0.026	0.014	0.000	0.08	0.17	0.00	0.00
72 IRON AND STEEL	0.626	0.000	0.000	1.91	0.00	0.00	0.00
73 IRON/STEEL PRODUCTS	0.000	0.025	0.000	0.00	0.29	0.00	0.00

Source of Data: U.S. Dept of Commerce, Bureau of the Census

LAWYERS IN DUSHANBE

Office of judicial consultation of the **Tsentralny district**,

#46A N. Karabayev Pr.; phone: 33-96-01:

1. Odinayev, Saidalimsho Khukumatovich 10 yrs, criminal

2. Burkhanova, Svetlana Pavlovna24 yrs, civil and criminal

3. Komilov, Saidakram Saidovich 19 yrs, criminal
home phone: 36-24-38

4. Yunusova, Alexandra Pavlovna19 yrs, civil
home phone: 33-22-69

5. Yatimov, K. criminal and civil

6. Sharipova, B. civil and criminal

Office of judicial consultation of the **Zheleznodorozhny (Railway) district**, phone: 27-85-04

1. Kurbanov, Saidkomil11 yrs, criminal
2. Khushvakhtova, Gulniso8 yrs, criminal
Abdullayevna
phone: 27-01-39

3. Urinbayev, Gani Odilovich9 yrs, criminal
4. Kurbonov, M. civil and criminal
5. Ms. Nusratova civil and criminal
6. Ms. Rasulova criminal
7. Mr. Yorov civil and criminal

Office of judicial consultation of the **Frunzensky district**,
#57 Ismoili Somoni Pr., phone: 36-18-30

1. Khametova Nailya11 yrs, criminal
Ismoilovna
2. Ubaydov, Nodirsho Saydulloevich11 yrs, civil and criminal
3. Beknazarov, S.
4. Mr. Anandiyev

Office of judicial consultation of **the October district**,
#91 Rudaki Pr., phone 21-76-51, 24-12-97:
1. Boboyeva, Zebo14 yrs, civil and criminal
2. Boturov, Bakhtiyor Mirzomuradovih9 yrs, civil and criminal
4. Faiziyev, Akbar20 yrs, civil and criminal
5. Ms. Soliyeva civil and criminal
6. Mr. Badriddinov criminal
7. Karimov, N. civil and criminal

Chairman of the Presidium of Collegiate of Lawyers of the Republic of

Tajikistan - Amirbekov, Naim Amirbekovich, phone: 21-24-03; 27-84-77, address: #12 Parhar St., Dushanbe
Vice chairman of the Presidium of Collegiate of Lawyers of the Republic of Tajikistan – Abduzoda, Mirzo, phone:
27-84-77
Commercial Law Project, Dushanbe, Akbar Muratov, some knowledge of English, phone: 21-26-50, 21-17-79, e-mail: Akbar79@hotmail.com
"Contract" judicial company - #54 Ostrovsky St., Dushanbe,
phones: 21-14-10, 21-27-38, 23-09-20

NEAR-BY REGIONS

Office of judicial consultation of **Leninskiy District:**

Ms. Umarova	civil and criminal

Office of judicial consultation of **Kofarnihon district**,
phone: 2-44-81, 2-41-05

Mr. Asatullayev	civil and criminal

Office of judicial consultation of **Ghissar district**

Mr. Rajabov	civil and criminal

Office of judicial consultation of **the City of Tursunzade**

Mr. Khojankulov	civil and criminal

Office of judicial consultation of **the City of Kughan-Tyube, Khatlon Region**

1. Ms. Amonova	civil and criminal
2. Mr. Nuritdinov	civil and criminal

OFFICIAL MATERIALS

CHALLENGES FACING THE TRANSITION ECONOMIES OF CENTRAL ASIA[2]

Thank you, President Akayev, Chairman Sultanov, ladies and gentlemen.

It is a great pleasure to join you at this conference marking the fifth anniversary of the introduction of the som. I say this for two reasons. First, you have given me a most welcome opportunity to visit the Kyrgyz Republic, a country which, under the leadership of President Akayev, has been at the forefront of reform within the countries of the former Soviet Union. The introduction of the som, which we are commemorating today, was one of many courageous and forward-looking decisions that have contributed to your country's economic progress.

Allow me to elaborate somewhat on that. The Kyrgyz Republic is now at a promising stage of its history. After several years of an extremely difficult transition, your country starts experiencing the benefits of its orientation toward a market economy. Not only has the dramatic decline in output been reversed, but for two years in a row growth of output has been around 7 percent, while the introduction of the som has been key in bringing inflation down from the destructive hyperinflation level of 1,259 percent, where it was in 1992, to the single digit level where it stands now, and you know that further progress is

[2] Address by Michel Camdessus Managing Director of the International Monetary Fund at a conference on "Challenges to Economies in Transition" Bishkek, Kyrgyz Republic - May 27, 1998

at hand. These achievements are still fragile and, in the framework of the new program on which we have just agreed, your government, Mr. President, wants to consolidate them, to make sure that the trends toward increased poverty are also reversed, and that the poorest in the country benefit particularly from the economic expansion of the years to come.

This is an ambitious but realistic program and, in visiting Bishkek today, I wanted to tell you and the people of this country our full determination to make a maximum effort to support this program and to convince the international community to join us in this endeavor. This is also a unique occasion to pay tribute, Mr. President, to your vision and leadership in conducting this transition, which not only has laid the grounds for a promising future, but has also been a source of inspiration for other countries in similar situations.

Second, your invitation also provides an excellent occasion to reflect upon the critical issues facing Central Asia. From the earliest days of the transition, the IMF has been providing policy advice, technical assistance, and financial support to help your countries develop efficient market economies and integrate themselves into the global economy. Thus, we have in some sense accompanied you during your "transition," sharing your pride in your achievements and your determination to overcome the problems you still face.

At the same time, however, the IMF is also in a continuous policy dialogue with its other member countries. So, our views on the issues facing Central Asia are colored not simply by our experience with your countries, or even by our involvement with transition economies in general, but by our experience in 182 countries at every stage of economic development, in every conceivable economic situation, and in every region of the world. It is from this broader perspective that I would like to discuss the issues facing your countries. Let me begin with a few words on the opportunities and challenges in the global economy and how various of our member countries have responded to them. Then I will turn to the implications for Central Asia.

Challenges in the global economy

It is frequently said that the world has entered the age of "globalization" or that we now live in a "global economy." But what does that really mean? For over fifty years, the world economy has been growing more closely integrated in terms of trade and capital flows. To a great extent, globalization is simply the continuation of that trend. But with greater freedom of trade and investment and new breakthroughs in telecommunication and information technology, markets have become much larger, more complex, and more closely linked than ever before. Moreover, capital now moves at a speed and in volumes that would have been inconceivable just a few years ago.

Asia, in particular, has been the showcase of the benefits of globalization. In 1996, private capital flows to developing and transition economies reached an all time high of $235 billion, of which nearly half went to Asia. Subsequent events have shown that some of those funds were not invested wisely. Nevertheless, over the last several decades, the forces of globalization have allowed many countries in Asia to accelerate investment and growth, create more jobs, reduce poverty, and attain other important human development goals. In Malaysia, for example, the share of the population living below the poverty line declined from almost 50 percent in 1970 to less than 10 percent in

1995. In Korea, the literacy rate increased from around 30 percent in the mid–1950s to over 95 percent today. Globalization has helped make such human progress possible.

But if globalization offers many opportunities, it also holds two major risks. The first can be seen in the recent experience of Thailand, Korea, and Indonesia, all of which have suffered major financial crises during the last year, when investors lost confidence in their economies and large capital inflows turned into massive capital outflows. Countries that attract large volumes of private capital are more vulnerable to sudden shifts in investor confidence, which can be very destabilizing to their own economies and have negative effects on other countries, as well. Indeed, some of your countries have felt a chill breeze from East Asia, as commodity prices weakened, conditions in international capital markets became less favorable, and some East Asian investors scaled back planned investments.

The second risk can be seen in the experience of many African countries. Countries that are unable to participate in the expansion of world trade or attract significant amounts of foreign capital risk becoming marginalized from the global economy and falling farther and farther behind the rest of the world in terms of growth and human development. This marginalization, in turn, poses the very real threat of economic stagnation and increasing poverty.

The challenge for all countries is how to make the most of the opportunities that globalization has to offer, while minimizing these risks. This is not an easy task. However, among the members of the IMF, there is a tremendous wealth of experience as to how countries can best meet this challenge. One purpose of the IMF is to help disseminate this experience as broadly as possible, so that countries can learn from each other's successes and failures. In this spirit, let me turn now to the lessons of our members' experience.

* * * * *

Ingredients of economic success

Experience shows that in order to be successful in the global economy, countries must first have properly functioning domestic economies. What does this involve? Let me mention three key requirements.

The first is to allow market forces to set prices and allocate resources so that the economy can operate efficiently. Progress in this area has been uneven in Central Asia, particularly in the agricultural sector, and private investment, labor productivity, output, and rural incomes have suffered. Countries that hesitate to liberalize agriculture, or indeed, other sectors of their economies, should consider the dramatic example of Vietnam, which went from being a net importer of about half a million tons of food annually in 1986–88 to being the world's third largest rice exporter in 1989, following sweeping reforms in the agricultural sector.[1] Today, Vietnam is still one of the world's leading rice exporters.

Of course, one key aspect of improving resource allocation—as well as taking advantage of the opportunities in global markets—is to open the economy up to foreign trade and hence to international price signals and competition. However, these benefits of trade liberalization will only materialize in the context of a unified exchange rate and the removal of restrictions on current transactions.

The second requirement for domestic economies to perform well is a stable macroeconomic environment, beginning with a relatively stable price level. There is now nearly universal consensus that low single-digit inflation is a necessary condition for sustained and equitable economic growth.

There is also wide agreement on the policies needed to achieve this objective—notably a disciplined fiscal policy that keeps government expenditure in line with government revenues, while providing for a satisfactory level of public investment in basic infrastructure and human capital and a well-targeted social safety net. In this regard, there is considerable scope for strengthening fiscal management in most transition economies—from improving tax systems and tax administration, establishing effective treasury systems, prioritizing public expenditure, and putting pension systems on a sustainable footing.

Such reforms are essential, among other reasons to ensure that the fiscal position is consistent with a non-inflationary monetary policy and a sustainable level of external debt. Yes, countries must also manage their external debt wisely. One needs only think about the debt crisis in Latin America during the 1980s and the so-called "lost decade" of economic stagnation that accompanied it, or the problems of heavily indebted poor countries in Africa today, to see how excessive external borrowing—or borrowing on inappropriate terms—can compromise a country's financial stability and economic growth for years to come.

Finally, for the private sector to fulfill its intended role as the main engine of growth and job creation, there is a third requirement, which for the most part is still missing here in Central Asia, and that is a suitable institutional framework that will give domestic and foreign entrepreneurs the confidence to invest. In particular, I would point to the need for:

- simple and transparent regulatory systems—so that businesses won't waste precious time and resources trying to find out what the rules are and how to comply with them; so that new firms can enter the market without complication or being driven underground; and so that foreign investors are encouraged to bring in their capital, technology, and skills;
- effective legal and judiciary systems that protect property rights, enforce contracts, and help create an atmosphere of law, order, and personal security—so that domestic and foreign investors will expand their businesses and create new ones; and
- tax systems that are simple and broad-based, with limited exemptions and reasonable and uniform rates—so that companies and individuals will not be discouraged from trying to fulfill their tax obligations; so that taxes can be more easily enforced; and so that governments receive the revenues they need to carry out their basic responsibilities in such areas as health and education.

Experience also shows that in order to make a decisive difference in the domestic economic climate, policies must be reasonably consistent and achieve a critical mass of reform, thereby convincing investors that reform is irreversible, and that the country is truly integrating into the international economy. Partial reform may not elicit much response if substantial impediments to economic activity remain in place.

As you may have surmised, meeting these three requirements implies a redefinition of the role of the State in the economy. In successful market economies, the State disengages from activities that markets and the private sector can perform more effectively, such as setting prices, allocating credit and other domestic resources and running commercial activities. Instead, it concentrates on carrying out a few core responsibilities well, such as upholding the rule of law, providing reliable public services, maintaining prudent macroeconomic policies, and establishing a fair and transparent regulatory framework for private sector activity. Of course, governments must also give their full attention to stamping out corruption in every form. These are all aspects of "good governance," which is an essential condition for saving, investment and sustained growth.

Lessons from East Asia

If these are the lessons of experience from developing and transition economies, what does the experience of the misfortunes of the "Asian tigers" imply for Central Asia?

First, it is worth noting that the reason why countries such as Thailand, Korea, and Indonesia were so successful economically for so many years is that they instituted many of the requirements I just mentioned—including macroeconomic stability, outward looking economic policies, and a high priority on human development—at a relatively early stage. So what went wrong? Put simply, domestic institutions were not strong enough, and domestic policies were not flexible enough, to meet the increasing demands of economic success. These institutional and policy shortcomings manifested themselves in various ways, including:

- in the failure to address the overheating pressures and the lack of sufficient exchange rate flexibility, which, along with implicit guarantees of support to banks and corporations, led to excessive external borrowing and exchange rate exposure, often at short maturities;

- in the high degree of inappropriate government intervention the economy, including lending based on personal connections and government directive, which led to inefficient investment and a deterioration in the quality of bank balance sheets, while prudential rules were lax and banking supervision was weak;

- in the lack of data and transparency, which concealed the extent of these countries' problems—and not just to the rest of the world, but also to their own eyes. This led to complacency on the part of the authorities, a false sense of security on the part of foreign investors, and later when the facts became known, to market panic.

From this experience, I would highlight three points that are particularly relevant for countries in Central Asia and, indeed, for every other country that hopes to tap international capital markets.

The first point concerns the need to maintain sound macroeconomic policies, correct macroeconomic imbalances promptly when they arise, and continue with the structural changes needed to sustain macroeconomic stability and high quality growth. Even countries that appear to have reasonably sound policies must be vigilant.

The second point concerns the importance of sound domestic financial systems. In Thailand, Korea, Indonesia, and many other countries, we have seen the tremendous human cost of allowing delaying key structural reforms, especially steps to strengthen the domestic financial system. Overcoming a domestic banking crisis is a very costly undertaking. We don't know yet what the price tag will be in East Asia, but I can tell you that the cost of the banking crisis in Chile, with all its indirect costs, exceeded 30 percent of GDP; the one in Venezuela, certainly more than 20 percent of GDP. Can you imagine the cost of this in terms of schools, health care centers, and basic infrastructure? The countries in Central Asia are in the process of reforming and restructuring their banking sectors; they should make sure that the systems they are creating are built on solid rock—not on sand—by establishing strong market incentives for prudent bank management and a framework of domestic regulation and supervision consistent with international standards.

The third point concerns the need for transparency. When governments are in the habit of providing the public with full information about their policies and the country's economic performance, policymakers have more incentive to pursue responsible policies, and costly policy mistakes and disruptive financial crises are less likely to occur. Moreover, when the financial markets have reliable economic and financial data, they are better able to distinguish between countries that have sound policies and those that do not, and the risk that a crisis will spill over from one country to another is reduced. Transparency also contributes to a more responsible use of public resources for the public good and reduces opportunities for corruption.

In this regard, and let me be very candid here again, one cannot help but observe the similarities between the relationships that existed among enterprises, banks, and government in some East Asian countries under the system of "crony capitalism" and the tendencies one can observe—which still survive or start developing again—in a number of transition economies. As we have seen in East Asia, when the structure of ownership is not transparent, when regulation is inadequate and unevenly applied, when too many ad hoc decisions are taken, and when market forces are prevented from playing their normal disciplining role, serious imbalances and deadly inefficiencies can build up. And, once exposed, these problems can provoke an abrupt market correction.

* * * * *

So these are some of the lessons of experience from other IMF members that face, or have faced, many of the same challenges confronting your countries. These lessons are particularly worthy of consideration today, as we commemorate the introduction of the som. A good currency can only be beneficial insofar as it is strong and stable. And, of course, all of that depends on the quality of the macroeconomic and structural policies that underpin it. In this regard, my remarks today have mostly concerned what the transition economies of Central Asia can learn from the experience of other IMF member countries. But when I come back for the tenth anniversary of the som, I hope to bring a different message—not what your countries can learn from, say, the East Asian "tigers," but what other countries can learn from the success of the "snow leopards" of Central Asia.

[1]These reforms included liberalizing agricultural prices, introducing competition among agricultural trading companies, granting families and individuals long-term rights to land use, and

removing internal barriers to trade. See: *Vietnam: Transition to a Market Economy*, IMF Occasional Paper no.135 (Washington: International Monetary Fund, March 1996).

PRIVATIZATION IN TADJIKISTAN

RESOLUTION ON THE STATE PROPERTY COMMITTEE OF THE REPUBLIC OF TAJIKISTAN

State Property Committee (SPC) is the privatization agency of the Republic of Tajikistan.
The SPC is headed by Mr. Davlatov, the Chairman.

I. General Provision

1. The State Property Committee of the Republic of Tajikistan, hereinafter referred as the Committee, is a republican entity of State management which within the limits of its rights delegated by the Government of the Republic of Tajikistan, manages the process of privatization of State property in the Republic of Tajikistan, statues on the order of possession, use, and disposal of State property.
2. The Committee's activity is regulated by the Constitution of the Republic of Tajikistan, the laws of the Republic of Tajikistan, resolutions of Majlisi Oli of the Republic of Tajikistan, Decrees of the President of the Republic of Tajikistan, resolutions and regulations of the Government of the Republic of Tajikistan, international-legal acts recognized by the Republic of Tajikistan, and the present Regulation.
3. The Committee's activity is subordinate to decisions of the Government of the Republic of Tajikistan.

II. Basic Tasks

4. The basic tasks of the Committee are to:

Organize and implement the privatization of state property in order to diversify the State's economy and the transformation of State property into other forms of property;

Manage State property matters of State entities throughout the territory of the Republic of Tajikistan;

Coordinate the activity of ministries, State Departments, and State Executive Authorities at the local basis on privatization of state property, including the development and realization of the programs of privatization of republican and communal property;
Participate in creation of stock exchanges and other structures associated with the process of privatization and realization of state policy in the attraction of investments;

Take under control the safety and effective use of State property and accordingly enforce legislation;

5. To fulfill its tasks, the Committee:

Develops programs of privatization of republican and communal property objects together with local Majlisis of People's Deputies, Ministries and State

Departments of the Republic of Tajikistan;

Organizes the implementation of the privatization programs, reports on the privatization process to the Government of the Republic of Tajikistan, and if necessary develops proposals to introduce changes and modifications in the programs;

Generalizes the implementation of the legislation related to its sphere, develops proposals to promote legislative and standard acts of the Republic of Tajikistan on privatization of objects of state property, bankruptcy of enterprises, issues within the limits of its competence as well as standards and other acts regulating the process of privatization and management of state property, and also carries out the control for their performance;

Provides protection of the property rights and interests of the State in the Republic of Tajikistan and abroad;

Carries out control for the proper use and safety of property by legal and physical persons and in case of infringement of the established rules and order on the use the property, the Committee takes necessary measures to enforce the law according to the legislation of the Republic of Tajikistan;

Participates within the limits of its competence in the development and realization of investment programs, elaboration of conditions for concession agreements, and also represents the interests of the proprietor in accordance to the legislation of the Republic of Tajikistan;

Acts on behalf of the Government of the Republic of Tajikistan as an authorized representative for matters related to the property of the former USSR;
Participates in the elaboration and fulfillment of measures to support privatized enterprises at the expense of the State Budget in accordance to programs related to post privatization support;

Participates in the elaboration and fulfillment of state policy on prevention of bankruptcy of State enterprises;

Officially approves State property status (whether republican or communal) of economic entities and State Management Authorities, agrees for the sale or lease of real estate property of economic entities, keeps track in a register book of lease contracts of objects of republican property;

Examines and carries out valuations of State property;

Manages Local State Property Committees and issues related to privatization of State Property of Local State Executive Authorities (hukumats);
Concludes agreements and contracts in the name of the Government of the Republic of Tajikistan, on interaction and cooperation in the management of property of the Republic of Tajikistan with foreign state entities and legal persons;
Carries out in accordance with its mandate, necessary actions to eliminate infringement of legislation of the Republic of Tajikistan related to the privatization of State property;

Supervises the privatization of state property carried out by Local Executive Authorities (hukumats). In cases of non abidance to the policy of privatization of state property, the Committee elaborates reasonable proposals to the Government;
Diffuses civic information on legislation of the Republic of Tajikistan on privatization of State property, organizes the training of the staff of the Committee in the headquarters and its local representations;
Determines main measures on privatization of state property and carries out the transformation of state property into other forms of property in accordance with other resolutions of the Government of Tajikistan;

May be the founder of joint-stock company, or other market structures transformed from state owned enterprises, or disposing state property;
Take decisions on the lease of state enterprises and other state property of republican property, organizes their sale to economic entities and individuals;
Organizes and conducts tenders and auctions on sale of state property;

Requests provision of proof and information on the fulfillment of privatization programs as well as information on the safe use of state property, from State Authorities and Local State Executive Entities (hukumats) and economic entities;
Requests provision of documents and information proving infringement of legislation of the Republic of Tajikistan on privatization issues, regulations and management of objects of Republican Property from Ministries, State Departments, and state enterprises, and undertakes appropriate corrective measures;

Stops the sale of property and actions related to the use of state property in case they do not conform to current legislation;

Contests in court decisions on privatization of state property violating the law;
Cancels decisions of Local Property Committees infringing legislation or of exceeding their powers;Publishes periodic printed editions on questions related to its field.

III. Organization of Work

6. The Chairman of the Committee directs the Committee and is appointed and relieved of his post by the President of the Republic of Tajikistan in accordance

with the Constitution of the Republic of Tajikistan and Decrees of the Majlisi Oli of the Republic of Tajikistan.

7. Deputy Chairmen are appointed and relieved of their posts by the Government of the Republic of Tajikistan upon request by the Chairman of the Committee. The distribution of duties between the Deputy Chairmen is carried out by the Chairman.

8. The chairman of the Committee bears personal responsibility for the fulfillment of the tasks and duties assigned to the Committee, the realization of its powers, and establishes the degree of the Deputy Chairmen's and Chiefs' of Departments' responsibility in the headquarters of the Committee for the organization and management of its respective spheres activity and the performance of duties assigned to them.

9. A Management Board is established within the Committee consisting of the Committee's Chairman, his deputies, chiefs of Departments in the headquarters, as well as other persons.

10. Members of the Management Board are approved and relieved of duty by the Government of the Republic of Tajikistan.

11. Major organizational issues on the development and improvement of the process of privatization of state property, selection and placing of Managerial Committee Staff and issues on the practical management of the activity of different departments and local representations are considered by the Management Board, provided that necessary accounts are given by Local Executive Authorities (hukumats), Ministries, State Departments, enterprises, organizations and other economic entities related to the field.

12. Resolutions of the Management Board are enforced as a rule by order of the Chairman of the Committee. In case of disagreements between the Chairman of the Committee and the Management Board, the Chairman enacts his decision, reporting disagreements to the Government of the Republic of Tajikistan; the members of Management Board may however, in their turn, inform the Government of the Republic of Tajikistan about their opinion.

13. In order to consider professional recommendations and proposals concerning the basic activity of the Committee, its improvement, methods and techniques of privatization of state property and important programs of privatization of state property, councils and commissions are created within the Committee by leading specialists and highly skilled experts without being additionally financed and with the consent of the chiefs of the bodies of state governing of industrial structures, and trade-union bodies.

14. The structure, number and payment fund for the central apparatus employees of the Committee are approved by the Government of Republic of Tajikistan. The Chairman of the Committee has the right to introduce changes and modifications in the structure of the Committee in the limits of established number and payment fund.

15. Manning table and estimate of the expenses of the central apparatus of the Committee and also regulations on structural divisions of the territorial bodies of the Committee are approved by the chairman of the Committee.

16. Running costs for the central apparatus of the Committee are made at the expense of the republican budget.
17. The Committee is a legal entity, has its own balance, accounts in the savings bank departments, a seal with the State Emblem of the Republic of Tajikistan and its name in the Tajik and Russian languages.

PRIVATIZATION PROCESS

While political and criminal violence are what generally place Tajikistan in the news, almost unnoticed is the dramatic progress the country has made in stabilizing the economy, promoting growth, and particularly in accelerating privatization. On the one hand, the Government is dealing with a myriad of factions and military groups, settling its own prolonged civil war, and working to maintain civil stability. Impressively, at the same time the Government, backed by the IMF and World Bank, is pushing through an aggressive and far reaching privatization program.

Small scale privatization is over 60% complete in the country, and will be complete in 1999, if the current pace is sustained. More small scale businesses have been privatized in the first 7 months of 1998 than in any other year, and the country currently plans to sell 1000 small scale businesses before the end of the year, about half of all those remaining.

The degree of medium and large scale enterprise privatization is not as high, but in the first 8 months of 1998,4 auctions were held for shares, and the Government's target is to reach 50 enterprises sold by end September. In 1998 147 state enterprises registered as corporations and prepared the necessary documents for sale, while in the previous 7 years of the privatization program, only 23 did so.

Much of the pressure for this acceleration of privatization comes from privatization conditions established by the World Bank and International Monetary Fund, which have transformed the privatization process over the last year and a half. In 1997, a new Privatization Law was passed, which changed the process from a bottom up, negotiated sale to collectives on an enterprise by enterprise basis to an open, competitive and top down program with more rapid wholesale transfer of assets into the private sector. Additional legal measures were adopted through 1997 and 1998 to support this new process, and the World Bank and IMF have kept up constant monitoring to ensure that the momentum continued.

Changing a privatization system that developed over 7 years into a corrupt, closed sales process cannot be achieved overnight. Privatization is always and everywhere a highly politically charged undertaking without a strong base of support, since the benefits (lower prices, lower taxes, better products or services) are widespread, while the costs (lost jobs, lost power) are concentrated. In Tajikistan these problems are further compounded by the presence of paramilitary groups and armed criminals, who are not afraid of using their muscle to take whatever they can.

While the auction process has accelerated, and has proven successful particularly in the more developed and commercial northern part of the country, in other areas auctions have not always been easy to implement. In the capital, an auction held in May featured soldiers shouting and waving their guns around, arguing that they had already paid for the object (in bribes). Further east, auctions have been canceled completely due to the fighting which still flares up occasionally. In one shares auction in Dushanbe, a single bidder was given two numbers, and proceeded to bid against himself (the law requires at least two bidders). When asked what he was doing, he replied candidly "My friend couldn't come."

Even when the small scale privatization process is declared "complete" in 1999, in fact there will remain many small scale enterprises which should be sold or whose ownership will have to change. The state property committee database contains 6974 small scale enterprises, of which 3178 are privatized, and 1694 not subject to automatic privatization. This database seems like a large number of small businesses until two other factors are considered: Tajikpotrebsoyuz, the nominally private consumer cooperative, and enterprises on farms, which are subject to privatization as the farm privatizes. The former controls about 12,000 enterprises all over the countryside, while the latter compromises about 2000 small enterprises. Until these issues are dealt with, the retail sector in the countryside will not develop fully.

In medium and large scale businesses, share sales are really just beginning, and the State Property Committee is still working out the kinks. Thus far, shares have been offered for sale in 125 enterprises. Of these, 47 have been privatized through auctions, with the criteria for privatization set at 75% sold. In September, the State Property Committee will be conducting at least two more auctions, in order to reach the Government's target of 50 medium and large enterprises sold by the end of September.

Share sales equally are not without their own specific problems. Many buyers of shares do not truly understand the nature of corporations, and there are continuing legal issues to be resolved within the securities market framework. The World Bank is providing technical assistance to assist the Government in this, and over the last year the laws on corporations and securities and stock exchanges have both been amended and improved. The basic framework for the securities market is therefore in place, while smaller technical questions will be solved in the coming months.

Privatization is a difficult undertaking in any environment. In Tajikistan, with continuing political and rule of law problems, provides even more challenges than usual. Prices received for enterprises are lower than could be expected, depriving a strapped budget of badly needed revenues, and increasing criticism of the process. Corruption and violence still affect the privatization process, though decreasingly. In spite of this, the process moves forward, creating a base of new entrepreneurs and owners who have a greater stake in peace and stability, which could, over the long run, contribute to solving the larger problems.

CURRENT SITUATION IN PRIVATIZATION

PROBLEMS AND RECOMMENDATIONS

I. OVERALL SITUATION

The current pace of privatization is very slow. Small scale privatization has made hardly any progress since September, and there are few objects scheduled until the end of the year. Incorporation of medium and large enterprises is going too slowly as well, and the target of 200 registered shares emissions will most likely not be met soon. Share auctions are taking place, but in many cases enterprises are being offered repeatedly and not sold, and in other cases enterprises are sold, but buyers refuse to pay in the end. Privatization of truck transport is very slow, and more trucks are becoming completely unusable each month than are being sold. Unfinished construction is not being sold at a reasonable pace. Cotton ginneries, the most important aspect of the privatization program, are not even registering as joint stock companies and a huge amount of work remains to be done in this sphere.

II. SMALL SCALE PRIVATIZATION - CURRENT SITUATION

Since September, when an IMF deadline caused a sharp increase in sales, only 42 small scale enterprises have been sold. At this time, if we do not count Dushanbe, only 4 auctions are being prepared, for 29 objects. At a time when not fewer than 100 objects per month should be sold, only 21 objects are being sold per month. The World Bank has set an overall target of 2000 small scale objects to be sold before the second tranche is given. Currently, 979 small scale objects have been sold in 1998. If the current pace continues, the second tranche, small scale privatization condition will be met in April 2004. The IMF and the Government's medium term economic program require that small scale privatization be completed by March 1999, which would require 250 small scale enterprises to be sold per month.

III. SMALL SCALE PRIVATIZATION - PROBLEMS

There are many problems with the small scale privatization process at this time. First among these is the fact that there is no consistent force requiring small scale privatization to move forward. Whenever an IMF target comes up, pressure is applied through telegrams from the Government. These telegrams have less effect each time, and more raions do not meet their targets. As soon as the deadline passes, privatization is forgotten until the next panic.

Related to this problem is that in spite of a clear legal framework giving the Government authority to delegate privatization authority to the SPC, no object is privatized without the approval and assent of some committee, ministry, torg or association. All these approvals and cooperations require additional time, and frequently petty officials refuse to cooperate, which means more objects are lost to the process.

Another problem is that for many, the primary focus of the privatization process is to raise revenues immediately. Thus, when an object is sold for a low price, officials begin to cry foul and create a scandal over it. In fact, many small scale objects still in state hands are completely closed and being robbed of their glass, window frames and anything else that can be removed. This emphasis on raising revenue means that small scale enterprises are not sold because the state authorities demand too much money for them. The recently approved inflation coefficients, which increase starting prices about 3 times over what they were before. Already, sales rates at auctions in the south are dropping (we are now selling about 30% of offered objects, compared to 50% before), and in some cases the local authorities simply don't bother organizing auctions because they know the prices will be too high.

Related to this is the fear of organizing Dutch auctions. Dutch auctions are a useful mechanism for selling a large number of objects quickly. As long as there is a focus on receiving high prices for objects, Dutch auctions cannot be used.

The focus of privatization is not to raise revenue, but to change ownership, encourage investment and maximize use of assets. Privatization builds a tax base and generates employment and these messages need to be emphasized over the revenue from sales. Ironically, the at the same time as officials complain about low prices received for objects, they also complain that the population does not have money to purchase enterprises. Basic economics teaches that low prices are precisely the result of this low purchasing power. Privatization gives the citizens the chance to make themselves rich, which is the point of the policy.

IV. SMALL SCALE PRIVATIZATION - RECOMMENDATIONS

The recommendations for the privatization process are simple, but not easy to implement. They are mostly political in nature.

a. Punish raions which do not meet their privatization target. Thus far, there has been no punishment for local officials who refuse to sell small scale objects. Unless they feel this is an important government policy, they will not bother to implement it.
b. Punish ministries or committee heads who refuse to cooperate with the privatization process. Again, many low level bureaucrats are simply stalling the privatization process, and nothing is done.
c. Insist on sale of Republican objects. Over 500 objects of Republican property exist which can be sold. The Chairman of the SPC has moved too slowly on selling these objects, and has increased prices to such an extent that there are no interested buyers. These objects must be sold if the Government is to meet its target.
d. Approve the sale of pharmacies and gas stations. Two draft decrees are in process to include pharmacies and gas stations in the privatization process. There are approximately 400 pharmacies which can be sold, and over 100 gas stations. The gas stations are technically already subject to privatization, and legally this decree is not necessary, but Tajiknefteprodukt is one example of the kind of organization which has stopped privatization of "its" enterprises so far.

V. INCORPORATION OF MEDIUM AND LARGE ENTERPRISES - CURRENT SITUATION

The World Bank requires that 600 medium and large enterprises be incorporated (register shares emissions) by end March 1999 (second tranche)

At this time, only 182 enterprises have registered their shares emissions since January 1998, and the pace of incorporation has slowed tremendously in recent months. Since September, only 32 emissions have been registered, and the process is slowing down. Ministries, enterprise directors, the Center for Valuation and the State Property Committee are all slowing the process down. Many enterprise directors are refusing to cooperate in registering their shares emissions, and others are refusing to register their enterprises as joint stock companies.

VI. INCORPORATION OF MEDIUM AND LARGE ENTERPRISES - PROBLEMS

The problems in incorporation of medium and large enterprises are similar to those with small scale privatization, and are related to pricing and political issues.

Enterprise directors are not interested in cooperating in the incorporation and shares emission process. In many cases they fear that someone else will buy their enterprise and they will lose their jobs. Because starting prices are set so high, the enterprise directors and collectives cannot purchase the enterprises, and so the process stops. In fact, 32 enterprises have documentation prepared for registering their shares emission (although in many cases this will have to be re-done, because of the new coefficients) and simply refused to submit their documentation.

Fees for enterprises registering as joint stock companies and registering their shares emission also prevent the process from moving forward. The Republican Center for Valuation charges for its services in many cases, and has a monopoly on the valuation process. Some enterprise directors insist that they cannot pay for these services, and the process stops.

VII. INCORPORATION OF MEDIUM AND LARGE ENTERPRISES - RECOMMENDATIONS

The problems with incorporation need to be solved at a high level, and line ministries and enterprise directors need to be forced to participate in the program. If problems with share sales can be solved (see below) then the process will likely move forward on its own.

a. First, line ministries must be given clear orders to require their enterprises to complete incorporation and registration of shares emission. This has recently been done, with letters signed by the Prime Minister. Close control needs to be maintained over these orders, and if there are non compliances, some form of punishment must be given out. Unless there is some punishment for failure, there will be no success.
b. Second, enterprise managers must be made to understand that they are required to complete this process, regardless of whether they will buy the enterprise or not.
c. Third, those organizations participating in the process (notaries, Center for Valuation, local authorities) must also be made to understand that this process is

of the highest priority and that they must not slow it down. The incorporation process involves many approvals and authorizations, and each step along the way is slowing the process.

VIII. PRIVATIZATION OF MEDIUM AND LARGE ENTERPRISES - CURRENT SITUATION

The requirement of the World Bank for second tranche, and of the IMF for the next ESAF, is that 70 enterprises be sold by end 1998 and 120 by end March 1999. At this time, only 30 medium and large enterprises have been privatized since January, according to the World Bank and IMF definition (75% shares sold and paid for). This means that in December, 40 companies must be sold, and in the first three months of 1999, another 30 companies must be sold.

There are currently 144 companies which are ready to sell, with prepared shares emissions registered. In fact, 150 of these companies have been offered at auction already once, 42 have been offered twice, 24 have been offered three times, and 13 have been offered four or more times. 10 auctions have been organized in 1998, and another auction is to be organized soon.

IX. PRIVATIZATION OF MEDIUM AND LARGE ENTERPRISES - PROBLEMS

There is only one main problem in the sale of shares in medium and large enterprises, and that is price. Price continues to be the most important issue in selling medium and large enterprises, and because the SPC is so concerned about selling enterprises for a high price, the Government risks losing the IMF and World bank supports.

The problem of too high prices also affects incorporation. Because the prices are too high, the enterprise directors refuse to participate in the incorporation process. They know they cannot afford to buy the enterprise, so they refuse to cooperate at all. If we can solve the problem of high prices, then the process will move forward.

X. PRIVATIZATION OF MEDIUM AND LARGE ENTERPRISES - RECOMMENDATIONS

The only way to increase sales of medium and large enterprises is to lower the prices of the enterprises. Until prices fall, the enterprises will remain unsold. There is not enough money in the population to buy the shares at the current prices. It is ironic that the SPC is trying to take more money from locals, and in the process losing money that could be gotten from the international organizations. The SPC is choking Tajiks for a few pennies while the foreigners are willing to give money.

XI. COTTON GINNERIES PRIVATIZATION - CURRENT STATUS

The privatization of cotton ginneries is the most important aspect of the privatization program at this time. The World Bank and the IMF require that the international tender for cotton ginneries begin in mid December, and the World Bank requires that the ginneries be privatized by end March 1999. At this time, only 7 ginneries have registered shares emissions. An additional 6 are incorporated but without registered shares emissions, an additional 4 are in the process of incorporation and 6 are not being prepared for incorporation at all. the status of the various ginneries is given in Attachment 1. A great deal of work remains to be done on these ginneries, but the directors of the ginneries refuse to cooperate, and Pakhtai Tojik has so far not ordered them to do so.

In addition, no progress is being made on the procedure for the international tender itself. The advertisement draft, which was left by the World Bank, contains quite specific information about the tender procedure. Before the advertisement is placed, these procedures must be agreed upon and established. Attachment 2 gives some ideas about what needs to be done.

XII. COTTON GINNERIES PRIVATIZATION - PROBLEMS

There are three fundamental problems with cotton ginnery privatization.

a. First, the ginneries are not cooperating with the incorporation process. Glavhlopkaprom has for a long time slowed the process, and other organizations are also slowing down the process as well.
b. Second, the Regulation on Case by Case Privatization is not passed. The sale cannot take place without this regulation approved by the Government.
c. Third, the advertisement for the international tender is not yet prepared, and the main policy decisions regarding this are not made. There are many important issues that must be decided, regarding the cotton ginnery privatization.

XIII. COTTON GINNERIES PRIVATIZATION - RECOMMENDATIONS

The problems with the privatization of cotton ginneries are not complicated to resolve, but it will take consistent attention from the highest levels of government.

First, the Government must order the immediate incorporation of all ginneries, and registration of their shares emissions. All intermediate organizations, such as Pakhtai Tojik, the Ministry of Agriculture, the Republican Center for Valuation, the notaries and others must be aware that nothing should delay this process.

Second, the Government must review and approve the Regulation on Case by Case Privatization. Without this, international investors will have no idea how the tender is to proceed.

Third, the Government must establish the Commission for the tender, which must immediately work out the exact procedures for the tender. Some sample questions are given in Attachment 2.

XIV. LIQUIDATION OF RCPT

The World Bank requires, as a second tranche condition, the sale of the RCPT, sale of its assets, and transfer of its non commercial functions to the Ministry of Agriculture by 1 January 1999.

No progress is being made on this issue, as far as we are aware.

XV. TRUCK TRANSPORT PRIVATIZATION - CURRENT SITUATION

The World Bank requirement for truck transport privatization is that 30,000 state owned trucks be either written off or sold by the time of the second tranche, which the World Bank and IMF envision as end March. Virtually no progress has been made on this issue at all, and the process has continued very slowly. Exact data is not known, since there is no centralized mechanism for monitoring privatization of truck transport. The only statistics available are from the GAI, and those will be known only in January. However, it is safe to say that it will require a massive national effort to meet this goal by end March.

At this time, an estimated 71 vehicles are falling out of use every day from the national truck fleet, and the state owned trucking enterprises cannot replace them for lack of funds. 51 transport enterprises, meanwhile, were amalgamated into 4 joint stock companies, and none of these could be privatized, because the charter fund was too high. The enterprises themselves cannot operate, because the new structure of the joint stock companies is exactly the same as that of the old ministry, and the enterprise managers have no freedom to restructure. This mistake seems to be slowly being corrected.

Recently, a decree on writing off and sale of trucks and means of transport was adopted, which will help accelerate the process. This will require a great deal of support from the line ministries to implement, however, and the problem of selling prices for vehicles will likely slow the process down once again.

XVI. TRUCK TRANSPORT PRIVATIZATION - PROBLEMS

The problems for truck transport privatization and writing off are still unknown, since the process has not started fully yet. However, certain problems can be anticipated.

Price will once again be a problem, most likely. Since the resolution specifies that trucks should be written off or sold, enterprise managers will probably be blamed or accused if they write off trucks, or if they sell them for low prices. Thus, once again, price will be an issue and the Government will risk losing IMF and World Bank credits because of some rusted vehicles.

Reporting will certainly be an issue. There is no centralized reporting system, and it will be very difficult to keep track of how many trucks have been sold or written off. Forms are being developed, but implementing of these forms is not certain.

Dissemination of information and mobilization of resources will be important problems. In order to complete this huge volume of work, it will be necessary to organize directors of all transport companies, many directors of farms and other organizations, and explain the procedure to them.

XVII. TRUCK TRANSPORT PRIVATIZATION - RECOMMENDATIONS

In order to implement the truck transport program, and overcome the problems mentioned above, certain steps need to be taken immediately.

a. The Ministers of Transport and Agriculture must be informed of the signing of the decree, and be required to inform their enterprises of the decree and the need to implement it.
b. Regional seminars must be organized with staff of the Ministry of Transport, Agriculture, State Property Committee and Carana Corporation giving consultation on how to implement the decree.
c. Reporting on the number of trucks written off and sold should be implemented through the ministries and seminars.

Unfinished Construction Privatization - Current Status, Problems and Recommendations

There are currently 343 unfinished construction sites remaining to be privatized. In 1998, 11 enterprises were sold, after 6 announcements were made for tenders. The last attempt to see unfinished construction sites was made on 9 October 1998.

It may be the case that, under current circumstances, there are no buyers for an unfinished construction site. However, that is rare, since for 0 dollars, someone would take the site and simply strip the building materials. Obviously, this is not the best result economically, but a crumbling unfinished construction site is also economically useless and only loses value.

Therefore, unfinished construction sites must be offered, in a well publicized announcement, with minimum starting prices. At first, conditions to complete the object may be attached, but in a second offering, no conditions should be attached.

XVIII. CONCLUSION

In spite of good progress on small scale privatization in 1998, the process not even half finished yet. Over 1000 objects remain to be sold, and this process should be completed in 4 months, which will mean a pace of small scale privatization almost as fast as than the period before the 15th of May deadline. Incorporation is also critical, and more enterprises now must register their shares emission each month than did in all of 1998, which was a fast year, in order to meet the World Bank and IMF conditions by March 1999. Sales of companies must accelerate also, and for this to happen, prices will have to drop dramatically, but there is no political will to do this at this time.

Most importantly of all, however, the privatization of the cotton ginneries, through international tender, must take place in the coming months, and this will require a concentrated effort in even in the next two weeks, in order to prepare the advertisement for the international tender. Carana Corporation is locating a consultant to advise the Government and SPC on the international tender, whom we hope will be able to travel immediately.

In the middle of 1998 there was the chance to keep the pace of privatization up, and meet the targets. That chance was lost, and unless a concentrated effort is made, the second tranches could slip further and further into the future

**DOCUMENT OF THE EUROPEAN BANK
FOR RECONSTRUCTION AND DEVELOPMENT**

STRATEGY FOR TAJIKISTAN

As approved by the Board of Directors on 1 July 2003

TABLE OF CONTENTS

I. EXECUTIVE SUMMARY

In the two years since the adoption of the last Country Strategy in August 2001, Tajikistan has been making progress in implementing the principles of multi-party democracy, pluralism and market economics as stipulated in Article 1 of the Agreement Establishing the Bank. After years of devastating civil war, stability and normality have returned to Tajikistan. The key elements of the Peace Agreement between the Government and the United Tajik Opposition, concluded in June 1997, have been implemented. A constitutional referendum, formation of a coalition government and presidential and parliamentary elections in 1999 and 2000, although not fully in conformity with international standards, were important benchmarks in this process.

Notwithstanding these achievements, many problems and challenges remain. The judiciary is weak and does not contribute to eradicating corruption. The extension of the limit of the presidential term in office is a concern. The opposition warned that this extension may give the incumbent President the possibility of remaining in office until 2020. Although the OSCE did not formally monitor the constitutional referendum of 22 June 2003, they welcomed the calm atmosphere in which the voting took place but noted shortcomings in the electoral framework. In the wake of the anti-terrorist campaign in neighbouring Afghanistan, the external security of Tajikistan has improved. However, the long common border continues to make Tajikistan vulnerable to developments in Afghanistan. Afghanistan also is the source of a large and increasing flow of drugs being trafficked via Tajikistan and other Central Asian countries to markets in Russia and Europe. Apart from the direct health and social risks associated with increasing drug use and drug traffic, its proliferation also contributes to a growing informal sector and carries the risk of an increasing criminalisation of society.

Macroeconomic performance has improved significantly. Economic growth has been strong, particularly in the last three years (9.2 per cent growth on average), supported by increased production of key commodities (mainly aluminium and cotton) and strong domestic demand fuelled by increasing remittances from Tajiks working abroad. Moreover, there have been improvements in fiscal management, reducing the fiscal deficit to near-balance in 2002. The exchange rate has been relatively stable, although concerns persist over inflation and the consistency of monetary policy. The recent bilateral debt rescheduling agreements have reduced the debt stock to US$ 985 million (82 per cent of GDP). The government also decided to limit public financed investments to 3 per cent of GDP (US$ 40 million for 2003) and not to allow non-concessional sovereign borrowings under the IMF programme. Tajikistan is one of the countries included in the CIS-7 Initiative.

Tajikistan remains the poorest country among the Bank's countries of operation with a per capita income of US$ 186 in 2002. Poverty is widespread (83 per cent of population is below the national poverty line[1]). The poor are predominantly engaged in agriculture, many of them at subsistence level, while the private sector outside farming has so far created only limited job opportunities for the poor. The government has prepared a Poverty Reduction Strategy Programme (PRSP), which was approved in July 2002, and has been based on a countrywide consultation process with significant input from the IFIs, including the Bank. In May 2003, Tajikistan hosted the first Consultative Group meeting on its own territory, at which

[1] Income below Tajik Rouble 20,000 (US$ 16) per month in 1999.

significant new aid commitments were received in support of the PRSP, but the authorities were urged to prioritise investments and emphasise their financial sustainability.

Despite significant reform progress in liberalisation, small-scale privatisation and the implementation of a land reform programme, the structural reform agenda for Tajikistan remains formidable. A key priority is poverty reduction and improved targeting of limited public resources, as well as improved revenue mobilisation. This is being addressed by other donors and the IFIs in the context of the PRSP. In relation to the Bank's area of expertise and comparative advantage, the critical transition challenges are to: (i) improve conditions for private sector development through restructuring and eventual privatisation or liquidation of large state-owned enterprises and through improvements in the investment climate in particular in the area of public governance; (ii) create a financial system that is able to service the financing needs of private domestic enterprises, in particular small and medium-sized companies which are likely to account for the bulk of job creation in the private sector; and (iii) improve financial and operational management in remaining public sector enterprises to reduce quasi-fiscal deficits and create the conditions for additional investment into the development of critical infrastructure.

Tajikistan's reform efforts alone will, however, not be sufficient to create the conditions for sustained growth and poverty reduction. The country is highly dependent on access to trade routes from Central Asia and to the markets of neighbouring countries. Its vast hydropower resources can only be efficiently developed in a regional context, whilst improved road and rail transport also relies on complementary regional investments. The Bank will continue to attempt to forge a regional policy dialogue for overcoming some of these constraints, noting, however, that given their severity Tajikistan is likely to remain dependent on concessional funding for a large proportion of its development needs for the foreseeable future.

Given the macro-economic environment and the stage of reforms mentioned above, the Bank will focus on the following during this strategy period.

1. Financing the Private Sector

The development of micro businesses and SMEs will form one of the pillars of the Bank's operational strategy. Despite the small size of individual projects, the support for entrepreneurship could have significant demonstration effects and spread to the economy at large through linkages. The Bank's main tools for the support of SMEs and micro-businesses will be credit lines administered through local banks, the Direct Investment Facility for equity investments, and the Trade Facilitation Programme for those enterprises engaged in foreign trade operations.

For enterprises larger than SMEs, the Bank's opportunities for financing alongside strategic foreign investors are limited due to the difficult investment climate and the geographical distance of the country from major source countries. Opportunities exist in agribusiness, cotton and natural resources, particularly mining of precious metals and aluminium smelting. Given the mixed experiences that the Bank or other financial institutions had with the private projects in the country, particular attention will need to be paid to the financial viability of proposed investments and the quality of the management and the sponsors.

2. Strengthening the Financial Sector

The banking sector in Tajikistan remains weak and undercapitalised and the number of banks, which are of sufficient quality to be considered as partners for the Bank, is limited. Those local banks chosen as partner institutions under credit lines and TFP facilities will benefit from the provision of a substantial amount of technical assistance to improve credit and financial management skills in general and in particular to introduce MSE and TFP financing as new products into the local banking sector.

The Bank is aware of the constraint placed on the expansion of its work in the financial sector by the high risk that many potential partner banks represent. Where possible and prudent, the Bank will seek to invest directly in the capital of existing or newly-established local banks to increase their ability to attract external funding as well as domestic deposits. However, given high risks, the Bank also expects to share risks with donors through the Central Asia Risk Sharing Special Fund (CARSSF) and other risk guarantee schemes, as a means to leverage its own resources and increase its exposure to the local financial sector.

3. Support for Critical Infrastructure

Investment needs in infrastructure are considerable in Tajikistan. Given limited public resources, however, prioritisation is essential among sovereign-guaranteed publicly financed projects. Since the Bank does not provide concessional funds, the Bank will concentrate on the financing of projects that would have cash flows sufficient to support debt without recourse to a sovereign guarantee. This could be the case in air transport, as well as some parts of the power sector. For other critical infrastructure projects, the Bank could, for example in the power and municipal infrastructure sectors, blend its resources with grants to achieve concessional terms if such funds are available. The Bank will proceed selectively with such an approach and coordinate closely with other donors and IFIs on the overall investment priorities of the country in the context of the PRSP. As an example of such coordination, the Bank will pay particular attention to project structures that combine the Bank financing with other IFIs as well as donor grant funds.

4. Policy Dialogue

During the strategy period, the Bank will continue to promote policy dialogue with the authorities in order to improve the investment climate and support their reform efforts. The Bank will closely co-ordinate with other IFIs and the business community to make such policy dialogue effective.

The Bank will also seek co-financing opportunities with other IFIs and bilateral institutions to mobilise greater resources into the country, especially projects that could enhance regional co-operation. The Bank's Environmental Policy and Public Information Policy will apply to all projects developed in Tajikistan.

LIST OF ABBREVIATIONS

ADB	Asian Development Bank
AKDN	Aga Khan Development Network
ALCO	Agency of Bank Liquidation and Credit Collection
BAS	Business Advisory Service
CAD	Civil Aviation Department
CARE	The Cooperative for American Remittances to Europe
CARSSF	Central Asia Risk Sharing Special Fund
CAS	Country Assistance Strategy
CG	Consultative Group
CIDA	Canadian International Development Agency
CIS	Commonwealth of Independent States
DAC	Development Assistance Committee
DFID	Department for International Development
DIF	Direct Investment Facility
ECFIN	Economic and Financial Affairs
ECHO	European Commission's Humanitarian Aid Office
EU	European Union
FDI	Foreign Direct Investment
FI	Financial Institutions
GDP	Gross Domestic Product
GEF	Global Environmental Facility
GSM	Global System for Mobile Communications
GtZ	Deutsche Gesellschaft für Technische Zusammenarbeit mbH
HIV/AIDS	Human Immunodeficiency Virus/Acquired Immunodeficiency Syndrome
IADI	International Association of Deposit Insurers
IAS	International Accounting Standard
IBRD	International Bank for Reconstruction and Development
ICT	Information and Communication Technology
IDA	International Development Agency
IFC	International Financial Corporation
IFI	International Financial Institution
IFRC	International Federation of Red Cross
ILO	International Labour Organisation
IMF	International Monetary Fund
IMU	Islamic Movement of Uzbekistan
IUCN	World Conservation Union
JSC	Joint Stock Company
JV	Joint Venture
MP	Member of Parliament
MSE	Micro and Small Enterprises
NAP	National Action Programme
NBT	National Bank of Tajikistan
NEAP	The National Environmental Action Plan
NGO	Non-Governmental Organisation
ODA	Official Development Assistance
OECD	Organisation for Economic Co-operation and Development
OGC	Office of the Secretary General
OSCE	Organisation for Security and Co-operation in Europe
PIP	Public Investment Programme
PRGF	Poverty Reduction and Growth Facility
PRSP	Poverty Reduction Strategy Programme

SAC	Structural Adjustment Credit
SDC	Swiss Agency for Development and Co-operation
SECO	State Secretariat for Economic Affairs
SME	Small and Medium – sized Enterprises
SMP	Staff Monitored Programme
TACIS	Technical Assistance for Commonwealth of Independent States
TADAZ	Tajik Aluminium Plant
TAM	Turn Around Management
TC	Technical Co-operation
TFP	Trade Facilitation Programme
TSA	Tajik State Air Company
TSOB	Tajiksodirot Bank
TT	Tajik Telecom
UN	United Nations
UNDP	United Nations Development Programme
UNESCO	United Nations Educational, Scientific and Cultural Organisation
UNICEF	United Nations International Children's Emergency Fund
US	United States
USAID	United States Agency for International Development
UTO	United Tajik Opposition
WB	World Bank
WFP	World Food Programme
WTO	World Trade Organisation

II. Country Strategy

1 The Bank's portfolio

1.1 Overview of the Bank's Activities to Date

Tajikistan became a member of the Bank in 1992. Until 1996 the Bank's operations had been limited to TCs. Since then the Bank approved seven investment projects (see Annex 5) involving both loans and equity. The signed commitments currently stand at EUR 27.5 million, out of which EUR 10.4 million have been disbursed. During the last strategy period the Bank signed two projects in transport and telecommunications. The current portfolio has a weighted project risk rating of 7.41 compared with a Bank average of 5.58.

Table 1. Tajikistan: Overview of the Bank's Activities to Date

	No. of Projects	Total Project Value (EUR million)	The Bank Finance (EUR million)	Debt (EUR million)	Equity (EUR million)	% share of Commitments
Private	2.3	20.2	9.8	8.0	1.8	33 %
State	3	25.3	17.7	17.7	0	67 %
Bank Equity	1	2.7	0.2	0	0.2[2]	1 %
Bank Lending	0.3[3]	3.6	3.6	3.6	0	12 %
Transport	2	12.5	6.7	6.7	0	25 %
Agribusiness	1	13.9	5.9	4.3	1.6	21%
Telecoms Info & M.	1	12.8	11.0	11.0	0	40 %
Totals	**5.3**	**45.6**	**27.5**	**25.7**	**1.8**	**100 %**

1.2 Assessment of the Last Strategy Period

The main operational focus of the last Strategy for Tajikistan (BDS/TA/01-1 (Final), 7 August 2001) was similar to that proposed in the current strategy period. The priorities were: (i) private sector development focusing on small and medium enterprises (SMEs) and micro-businesses; (ii) support for the financial sector to alleviate a key constraint for private sector growth in particular of SMEs; and (iii) selective support for critical investments in infrastructure.

During the last strategy period, the Bank signed two projects: (a) Tajiktelecom Modernisation project; and (b) TSA Air Navigation Systems project. They met the third objective of the strategy mentioned above which was to support critical investments in infrastructure. Their transition impact is explained below (Section 1.3) and is positive in both cases. For these projects, the Bank adopted an approach of blending its resources with grants from donors (Japan and Switzerland) to achieve concessional lending terms. The Bank has not yet implemented a non-sovereign guaranteed project in the public sector, but the blending approach has allowed the Bank to substantially increase its portfolio in Tajikistan and demonstrate its commitment to the country.

[2] The Bank and IFC exited from this equity investment in TSOB bank in March 2003.
[3] In case of framework arrangements for projects, the Bank calculates number of projects by dividing the committed amount by the framework amount approved.

Promoting SME and micro-business financing and supporting the financial sector proved to be more difficult to achieve. The main reason for the difficulty was that the Tajik banking system did not improve sufficiently for the Bank to increase its exposure to the sector. In particular, the depreciation of the Tajik currency had led to a continuous erosion of the capital base of most banks before the depreciation significantly decelerated in the recent past. The currency risk, however, remains an important risk factor. For instance, the Bank could not disburse the second tranche of the existing SME Credit Line with Orienbank because the capital base of the bank did not reach the minimum level required for such disbursement. In addition, the Bank was recently forced to exit from its equity investment in Tajiksodirot Bank (TSOB) for reasons explained below (see the last paragraph in Box 1 in Section 1.4 below).

Despite the improvements recorded in the political and macroeconomic situation, the investment climate remains too weak and the country is seen as being too remote to be of interest to western strategic investors. This was the main reason why the Bank was unable to sign a direct loan or equity investment in the private sector. The Bank will continue to explore such opportunities and market them actively during the current strategy period.

1.3 Transition Impact of the Bank's portfolio

The transition impact has been positive and significant in telecommunications and aviation. In the financial sector, the Bank's impact was mainly through technical assistance to the participating bank in the SME programme. In the private manufacturing sector the Bank's transition impact has been insignificant due to the difficult economic environment and lack of quality sponsors in the two projects in which the Bank invested.

In telecommunications, technical assistance in connection with the Tajik Telecom Modernisation project contributed to the development of the legal and regulatory framework including tariff reform and the creation of an independent regulator. It also facilitated the early-stage preparation of Tajik Telecom (TT) for a potential privatisation through improvements in corporate and financial management as well as upgrading of the physical facilities.

In aviation, the Bank's TC study on Aviation Restructuring was undertaken in connection with the Khoujand Airport Rehabilitation and TSA Air Navigation Systems projects for Tajikistan State Air Company (TSA). This led to the introduction of the Transport Law in October 2000 by which the regulatory functions of TSA were transferred to a newly-created Civil Aviation Department (CAD).[4] In addition, TSA with the Bank's assistance is in the process of preparing separate business units within TSA and introducing IAS accounts for each business units.

The performance of the Credit Line to Orienbank was mixed due to the difficult economic environment and the frequent changes of its management. However, the SME Credit Advisor TC provided by the Bank to Orienbank and the Institution Building TC provided to TSOB have helped to improve management, credit risk assessment capabilities and financial transparency in these banks, with the potential to achieve demonstration effects on the rest of the sector if recent improvements are sustained.

[4] The transfer of CAD, however, entailed another issue related to the corporate governance in aviation. The distinction between regulatory functions and TSA's operational functions has not been clearly understood by the CAD. This resulted in the frequent interference by CAD on TSA's day-to-day operations. The Bank is examining measures to improve the situation.

1.4 Lessons Learned

The success of the Bank's investments in the public sector suggests that significant transition impact can be achieved by leveraging the Bank's resources with grant funds and cross-checking reform covenants with other IFIs to ensure consistent implementation. Looking forward, the challenge will be to repeat these successes in the light of limited implementation capacity of the government through close coordination among all donors.

The financial difficulties of the two private sector investments underscore the importance of ensuring that such projects have quality management and good sponsors who are fully committed to the project (see Box 1).

The Bank experienced the country's weak investors' rights protection with the equity investment in TSOB. It also highlighted the importance of the corporate governance issues. While the Bank exited from the investment, it will continue to undertake policy dialogue with the authorities on these issues as they are crucial to allowing additional private and financial sector investments to be undertaken.

Box 1: Specific lessons from private sector investments

Khoujand Packaging was negatively affected during the early stage of the project by the Russian crisis since the company had originally planned to direct more than 85 per cent of its sales to the Russian market. The management did not react appropriately to the crisis and to date has not made sufficient efforts to turn the situation around. Due to the deterioration of the financial position of the company, the foreign sponsors have long lost interest. Both TAM and the BAS consultants assisted the Company without success. The lack of competent management open to external advice would appear to be the key problem in this project.

Obi-Zulol project started full production in February 2001. The project was expected to increase the country's export revenues. However, due to extended delays to the start of production and lower-than-expected sales in export markets, Obi-Zulol has not generated enough cash to service principal and interest payments. The Bank has been assisting the company's management in reaching a break-even level of sales and expanding to export markets. One of the problems behind the present situation was the difficulties of the marketing analysis and as a result the size of the investment was larger than could be supported by the current market. Market access restrictions to neighbouring Uzbekistan also played a role in depressing the company's sales performance.

The Bank made an equity investment (US$ 200,000) in **TSOB** in November 2000[5]. In 2002 the Bank encountered a serious problem as TSOB issued free shares to some of the shareholders in April 2002 without informing the other shareholders. This resulted in the dilution of the Bank's shares to 8.3 per cent from the original 19.4 per cent. The Bank conducted a number of negotiations with the management of TSOB and consulted with the Central Bank without success. In March 2003, the Bank exited from the equity investment. The apparent weakness of investor right protection in Tajikistan underscores the importance of carefully choosing partner institutions, as well as continuing policy dialogue with the Central Bank to improve its regulatory enforcement capacity.

[5] Subsequently the IFC invested in TSOB's equity for US$ 200,000 in April 2002.

1.5 Portfolio Ratio

Thirty three per cent of the Bank's cumulative commitments are in the private sector. Because of the small size of the Bank's operations in the country, the portfolio ratio is significantly influenced by the two recent public sector transactions. The Bank's private sector focus in the current strategy period is expected to move the portfolio ratio gradually towards the 60 per cent target.

2 Operational Environment

2.1 The General Reform Environment

2.1.1 Political Conditions

The political situation has stabilised in recent years. For detailed political assessment, see Annex 1.

2.1.2 Social Conditions and Labour Issues

Tajikistan remains the poorest country in the former Soviet Union. Per capita GDP in 2002 was US$ 186 at current exchange rates and US$ 1,374 at PPP exchange rates. Tajikistan has been classified as IDA only by the World Bank. According to the Tajikistan Living Standard Survey, conducted in 1999 by the World Bank, 83 per cent of the population were below the official poverty line[6], of which 17 per cent lived in extreme poverty.[7] Poverty is highest in rural areas and among those without regular work. Average incomes were just US$ 10.6 per month in 2001, meaning that a significant proportion of the working population earns less than a subsistence wage. The legislation on labour rights is largely in accordance with ILO conventions although it may not be fully enforced in practice (see Annex 1 for details).

To increase real incomes and living standards and to target better government assistance to the poor, the government approved a Poverty Reduction Strategy Paper (PRSP) in May 2002.[8] This strategy forms the basis for future official donor assistance and outlines key policy priorities over the medium term. Particular emphasis is placed on improving the rural economy and the agriculture sector on which the majority of poor people depend. The PRSP does not contain a strong focus on private sector development, although both the government and donors realise that ultimately effective poverty reduction will require sustained growth and new employment opportunities in the private sector, which remains small outside the rural economy. Given the limited sovereign debt capacity, a key task for the government is to prioritise the investments envisaged under the PRSP and the public investment programme.

2.1.3 Regional Co-operation

Tajikistan is a small and land-locked country. It is highly dependent on good neighbourly relations for market access and significantly affected by regional security issues related to drug transit and the political situation in Afghanistan. Tajikistan's major export routes are through Uzbekistan and Kazakhstan to Russia. Limited trade also takes place with China through a road link in the East of the country. The routes south through Afghanistan into the Indian subcontinent have potential in the future, but have remained underdeveloped due to the instability in Afghanistan. Concerns over regional security and drugs have repeatedly disrupted trade flows from Tajikistan through border closures (and the mining of border areas) with Uzbekistan and transit restrictions in Kazakhstan. Uzbekistan's protectionist trade policies have also hampered market access for Tajik goods. As a result regional trade has declined significantly. While regional leaders have repeatedly made commitments to improve regional cooperation in trade and transit matters, this has not translated into concrete steps so far.

One of Tajikistan's main economic assets and a key export is hydropower. Tajikistan's trade in water and electricity is guided by complex bilateral barter arrangements. For example,

---

[6] Tajik Rouble 20,000 (approximately US$ 16) in 1999.

[7] PPP US$ 1.075 a day.

[8] The main contributions of the Bank are indicated in the aviation and telecommunication sectors.

under annually negotiated bilateral agreements, Tajikistan purchases power from Uzbekistan and Turkmenistan during winter time and releases water in summer used for irrigation purposes. Tajikistan also exports surplus power in summer. The pricing arrangements implicit in these barter deals do not reflect true opportunity costs, and disagreements over terms have led to the accumulation of debts and repeated supply disruptions. Creating the economic conditions for efficient regional trade in power and water is a key challenge for Tajikistan's future and for the whole of Central Asia. The international community has recently stepped up its efforts to encourage regional cooperation in Central Asia. The EBRD's Annual Meeting also provided an important focal point for these efforts, and the IFIs have since created a working group to pursue joint policy initiatives, including thorough support to the ADB's Ministerial Conference on Regional Cooperation.

The Bank is also currently preparing the Regional Power Transmission Project to be co-financed with the ADB. The objective of the project is to promote cross-border power trade between Tajikistan and Uzbekistan. The ADB approved the Tajik component of the project and the Bank plans to finance the Uzbek component.

2.1.4 Legal environment

Tajikistan's legal environment is among the least developed of the EBRD's countries of operation. Other than a new leasing law introduced in April 2003, certain environmental protection laws in 2001 and in 2002, and a telecommunications law adopted in 2002, commercial law is substantially inadequate and the reform of the secured transactions laws has been minor. There have been no major legal reforms implemented since the adoption of parts I and II of a new Civil Code, in 1999, certain provisions of which now conflict with existing laws which govern secured transactions.

Bankruptcy laws are in place, and while further reform is being considered, the country lacks effective bankruptcy courts, trustees and enforcement mechanisms. The lack of implementation of laws and the problem of corruption in the judiciary are among the most serious constraints on Tajikistan's transition to a functioning market economy.

2.1.5 Environmental issues

Annex 2 contains a summary of environmental issues in Tajikistan.

2.1.6 Integrity issues

Tajikistan faces serious problems of weak governance and low government capacity. It ranks 175 among 195 countries according to the 2001 World Bank Governance Indicators on control of corruption. According to the 2002 Business Environment and Enterprise Performance Survey, 35 per cent of surveyed firms were paying bribes frequently, which is in line with other countries in the CIS. The average share of revenues paid in unofficial payments was 2.6 per cent, again similar to levels in other CIS countries.

Tajikistan's institutional environment is among the weakest in the region, despite good progress in economic reforms. The absence of qualified local personnel, for instance in accounting or corporate law, is a significant constraint on business, as many Tajiks have emigrated to Russia in search of higher incomes. Government capacity to implement and enforce legislation is relatively weak, given low public sector wages. The growing drug transit remains a problem. As examples from around the world demonstrate, drug traffic has the potential to criminalise society with serious negative implications for private investment.

There is no specific legislation on money laundering, but the law on external economic activity addresses the consequences of illegal financial activities.

2.2 Macroeconomic conditions relevant for the Bank's operations

Since the end of the civil war, Tajikistan has experienced rapid growth. The average growth rate in the last five years (1998-2002) was 7.3 per cent, driven by strong industrial and agricultural output (five year average of 9.2 per cent and 9.4 per cent respectively) and domestic demand fuelled by increasing remittances (estimated at some US$ 80 million in 2002). Cotton and aluminium continue to account for the bulk of production, but there is some evidence of economic diversification and productivity increases in other sectors. GDP grew by 10.2 per cent in the four months of 2003. However, growth is expected to decelerate in the medium term, as early gains based on improved capacity utilisation are exhausted. Aluminium production at the TADAZ[9], in particular will soon face capacity constraints.

Inflation has been on a downward trend since 2000 ending last year at 14.5 per cent. However, public sector wage increases, growing energy and food prices and a temporary resumption of directed credits kept inflation above target throughout 2002 and inflation spiked during the first quarter of 2003. Looking forward, there remain some inflationary pressures this year due to planned utility tariff increases and a 20 per cent wage increase in the public sector (April 2003).

Due to low tax collection rates and lapses in expenditure management, the fiscal balance was chronically in deficit in the past decade. However, in 2002 the government achieved a near budget balance. Strong economic growth and the establishment of a Ministry of State Revenues and Customs in early 2002 have improved tax collection, while restraints on spending have contained the growth of expenditures. However, with fiscal revenues at 16.1 per cent of GDP and external debt over 80 per cent of GDP, further improvements in fiscal management are required to achieve sustainable public finances. To achieve fiscal sustainability, the IMF imposed a ceiling of 3 per cent of GDP (about US$ 40 million for 2003) on the externally financed PIP. Moreover, quasi-fiscal activities remain problematic as the quasi-fiscal deficit in the energy sector is estimated at 5.3 per cent of GDP in 2001 (1.9 per cent for gas, 3.0 per cent for electricity and 0.5 per cent for heating), although there were significant tariff increases and improvements in cash collection recently.

Tajikistan, as a small land-locked country, has a fairly open economy with share of trade[10] in GDP of 123 per cent in 2002. However, exports are highly concentrated in a few commodities (cotton and aluminium) and are affected by price fluctuation of these commodities. The trade deficit narrowed and FDI inflows increased in 2002, but repayments to the IMF because of earlier misreporting kept gross reserves unchanged. On the institutional side, the country made some progress in WTO accession. In May 2002, tariffs and the number of tariff-exempt goods were further reduced and a WTO memorandum on the trade regime was approved by the parliament in December 2002 and submitted to the WTO in February 2003. Moreover a new customs code and tax code are being introduced in compliance with international practices.

The informal economy in Tajikistan appears to be large. A large number of small/micro enterprises, especially in rural areas and in the agriculture sector, do not pay appropriate taxes

[9] A state owned aluminium smelter, which accounts for around 60 per cent of export revenues.
[10] Imports plus exports over GDP.

and barter transactions are substantial. Moreover, drug trafficking probably accounts for substantial part of the informal economic activities.[11]

Bilateral debt rescheduling agreements in 2002, most importantly with Uzbekistan, Kazakhstan and Russia, have reduced the debt stock to US$ 985 million (82 per cent of GDP), from a peak of US$ 1,226 million (124 per cent of GDP) in 2000. Debt service due is expected to decline in the next few years (from 25.6 per cent of exports in 2001 to 13.4 per cent in 2004) due to the grace periods agreed under the new agreements, but it will increase again from 2005 (a peak of 19 per cent of exports in 2007). Nonetheless, external debt in net present value terms accounted for 129 per cent of exports and 339 per cent of fiscal revenues in 2002. Tajikistan thus remains vulnerable to debt servicing problems and highly dependent on continued access to concessional international financing (see Section 2.4 below).

2.3 Progress in Transition and Remaining Challenges

Tajikistan has made impressive gains in economic reform over the past five years, since the end of the civil war. However, the country faces enormous challenges in moving forward, related to a complex political situation in a potentially volatile region, and the combination of fundamental development issues with specific transition challenges. Government capacity to implement and enforce new legislation is poor and the functioning of domestic markets still impeded by many informal and physical barriers.

The biggest gains in structural reforms have been made since 1997 in the areas of price and trade liberalisation and the privatisation of small scale enterprises (see Chart 2.1). Tajikistan maintains a floating exchange rate regime with full currency convertibility and relatively open trade policies and applied for membership in the WTO in May 2001. The government is also making efforts to meet all requirements for acceptance of the IMF's article VIII on full current account convertibility. However, the transition progress of the financial sector, infrastructure as well as corporate restructuring and privatisation of large scale firms has been slow. Recent progress and detailed challenges in the three areas of private sector development, financial sector reform and infrastructure improvement are examined below.

[11] According to the ICG report (April 2003), as much as 30 per cent of the population are in some way associated with the drug business. It is estimated that it accounts for 10-15% of GDP.

Chart 1 Progress in Transition (EBRD transition indicators, 2002)

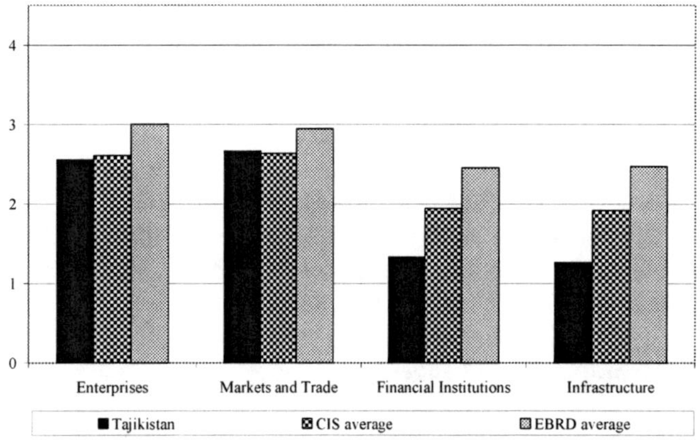

Note: 1 indicates little or no progress and 4+ indicates a standard similar to advanced market economies (see Transition Report for more details).

It is apparent that Tajikistan's main economic challenges go beyond the establishment of well-functioning markets and supporting market institutions. The country faces fundamental tasks of overcoming poverty and breaking out of its geographical isolation.

The Bank needs to define its role in this larger process in close collaboration with other partners. Many of the pressing social needs are of a kind that cannot be directly addressed with commercial funding, and instead will rely on grants. The country's high external debt puts a severe constraint on commercial funding for public sector infrastructure projects, including in the critical transport and energy sectors, although opportunities of co-financing with donor grants and other concessional lenders may exist. In the light of this, the Bank's most important contribution will be to promote private investment in Tajikistan:

The three critical transition challenges that the Bank can help to address directly are:

- to ***improve conditions for private sector development*** through improvements in the investment climate in particular in the area of public governance. Promoting private investment and entrepreneurship in the micro and SME sector is particularly important since it will directly contribute to poverty alleviation.

- to ***create a financial system*** that is able to service the financing needs of private domestic enterprises, in particular small and medium-sized companies which are likely to account for the bulk of job creation in the private sector.

- to ***improve financial and operational management in public sector enterprises***. Sovereign operations are constrained, but possibilities exist for non-sovereign operations in air transport, and grant co-financing in other areas of critical infrastructure, such as power water and other municipal utility services. The Bank's approach to infrastructure financing is based on cost recovery, taking into account affordability constraints and addressing these through targeted income support.

2.3.1 Privatisation and Enterprise Reform

As of end-2002, small-scale privatisation was almost complete. The private sector share in GDP is estimated to have increased from 30 per cent in 1997 to 50 per cent in 2002. However, only half of the medium and large-scale state enterprises scheduled for privatisation have been privatised so far (including all 22 cotton ginneries) and 300 medium and large-scale entities are to remain fully state-owned.[12]

Moreover, weak governance structures and government interference impede effective restructuring. With the exception of gold mining, where there has been some inflow of FDI, most branches of industry suffer from the lack of outside funding and management expertise, particularly in those firms sold to insiders. Moreover, the restructuring of TADAZ, in which the World Bank has been involved, has been delayed due to disagreements over a required financial audit of the company. A new privatisation strategy was approved by the parliament in December 2002, but was unsatisfactory to the World Bank as the majority of the listed enterprises are not operating.

With over half of the population dependent either directly or indirectly on agriculture, rural reforms are critical to improve economic opportunities and the standard of living for the majority of the population. After a slow start, land reform has been progressing well as around 50 per cent of co-operative farm lands have been converted into dekhan farms (individual land plots). A land registry has been established and land registration fees have been reduced. Private plots achieve significantly higher yields as those managed by cooperatives or state-owned farms and land reform have been one source of agricultural growth. However, many private plots are too small to achieve scale economies and have relied, so far, on the availability of cheap family labour. Improvements in rural credit and input markets as well as marketing of rural produce and reductions in internal trade barriers will be needed to sustain recent productivity gains. Moreover, Tajikistan's irrigation infrastructure is in significant disrepair, as the previous system relied on cheap energy to fuel the extensive system of pumps. This is an area of donor focus, with efforts going into improved water management and the design of technologically more appropriate irrigation systems.

The key challenge in the enterprise sector remains the attraction of foreign investment, in sectors such as mining, cotton processing and possibly some areas of infrastructure, where potential returns are sufficient to compensate for the significant country risks; and from domestic sources for the many SMEs that will be the backbone of the economy's sustained recovery in the future. Large scale enterprise restructuring, including TADAZ, needs to proceed in parallel to reduce the drain on public resources and create a level playing field for all investors.

2.3.2 Financial Sector Development

The banking sector remains fragile and underdeveloped. Bank deposits account for only 4 per cent of GDP, with the bulk of sector liabilities in the form of foreign loans. Domestic credit accounts for 18.6 per cent of GDP. These ratios are comparable to other low-income CIS countries but significantly lower than in other transition economies. Both deposits and credits have been growing quite rapidly in recent years, as the economy has enjoyed some

---

[12] Most of the medium-scale privatisations are considered too small for the Bank to participate (e.g. the largest ones in 2002 were a sewing factory for US$ 0.5 million and a construction company for US$ 0.4 million). All utility and infrastructure companies are state-owned.

remonetisation and has benefited from the inflow of remittances. The majority of bank assets are held by four large banks[13], with cotton financing the largest single exposure of the sector.

The consolidation of the banking sector has progressed in recent years (the number of commercial banks declined from 24 in 1994 to 13 in March 2003). However, banking supervision continues to be weak and the restructuring of the largest banks remains slow. Only five banks have achieved the minimum capital requirement of US$ 1.5 million by mid-2002. This requirement will be raised to US$ 2 million by end-2003 and US$ 3 million at end-2005, but many banks, including well-managed small banks, might face serious difficulties in meeting these targets. Many banks are still effectively operating as "pocket banks" for specific branches of the economy, limiting the scope for competition, and making outside investments into the sector more difficult.

The National Bank of Tajikistan (NBT) has prepared restructuring plans for the two largest banks (Agroinvestbank and Savings Bank). Agroinvestbank will be separated into one commercial bank (non-cotton) and one credit union (cotton finance) while the state owned Amonatbank, currently serving as a fiscal agent for the government, will be financially restructured and operated on a commercial basis. Moreover, the Agency of Bank Liquidation and Credit Collection (ALCO), which was created to deal with the assets of the liquidated banks, will be closed as it proved inefficient. From April 2003 the government has decreed a two-month capital amnesty, aimed at bringing some of the estimated large private holdings of cash into the banking system and make it available for investments in the economy. After ten days extension and lifting the frozen period, approximately US$ 170 million were legalised but most of the deposited money were withdrawn immediately. This amnesty has increased deposit growth in the banking sector and decrease the size of the unofficial economy, but raises significant concerns over: (i) the legalisation of money obtained from criminal activities and (ii) moral hazard and hence the encouragement of future tax evasion.[14]

The critical challenge in the sector remains the improvement in the functioning of the domestic financial institutions, to increase confidence and attract additional domestic deposits, and to provide competitive access to finance for domestic enterprises. This will need to be addressed both with additional capital contributions into the sector (including possibly through the creation of new banks) and continued technical support to increase credit skills among existing banks. Further improvements in macroeconomic management and in the supervisory capacity of the NBT will also be critical to allow additional investment in the financial sector to take place.

2.3.3 Infrastructure reforms

Tajikistan inherited an infrastructure from Soviet times that required extensive investment in rehabilitation and modernisation. However, the civil war and the collapse of state revenues have meant that the government has been unable to fund even basic maintenance expenditures and the quality of the existing assets has consequently sharply deteriorated. A particular concern is the quality of irrigation, which is being addressed by a number of donor initiatives, with limited scope for commercial financing. Other priority areas are transport, water supply and power.

[13] Agroinvestbank, Orien Bank, Savings Bank (Amonatbank) and TSOB hold about 85 per cent of assets and 70 per cent of household deposits.
[14] Amnesty has been extended for 10 days until 10 June 2003.

Over the past 2-3 years, the government has begun to implement a series of institutional and tariff reforms to lay the foundations for future investment in infrastructure. With the establishment of a Ministry of Energy and Ministry of Transport, regulatory functions were essentially separated from operations but the regulators remain under-resourced. The government's Public Investment Programme includes numerous infrastructure projects, and the authorities are aware of the need for further tariff and institutional reform if such investments are to be financial in a sustainable manner over the medium term. There is increased interest among donors and in the government for combining concessional funds with a commercial approach, which tries to attract private risk capital to the sector to enhance its efficiency and put it on a more solid financial basis.

Notable progress has recently been made in tariff reform. In the power sector, under an ADB supported programme, average prices rose substantially over the last few years. Barki Tajik, the state owned electricity company, has reached a 95 per cent collection ratio and payment arrears from budgetary organisations and public enterprises have been significantly reduced. In the telecom sector, tariff reform has also begun, with monthly subscription, local call and related charges increasing by 174 per cent in June 2002. A formula for automatic adjustments of tariffs has been agreed by the Ministry of Communications and the Anti-monopoly Committee, which will reflect the financing costs for new investments undertaken by the incumbent operator, Tajiktelecom. Tajiktelecom has also made strenuous efforts to increase its revenue collections, which reached 88 per cent of total billings in the first half of 2002. However, collections from state entities are much lower and substantial payment arrears remain from previous years, affecting the financial health of the company. Privatisation is regarded as premature under the present environment, as a tender would be unlikely to attract competent private bidders.

In the aviation sector, the regulatory functions of Tajikistan State Air Company (TSA) have been transferred to a newly created Civil Aviation Department (CAD) within the Ministry of Transport. Moreover, it is envisaged that three business units (air transport services, airport services and air navigation services) will be financially separated and cross-subsidisation is expected to be minimised. With the entry of non-Tajik airlines, competition is also expected to increase in the near future.

The critical challenge in infrastructure is to prioritise investments given limited public funds and to promote private investment in the modernisation of infrastructure. The Bank can contribute to meeting this challenge through its commercial approach, and related support to institutional development. However, it will coordinate its activities closely with the other donors and IFIs to invest in line with the government's priorities.

2.4 Access to Capital

Tajikistan remains essentially dependent on official financing from donors and IFIs for most of its public investment as well as to finance a structural current account deficit. Although FDI has been increasing in 2002, it remains significantly below the level of official flows and is unlikely to replace such flows anytime soon. Commercial bank lending has been provided to the cotton and aluminium sectors, largely for working capital purposes, but at terms that are not always advantageous for Tajikistan.

Tajikistan has held two successful Consultative Group meetings in Tokyo in 2001 and in Dushanbe in 2003, with donors' commitments of around US$ 400 million and US$ 900 million respectively. However, the experience over the past two years has been that only around 60 per cent of commitments made were disbursed, with donors concerned in particular about weak implementation capacity in the government. Moreover, slow progress in some critical reform areas has delayed IMF and World Bank financing over the 2001-2003 period, further reducing the actual flow of disbursements to some estimated US$ 250 million (of which US$ 130 million if IFI financing is excluded) over the two-year period. Assuming a similar disbursement ratio under the 2003 CG commitments would imply annual disbursements of US$ 150 million – around 15 per cent of GDP. The PRSP envisaged a total of US$ 689 million for the next two years, of which US$ 543 million should be raised externally, although donors continue to be concerned over the lack of prioritisation in the PIP, which may limit financing.

Private sector access to medium and long-term finance is extremely limited in Tajikistan. Interest rates remain high and most bank lending is short-term (up to three months). Access to bank lending is especially difficult for micro and small/medium enterprises (which account for more than 90 per cent of total enterprises in terms of number). The 2003 International Crisis Group report on Tajikistan notes that most existing donor supported micro-finance programmes are too small to benefit the more dynamic urban firms, while existing SME credit lines are insufficient to fill the demand for credit among such enterprises.

One sector, which has attracted private financing is the cotton sector. In 2002, reportedly US$ 90 million in commercial, non-guaranteed credits were provided to the sector by foreign investors and on-lent to cotton producers at a rate of 12 per cent. Another sector is aluminium. The state owned aluminium company (TADAZ) holds around US$ 110 million in commercial debt, much of this working capital finance from alumina suppliers. There are no functioning domestic equity markets and access to international debt/equity markets by Tajik enterprises remains almost impossible.

3 Strategic Orientations

3.1 Bank's Priorities for the Strategy Period

In line with the difficult investment and transition challenges facing Tajikistan, the Bank's main priorities in the strategy period will be:
(i) financing the private sector, focusing on small and medium sized enterprises and micro businesses,
(ii) strengthening the financial sector through technical assistance and where possible additional capital injections, and
(iii) supporting critical infrastructure projects with a clear focus on high priority, commercially oriented investments in close collaboration with other donors and IFIs.
(iv) maintaining policy dialogue.

Considering the difficulties in implementing investment projects in the country, the Bank will actively utilise the Central Asia Risk Sharing Special Fund (CARSSF), introduced in June 2002, to support private sector development through facilitating broader participation of local banks in financing, thus enhancing financial sector development. The Bank will also seek to develop further co-operation with other donors, who have shown their growing interest in the country on such occasions as the CIS7 initiative and the recent CG meeting in Dushanbe. These areas of co-operation will include (i) active utilisation of co-financing grants, which will enable the Bank to implement critical infrastructure projects, and (ii) further contributions to CARSSF[15].

During the strategy period, the Bank will continue to promote policy dialogue with the authorities in order to improve the investment climate and support their reform efforts. The Bank will closely co-ordinate with other IFIs and the business community to make such policy dialogue effective. The Bank will also seek co-financing opportunities with other IFIs and bilateral institutions to mobilise greater resources into the country, especially projects that could enhance regional co-operation.

3.2 Sectoral Challenges and Bank Objectives

3.2.1 Financing the Private Sector

<u>Transition Goals</u>

The Bank's main transition goal in this sector is to strengthen the private sector base of the economy. Despite the recent encouraging expansion of private sector employment, making this expansion sustainable will be key to absorbing Tajikistan's rapidly expanding and largely rural population. Although the Bank's investment through its SME and micro-business credit lines or through DIF projects will be small relative to the needs of the country, they could serve to generate significant demonstration effects and encourage entrepreneurial activity. The Bank will also aim to strengthen Tajikistan's integration into the world economy through

[15] So far Swiss Government contributed EUR 6 million (TFP, MSE and DIF) and German Government EUR 2.45 million (TFP) for the total of EUR 8.45 million. The Swiss Government is considering further contribution of EUR 2 million to the MSE programme in Tajikistan.

its TFP facility. For a country as geographically isolated as Tajikistan, reducing the costs to foreign trade can be critical for facilitating exchange.

The second major goal of the Bank in the private sector is to attract additional foreign investment into larger local enterprises. Tajikistan is not an attractive investment location for reasons to do with geography and market access, recent experiences of political instability, weaknesses in governance and state capacity, and general levels of poverty. Yet, opportunities do exist, primarily in extraction and processing of natural resources, including agricultural products and the Bank will seek to market these actively. As medium and large scale privatisation and restructuring gathers pace, additional investment opportunities may become available and allow the Bank to support these critical reforms.

Operational Focus

Entrepreneurship development

The Bank will support micro and small enterprises by providing credit lines through selected local banks. The programme provides small, mainly short-term loans to various entrepreneurs including manufacturing, trading and services. The Bank is negotiating with two local banks, which will be qualified as the first participating banks, and other banks are expected to be invited during the strategy period, if they are qualified. The programme will be supported by comprehensive TC for participating banks.

The Bank is actively looking for small investment projects with local entrepreneurs through the Direct Investment Facility. In the selection process, the Bank will consider lessons learned with the existing private projects and will undertake thorough due diligence, market analysis and monitoring. The Bank also will consider utilising the CARSSF to share project risks, if the project demonstrates excellent transition impact.

Trade Facilitation

The Bank will consider establishing a TFP facility, which provides guarantees against letters of credit of local banks to importers and exporters to and from Tajikistan. The programme will help Tajik enterprises' access to international and regional markets and enhance Tajikistan's integration to international market. The Bank will select appropriate local banks to administer the programme and support them by comprehensive TC to develop trade finance skills. Other than the standard TFP, the Bank will study the possibility to provide export-finance to the agricultural sector, such as input financing and equipment leasing to cotton producers, together with commercial banks already active in the region.

Support for FDI, Privatisation and Restructuring

Because of the difficulties in the operational environment, foreign investors' interest in Tajikistan has remained limited, and is concentrated on small scale investment opportunities in the textiles, agribusiness and manufacturing sector. However, the Bank considers that opportunities exist in the agribusiness and cotton sector, where a positive impact will influence a large number of the rural population, as well as natural resources, particularly mining of precious metals. The Bank will explore possibilities to enhance foreign investments in such sectors. In the mining sector, in view of the challenging conditions and mixed results experienced by other financial institutions, the Bank's operations will be limited to supporting viable joint venture companies with suitable foreign sponsors. Moreover, the Bank will study the possibility of utilising such schemes as machinery leasing or export financing. Regarding private sector projects, particular attention will need to be given to the financial viability of proposed investments and the quality of the management and the sponsors.

While the Bank's operational focus will remain concentrated on small private projects, the Bank will also seek to support privatisation and restructuring of large state enterprises. The Bank will continue to co-operate with WB/IFC on restructuring and privatisation of the state aluminium company, TADAZ. Among the critical issues to be considered in the restructuring of TADAZ are i) the smelter's viability at full cost energy prices (an IFC sponsored study seems to indicate that TADAZ would be profitable at full cost prices) ii) the financial situation of the company, given its high level of debt on the balance sheet and iii) its corporate governance and the role of the existing input supplier and off taker in the future restructuring and possible privatisation of TADAZ. The Bank supports the World Bank's Action Plan, which requires, as a first step, the publication of a full financial audit.

3.2.2 Strengthening the Financial Sector

Transition Goal

The transition goal in this sector is to work selectively with local financial institutions to improve their performance and provide safe intermediaries for the Bank's MSE, SME and TFP facilities. By asking for high standards of corporate governance and financial transparency, and potentially through participating in existing or newly-created financial institutions in Tajikistan, the Bank expects to strengthen competition in the sector and achieve demonstration effects, as other financial institutions attempt to emulate the success of the Bank's partner banks. It should be noted, however, that given the challenging conditions in the sector at present, progress will necessarily be gradual and is likely to suffer from occasional setbacks.

Operational Focus

Micro Financing and Trade Facilitation
The key tools for the Bank to improve the operational performance of local banks will be the provision of short to medium term funding through MSE lines, medium and long-term funding through SME lines and TFP facilities, all combined with technical assistance components. The Bank will undertake thorough due diligence of selected local banks to identify viable partner banks for establishing such facilities. In addition, for TFP in particular, the CARSSF will be a crucial tool to increase the Bank's opportunities to work with local banks that satisfy the Bank's conditions on financial transparency and corporate governance but that have insufficient capital to support the Bank's exposure.

Partner banks will also be requested to improve their performance with respect to corporate governance, transparency, and anti-money laundering procedures as part of a Corrective Action Plan that will be combined with the implementation of the MSE credit line.

Technical Assistance to Banking Sector
MSE and TFP envisage provision of substantial technical assistance to improve credit assessment and financial management skills and to help to introduce these new products to the local banks.

The Bank will also continue policy dialogue to improve regulatory and supervisory conditions in the sector. One instance of these ongoing efforts was the Seminar on Deposit Insurance System for Central Asia, which was co-organised by the Bank and IADI (International Association of Deposit Insurers) in January 2003 in Basle, mainly funded by the Swiss Government in cooperation with the Japanese Deposit Insurance Corporation. The seminar provided a unique opportunity for bank regulators, including NBT (who currently prepares law on deposit insurance), to understand the benefits and risks involved in Deposit Insurance Schemes and contributed to establish well-functioning systems in the Central Asian countries.

Strengthening the Capital Base in the Sector
Although the Bank experienced serious corporate governance issues arising from the dilution of the Bank's equity in TSOB, the Bank will seek opportunities, with caution, to participate in the equity of selected existing or newly-established banks in order to increase the capital base and the level of financial intermediation in the Tajik banking sector. Thorough due diligence on selected partner institutions will be key to these efforts, as will be the ongoing policy dialogue with the NBT to enhance mutual understanding of the conditions necessary to promote direct private investment in the banking sector. The Bank will strengthen policy dialogue with regard to the issues related to corporate governance, banking regulations and supervision, considering the experiences with the TSOB. Where possible, the Bank will seek to mobilise additional official and private sources of co-investment into the capital of selected banks.

3.2.3 Support for Critical Infrastructure

Transition Goals

The main transition goal in this sector is to improve the quality of infrastructure in a way that is commensurate with the limited public resources available and that creates the basis for sustainable future operation of infrastructure enterprises, where possible through the attraction of private investment. As mentioned in Section 2.3.3, the state of infrastructure deteriorated sharply during the last decade due to the poor maintenance and lack of new investments. The Bank will aim to support new investment selectively in the light of the limited borrowing capacity of the country. By advocating a commercially oriented approach, combining investments in rehabilitation and modernisation with tariff and regulatory reforms, the Bank will aim to contribute to reduce quasi fiscal deficits in the public sector (particularly in energy) and set free resources for critical social spending priorities. The Bank will be consistent with the Government priorities of the projects in its Public Investment Programme and seek, where possible, co-financing from donors, private investors and other IFIs to optimally allocate project risks among parties, and achieve a maximum degree of leverage for intended transition impact.

Operational Focus

Aviation continues to be a priority sector for the Bank's operations in Tajikistan. The sector occupies a vital position due to the country's geographical remoteness and the current lack of economic integration with the rest of the region and the world. Aviation projects will provide transition impact to the Tajik economy on trade, labour mobility, information and communications through increased traffic. There has been a sharp increase of passenger traffic and the current fleet of TSA cannot cope with the underlying demand. Since the Government's ability to provide sovereign guarantee is limited due to its borrowing capacity, the Bank will seek to introduce non-sovereign guaranteed operations with the Tajikistan State Air Company, a commercially managed entity, and rely on its cash generation. The Bank is financing a feasibility study to review the viability of the project.

Another priority area, both to the Bank and the Government, relates to municipal and environmental infrastructure. Specifically the Bank will support such sectors as water supply and urban transport in major cities where the population suffers severely from the poor quality of services. The Bank will support, within the existing tight affordability constraints, a commercial approach by municipal entities to improve service delivery and cost control, while introducing gradually cost recover tariffs and improved collection practices to enable these utilities to provide a financially sustainable service in the medium term. This will require significant organisational restructuring while municipalities need to ensure that adequate project implementation and supervision capacity at enterprise and municipal level is in place to undertake new investments.

In order to fund such projects within the affordability constraints of Tajikistan, grant co-financing will be required. In addition such grant components are also necessary to achieve the concessional terms, required for the public sector borrowing and to ensure that the funding will be consistent with the restrictions on new public debt and annual public debt service allocation agreed between the Government of Tajikistan and the IMF. The Bank needs to approach the donor community for potential grant co-financing and technical co-operation to leverage the loan financed capital investments with grants.

The Bank will select other infrastructure projects with a view to promoting a commercial approach to projects that would lead to financially sustainable entities as mentioned above. In light of the rich hydro power resources, the Bank could explore possibilities in small scale power projects. The Bank needs to be innovative to structure such projects and mobilisation of grant funding could be an important element for a viable solution.

3.2.4 Policy Dialogue

During the strategy period, the Bank will continue to promote policy dialogue with the authorities in order to improve the investment climate and support their reform efforts. The Bank will closely co-ordinate with other IFIs and the business community to make such a policy dialogue effective, including in the context of the development of the PRSP.

3.2.5 Environmental Impact of Bank Strategy

The Tajikistan Strategy provides a mix of projects, many of which have environmental benefits. Microbusiness and SME investments can contribute to sustainability, and MEI projects, including water supply and urban transport, can provide opportunities for environmental benefits. Projects in aviation are likely to lead to improvements in air safety in the region.

In contrast to projects with primary environmental or safety benefits, the Bank will need to select projects carefully in natural resources or cotton sectors. This is particularly important for smaller funding amounts where leverage may be weak. The irrigation associated with the cotton sector in the Central Asian Republics is linked to depletion of water in the Aral Sea and the associated concerns, so any projects proposed in this sector will need particular scrutiny to ensure they meet the Bank's policy requirements. It is likely that projects in the cotton sector would need to be associated with capacity-building initiatives, such as technical cooperation projects to assist with environmental management, water management, integrated pest management, and other key issues.

The Bank's 2003 Environmental Policy and Public Information Policy will also help increase transparency associated with EBRD projects.

4 Co-operation with other International Organisations

Given the level of poverty and limited budget of the government, Tajikistan needs substantial aid, particularly in the form of non repayable grants. During the fourth Consultative Group meeting in May 2003, multilateral and bilateral donors pledged US$ 900 million over the next three years, including US$ 200 million of humanitarian aid. This amount is much greater than that of the last consultative meeting held in Tokyo in 2001 (around US$ 400 million of commitments, but only US$ 233 million disbursed by May 2002). The aid programmes are based largely on the PRSP, focusing on improving social conditions (health, education, and poverty), infrastructure, governance and public services. The emphasis on the private sector is relatively smaller in the PRSP, but other donors recognise the critical importance of private investments and the complementarity between their investments and those of the EBRD. In the public sector, despite the generous commitments, there is concern among some donors that projects are so far not sufficiently prioritised and need to be designed in ways that would reduce over time the reliance on outside grant financing. In infrastructure, these concerns point to the benefits of a commercial approach, combining private investment and IFI funding with donor grants to alleviate any affordability constraints.

Tajikistan is one of the countries under the CIS-7 initiative, an international initiative to promote poverty reduction, growth and debt sustainability in low-income CIS countries. The Initiative brings together the seven low income and indebted CIS countries, with a support from the four sponsoring organizations (ADB, EBRD, IMF and World Bank) and a group of bilateral creditors/donors.

4.1 International Monetary Fund (IMF)

The IMF has worked with Tajikistan since May 1996. Since 1998, the government of Tajikistan has been implementing an economic reform programme with the support of a three-year arrangement under the Poverty Reduction and Growth Facility (SDR 100.3 million). The PRGF, which had disbursed a total of SDR 78.3 million, went off track in December 2001 due to delays in structural reforms. But the government satisfactorily implemented a Staff Monitored Programme (SMP) that covered the first half of 2002. During a series of Article IV consultation, the Fund welcomed Tajikistan's strong economic growth but expressed concerns about continued high inflation and structural reforms. The IMF approved a new PRGF for SDR 65 million (US$ 87 million) in December 2002 for the next three years. The programme remains on track and the first review is expected to be completed by July 2003. The Bank has maintained close contacts with the IMF on issues related to macroeconomy.

4.2 Word Bank Group

Tajikistan became a member of IBRD and IDA in 1993 and of the IFC in 1994. To date, World Bank Group assistance has consisted of poverty reduction, policy advice, institutional capacity building, financing of post-conflict needs through rehabilitation and reconstruction operations and resource mobilization. To benefit the most vulnerable groups in rural areas, the emphasis is put on creating ways of transferring agricultural assets from public to private hands, enhancing incentives, and investing in rural infrastructure. This is complemented by investments in health, education, and social funds. As of September 2002, IDA had committed US$ 302 million for 20 operations, of which US$ 45.5 million has been disbursed. There are 11 on-going operations with a commitment of US$ 151.5 million. As for the Structural Adjustment Credit (SAC II), the government failed to meet two important conditions and its second tranche has been pending subject to fulfilment of the following conditions; completing an IAS audit of TADAZ and developing a new privatisation plan for TADAZ. The government is currently working to meet these conditions. The Bank has supported the preparations of the SAC II in particular in telecommunications and aviation.

To date the IFC has financed the following: (i) a large gold mining operation (Zeravshan Gold/Nelson gold) from which it recently withdrew after suffering setbacks, (ii) two commercial operations (a supermarket project and a marble/granite processing facility), (iii) a Tajik/Italian auditing firm, and (iv) equity investment in Tajiksodirot Bank (TSOB from which IFC exited at the same time at the Bank). The Bank's co-operation with IFC includes the TSOB investment, co-financing on the MSE project under preparation and the policy dialogue with the Government on TADAZ.

A new World Bank Country Assistance Strategy (CAS) was approved recently (US$ 80 million for 2003-2005), which focuses on three key objectives; improving community-based support, fostering private sector activities, and strengthening the institutions needed for a market economy.

4.3 Asian Development Bank

Tajikistan became a member of the Asian Development Bank (ADB) in April 1998 and ADB has financed projects for a total of US$ 172.9 million to date. In 1998, the ADB approved the first project for a post conflict infrastructure programme loan (US$ 20 million) to support reforms in the transport and energy sectors. In 1999 the ADB approved two projects: Social sector rehabilitation project (US$ 20 million) and an emergency flood rehabilitation project (US$ 5 million). In 2000 they approved three projects for a total of US$ 57.6 million: a road rehabilitation project, a power rehabilitation project and the emergency restoration of Yavan water conveyance system. In 2002 the ADB approved four projects (total of US$ 70.3 million): emergency rehabilitation assistance, regional trade facilitation and customs cooperation program, agriculture rehabilitation, and regional power transmission modernisation. The latest country strategy and program (for 2003-2005) envisages annual commitments of US$ 40 million for assistance in social development, energy, agriculture, governance, and infrastructure. As mentioned earlier (Regional Cooperation), the Bank is preparing a co-financing project on Regional Power Transmission with the ADB.

4.4 United Nations Development Programme

The United Nations Development Programme (UNDP) has been in Tajikistan since 1994. The UNDP focuses on three broad areas: good governance and capacity building at the national level, rehabilitation, reconstruction and development, and protection and sustainable management of natural resources. Moreover, the UNDP is keen to achieve the Millennium Development Goals and focuses on these areas, including democratic governance, poverty reduction, crisis prevention, energy and environment, ICT and HIV/AIDS.

4.5 The Aga Khan Development Network

The Aga Khan Development Network (AKDN) has been active in Tajikistan since 1992, mobilising over US$ 150 million for its various programmes from its own resources, from the Ismaili Imamat and Ismaili Community around the world and its own donor partners. The activities were initially focused on drug issues and humanitarian aid and are now being expanded into agricultural reforms, health, education, physical infrastructure improvement and culture. In addition, AKDN is starting to invest in the financial sector, including micro finance on which the Bank has been exploring a potential co-operation with AKDN.

Tajikistan

	Item	1984	1985	1986	1987	1988	1989	1990	1991
001	**POPULATION** *million; as of 1 July*	4.45	4.58	4.72	4.87	5.03	5.18	5.30	5.46
002	**LABOR FORCE** *thousand; calendar year*	...	...	...	...	...	...	...	...
003	Employed	...	1681	1714	1775	1820	1879	1934	1970
004	Agriculture	...	722	722	745	765	792	833	881
005	Mining }								
006	Manufacturing [a] }	...	359	373	382	384	417	422	405
007	Others	...	600	619	648	671	670	679	683
008	Unemployed [b]	...	...	...	...	...	...	...	...
009	Unemployment rate, %	...	...	...	...	...	...	...	...
	NATIONAL ACCOUNTS [c] *Bn Russian Rubles* **I** *Mn Somoni; calendar year*								
	At Current Factor Cost								
010	GDP by Industrial Origin	...	...	...	...	...	...	...	...
011	Agriculture	...	...	...	...	...	...	...	...
012	Mining }								
013	Manufacturing }	...	...	...	...	...	...	...	...
014	Electricity, gas and water }								
015	Construction	...	...	...	...	...	...	...	...
016	Trade	...	...	...	...	...	...	...	...
017	Transport and communications	...	...	...	...	...	...	...	...
018	Finance }								
019	Public administration }								
020	Others [d] }	...	...	...	...	...	...	...	...
021	Indirect taxes less subsidies	...	...	...	...	...	...	...	...
022	GDP at current market prices	...	...	...	...	...	...	...	...
023	Net factor income from abroad	...	...	...	...	...	...	...	...
024	GNP at current market prices	...	...	...	...	...	...	...	...
	At Current Market Prices								
025	Expenditure on GDP	...	...	...	...	...	...	...	...
026	Private consumption	...	...	...	...	...	...	...	...
027	Government consumption	...	...	...	...	...	...	...	...
028	Gross fixed capital formation	...	...	...	...	...	...	...	...
029	Increase in stocks	...	...	...	...	...	...	...	...
030	Exports of goods and services	...	...	...	...	...	...	...	...
031	Less: Imports of goods and services	...	...	...	...	...	...	...	...
032	Statistical discrepancy	...	...	...	...	...	...	...	...
	At Current Market Prices, *Russian Rubles* **I** *Somoni*								
033	Per Capita GDP	...	...	...	...	...	...	...	...
034	Per Capita GNP	...	...	...	...	...	...	...	...
	PRODUCTION *thousand metric tons; calendar year*								
	Agriculture, *crop year*								
035	1. Seed cotton	...	...	922	872	964	921	842	826
036	2. Wheat [e]	...	...	99	175	191	109	143	153
037	3. Potatoes	...	...	199	192	183	217	207	181
038	4. Cotton (lint)	...	...	293	276	294	290	256	247
039	5. Grapes	...	...	199	132	178	174	190	121
040	6. Rice	...	...	27	27	30	28	29	26
041	7. Barley	...	...	27	43	43	34	48	51
042	8. Maize	...	...	73	85	88	109	85	60
	Mining								
043	1. Hard coal	22	24	29	23	52	39	42	38
044	2. Crude petroleum	376	387	367	322	271	190	144	108
045	3. Natural gas, *Mn cu. m.*	293	303	292	280	235	194	111	93
	Manufacturing								
046	1. Cement	1103	1080	1102	1094	1109	1110	1067	1013
047	2. Wheat flour	464	465	461	649	719	672	729	756
048	3. Aluminum	271	316	356	384	447	456	450	380

1992	1993	1994	1995	1996	1997	1998	1999	2000	2001	
5.57	5.64	5.75	5.84	5.93	6.02 *	6.11 *	6.20 *	6.29 *	6.38 *	001
1915	1876	1886	1891	1777	1842	1855	1780 *	1794 *	1717 *	002
1908	1854	1854	1853	1731	1791	1796	1726 *	1745 *	1674 *	003
892	949	1002	1095	1026	1145	1080	1118 *	1120 *	...	004
										005
382	335	315	264	249	216	200	174 *	170 *	...	006
634	570	538	494	456	430	516	434 *	455 *	...	007
7	22	32	38	46	51	59	54 *	49 *	44 *	008
0.4	1.2	1.7	2.0	2.6	2.8	3.3	3.0 *	2.7 *	2.5 *	009
69.4	636.9	1421.8	66.6	285.1	468.5	947.3	1246.9	1657.0	2270.2 *	010
18.8	148.3	339.7	25.6	111.1	165.8	257.2	341.3	487.9	553.8 *	011
										012
25.3	231.7	393.8	23.8	79.3	114.0	206.1	291.5	431.7	470.7 *	013
										014
6.3	63.5	185.6	2.2	7.9	14.3	39.5	73.0	61.0	64.3 *	015
2.2	23.4	232.5	5.3	45.1	106.2	226.4	265.3	330.0	257.3	016
3.2	9.2	42.6	3.1	12.4	15.1	42.7	99.0	88.3	70.0 *	017
										018
										019
13.6	160.8	227.6	6.7	29.3	53.1	175.4	176.8	258.1	854.1 *	020
0.1	70.1	364.7	3.2	23.3	49.8	77.8	98.0	149.7	241.9 *	021
69.6	707.1	1786.5	69.8	308.5	518.4	1025.2	1345.0	1806.7	2512.1 *	022
...	...	...	...	...	...	...	...	...	...	023
...	...	...	...	...	...	...	...	...	...	024
69.6	707.1	1786.5	69.8	308.5	518.4	1025.2	1345.0	1806.7	2512.1 *	025
...	...	...	...	194.9	334.9	743.8	1021.6	1561.5	...	026
...	...	...	...	14.8	31.8	42.6	62.7	86.0	...	027
...	...	...	...	68.8	102.0	158.1	233.1	209.2	...	028
...	...	...	...							029
...	...	...	...	225.5	424.0	509.6	913.5	1537.6	...	030
...	...	...	...	195.7	442.8	589.3	893.6	1353.4	...	031
...	...	...	...	0.0	68.8	160.4	7.6	-234.2	...	032
12493	125417	310642	12	52	86	168	217 *	287 *	394 *	033
...	...	...	...	...	...	...	...	...	...	034
513	524	531	412	318	353	383	313	335	453	035
156	159	182	174	548	559	500	483	550	494	036
167	147	134	112	108	128	175	240	303	318	037
174	180	167	130	120	104	108	103	107	123	038
100	88	80	96	122	127	46	54	110	110	039
20	23	20	24	21	44	40	47	82	40	040
39	30	25	22	17	23	26	25	19	16	041
32	34	18	19	90	30	36	36	38	42	042
31	13	3	7	14	9	8	9	9	11	043
61	42	33	26	26	26	19	19	18	16	044
72	49	33	39	47	42	32	36	40	52	045
447	262	178	78	49	36	18	33	55	69	046
628	667	360	304	271	322	417	341	307	312	047
345	252	237	237	198	189	196	229	269	289	048

Tajikistan

	Item	1984	1985	1986	1987	1988	1989	1990	1991
	Production Indexes *period averages*								
049	Agriculture, *1989-91 = 100*	...	...	...	...	...	...	...	...
050	Mining, *1990 = 100*	...	...	92.1	94.3	96.4	98.1	100.0	96.0
051	Manufacturing, *1990 = 100*	...	...	88.3	92.3	96.9	99.8	100.0	96.0
	ENERGY *annual values*								
	Crude petroleum, *'000 m.t.*								
052	Production	...	...	...	...	...	...	...	99
053	Exports	...	...	...	...	...	...	...	...
054	Imports	...	...	...	...	...	...	...	...
055	Consumption	...	...	...	...	...	...	...	...
	Coal, *'000 m.t.*								
056	Production	...	...	...	...	...	...	...	313
057	Exports	...	...	...	...	...	...	...	274
058	Imports	...	...	...	...	...	...	...	649
059	Consumption	...	...	...	...	...	...	...	688
	Natural gas, *Mn cu. m.*								
060	Production	...	...	...	...	...	...	...	93
061	Exports	...	...	...	...	...	...	...	...
062	Imports	...	...	...	...	...	...	...	2
063	Consumption	...	...	...	...	...	...	...	...
	Electricity, *Mn kWh*								
064	Production	...	15700	13600	15900	18800	15300	18200	17600
065	Exports	...	5900	4400	5500	6000	4200	5700	5400
066	Imports	...	5500	7400	6500	5500	8000	6900	6900
067	Consumption	...	15300	16600	16900	18300	19100	19400	19100
	MONEY AND BANKING [c] *Mn Russian Rubles I Thousand Somoni; as of end of period*								
068	Money supply (M1)	...	...	...	...	...	...	...	...
069	Currency in circulation	...	...	...	...	...	...	...	...
070	Demand deposits	...	...	...	...	...	...	...	...
071	Quasi-money [f]	...	...	...	...	...	...	...	...
072	Money supply (M2)	...	...	...	...	...	...	...	...
073	Foreign assets (net)	...	...	...	...	...	...	...	...
074	Domestic credit	...	...	...	...	...	...	...	...
075	Claims on gov't. sector (net)	...	...	...	...	...	...	...	...
076	Claims on private sector	...	...	...	...	...	...	...	...
077	Claims on other financial insts.	...	...	...	...	...	...	...	...
078	Other items	...	...	...	...	...	...	...	...
	GOVERNMENT FINANCE *Mn Russian Rubles I Thousand Somoni; fiscal year ending 31 December*								
	Central Government (Consolidated Central and Local Governments) [c, g]								
079	Current revenue	...	...	...	...	...	...	...	...
080	Taxes	...	...	...	...	...	...	...	...
081	Non-taxes	...	...	...	...	...	...	...	...
082	Current expenditure	...	...	...	...	...	...	...	...
083	Current surplus/deficit	...	...	...	...	...	...	...	...
084	Capital receipts	...	...	...	...	...	...	...	...
085	Capital expenditure	...	...	...	...	...	...	...	...
086	Capital account surplus/deficit	...	...	...	...	...	...	...	...
087	Net lending	...	...	...	...	...	...	...	...
088	Overall surplus/deficit [h]	...	...	...	...	...	...	...	...
	Financing								
089	Domestic borrowing [i]	...	...	...	...	...	...	...	...
090	Foreign borrowing [j] }	...	...	...	...	...	...	...	...
091	Foreign grants }								
092	Use of cash balances [k]	...	...	...	...	...	...	...	...
	Expenditure by Function, Central Gov't. [c, g]								
093	Total [h]	...	...	...	...	...	...	...	...
094	General public services [l]	...	...	...	...	...	...	...	...
095	Defence	...	...	...	...	...	...	...	...

1992	1993	1994	1995	1996	1997	1998	1999	2000	2001	
75.9	71.5	69.2	60.4	52.8	50.4	47.2	46.0	46.2	49.2	049
73.0	67.0	50.0	43.0	33.0	76.4	84.2	83.9	79.6	...	050
73.0	66.0	49.0	41.0	29.8	26.6	28.1	31.7	35.5	...	051
57	39	33	26	26	26	19	19	18	16	052
...	...	...	...	...	...	5	6	3	3	053
...	...	...	...	...	...	...	...	...	...	054
...	...	...	...	...	...	...	...	...	...	055
214	174	106	34	20	17	19	19	22	24	056
186	80	42	...	14	–	–	...	–	–	057
422	33	14	...	...	12	6	2	5	5	058
450	127	78	...	...	5	3	2	1	1	059
72	49	33	39	47	42	32	36	40	52	060
...	...	...	...	...	...	...	...	...	...	061
1	1	1	1	1	2	1	1	1	1	062
...	...	...	...	...	...	...	...	...	...	063
16800	17700	17000	14800	14980	14005	14422	15797	14247	14336	064
5600	6400	5800	4200	4890	4247	3724	3831	3909	4047	065
6400	5200	4900	4900	3978	4345	3969	3641	5242	5396	066
17600	16500	16100	15500	14068	14103	14667	15607	15580	...	067
33000	562000	1442000 I	8884	21557	46813	55600	71827	106761	121137 *	068
16000	159000	131000 I	5521	15720	37336	46622	62032	86773	82597 *	069
17000	403000	1311000 I	3363	5837	9477	8978	9795	19988	38540 *	070
250000	10000	44000 I	4416	4138	7319	27702	27890	42104	...	071
283000	572000	1486000 I	13300	25695	54132	83302	99716	148866	...	072
325000	-141000	147000 I	8035	2483	-5281	-202812	-153497	-168183	-140367 *	073
71000	828000	1866000 I	13832	26834	77644	365005	325446	351804	387069 *	074
...	...	... I	...	...	...	...	...	...	...	075
...	...	... I	...	...	...	...	...	...	...	076
...	...	... I	...	...	...	...	...	...	...	077
-113000	-115000	-527000 I	-8567	-3622	-18231	-78892	-72233	-34755	...	078
17235	171224	765290 I	6977	37335	76720	115201	164721	217115	...	079
16622	159195	725086 I	5849	35953	74452	111264	158244	205409	354192 *	080
613	12029	40204 I	1128	1382	2268	3937	6477	11706	...	081
31587	288951	689624 I	11019	52066	92570	117036	153469	176209	308976 *	082
-14352	-117727	75666 I	-4042	-14731	-15850	-1835	11252	40906	...	083
–	–	– I	–	–	–	–	–	–	...	084
5866	40105	255621 I	1114	2275	3764	29011	46204	47802	...	085
-5866	-40105	-255621 I	-1114	-2275	-3764	-29011	-46204	-47802	...	086
–	–	– I	–	832	1499	-3490	93	1399	...	087
-20218	-157832	-179955 I	-5156	-17838	-21113	-27356	-35045	-8295	-2512 *	088
19796	156419	174871 I	4931	6980	10198	5208	-12405	-19227	-5024 *	089
–	–	– I	–	10230	6940	16948	33063	7470	7536 *	090
3582	1688	... I								091
422	1413	5084 I	225	628	3975	5200	10805	18364	...	092
37453	329056	945245 I	12132	55173	97833	142557	199766	225410	416992 *	093
2080	18364	94469 I	441	2678	7904	10135	32473	71365	...	094
256	24338	34744 I	482	3977	10713	13562	18723	21097	...	095

Tajikistan

	Item	1984	1985	1986	1987	1988	1989	1990	1991
096	Education	...	...	...	...	...	...	...	...
097	Health	...	...	...	...	...	...	...	...
098	Social security and welfare	...	...	...	...	...	...	...	...
099	Housing and community amenities	...	...	...	...	...	...	...	...
100	Economic services [m]	...	...	...	...	...	...	...	...
101	Agriculture	...	...	...	...	...	...	...	...
102	Industry	...	...	...	...	...	...	...	...
103	Electricity, gas and water	...	...	...	...	...	...	...	...
104	Transport and communications	...	...	...	...	...	...	...	...
105	Other economic services	...	...	...	...	...	...	...	...
106	Others [n]	...	...	...	...	...	...	...	...
	EXTERNAL TRADE *Mn US dollars; calendar year*								
107	Exports, fob	...	...	...	...	...	...	...	...
108	Imports, cif	...	...	...	...	...	...	...	...
109	Trade balance	...	...	...	...	...	...	...	...
	Direction of Trade *Mn US dollars; calendar year*								
110	Exports, Total	...	...	...	...	...	...	...	...
111	1. Netherlands	...	...	...	...	...	...	...	...
112	2. Uzbekistan	...	...	...	...	...	...	...	...
113	3. Russia	...	...	...	...	...	...	...	...
114	4. Switzerland	...	...	...	...	...	...	...	...
115	5. Turkey	...	...	...	...	...	...	...	...
116	6. Italy	...	...	...	...	...	...	...	...
117	7. Iran	...	...	...	...	...	...	...	...
118	8. Belgium	...	...	...	...	...	...	...	...
119	9. Moldova	...	...	...	...	...	...	...	...
120	10. Kazakhstan	...	...	...	...	...	...	...	...
121	Imports, Total	...	...	...	...	...	...	...	...
122	1. Uzbekistan	...	...	...	...	...	...	...	...
123	2. Russia	...	...	...	...	...	...	...	...
124	3. Switzerland	...	...	...	...	...	...	...	...
125	4. Kazakhstan	...	...	...	...	...	...	...	...
126	5. Azerbaijan	...	...	...	...	...	...	...	...
127	6. United Kingdom	...	...	...	...	...	...	...	...
128	7. Turkmenistan	...	...	...	...	...	...	...	...
129	8. Romania	...	...	...	...	...	...	...	...
130	9. Ukraine	...	...	...	...	...	...	...	...
131	10. United States	...	...	...	...	...	...	...	...
	Trade Indexes *1993 = 100; period averages*								
	Quantum index								
132	Exports	...	...	...	...	...	...	...	...
133	Imports	...	...	...	...	...	...	...	...
	Unit value index								
134	Exports	...	...	...	...	...	...	...	...
135	Imports	...	...	...	...	...	...	...	...
136	Terms of trade	...	...	...	...	...	...	...	...
	BALANCE OF PAYMENTS *Mn US dollars; calendar year*								
137	Merchandise exports, fob	...	...	...	...	...	...	...	...
138	Merchandise imports, fob	...	...	...	...	...	...	...	...
139	Trade balance	...	...	...	...	...	...	...	...
140	Other goods, services and income	...	...	...	...	...	...	...	...
141	Credit	...	...	...	...	...	...	...	...
142	Debit	...	...	...	...	...	...	...	...
143	Unrequited transfers	...	...	...	...	...	...	...	...
144	Private	...	...	...	...	...	...	...	...
145	Official	...	...	...	...	...	...	...	...
146	Current balance	...	...	...	...	...	...	...	...
147	Direct investment [o]	...	...	...	...	...	...	...	...

1992	1993	1994	1995	1996	1997	1998	1999	2000	2001	
7207	55653	149007	1521	6516	13166	22091	28363	41354	...	096
3696	34379	110763	943	4011	8259	11733	13893	16652	...	097
1971	9086	9310	71	299	1354	2014	2500	2087	...	098
...	...	...	...	...	...	...	...	...	...	099
18783	117051	404214	2717	11376	21360	40305	47518	51950	...	100
...	...	...	...	...	...	...	...	...	...	101
...	...	...	...	...	...	...	...	...	...	102
...	...	...	...	...	...	...	...	...	...	103
...	...	...	...	...	...	...	...	...	...	104
...	...	...	...	...	...	...	...	...	...	105
3460	70185	142738	5957	26316	35077	42717	56296	20905	...	106
185	456	559	839	770	746	597	689	784	652	107
240	660	707	880	668	750	711	663	675	688	108
-55	-204	-148	-41	102	-4	-114	26	109	-36	109
29.3	349.8	491.9	748.6	771.5	803.4	596.6	688.7	784.3	595.1	110
–	1.1	147.6	255.2	218.0	229.4	221.4	222.3	178.2	0.5	111
...	20.3	22.7	132.0	190.7	172.5	125.7	181.0	97.8	97.8	112
...	62.5	46.2	95.3	79.0	63.5	47.8	115.1	258.8	116.9	113
0.4	5.8	44.9	37.2	83.5	140.7	94.9	75.1	72.2	72.2	114
...	5.2	7.6	8.1	1.9	8.2	0.4	1.0	58.4	115.8	115
6.8	2.5	0.4	2.4	6.6	7.8	9.8	5.1	21.4	23.5	116
...	–	1.4	0.7	1.7	3.5	13.6	13.5	12.5	12.5	117
...	...	...	...	...	14.7	12.7	7.0	5.1	6.4	118
...	3.4	1.4	–	0.1	0.5	0.0	0.0	14.3	28.6	119
...	16.3	10.1	7.0	24.3	10.0	10.0	3.6	5.7	7.8	120
72.9	532.1	547.0	809.9	668.1	750.3	711.0	663.1	675.0	727.4	121
...	65.4	83.2	251.4	198.9	261.6	227.3	264.4	185.6	185.6	122
...	83.8	60.7	136.0	74.4	115.1	102.2	92.4	105.1	75.8	123
0.1	4.3	100.4	51.7	99.8	185.1	157.9	25.1	0.6	0.6	124
...	65.5	32.8	26.5	52.4	42.0	51.9	78.8	82.4	86.0	125
...	1.1	0.2	1.2	0.0	3.2	1.8	15.6	63.1	110.6	126
–	16.4	68.0	161.2	78.3	10.1	3.8	70.5	86.9	5.0	127
...	26.0	39.4	57.4	26.3	29.7	31.3	15.2	29.3	43.4	128
...	–	–	0.1	0.1	0.0	0.0	3.3	41.0	78.7	129
...	4.4	13.6	2.2	19.2	20.7	16.6	37.7	–	–	130
9.7	8.7	31.9	25.3	16.0	3.2	32.8	1.7	1.3	31.8	131
...	100	89	82	90	88	80	86	95	...	132
...	100	75	74	67	72	72	68	76	...	133
...	100	138	182	153	154	163	169	180	143	134
...	100	158	158	173	164	158	162	175	104	135
...	100	88	115	89	94	103	104	103	138	136
185	456	559	779	770	746	586	666	792	652	137
-240	-639	-686	-838	-786	-809	-731	-693	-839	-766	138
-55	-183	-127	-59	-16	-63	-145	-27	-47	-114	139
2	-51	-68	-55	-84	-33	-20	-44	-47	-26	140
...	...	...	...	...	...	...	...	...	65	141
...	...	...	...	...	...	...	...	...	-91	142
–	25	25	25	30	40	57	35	33	79	143
...	...	...	...	...	...	...	...	...	-14	144
...	...	...	...	...	...	...	...	...	93	145
-53	-208	-170	-89	-70	-56	-108	-36	-61	-61	146
8	9	12	20	25	30	24	21	22	10	147

Tajikistan

	Item	1984	1985	1986	1987	1988	1989	1990	1991
148	Portfolio investment	...	...	...	...	...	...	...	...
149	Other long-term capital [p]	...	...	...	...	...	...	...	...
150	Other short-term capital }	...	...	...	...	...	...	...	...
151	Net errors and omissions }								
152	Change in net foreign assets - commercial banks	...	...	...	...	...	...	...	...
153	Overall balance	...	...	...	...	...	...	...	...
154	Allocation of SDRs }								
155	Monetary movements }	...	...	...	...	...	...	...	...
	INTERNATIONAL RESERVES *Mn US dollars; as of end of period*								
156	Total [q]	...	...	...	...	...	...	...	...
157	Gold, national valuation	...	...	...	...	...	...	...	...
158	Foreign exchange	...	...	...	...	...	...	...	...
159	Reserve position in the Fund	–	–	–	–	–	–	–	–
160	SDRs	–	–	–	–	–	–	–	–
	EXCHANGE RATES *Tajik Rubles I Somoni per US dollar*								
161	End of period	...	...	...	...	...	...	...	...
162	Average of period	...	...	...	...	...	...	...	...
	EXTERNAL INDEBTEDNESS *Mn US dollars; as of end of year*								
163	Total outstanding and disbursed	...	...	...	...	...	...	...	...
164	Long-term	...	...	...	...	...	...	...	...
165	Public and publicly guaranteed	...	...	...	...	...	...	...	...
166	Private non-guaranteed	...	...	...	...	...	...	...	...
167	Short-term	...	...	...	...	...	...	...	...
168	Use of IMF credit	...	...	...	...	...	...	...	...
	Debt service *transactions during the year*								
169	Principal repayments on LT debt	...	...	...	...	...	...	...	...
170	Interest on long-term debt	...	...	...	...	...	...	...	...
171	Interest on short-term debt	...	...	...	...	...	...	...	...
	Average terms of new commitments								
172	Interest (%)	...	...	...	...	...	...	...	...
173	Maturity (years)	...	...	...	...	...	...	...	...
174	Grace period (years)	...	...	...	...	...	...	...	...
175	Grant element (%)	...	...	...	...	...	...	...	...

FOOTNOTES:

a Refers to those employed in industry and construction.
b Refers to employed in transport and communications, trade, finance, public administration and other sectors.
c For 1992 to 1994, currency was in Russian ruble. From 1995, currency is in Tajik ruble. The new national currency, the Somoni, has been circulated since 30 October 2000 and fully replaced the Tajik ruble on 1 April 2001 at the exchange rate of TJS1.00=TJR1,000.
d Includes supplies, procurement, other material sectors, and nonmaterial services.
e Refers to cereal.
f Refers to foreign currency deposits.
g Data for 1995 covers only the period May 11 to December 31 when currency is in Tajik ruble.
h On cash basis.

1992	1993	1994	1995	1996	1997	1998	1999	2000	2001	
...	...	...	...	...	...	...	...	...	...	148
44	56	25	-81	-90	-17	28	5	16	-32	149
140	-95	-87	32	-53	3	24	18	-17	74	150
									-13	151
...	...	-2	-7	7	7	72	-35	21	3	152
139	-238	-223	-126	-181	-33	40	-26	-21	-20	153
										154
-139	238	223	126	181	33	-40	26	21	20	155
1.0	2.0	1.0	4.1	14.0	30.0	65.0	58.0	87.0	94.7	156
...	...	...	...	...	...	...	...	1.0	1.7	157
...	...	...	...	...	...	...	...	78.0	88.2	158
–	0.0	0.0	0.0	0.0	0.0	0.0	0.0	0.0	0.0	159
–	–	–	–	3.2	12.2	2.9	0.0	7.8	4.8	160
...	...	...	288.00	334.00	747.00	918.00	1436.00 I	2.20	2.55	161
...	...	...	135.00	298.30	564.00	773.30	1240.50 I	1.83	2.36	162
9.7	385.2	580.3	633.6	699.4	1065.0	1249.7	1134.1	1170.0	...	163
9.7	384.9	562.0	590.4	656.8	961.0	1003.4	942.7	995.3	...	164
9.7	384.9	562.0	590.4	656.8	669.0	709.1	611.7	625.6	...	165
0.0	0.0	0.0	0.0	0.0	292.0	294.3	331.0	369.7	...	166
0.0	0.3	18.3	43.2	21.0	73.7	147.2	90.9	64.0	...	167
0.0	0.0	0.0	0.0	21.6	30.4	99.0	100.5	110.8	...	168
0.0	0.0	0.0	0.0	0.0	28.9	60.3	39.1	46.1	179.2	169
0.0	0.8	0.4	0.0	0.3	16.6	28.0	19.3	27.2	29.5	170
0.0	0.0	0.0	0.0	0.4	1.2	1.2	3.8	2.3	...	171
3.9	3.9	7.3	0.0	0.8	0.5	0.6	0.7	0.8	...	172
9.3	16.6	7.2	0.0	39.8	38.0	35.8	35.1	38.0	...	173
4.2	5.3	2.1	0.0	10.3	9.9	9.4	9.1	9.8	...	174
26.4	34.4	9.6	0.0	80.7	81.5	78.4	77.5	78.7	...	175

i Refers to credit from banks and domestic non-bank financing (T-bills).
j Refers to external financing.
k Refers to privatization proceeds.
l Refers to State administration.
m Refers to expenditures of the national economy.
n Includes also culture, allowances, science, law and judicial bodies and interest payments.
o Refers to net foreign direct investment.
p Refers to loans.
q Refers to gross official reserves.

USAID/CAR	Country Profile: Tajikistan

Area: 143,100 sq km
Capital: Dushanbe
Population: 6,578,681
Population Growth Rate: 2.12% (2001 est)
Ethnic groups: Tajik 64.9%, Uzbek 25%, Russian 3.5% (declining because of emigration), other 6.6%
Life Expectancy: male 61.09 yrs; female 67.42 yrs
Birth Rate: 33.23 births/1,000 population
Infant Mortality: 116.09 deaths/1,000 live births
Per Capita Income: $286 (IMF World Economic Outlook; 2002 estimate)
Religion: Sunni Muslim 80%, Shi'a Muslim 5%
Language: Tajik (official), Russian widely used in government and business
Literacy: total 98%; male 99%; female 97%

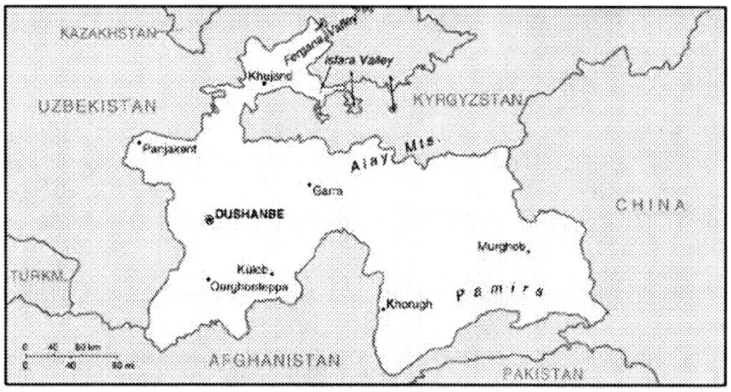

President: Emomali Rahmonov
Prime Minister: Oqil Oqilov
Ambassador to the US: Rashid Alimov

Development Challenge

Tajikistan is a front line state in the War on Terrorism and, despite risks from its own Islamists, quickly gave the U.S. necessary access for the intervention in Afghanistan. Its role in the conflict and humanitarian relief has been essential. The most disadvantaged of the Central Asian republics, Tajikistan has limited resources, is landlocked with few transportation links, was ravaged by several years of civil war, and is one of the poorest countries in Asia. Lawlessness and trafficking in both arms and drugs remain a U.S. concern.

Notwithstanding its disadvantages, Tajikistan is successfully, if haltingly, making a transition to normalcy, civil order and democracy. Despite several potentially destabilizing events during 2001, such as the assassination of cabinet officials by unknown assailants, the various parties remain committed to peace even as they struggle for influence within the political landscape. The government continues to work to maintain a balance between various factions, including from the president's party and former opposition members integrated into the government following the 1997 Peace Accord. The peace process resulted in a unique coalition government (of Islamists and former Communists), and the Islamists are a vocal opposition. Yet, governance and rule of law remain weak. In 2001, Freedom House characterized Tajikistan as "not free", and its political rights and civil liberties ratings are both 6 out of 7, with 7 the lowest degree of freedom.

Corruption and local abuse of power are pervasive. Anecdotal evidence suggests that bribery is necessary for most transactions with the government, as well as for health services and training. Weak government institutions, deteriorated infrastructure and social services, and a largely subsistence (and criminalized) economy limit the pace of reform. Reforms are, however, moving forward, and economy grew modestly by about 10% last year. Since privatization began in 1991, Tajikistan has privatized nearly 5,500, an estimated 83%, of its small state-owned properties. The agricultural sector, which employs over 60% of the population, is seriously constrained by the deterioration of the country's irrigation infrastructure and a lack of quality inputs. The economy as a whole remains overly dependent on its two main exports, cotton and aluminum, the earnings from which are controlled by politically connected elites. Tajikistan has the lowest per capita GDP ($286) among the 15 former Soviet republics, and inflation in 2001 was 35.5%. Thus far, the government has not been able to establish the rule of law sufficiently to attract the domestic and foreign investment needed to spur economic growth. The perceived inability of the government to prevent either Islamic extremists or drug traffickers from transiting prompted the Government of Uzbekistan to severely restrict movements across their common border, effectively shutting off much of Tajikistan's international trade and migratory labor. Two successive years of drought have further set back the country's economic recovery.

Tajikistan's social indicators reflect the seriousness of the problem it faces: 80% of the population is below the poverty line, with 17% in extreme poverty. A recent national nutritional assessment found 17.3% acute malnutrition, with 4.2% severe malnutrition, and 37.9% chronic malnutrition. Tajikistan has the highest rates of infant mortality in Central Asia, with an estimated 116 deaths per every 1,000 live births. According to World Bank estimates, Tajikistan's total external debt is slightly over $1.2 billion, 129 percent of GDP, mostly to Russia and Uzbekistan. Debt servicing is expected to require 50% of total government revenues in 2002.

Contact Information

USAID/Central Asia Region (CAR)
Mission Director George Deikun
Park Palace Building
41 Kazibek Bi Street
Almaty, Kazakhstan 480100
Tel: 011-7-3272-50-76-12/17
Fax: 011-7-3272-50-76-35/36

Tajikistan Country Representative
Michael Harvey
Park Palace Building
41 Kazibek Bi Street
Almaty, Kazakhstan 480100
Tel: 011-7-3272-50-76-12/17
Fax: 011-7-3272-50-76-35/36

USAID/Washington
Central Asia Desk Officer Tim Alexander
Tel: 202-712-1669

USAID/CAR website: http://www.usaid.gov/regions/europe_eurasia/car/index.html

Overview of USAID's Focus in Tajikistan

Economic Reform and Private Sector Development Despite the government's willingness to reform its economy, political, and social instability remained a serious obstacle to the successful implementation of USAID reforms. In FY 2001, 735 Tajik entrepreneurs were trained in western business methods, and USAID training also helped 622 (49% women) bookkeepers become professional accountants, practitioners, and technicians. Similarly, EdNet watched network membership grow to 14 universities in less than a year, and supported two Visiting International Professors (VIPs). These VIPs helped develop their respective departments and delivered training and seminars to students and faculty in modern business principles and market economics. Tajikistan's leading accounting association qualified for membership in the International Council of Certified Accountants and Auditors (ICCAA). ICCAA is establishing an internationally recognized education, examination, and certification program in the Russian language. USAID worked broadly with the Tajik judiciary to create a more transparent and orderly system of justice. Advisors created a legal database of Tajik laws and normative acts that is the most comprehensive collection of its kind in Tajikistan. USAID advisors also assisted in the preparation of draft language for Intellectual Property Rights in the Tajik Civil Code. USAID played a key role in developing and implementing a successful examination process for prospective and sitting Tajik judges in FY 2001 and trained a core group of Tajik judges to establish an institutional judicial training mechanism. A court computerization program was launched at the City Court of Dushanbe, and training was provided to Dushanbe City Court and Council of Justice personnel which enables them to effectively use the legal database and computer equipment.

Water and Energy Management Up until now, USAID has had very few water and energy activities in Tajikistan due to security concerns and limited access to water and energy officials by advisors. Out of country training was the main focus of activities. With the easing of travel restrictions, we expect a significant increase in activities, especially in water. Staff of the Tajik National Hydromet Service are full participants in the regional snowmelt runoff committee that meets semi-annually to improve water allocations for the Central Asia region. They have begun collecting and processing water data for which USAID provided equipment and training. Several water courses were funded by USAID in cooperation with the Canadian Agency for International Development, through which Tajik water officials and managers better acquainted themselves with international water law, transboundary water management, and integrated water practices to improve irrigation efficiency. By the completion date of the activity, water managers should have the necessary tools and training to better collect, communicate and process water data resulting in improved allocations and overall management of the resource. Also, water and energy agreements will be based more on objective data and standards, thereby mitigating their potential for conflict.

Strengthening Democratic Culture and Institutions Despite the difficult travel situation to and within Tajikistan (and the security situation which demands restricted travel), support to Tajikistan's NGOs led to a marked improvement in NGO advocacy, service provision, and organizational capacity. The first independent radio station in Tajikistan, Radio Tiroz, opened in Khojand. Recommendations made by the Poverty Reduction Strategy Working Groups on public sector reform and improving parliamentary and judicial professionalism and independence were accepted by the President. USAID implementing partners ensured the participation of parliamentarians, judges, and NGOs in the process. This more participatory process resulted in recommendations including opening the parliamentary committee process and removing the judiciary from the control of the Ministry of Justice. Open meetings and seminars bringing together parliamentarians and NGOs on specific legislation are being held more frequently. Topics have included the family code, criminal procedure code, law on registering legal entities, and others. Three NGOs that received coalition-building technical assistance from USAID's local NGO resource center joined together to battle drug addiction among youth. Youth Initiative Center Ittifok, No Drugs, and Public Television SM1 created the coalition Youth Against Drugs to prevent further increases in drug addiction among youth. USAID-funded interactive training and roundtables by the coalition on the harmful effect of drugs has resulted in a marked decrease in drug addiction in the area. By working with political parties and the parliament, encouraging participation of and open meetings with NGOs in legislative decision making, USAID will help stabilize the post-conflict situation in Tajikistan. NGOs will have the necessary advocacy skills to help local communities address pressing social problems and mitigate the potential for conflict.

Quality Primary Health Care USAID's primary health care efforts in Tajikistan were strengthened with the opening of a new institutional partner under USAID's expanded health program – The Republican Training Center for Family Medicine in Dushanbe. In FY 2001 the USAID-funded partnership between the Ministry of Health and the Community Hospital in Boulder, Colorado provided equipment and skills-based training for primary care providers in family medicine and emergency medical services. USAID, in collaboration with the World Health Organization (WHO), conducted an assessment of TB prevention and control in Tajikistan to plan for a donation of TB drugs by the WHO Global Drug Funds (GDF). The assessment also led to the initiation of two pilot sites in Dushanbe for DOTS implementation. USAID helped the GOT successfully apply for funding from the Global Alliance Vaccines Initiative, which will extend universal Hepatitis B immunization at birth. Since independence, malaria in Tajikistan has reached epidemic proportions. Estimates are that the true number of cases is over 250,000. Since 1990, this is the first effort at reasonable estimation of malaria incidence in Tajikistan. WHO indicates that reported incidence of malaria dropped by 30 percent from 1997 to 2001, from 30,000 to 19,064. Research and training in HIV/AIDS surveillance have begun. USAID supported a study tour of government officials to a model Harm Reduction site in Lithuania; a Central Asian Condom Social Marketing Assessment and Workshop were conducted; and the Central Asian Initiative Conference on the Prevention of HIV/AIDS/STIs was held jointly with UNICEF and UNAIDS. Children and women of reproductive age in Varzob have benefited from improved reproductive health services for women. CARE's midwives and birth attendants see to the delivery of a high proportion of babies in Tajikistan, as hospitals and health facilities have fallen into extreme disrepair. Almost 5,000 women attended nurse-led education sessions on breast-feeding and infant feeding practices. USAID's efforts in child malnourishment surveillance and identification were supported through a new supplementary feeding center in Ayronom (with 16 more planned) using WFP food commodities.

Map No. 3765 Rev. 9 UNITED NATIONS
October 1997

Department of Public Information
Cartographic Section

US FEDERAL GOVERNMENT LIBRARY-2003

ULTIMATE INFORMATION ON US FEDERAL GOVERNMENT AGENCUES

The ultimate handbook with detailed information on US Federal Government Agencies and more

Price: $99.95 each

Title *	ISBN
1. Overseas Private Investment Corporation (OPIC) Handbook	0739731835
2. The White House Handbook	0739731815
3. U.S. House Committee on Agriculture	0739727370
4. U.S. House Committee on Appropriations	0739727389
5. U.S. House Committee on Armed Services	0739727397
6. U.S. House Committee on Education and the Workforce	0739727710
7. U.S. House Committee on Energy and Commerce	0739727435
8. U.S. House Committee on Financial Services	0739727745
9. U.S. House Committee on Government Reform	0739727443
10. U.S. House Committee on House Administration	0739727788
11. U.S. House Committee on International Relations	0739727451
12. U.S. House Committee on Resources	0739727486
13. U.S. House Committee on Rules	073972780X
14. U.S. House Committee on Science	0739727494
15. U.S. House Committee on Small Business	0739727729
16. U.S. House Committee on Standards of Official Conduct	0739727737
17. U.S. House Committee on the Budget	0739727419
18. U.S. House Committee on the Judiciary	073972746X
19. U.S. House Committee on Transportation and Infrastructure	0739727453
20. U.S. House Committee on Veterans Affairs	0739727761
21. U.S. House Committee on Ways and Means	073972777X
22. U.S. House Joint Committee on Printing	0739727699
23. U.S. House Joint Committee on Taxation	0739727362
24. U.S. House Joint Economic Committee	0739727354
25. U.S. House Permanent Select Committee on Intelligence	0739727796
26. U.S. Senate Agriculture, Nutrition, And Forestry Committee	0739727818
27. U.S. Senate Appropriations Committee	0739727826
28. U.S. Senate Armed Services Committee	0739727834
29. U.S. Senate Banking, Housing, And Urban Affairs	0739727842
30. U.S. Senate Budget Committee	0739727850
31. U.S. Senate Commerce, Science, And Transportation	0739727869
32. U.S. Senate Committee On Indian Affairs	0739727990
33. U.S. Senate Energy And Natural Resources Committee	0739727877
34. U.S. Senate Environment And Public Works Committee	0739727885
35. U.S. Senate Finance Committee	0739727893

To order and for additional analytical and marketing information, please contacrt
International Business Publications, USA at:
P.O. Box 15343, Washington, DC 20003, USA. Phone: (202) 546-2103. Fax: (202) 546-3275.
E-mail: rusric@erols.com

Title *	ISBN
36. U.S. Senate Foreign Relations Committee	0739727907
37. U.S. Senate Governmental Affairs Committee	0739727915
38. U.S. Senate Health, Education, Labor And Pensions Committee	0739727931
39. U.S. Senate Joint Committee On Taxation	0739728644
40. U.S. Senate Joint Economic Committee	0739728636
41. U.S. Senate Judiciary Committee	0739727923
42. U.S. Senate Rules And Administration Committee	073972794X
43. U.S. Senate Select Committee On Ethics	0739727982
44. U.S. Senate Select Committee On Intelligence	0739727974
45. U.S. Senate Small Business Committee	0739727958
46. U.S. Senate Special Committee On Aging	0739728628
47. U.S. Senate Veterans' Affairs Committee	0739727966
48. US African Development Fund Handbook	073973184X
49. US AGENCY FOR INTERNATIONAL DEVELOPMENT BUSINESS OPPORTUNITIES HANDBOOK	0739731866
50. US Agency for International Development Handbook	0739731874
51. US Arms Control and Disarmament Agency Handbook	0739739832
52. US CENTRAL INTELLIGENCE AGENCY (CIA) HANDBOOK	0739732757
53. US Civil Rights Policy Handbook	073976201X
54. US Commodity Futures Trading Commission Handbook	0739762028
55. US Congressional Budget Office Handbook	0739762036
56. US Defense Intelligence Agency Handbook	0739711709
57. US Department of Agriculture Business Opportunities Handbook	0739762044
58. US Department of Agriculture Handbook	0739762052
59. US Department of Commerce Handbook	0739762079
60. US Department of Defense Handbook	0739762087
61. US Department of Energy Business Opportunities Handbook	0739762095
62. US Department of Energy Handbook	0739762109
63. US Department of Health and Human Services Handbook	0739762117
64. US Department of Housing and Urban Services Handbook	0739762125
65. US Department of Interior Handbook	0739762133
66. US Department of Justice Handbook	0739762141
67. US Department of Labor Handbook	073976215X
68. US Department of State Handbook	0739762168
69. US Department of the Air Force Handbook	0739762060
70. US Department of the Army Handbook	0739762176
71. US Department of the Navy Handbook	0739762184
72. US Department of the Treasury Handbook	0739762192
73. US Department of Transport Handbook	0739762206
74. US Department of Veteran Affairs Handbook	0739762214
75. US Environmental Protection Agency Handbook	0739762222
76. US Export-Import Bank Handbook	0739762230

To order and for additional analytical and marketing information, please contacrt
International Business Publications, USA at:
P.O. Box 15343, Washington, DC 20003, USA. Phone: (202) 546-2103. Fax: (202) 546-3275.
E-mail: rusric@erols.com

Title *	ISBN
77. US FBI ACADEMY HANDBOOK	0739731858
78. US Federal Bureau of Investigation (FBI) Business Opportunities Handbook	0739762370
79. US Federal Bureau of Investigation (FBI) Handbook	073976246X
80. US Federal Communication Commission Handbook	0739733494
81. US Federal Election Commission Handbook	0739762400
82. US Federal Energy Sector Regulations Handbook	0739762419
83. US Federal Executive Government Handbook	0739731823
84. US Federal Maritime Commission Handbook	0739762427
85. US Federal Mine Safety and Health Commission Handbook	0739762435
86. US Federal Reserve System Handbook	0739762532
87. US Federal Trade Commission Handbook	0739762451
88. US Food and Drug Administration Handbook	0739762397
89. US Food Assistance to Russia Handbook	0739762478
90. US Information Agency Handbook	0739762486
91. US Intelligence Policy Handbook	0739762494
92. US Internal Revenue Service Handbook	0739762508
93. US Libraries and Information Science National Commission Handbook	0739762516
94. US National Academy of Science and Research Policy Handbook	0739762524
95. US National Aeronautics and Space Administration Handbook	0739762249
96. US National Drug Control Policy Handbook	0739762389
97. US National Institute of Health Handbook	0739762443
98. US National Science Foundation Handbook	0739762362
99. US National Security Policy Handbook	0739762354
100. US Navy Seals Handbook	0739762540
101. US Office of Management and Budget Handbook	0739762346
102. US Office of Personnel Management Handbook	0739762338
103. US Peace Corp Handbook	073976232X
104. US Postal Service Handbook	0739762311
105. US Science and Technology Policy Handbook	0739762303
106. US Securities and Exchange Commission Handbook	073976229X
107. US Small Business Administration Handbook	0739762281
108. US Special Combat Fources Handbook	0739762001
109. US Submarine Force Hnadbook	0739764136
110. US Trade and Development Agency Handbook	0739762273
111. US Trade Representative Office Handbook	0739762265
112. WORLD BANK BUSINESS OPPORTUNITES HANDBOOK	0739762257

To order and for additional analytical and marketing information, please contacrt
International Business Publications, USA at:
P.O. Box 15343, Washington, DC 20003, USA. Phone: (202) 546-2103. Fax: (202) 546-3275.
E-mail: rusric@erols.com

NEW WORLD POLITICAL LEADERS LIBRARY-2003

ULTIMATE INFORMATION ON LOLITICAL AND BUSINESS LEADERS OF FOREING COUNTRIES

The ultimate handbook with detailed information on foreign leaders, including biographic data, position on domestic and international issues, economic policy and more

Price: $99.95 each

	TITLE
1.	Albania President Rexhep Meidani Handbook
2.	Angola President José Eduardo dos Santos Handbook
3.	Armenia President Robert Kocharian Handbook
4.	Austria President Dr. Thomas Klestil Handbook
5.	Azerbaijan President Heydar Aliyev Handbook
6.	Bangladesh Prime Minister Khaleda Zia Handbook
7.	Belarus President Alexander LUKASHENKO Handbook
8.	Brunei Sultan Haji Hassanal Bolkiah Mu'izzaddin Waddaulah Handbook
9.	Canada Prime Minister Joseph Jacques Jean Chrétien Handbook
10.	China President Jiang Zemin Handbook
11.	Cuba President Fidel Castro Handbook
12.	Egypt President Hosny Mubarak Handbook
13.	France President Jacques Chirac Handbook
14.	Germany President Johannes Rau Handbook
15.	Guyana President BHARRAT JAGDEO Handbook
16.	Iran President Hojjatoleslam Seyed Mohammad Khatami Handbook
17.	Iraq President Saddam Hussein Handbook
18.	Israel Prime Minister Ariel Sharon Handbook
19.	Japan Prime Minister Junichiro Koizumi Handbook
20.	Korea North General Secretary Kim Jong Il Handbook
21.	Korea South President Kim Dae-jung Handbook
22.	Libya President Muammar Muhammad Abd as-Salam al-Gaddafi Handbook
23.	Norway Queen Sonja Handbook
24.	Pakistan President Pervez Musharraf Handbook
25.	Palestine President Yasser Arafat Handbook
26.	Philippines President Gloria Macapagal Arroyo Handbook
27.	Poland President Aleksander Kwasniewski Handbook
28.	Russia President Vladimir Putin Handbook
29.	Saudi Arabia King Fahd bin Abdul Aziz Handbook
30.	Syria President Bashar Hafez Al-Assad Handbook
31.	Taiwan President Chen Shui-bian Handbook
32.	Thailand King Bhumibol Adulyadej Handbook
33.	United Arab Emirates Ruler Sheikh Zayed bin Sultan Al Nahyan Handbook
34.	United States President George W. Bush Handbook
35.	Uzbekistan President Islam Karimov Handbook
36.	Yugoslavia President Vojislav Koštunica Handbook

To order and for additional analytical and marketing information, please contacrt
International Business Publications, USA at:
P.O. Box 15343, Washington, DC 20003, USA.
Phone: (202) 546-2103. Fax: (202) 546-3275. E-mail: IBPUSA@comcast.net

TITLE *	ISBN
Netherlands Export-Import and Business Directory	0739742345
Pakistan Expoprt-Import and Business Directory	0739742353
Portugal Export-Import and Business Directory	0739742361
Russia Export-Import and Business Directory	073974237X
Spain Export-Import and Business Directory	0739742388
Switzerland Export-Import and Business Directory	0739742396
Syria Export Import & Business Directory	073974240X
Tajikistan Export-Import and Business Directory	0739742418
Turkmenistan Export-Import and Business Directory	0739742426
Ukraine Export-Import and Business Directory	0739742434
United Kingdom Export-Import and Business Directory	0739742469
US Export-Import and Business Directory	0739742442
Uzbekistan Export-Import and Business Directory	0739742450

38. Common Fund for Commodities Handbook
39. Common Market for Eastern and Southern Africa (COMESA) Handbook
40. Cooperation Council for the Arab States of the Gulf (GCC) Handbook
41. Council of the Baltic Sea States (CBSS) Handbook
42. Council of Europe Development Bank (CEB) Handbook
43. East African Development Bank (EADB) Handbook
44. Eastern Caribbean Central Bank (ECCB) Handbook
45. Economic Community of West African States (ECOWAS) Handbook
46. Economic Cooperation Organization (ECO) Handbook
47. European Bank for Reconstruction and Development (EBRD) Handbook
48. European Central Bank (ECB) Handbook
49. European Free Trade Association (EFTA) Handbook
50. European Investment Bank (EIB) Handbook
51. European Investment Fund (EIF) Handbook
52. European Union, The (EC) Handbook
53. Financial Fund for the Development of the River Plate Basin (FONPLATA) Handbook
54. Food and Agriculture Organization of the United Nations (FAO) Handbook
55. Fund for Co-operation, Compensation and Development (ECOWAS Fund) Handbook
56. Inter-American Development Bank (IDB) Handbook
57. Inter-American Institute for Cooperation on Agriculture (IICA) Handbook
58. Inter-Arab Investment Guarantee Corporation (IAIGC) Handbook
59. International Atomic Energy Agency (IAEA) Handbook
60. International Civil Aviation Organization (ICAO) Handbook
61. International Cocoa Organization (ICCO) Handbook
62. International Coffee Organization (ICO) Handbook
63. International Confederation of Free Trade Unions (ICFTU) Handbook
64. International Cotton Advisory Committee (ICAC) Handbook
65. International Fund for Agricultural Development (IFAD) Handbook
66. International Grains Council Handbook
67. International Labour Organization (ILO) Handbook
68. International Lead and Zinc Study Group Handbook
69. International Monetary Fund (IMF) Handbook
70. International Olive Oil Council (IOOC) Handbook
71. International Rubber Study Group Handbook
72. International Sugar Organization (ISO) Handbook
73. International Telecommunications Union (ITU) Handbook
74. International Tropical Timber Organization (ITTO) Handbook
75. Islamic Development Bank Group (IsDB) Handbook
76. Islamic Research and Training Institute (IRTI) Handbook
77. Joint Vienna Institute (JVI) Handbook
78. Kuwait Fund for Arab Economic Development Handbook
79. Lake Chad Basin Commission (LCBC) Handbook
80. Latin American Association of Development Financing Institutions (ALIDE) Handbook
81. Latin American Economic System (SELA) Handbook
82. Latin American Energy Organization (OLADE) Handbook
83. Latin American Export Bank (BLADEX) Handbook
84. Latin American Integration Association (ALADI) Handbook
85. Latin American Reserve Fund (LARF) Handbook
86. League of Arab States Handbook
87. Mekong River Commission (MRC) Handbook
88. Nordic Development Fund (NDF) Handbook

89. Nordic Investment Bank (NIB) Handbook
90. OPEC Fund for International Development Handbook
91. Organisation for Economic Co-operation and Development (OECD) Handbook
92. Organisation of Eastern Caribbean States (OECS) Handbook
93. Organization of American States (OAS) Handbook
94. Organization of Arab Petroleum Exporting Countries (OAPEC) Handbook
95. Organization of the Petroleum Exporting Countries (OPEC) Handbook
96. Pacific Financial Technical Assistance Centre Handbook
97. Pacific Islands Forum Secretariat Handbook
98. Pan American Health Organization (PAHO) Handbook
99. Regional Association of Oil and Natural Gas Companies in Latin America and the Caribbean (ARPEL) Handbook
100. Regional Electrical Integration Commission (CIER) Handbook
101. Saudi Fund for Development (SFD) Handbook
102. Secretariat for Central American Economic Integration (SIECA) Handbook
103. Secretariat of the Pacific Community Handbook
104. Sectorial Commission for the Common Market of the South (MERCOSUR) - Uruguay Handbook
105. South Asian Association for Regional Cooperation (SAARC) Handbook
106. South-East Asian Central Banks (SEACEN) Research and Training Centre Handbook
107. Training Centre for Regional Integration (CEFIR) Handbook
108. United Nations African Institute for Economic Development and Planning (IDEP) Handbook
109. United Nations Conference on Trade and Development (UNCTAD) Handbook
110. United Nations Development Program (UNDP) Handbook
111. United Nations Economic and Social Commission for Asia and the Pacific (ESCAP) Handbook
112. Asian and Pacific Centre for Transfer of Technology (APCTT) Handbook
113. Regional Coordination Centre for Research and Development of Coarse Grains, Pulses, Roots and Tuber Crops in the Humid Tropics of Asia and the Pacific (ESCAP CGPRT Centre) Handbook
114. Statistical Institute for Asia and the Pacific (SIAP) Handbook
115. United Nations Economic and Social Commission for Western Asia (ESCWA) Handbook
116. United Nations Economic Commission for Africa (UNECA) Handbook
117. United Nations Economic Commission for Europe (UN/ECE) Handbook
118. United Nations Economic Commission for Latin America and the Caribbean (ECLAC) Handbook
119. United Nations Educational, Scientific and Cultural Organization (UNESCO) Handbook
120. United Nations Industrial Development Organization (UNIDO) Handbook
121. United Nations Latin American and Caribbean Institute for Economic and Social Planning (ILPES) Handbook
122. Universal Postal Union (UPU) Handbook
123. West African Development Bank (BOAD) Handbook
124. West Africa Economic and Monetary Union Handbook
125. World Bank Group Handbook
126. World Food Program (WFP) Handbook
127. World Health Organization (WHO) Handbook
128. World Trade Organization (WTO) Handbook

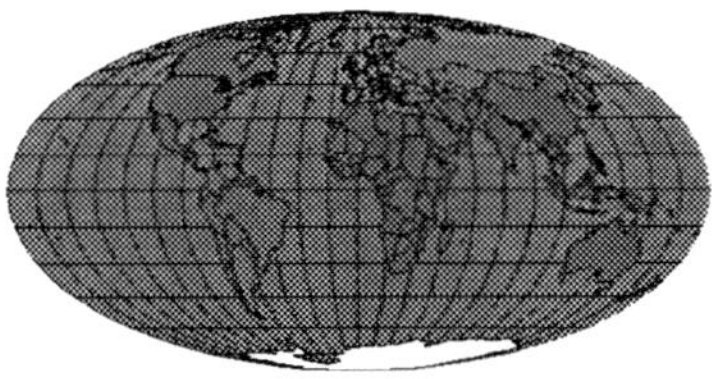

COMMONWEALTH OF INDEPENDENT STATES INDUSTRIAL AND BUSINESS DIRECTORIES LIBRARY 2004

Price: $129.95 Each

TITLE
Commonwealth of Independent States (CIS) Industry: Automobile Industry
Commonwealth of Independent States (CIS) Industry: Building Materials Industry
Commonwealth of Independent States (CIS) Industry: Chemical Pharmaceutical and Microbiology Industry
Commonwealth of Independent States (CIS) Industry: Civil Engineering and Transport Industry
Commonwealth of Independent States (CIS) Industry: Clothing Industry
Commonwealth of Independent States (CIS) Industry: Coal Mining and Peat Industry
Commonwealth of Independent States (CIS) Industry: Consumer Goods Household and Cultural Goods Industry
Commonwealth of Independent States (CIS) Industry: Electrical Engineering Industry
Commonwealth of Independent States (CIS) Industry: Fishing and Fish Processing Industry
Commonwealth of Independent States (CIS) Industry: Food and Food Processing Industry
Commonwealth of Independent States (CIS) Industry: Footwear and Tanning Industry
Commonwealth of Independent States (CIS) Industry: Forestry and Timber Industry
Commonwealth of Independent States (CIS) Industry: Gold Mining and Mining Industry
Commonwealth of Independent States (CIS) Industry: High-Tech Products PC Research and Design Industry
Commonwealth of Independent States (CIS) Industry: 1000 Largest Industrial Companies
Commonwealth of Independent States (CIS) Industry: 500 Largest Industrial Companies
Commonwealth of Independent States (CIS) Industry: Machine Building Industry
Commonwealth of Independent States (CIS) Industry: Medical Equipment Industry
Commonwealth of Independent States (CIS) Industry: Metallurgy Industry
Commonwealth of Independent States (CIS) Industry: Metal-Working Industry

TITLE
Commonwealth of Independent States (CIS) Industry: Mining (Building Materials) Industry
Commonwealth of Independent States (CIS) Industry: Oil and Gas Industry
Commonwealth of Independent States (CIS) Industry: Oil Refining and Gas Processing Industry
Commonwealth of Independent States (CIS) Industry: Power Industry
Commonwealth of Independent States (CIS) Industry: Publishing and Printing Industry
Commonwealth of Independent States (CIS) Industry: Pulp and Paper Industry
Commonwealth of Independent States (CIS) Industry: Radio-Electronic Industry
Commonwealth of Independent States (CIS) Industry: Rubber and Plastic Industry
Commonwealth of Independent States (CIS) Industry: Scrap and Waste Industry
Commonwealth of Independent States (CIS) Industry: Textile Industry
Commonwealth of Independent States (CIS) Industry: Tobacco Industry

CIS & BALTICS BUSINESS & INDUSTRIAL DIRECTORIES

Export-import opportunities, local industrial companies, government and business contacts, strategic and practical information for conducting business and more...

Price: $129.95 each

TITLE
Armenia Business and Industrial Directory
Azerbaijan Industrial and Business Directory
Belarus Business and Industrial Directory
Central Ukraine Business and Industrial Directory
Eastern Ukraine Business and Industrial Directory
Estonia Business and Industrial Directory
Georgia Business and Industrial Directory
Kazakhstan Business and Industrial Directory
Kyrgyzstan Business and Industrial Directory
Latvia Business and Industrial Directory
Lithuania Business and Industrial Directory
Moldova Business and Industrial Directory
Russia Business and Industrial Directory
South Ukraine Business and Industrial Directory
Tajikistan Business and Industrial Directory
Turkmenistan Business and Industrial Directory
Ukraine Business and Industrial Directory

CIS & BALTICS EXPORT-IMPORT & BUSINESS DIRECTORY DIRECTORIES

Export-import opportunities, local industrial companies, government and business contacts, strategic and practical information for conducting business and more...

Price: $129.95 each

TITLE
Armenia Export-Import & Business Directory
Azerbaijan Export-Import & Business Directory
Belarus Export-Import & Business Directory
Central Ukraine Export-Import & Business Directory
Eastern Ukraine Export-Import & Business Directory
Estonia Export-Import & Business Directory
Georgia Export-Import & Business Directory
Kazakhstan Export-Import & Business Directory
Kyrgyzstan Export-Import & Business Directory
Latvia Export-Import & Business Directory
Lithuania Export-Import & Business Directory
Moldova Export-Import & Business Directory
Russia Export-Import & Business Directory
South Ukraine Export-Import & Business Directory
Tajikistan Export-Import & Business Directory
Turkmenistan Export-Import & Business Directory
Ukraine Export-Import & Business Directory
Uzbekistan Export-Import & Business Directory

Printed in the United States
76935LV00009B/4

9 780739 760130